THE WAR ON
FREEDOM

How and Why America was Attacked,

September 11th, 2001

Nafeez Mosaddeq Ahmed

Tree of Life Publications
Joshua Tree, California

A Media Messenger Book

In cooperation with
Media Monitors Network

The War on Freedom:
How and Why America was Attacked, September 11th, 2001

www.Thewaronfreedom.com,
http://groups.yahoo.com/group/WarOnFreedom

Edited & Published by
Tree of Life Publications, PO Box 126, Joshua Tree, CA 92252
E-mail: publishing@mediamonitors.org, Web: www.treeoflifebooks.com

In cooperation with
Media Monitors Network, www.mediamonitors.net

Cover Design
Michael Mursell, a fish in sea
PO Box 22398, London, W13 9XL, England
info@afishinsea.co.uk

International Standard Book Number (ISBN): 0-930852-40-0

Library of Congress Catalog Number: 2002107291

A Media Messenger Book

Printed in the United States of America
by BooksJustBooks.com
First printing, June 2002
Unabridged edition.

Critical acclaim for
THE WAR ON FREEDOM

"On the subject 'How and Why America was Attacked on 11 September, 2001', the best, most balanced report, thus far, is by Nafeez Mossadeq Ahmed ..."
Gore Vidal, in his new book, *Dreaming War*.

"This riveting and thoroughly documented study is a 'must' resource for everyone seeking to understand the attack on the World Trade Center of New York on September 11, 2001 and 'America's New War' since. It connects together over 10 years of relevant covert actions and decisions by top-level U.S. security-state operations, and organises the whole into a coherent and devastating exposé of the real meaning and construction of the historic turn of 'the war against terrorism' now rewriting laws and constitutions across borders. For those who have seen or filed facts on these matters from web-disclosures and scattered revelations of newspapers, this volume provides the detailed documentation in a definitive and masterful record."
Professor John McMurtry, Department of Philosophy, University of Guelph, Ontario; Fellow at the Royal Society of Canada; Chair of Jurists, War Crimes and Crimes Against Humanity Tribunal at the Alternative World Summit in Toronto, 1989 (Canada)

"The most complete book I know of, summarizing the relevant background and foreground intersecting upon the events of September 11, 2001... A tour de force in every respect: organization, methodology, timeliness, clarity of purpose and of scope, activist commitment to more inquiry, evenness, relative comprehensiveness... I can't say how much I admire this work. It must be seen by as many people as possible all over the world as soon as possible."
Barry Zwicker, Producer and Host, MediaFile, Vision TV Insight; award-winning journalist on *CBC-TV* and *CTV* (Canada)

"The material you have collected is immensely important and useful. You look at the right subjects and report a number of things I had missed entirely... We need more people doing the important research that you have done."
Professor Peter Dale Scott, Co-Founder of the Peace and Conflict Studies Program, University of California, Berkeley (United States)

"A meticulous investigation of circumstances, events and circumstantial evidence of what really happened before and on September 11. There aren't many people who still take the task of following the trails of their own doubts... Your excellent report goes deep into what really happened and what the American defense machinery had let happen."
Peter G. Spengler, Editor, *Contemporary Studies* (Germany)

Dedication

This study is dedicated to the innocent civilians murdered

in the terrorist attacks against the United States on

11th September 2001, their families, their friends,

and to all the other victims of terrorism around the world,

including those killed, injured and starving in Afghanistan.

ABOUT THE AUTHOR

Nafeez Mosaddeq Ahmed, a British political scientist and human rights activist, is Executive Director of the Institute for Policy Research & Development in Brighton, UK, www.globalresearch.org, a 'think tank' dedicated to the promotion of human rights, justice and peace.

Ahmed is the author of many internationally acclaimed research papers and reports on human rights practices and Western foreign policy. He has been invited to lecture on U.S. foreign policy in various universities and educational establishments around the world. He has been an Oxfam Campaigner since 1996.

Ahmed's work on the history and development of the conflict in Afghanistan as a consequence of international policies, has been recommended as a resource by Harvard University's Program on Humanitarian Policy and Conflict Research, the Department of Communications Studies at California State University, and the English Department at Warren College on Staten Island. His archive of political analyses, published on the Web by Media Monitors Network in Los Angeles, has been nominated a Cool Site on the Netscape Open Directory Project. He was also recently named a Global Expert on War, Peace and International Affairs by The Freedom Network of The Henry Hazlitt Foundation in Chicago. A rising star, Ahmed is still only 23 years old, is married and lives in Brighton.

Acknowledgements

I would like to thank Professor Andre Gunder Frank, currently at the Department of History in the University of Nebraska, for reading various successive drafts of my manuscript and providing detailed advice on content and structure. Relevant data that he also provided was very useful in following up specific leads and uncovering pertinent facts. I am indebted to social philosopher Professor John McMurtry of the Department of Philosophy at the University of Guelph, Ontario, for his thorough review of the manuscript shortly prior to publication. I must also express my gratitude to the former Canadian diplomat and leading political scientist Professor Peter Dale Scott of the University of California, Berkeley, for pointing out some potential holes and flaws in my argument. My friend, Johnathan G. Baston (Abdul Nasser), a British local government health officer and active human rights campaigner, must be credited for his initial analysis and speculations that led me to embark on this project in the first place. Baston must also be thanked for assessing an early draft of the manuscript and making invaluable suggestions for further research. Kamran Naqui, another good friend, deserves due praise for scouring an early, messy draft of the manuscript with a fine-tooth comb. I cannot forget to mention Aamir Jiwa, who looked through the earliest pilot version of this study and gave me welcome encouragement. I must express my heartfelt appreciation to John Leonard, without whose indefatigable efforts this study would not be published. A special thanks is due to Mrs. Erika Anderson, without whose unexpected and invaluable contributions, this book could never have got to the printers. Media Monitors Network Chief Editor Ali Khan was also a constant source of invaluable support and advice. I must also thank Michael Mursell (www. afishinsea.co.uk) for his inspired cover designs. Others who deserve thanks include Mark Jones, who dropped an early draft of this study into his A-List, thus leading to highly useful comments and criticisms, and Louis Proyect, whose rigid opposition to my thesis provided me with crucial insight into how to formulate it properly. I also thank Greg Bates of Common Courage Press, who kindly took the time to assess the manuscript and offer very useful criticisms and suggestions. I should also mention my father-in-law, whose support, advice and pointers throughout this project and beyond, have been priceless. My mother and father also deserve due recognition for putting up with me while I was struggling to discover my true vocation; if they hadn't put up with me then, this study would not exist. In connection with the task of enduring my vocation, I must most of all thank my wife, who has been a constant source of support, advice, inspiration and peace. Without her ideas, pointers, and provision of important data, this study would not be what it is. Last but not least, I would like to thank our baby, who has been a source of strength and resolve for the future. Needless to say, as the author, I bear sole responsibility for the contents of this work.

Table of Contents

"In the councils of government, we must guard against the acquisition of unwarranted influence, whether sought or unsought, by the military-industrial complex. The potential for the disastrous rise of misplaced power exists and will persist. We must never let the weight of this combination endanger our liberties or democratic processes. We should take nothing for granted. Only an alert and knowledgeable citizenry can compel the proper meshing of the huge industrial and military machinery of defense with our peaceful methods and goals, so that security and liberty may prosper together."

Dwight D. Eisenhower, President of the United States of America, Farewell Address (17 January 1961)

"Turkistan, Afghanistan, Transcaspia, Persia... are the pieces on a chessboard upon which is being played out a game for the dominance of the world."

Lord George Curzon, British Foreign Secretary, Russia in Central Asia (1889)

"Power tends to corrupt, and absolute power corrupts absolutely."

Lord John Acton, Regius Professor of Modern History at Cambridge University (1887)

"Those who would sacrifice liberty for security deserve neither."

Benjamin Franklin, Founding Father of the United States of America, Historical Review of Pennsylvania (1759)

Preface

On the 11th September 2001, a catastrophe occurred which signaled unprecedented transformations in world order. Two hijacked jetliners hit the World Trade Center (WTC) in New York City, a third hit the Pentagon outside Washington, and a fourth hijacked plane crashed into a field in Pennsylvania. Trading on Wall Street stopped. The Federal Aviation Administration (FAA) halted all flight operations at U.S. airports. President Bush addressed the nation, vowing to "find those responsible and bring them to justice." Hundreds of New York City firemen and policemen sent to rescue WTC workers were lost when the WTC Twin Towers collapsed. So far, the confirmed death toll appears to be just under 3,000.

The world has, indeed, changed forever—but not necessarily in the way slavishly described by the majority of academic and media commentators. This study analyses the events of 11th September 2001, the responses of U.S. government, military, and intelligence agencies, as well as the historical, strategic and economic context of current U.S. policy. The study examines the development of U.S. policy prior to, and in the aftermath of, the 11th September attacks, in relation to Afghanistan and the surrounding region, as well as within the U.S. It builds on the conclusions of previous papers by this author, *Afghanistan, the Taliban and the United States: The Role of Human Rights in Western Foreign Policy*[1] and *Distortion, Deception and Terrorism: The Bombing of Afghanistan,*[2] as well as the work of other researchers.

The study begins by examining the history of U.S. policy in Afghanistan from the 1980s to the year 2001. It highlights evidence that a war on Afghanistan had been planned for several years prior to the terrible tragedy that occurred on 11th September on U.S. soil. It attempts to explore the interests from which these U.S. military plans may have sprung, principally those related to the strategic and economic domination of Central Asia and the Caspian. The study further investigates the multiple warnings of the 11th September attacks received by the U.S. intelligence community, and in that context considers in detail the U.S. response to those attacks. It also investigates the history of relations between the U.S. and Osama bin Laden, and their possible impact on the events of the 11th September.

The study then considers the developments in Afghanistan as well as within the United States, as a consequence of the U.S.-led military intervention that began in October 2001. The purpose of this study is not to provide exhaustive conclusions, but to point to the most pertinent questions and issues that have as yet to be thoroughly examined in a comprehensive manner, by assessing the facts on record.

Nevertheless, I do outline a variety of conclusions based on examination of the facts surrounding the 11th September attacks. Neither the facts themselves, nor the inferences I draw therefrom, are palatable. However, they are worthy of urgent consideration, not only by members of the public, but by our purported political leaders and representatives. In the final analysis, this study is an attempt to collate the facts on the 11th September attacks, no matter how unsavory they may be. While I frequently analyse these facts to derive their logical implications, thus arguing and articulating my conclusions, ultimately I leave it to the reader to make up their mind as to what they believe the facts suggest. My hope is that the reader will find the most value in this study in the scandalous facts recorded herein, rather than merely in my logical inferences therefrom.

Notes

[1] Ahmed, Nafeez M., 'Afghanistan, the Taliban and the United States: The Role of Human Rights in Western Foreign Policy,' Institute for Afghan Studies, January 2001. Republished by Media Monitors Network, April 2001. Featured on Central Asia section of Conflict Prevention Initiative, Program on Humanitarian Policy and Conflict Research, Cambridge MA, Harvard University, www.preventconflict.org/portal/centralasia/research_taliban. php.

[2] Ahmed, Nafeez, 'Distortion, Deception and Terrorism: The Bombing of Afghanistan,' Media Monitors Network, October 2001. Republished by Global Issues, October 2001, www.globalissues.org. Republished in revised format by *International Socialist Review*, November-December 2001.

Foreword: a Synopsis

In *The War on Freedom*, brilliant British scholar Nafeez M. Ahmed writes with cool, factual understatement a story that begs comprehension: *compelling evidence that the U.S. government instigates terrorism as the perfect pretext to justify an aggressive foreign policy—up to and including the September 11 attacks on the World Trade Center and Pentagon.* Astonishing as his thesis may seem, the thoughtful reader will find that it explains many obvious puzzles:

- How could our intelligence services fail to thwart such an ambitious project as 9/11?

- Why did our government immediately point the finger at Bin Laden, yet refuse to release the evidence? Were they loath to reveal their complicity, if they had been monitoring the 'Boeing Bombing' plot all along, and let it happen?

- Why did the White House ram through legal measures immediately after the attacks that essentially repeal the Bill of Rights and the Freedom of Information Act?

Ahmed's extensive research also brings to light some less well-known puzzles. Isn't it strange that:

- An investment from the bin Laden family started George Bush Jr. in business, and the war in Afghanistan will make the Bush family richer.

- The activities of a former U.S. Army Sergeant who trained Al-Qaeda and participated in the Embassy bombings suggest that the U.S. continues to protect bin Laden as a strategic asset.

- Members of Al-Qaeda were trained in terrorism by the CIA in the USA, and the hijackers themselves were trained by the U.S. military.

- The U.S. financially supported the Pakistani secret services, which funded presumed hijacker Mohammed Atta.

- A crescendo of warnings from intelligence services around the world in early September were selectively ignored, while high-level orders were issued to block investigations of suspected terrorists linked to Bin Laden.

- Three FBI officers testified that they had known the names of the hijackers and the date of the planned attack weeks before it happened, but were muzzled by superiors under threat of prosecution; their counsel was the U.S. Congress' chief prosecutor in the Clinton impeachment case.

- Standard operating procedure is for Air Force fighters to intercept hijacked planes immediately, but this was not done until it was all over on September 11, an hour and a half after the World Trade Center was hit.

- Intelligence experts deride the possibility that Bin Laden could have carried out such sophisticated, precise attacks without the support of a state-run intelligence organization.

Bin Laden got away, and the war on him remains an open-ended campaign, justifying any presidential policy, from attacking Iraq to plundering Social Security.

Loyal, law-abiding American readers may find all this too difficult to believe. We are taught certain civic values, and we believe our democratically elected government upholds them. Yet, even General Dwight D. Eisenhower warned us against the military-industrial complex...

How and why could the American presidency in effect wreak terror on its own citizens? The WTC attack, widely considered epoch-making, was certainly an immense opener for the war and oil lobbies, and for the projection of naked power. Ahmed unveils the linkages between the Bush, Cheney, Saudi, and Iraqi oil fortunes, as well as the shared anti-Soviet geopolitics of the CIA and the Islamic mujahideen in Central Asia.

How much of U.S. history and foreign policy has been made by manufacturing a pretext to attack a weaker enemy? Ahmed answers the question here in reference to the Afghan war, as he has earlier in a series of brilliant articles on U.S. intervention in Latin America and other regions (see http://nafeez.mediamonitors.net.)

I am not an historian by trade, but I remember not only the Alamo, but the Maine, which we found out 100 years later the Spanish didn't blow up; our intercession in WWI, from which Europe never recovered; and how FDR invited the Japanese to demolish our navy at Pearl Harbor. Isn't it time to investigate this subversive government within a government, the war party with its ruthless secret services?

People around the world are saying they like America and Americans—it's our government they can't stand. Yet it is *our* civic responsibility to keep an eye on it, and not hide our heads in the sand of so-called patriotism.

God willing, Ahmed's call for an investigation will be heard and the evidence he has so diligently gathered will be examined. If his thesis is proved right, then the September 11 attacks will truly be epoch-making for freedom and democracy.

John Leonard

Tree of Life Publications
February 2002

Executive Summary[3]

The current state of affairs in Afghanistan has its roots in a history that can be traced back to at least the end of the 19th century. Afghanistan has been the victim of numerous catastrophic interventions by the world's superpowers, from the British Empire, to the Soviet Union and the United States, which have left the country devastated and in ruins. Yet even a brief historical overview of these interventions makes it clear that the superpowers had no intention to improve the affairs of the people of Afghanistan. Rather, their involvement was motivated by their own interests, that were primarily strategic and economic in nature.

During the late 1970s, the USSR installed a puppet regime, the People's Democratic Party of Afghanistan (PDPA), that served its own interests and trampled upon those of the common people. A Communist party, the PDPA came to power through a coup d'etat that was largely sponsored and supported by the Soviet Union, although it did implement a variety of modernisation programmes. However, there was a general discontent with this regime which, despite some beneficial reforms, consolidated its power through a variety of brutal policies.

Fearing that it would lose its influence in the region, the Soviet Union sent troops into the Afghan capital, Kabul, in a full-fledged invasion of the country. Contrary to conventional wisdom, which presupposes that American support for the Afghan resistance against Soviet occupation was triggered by the USSR's invasion, historical records prove otherwise. In reality, the U.S. had been sponsoring rebel movements within Afghanistan prior to the Soviet invasion. The result, anyhow, was a brutal civil war in the country effectively engineered by both superpowers to secure their influence and control. There was no regard for either human rights or democracy, despite the jingoistic lip service paid to these by top U.S. and Soviet officials.

The U.S. supported the Afghan rebels in their fight against the Soviet Union throughout the 1980s, until Soviet forces pulled out of Afghanistan. This support from Washington came in overt forms, such as allowing and encouraging client states, Saudi Arabia and Pakistan, to sell arms to the Afghan mujahideen, and covertly, through direct CIA involvement, such as funds and training. After the Soviet withdrawal from Afghanistan in 1988, the country fell into a chaotic civil war between the various rebel factions previously supported by the U.S. Eventually, one of these factions, the Taliban, gained control over most of the country by the mid-1990s.

The Taliban, like their Northern Alliance predecessors, were no democrats, no agrarian reformers. Their policies of cruel oppression towards women, their ethnic cleansing of minorities such as the Hazaras of the north, their indiscriminate use of torture against prisoners, and many other such atrocities, are well-documented by numerous human rights groups. But such issues were irrelevant in the eyes of the U.S. government, whose only interest in the region was that a "stable" regime emerge, which in official doublespeak means a regime that serves U.S. strategic and economic interests, even if that be at the expense of the Afghan population.

Also well documented is the crucial factor of the abundant oil and gas resources recently discovered in the Caspian Sea. Afghanistan is considered the prime trans-shipment route for pipelines to these energy deposits. From another perspective, Afghanistan has great strategic value to those powers who desire to expand their hegemony[4] to global proportions. In fact, Afghanistan has long been recognised as the principal gateway to Central Asia, which was described in a 1997 Council on Foreign Relations (CFR) study as the instrument of control of Eurasia, and thus the world.

In other words, there could be no claim to 'democracy' or 'human rights' when the U.S. government was covertly supporting the Taliban. The cozy relationship between certain U.S. high-ranking officials and Taliban members in the later half of the 1990s is not a secret. Indeed, when strategic and economic interests were weighed in contrast to ideals such as human rights and freedom, the former took precedence. We see this played out perfectly in American policy towards Afghanistan.

Indeed, the anti-Taliban stance of the U.S. government grew, not out of any specific concern for the human rights of the Afghan people, but out of a more general and growing realisation that the Taliban regime would be incapable of serving as a vehicle of U.S. entry into Central Asia. In relation to this, extensive U.S. government and corporate planning for the establishment of pipelines to the vast oil and gas reserves of the Caspian basin were put on hold, because of the insufficient security in Afghanistan under Taliban rule. As confirmed in 1998 Congressional hearings on U.S. interests in Central Asia, a unified, stable and friendly regime in Afghanistan was needed to allow the pipelines to be built and remain safe.

A number of factors were critical in the growing U.S. recognition that the Taliban could not provide any such security. By the year 2001, while formulating specific plans to invade Afghanistan and topple the Taliban, George W. Bush Jr.'s administration began a series of negotiations with the Taliban to save its relationship with that regime. U.S. officials called for a government of national unity, in which all factions, including the Taliban, would participate—but the Taliban were unwilling to compromise their own power.

Accordingly, U.S. officials promised the Taliban that they would suffer the consequences by facing "a carpet of bombs," and further noted privately that the military plans would be implemented by October 2001. Extensive evidence on record indicates that the Bush administration intended to invade Afghanistan and overthrow the Taliban regime quite independently of the events of 11th September. The war on Afghanistan was thus not a response to 11th September. On the contrary, there is a long record of in-depth strategic planning at the root of U.S. military plans to invade Afghanistan. Much of this evidence is available in a 1997 CFR study by former National Security Adviser Zbigniew Brzezinski, who discusses in detail U.S. plans to secure hegemony over Central Asia as a means to the control of Eurasia, and thereby the expansion and consolidation of global U.S. hegemony, unhindered by potential rivals, such as Russia and China.

Against this backdrop, there is considerable evidence that, from 1995 to 2001, the American intelligence community was in receipt of multiple credible warnings of a terrorist attack on U.S. soil orchestrated by Osama bin Laden. Contrary to the official line of the Bush administration, this information, which was taken seriously by the U.S. intelligence community, specified the hijacking of civilian airplanes to be flown into key U.S. buildings in Washington, DC and New York City, including the World Trade Centre. The nature of these urgent warnings converged in a manner specifying that the attacks would occur between early and mid-September, while other credible information pinpointed 11th September as a likely watch date. Yet despite this extensive forewarning of the attacks, the Bush administration failed to act.

The failure to act was even more apparent on 11th September itself. There are clear rules established by the Federal Aviation Administration and the Department of Defense for responding to emergency situations, including hijacking. Yet, although four planes were almost simultaneously hijacked on 11th September, the U.S. Air Force systematically failed to respond in accordance with these rules, which are normally adhered to with routine, since they constitute Standard Operating Procedures (SOP). Subsequently, various official government accounts and statements have been issued attempting to deflect public attention from, thus denying the reality of, the collapse of SOP on 11th September.

In this context, the systematic violation of Standard Operating Procedures by the U.S. Air Force is an event that appears to have occurred with the complicity of key government and military officials in the Bush administration. This notion is supported by evidence that both President George W. Bush Jr. and Chairman of the Joint Chiefs of Staff Richard B. Myers displayed utter indifference to notification they received of the commencement of an air attack on the World Trade Centre, despite their responsibility at that time to ensure the security of the American nation.

The ominous implications of these facts are exacerbated in light of various revelations about the long-standing financial, diplomatic, military and intelligence ties between the members of the Bush administration and figures linked to Osama bin Laden–not to mention Osama himself. Reports indicate that until just after 11th September, the Bush family had close financial ties to the bin Laden family, and both were set to reap substantial profits from the war on Afghanistan through their mutual involvement in the U.S. defence industry. This has been accompanied by credible reports that Osama bin Laden has not broken away from his family and maintains ties with them. Further reports show that the Bush administration has systematically blocked attempts to apprehend Osama bin Laden, along with intelligence investigations of the terrorist connections of the bin Laden family and Saudi royals implicated in supporting Osama.

This state of affairs has largely continued in the aftermath of 11th September, despite the fact noted by former Deputy Director and Director of Antiterrorism for the FBI, John O'Neill, that the key to Osama bin Laden lies in Saudi Arabia. Indeed, abundant evidence indicates that the U.S. government has simultaneously maintained ties with figures in Saudi Arabia and Pakistan who support Osama bin Laden and Al-Qaeda, while blocking all meaningful investigations of those figures.

A particularly damning example is the U.S. response to revelations first in India, and then in Pakistan, that the then Director-General of Pakistani military intelligence, Mahmoud Ahmad, had funneled $100,000 to the lead hijacker, Mohamed Atta, shortly before 11th September. The Bush administration, on confirming this fact through the FBI, blocked any further inquiry into the role of Pakistani military intelligence in supporting Al-Qaeda by requesting that Ahmad, from behind-the-scenes, quietly pursue early retirement as a purported consequence of routine re-shuffling.

In the aftermath of 11th September, the Bush administration embarked on a devastating bombing campaign in Afghanistan, killing up to 5,000 Afghan civilians—almost double the number of civilians killed in the World Trade Center and Pentagon attacks. This massive bombardment of the country resulted in the destruction of the Taliban regime, making way for the installation of a new, interim government.

The new regime effectively constituted a return to the pre-Taliban era, when Northern Alliance factions ruled most of Afghanistan, brutalising and repressing the civilian population in the same manner as the Taliban. Now, however, Northern Alliance warlords have been bound by U.S.-UN brokered agreements designed to ensure the minimisation of civil war breaking out between rival warlords, the idea being to create the regional stability essential to lending an appropriate degree of security for proposed pipelines to Caspian oil and gas. The rights and wishes of the Afghan people, meanwhile, have been ignored.

Subsequently, on the pretext of entering into a new "war on terror," the Bush administration successfully secured unlimited war powers, free from Congressional accountability. This has established an open-ended militarisation of foreign policy in which any country can be targeted at will on the pretext of harbouring terrorists.

In the U.S., this has been accompanied by unprecedented curbs on civil liberties and basic human rights, the crushing of domestic dissent, and the criminalisation of legitimate protest. Many authoritative commentators have described these domestic measures as moves toward the establishment of an American police state. The combination of militarisation abroad and repression at home has granted the Bush administration a free hand to pursue its strategic and economic interests, consolidating a permanent military presence in Afghanistan and Central Asia, and moving swiftly to establish lucrative pipeline deals to secure access to regional resources and energy deposits. It has allowed the Bush administration to challenge its principal rivals—Europe, China and Russia—in the pursuit of control of Central Asia, with the final objective of consolidating U.S. hegemony over the entirety of Eurasia, thus moving toward the establishment of unrivalled global hegemony.

Prior to 11th September, all of this was inconceivable. The tragic catastrophe of 11th September, which was apparently permitted to occur by the Bush administration—and further effectively pushed forward by the administration through its ongoing support of key allies in Saudi Arabia and Pakistan who support bin Laden and Al-Qaeda—allowed the U.S. to expand, consolidate and empower its hegemony, both at home and abroad, to an unprecedented level.

In the epilogue, John Leonard gives a historical perspective on the Federal executive's repeated, clandestine use of staged provocations to get America into foreign wars, and presents published evidence pointing to the involvement of Mossad, Israeli military intelligence, in September 11.

Notes

[3] Mohamed Ahmad, a Researcher for the Institute for Policy Research & Development, contributed to this Executive Summary.

[4] Hegemony: The predominant influence or rule, as of a state, region, or group, over another or others.

1. The Role of the International Community in the Afghan Crisis

"Civilians are the targets of human rights abuses in a war they have not chosen, by one faction after another... They are pawns in a game of war between armed groups inside Afghanistan backed by different regional powers. Meanwhile, the world has watched massacres of civilians without making any meaningful effort to protect them."

(Amnesty International News Release,
'Civilians in a game of war they have not chosen,'
27th May 1999)

Many opinion-makers deride the idea that the September 11th terrorist attacks could have been somehow linked to American foreign policy. To seek such connections may be seen as adding insult to injury, or unpatriotic.

At the same time, it is clear that such an outrage could not appear simply out of the blue. We have the explanation of George W. Bush, that it was an attack on freedom, by terrorists who hate freedom. While this makes an excellent formula for a speech to elementary schoolers, little evidence to support such a simple theory was found, during this author's extensive research on the origins of the 9-11 attacks.

The abundant documentation provided in the following analysis does show how global terrorism is intimately interconnected with U.S. foreign policy, in complex and surprising ways. To fully understand how and why New York City and the Pentagon could have been targeted by Al-Qaeda terrorists out of Afghanistan, we need to grasp the roots of this terrorism, and the thrust of U.S. policy in Afghanistan, both before and after September 11, 2001.

To plumb the wellsprings of U.S. and Al-Qaeda policies, we will need some familiarity with the historical context that gave rise to them, from the severe crises that have ravaged Afghanistan for many decades; the impact of U.S. and Soviet strategy and intervention during and since the Cold War; the rise of extremist religious factions, of Al-Qaeda, and the Taliban in Afghanistan, during the 1990s; the rise of global "Islamic terrorism," and finally, to the logistics of the devastating terror attacks that brought down the Twin Towers. To do justice to the task of uncovering how and why the September 11th terrorist attacks took place, we start at the beginning of both how and why, with an inspection of the political changes in Afghanistan during the Cold War.

Cold War Imperialism

The decades-long Afghan crisis is a direct result of self-seeking interference by the two leading superpowers, the United States and the Soviet Union, during the Cold War. The roots of this interference can be found in Afghanistan's coup of 1978, which brought a new government to power in the Afghan capital, Kabul, headed by Nur Muhammad Taraki. This coup d'etat by Taraki's party—the People's Democratic Party of Afghanistan (PDPA)—had been precipitated by the previous government's arrest of almost the entire leadership of the PDPA. That had been an attempt to annihilate any viable opposition to the government of the time, which was led by Muhammad Daud.

The leader of the PDPA, Taraki, had then been freed in an uprising by the lower ranks of the military. Within a day, Daud and his government were overthrown, with Daud killed in the process. Many of the leaders of the PDPA had studied or received military training in the USSR; moreover, the Soviet Union had pressured the PDPA—which had split into two factions in 1967—to reunite in 1977. So the PDPA was the main Soviet-orientated Communist organisation in Afghanistan.

The military coup of 1978 was thus effectively engineered by the USSR, which had significant leverage over the PDPA and its activities. Afghanistan subsequently became exclusively dependent on Soviet aid, unlike previous governments that had attempted to play off the U.S. and USSR against each other, refraining from exclusive alignment with either.

Like the previous government, the PDPA did go on to implement certain programmes of social development and reform—although these were primarily related to urban areas. For example, Daud's government had used foreign aid from both the USSR and the U.S. (primarily the USSR) to build roads, schools and implement other development projects, thereby increasing the mobility of the country's people and products—not that this necessarily eliminated the severe problems faced by masses of the Afghan population.

For instance, 5 per cent of Afghanistan's rural landowners still owned more than 45 per cent of arable land. A third of the rural people were landless labourers, sharecroppers or tenants, and debts to the landlords were a regular feature of rural life. An indebted farmer ended up turning over half his annual crop to the moneylender. Illiteracy in rural areas was 90.5 per cent, and literacy was four times rarer among women than men, with a female illiteracy at 96.3 per cent.

The Communist PDPA government under Taraki had similarly imposed some social programmes like Daud's government: It moved to remove both usury and inequalities in land-ownership and cancelled mortgage debts of agricultural labourers, tenants and small landowners. It established literacy programmes, especially for women, printing textbooks in many languages, training more teachers, building additional schools and kindergartens, and instituting nurseries for orphans.

Nonetheless, the new regime was the result of a violent military coup by a tiny faction, without rapport with the wishes of the majority of the Afghan people, and it did not gain their support or participation. PDPA policies, as a stage in a revolutionary programme imposed by force and without the approval of the people, served instead to destroy even the state institutions established over the previous century.

The new government, like previous ones, was essentially illegitimate, with no substantial representation of the Afghan population. It was, for example, responsible for arresting, torturing and executing both real and suspected enemies, setting off the first major refugee flows to neighbouring Pakistan. Such policies of repression and persecution, resulting in the killing of thousands, as well as the forceful imposition of a Communist revolutionary programme that was oblivious to the sentiments of the majority of the Afghan masses, sparked off popular revolts led by local social and religious leaders—usually with no link to national political groups. These revolts broke out in different parts of the country in response to the government's atrocities. Furthermore, during the Soviet occupation, despite the modest 'modernising' policies that were primarily urban in character, the bifurcation[5] of Afghan society and economy deepened greatly.[6]

The PDPA was, therefore, essentially a Communist dictatorship allied with the Soviet Union. This was unlike the previous government of Daud's, that was not exclusively allied to either superpower (neither the U.S. nor the USSR). However, each superpower wished Afghanistan to remain within its own sphere of influence, due to the traditional brand of political, economic and strategic interests. Their wishes resulted in one of the last brutal episodes of the Cold War: the Afghanistan war, that began several months after the 1978 Saur coup (named after the Afghan month when the coup took place), and was a manifestation of the two superpowers' attempts to gain control of a region of very high geostrategic significance.

Although the USSR had been interfering in Afghan affairs long before the United States, it is worth noting that, contrary to conventional wisdom, the U.S. appears to have begun operations in Afghanistan before the full-fledged Soviet invasion. Former National Security Adviser under the Carter Administration, Zbigniew Brzezinski, has admitted that an American operation to infiltrate Afghanistan was launched long before Russia sent in its troops on 27th December 1979. Agence France Press reported that: "Despite formal denials, the United States launched a covert operation to bolster anti-Communist guerrillas in Afghanistan at least six months before the 1979 Soviet invasion of the country, according to a former top U.S. official."[7]

Elaborating, Brzezinski confirmed that: "We actually did provide some support to the mujahideen before the invasion."[8] "We did not push the Russians into invading, but we knowingly increased the probability that they would." He also bragged: "That secret operation was an excellent idea. The effect was to draw the Russians into the Afghan trap."[9] Former CIA Director Robert Gates similarly affirmed in his memoirs *From the Shadows* that U.S. intelligence began to aid rebels in Afghanistan six months before the Soviet intervention.[10]

In other words, the U.S. appears to have been attempting to foster and manipulate unrest amongst various Afghan factions to destabilise the already unpopular Communist regime and bring the country under the U.S. sphere of influence. This included the recruitment of local leaders and warlords to form mercenary rebel groups, who would wage war against the Soviet-backed government in order to institute a new regime under American control.

In December 1979, Russia intervened in order to reinforce its dominance over Afghanistan because the PDPA was, according to Brzezenski's testimony, being destabilised by a U.S. operation to infiltrate Afghanistan that had commenced at a much earlier date. The U.S. had evidently also wished to bring this strategic region under its own hegemony. Anticipating this attempt by the U.S. to destabilise the pro-Soviet PDPA and install a new pro-American regime in Afghanistan, Russia undertook a full-fledged invasion to keep the country under its own sphere of influence. Afghan analyst Dr. Nour Ali observes of the ensuing U.S. policy:

"Following the invasion of Afghanistan by the former Soviet Union in late December 1979, hundreds of high ranking Afghan politicians and technocrats as well as army officers including generals entered into Pakistan with the hope of organizing the needed resistance to oppose the invader in order to liberate Afghanistan. Unfortunately and regrettably the U.S. Government in collusion with Pakistan's leaders took abusive advantage of the opportunity so as to exploit it fully and by all manner of means to their own and exclusive illegitimate benefits and objectives, which had been threefold: (i) to rule out the creation of any responsible and independent Afghan organization among Afghans, interacting directly with Washington, to support Afghan resistance, (ii) to repulse the Red Army by using exclusively the blood of Afghans, and (iii) to make of Afghanistan a satellite if not an integrated part of Pakistan in return for Pakistani leaders' services, but in complete disregard to Afghan people's sovereignty and sacrifices."[11]

The CIA, in alliance with Pakistani military intelligence, did provide covert military aid, training and direction to the Afghan rebels. The U.S.-sponsored operation also involved the creation of an extremist religious ideology derived from, but distorting the actual teachings of, Islam: "Predominant themes were that Islam was a complete socio-political ideology, that holy Islam was being violated by the atheistic Soviet troops, and that the Islamic people of Afghanistan should reassert their independence by overthrowing the leftist Afghan regime propped up by Moscow."[12] The overall result was a brutal civil war manipulated by the two superpowers that drove 6 million Afghan people from their homes.

Afghanistan After the Cold War

By 1991-92, the U.S. and the USSR finally reached an agreement that neither would continue to supply aid to any faction in Afghanistan. However, the numerous militant factions previously funded and armed by the U.S. have been vying for supremacy. Out of these factions funded by the CIA, various elements went on to form the Taliban, an apparently Islamic movement. With the departure of Soviet troops in 1989, these factions began competing with one another for dominance, the Taliban eventually arising as the most powerful force in Afghanistan. As a coherent politico-military faction or movement, the Taliban did not exist prior to October 1994, but were members of other factions, such as Harakat-e Islami and Mohammad Nabi Mohammadi, or operated independently without a centralised command centre.

The ultimate result was that post-Cold War Afghanistan remained in a state of anarchical civil war, with the Taliban emerging as the most powerful faction in the country by the mid-1990s. One can therefore conclude that, as a result of a string of proxy wars that were the result of manipulation by both the U.S. and the former USSR, Afghanistan has been plunged into a state of perpetual humanitarian catastrophe.

Development specialist Dr. J. W. Smith, founder and Director of Research for the California-based Institute for Economic Democracy, summarises the humanitarian catastrophe of Afghanistan, commenting on Brzezinski's admission of the U.S. operation in the country:

> "Afghanistan was also a U.S. destabilization. In 1998, Zbigniew Brzezinski, President Carter's National Security Advisor... admitted that covert U.S. intervention began long before the USSR sent in troops... Take note of what was 'an excellent idea': A country rapidly developing and moving towards modernization was politically and economically shattered, almost 2 million Afghans were killed, the most violent and anti-American of the groups supported by the CIA are now the leaders of Afghanistan, these religious fundamentalists set human rights back centuries to the extent they are even an embarrassment to neighboring Muslim fundamentalists, and both Muslim and non-Muslim governments within the region fear destabilization through Taleban fundamentalism."[13]

Smith fails, however, to take into account the illegitimacy of the Soviet puppet regime and its policies of repression. The fact is, both the U.S. and USSR bear responsibility for having attempted to control Afghanistan, thereby shattering the country in the process. If these powers had merely attempted to help the Afghan people develop their country, rather than enforce hegemony over the country for their own self-interested strategic designs, there would have been no such humanitarian crisis.

Thus, as Barnette Rubin of the U.S. Council on Foreign Relations reports: "Despite the end of the proxy war, the massive arms supplies still held by both the Soviet-aided army and the Islamic resistance fighters (backed by the U.S., with help from Pakistan, Saudi Arabia and others) continue to fuel the fighting."[14]

Northern Alliance Rule 1992-1996

By August 1992, ongoing rocketing by the forces of Gulbuddin Hekmatyar—a one-time favourite of Pakistan and the U.S.—had driven half a million civilians from the capital city, Kabul, and killed over 2,000 people. HRW reports that by the end of the year, "international interest in the conflict had all but vanished and Afghanistan appeared to be on the brink of a humanitarian catastrophe," while the U.S.-Pakistani favourite masterminded the escalation of terror, "carried out with U.S. and Saudi financed weaponry." *The Economist* reported that, by summer 1993, about 30,000 people had been killed and 100,000 wounded in the capital. The bombardment of civilian targets has continued ever since, with casualty and refugee figures rising rapidly and steadily.[15]

It is important to note that the Taliban and the forces of Hekmatyar were two separate factions. Moreover, it should also be emphasised that Hekmatyar and his forces are not solely responsible for the deaths of thousands in Kabul or for the city's destruction. While Hekmatyar's forces may have killed and destroyed more than other groups, factions under Ahmed Shah Masoud, Burhanuddin Rabbani, Abdul Rashid Dostum, Abdul Ali Mazari and Abdul Karim Khalili are equally responsible for the violence that raged between 1992 and 1996.

Indeed, atrocities by the Northern Alliance factions against the Afghan people were of exactly the same nature as those committed by the brutal Taliban regime that, by the late 1990s, ruled the majority of Afghanistan. British Middle East specialist Robert Fisk refers in *The Independent* to "the whole bloody, rapacious track record of the killers in the 'Alliance,'" a "gang of terrorists... The Northern Alliance, the confederacy of warlords, patriots, rapists and torturers who control a northern sliver of Afghanistan,... have done their [fair share of] massacres on home turf, in Afghanistan. Just like the Taliban..."[16] He points out that: "... it remains a fact that from 1992 to 1996, the Northern Alliance was a symbol of massacre, systematic rape, and pillage... The Northern Alliance left the city in 1996 with 50,000 dead behind it."[17]

Human Rights Watch (HRW) has also documented the anti-humanitarian policies of the Northern Alliance which, after 1996, also came to be known as the 'United Front.' Sidney Jones, Executive Director of the Asia division of HRW, noted that the Alliance "commanders whose record of brutality raises questions about their legitimacy inside Afghanistan," were responsible for gross violations of human rights in late 1999 and early 2000, including "summary executions, burning of houses, and looting, principally targeting ethnic Pashtuns and others suspected of supporting the Taliban." HRW also describes the parties comprising the 'United Front' as having "amassed a deplorable record of attacks on civilians between the fall of the Najibullah regime in 1992 and the Taliban's capture of Kabul in 1996."[18]

HRW has provided a detailed but concise overview of the systematic abuses committed by Northern Alliance/United Front forces in areas under their control, and in their war against Taliban forces:

"Late 1999–early 2000: Internally displaced persons who fled from villages in and around Sangcharak district recounted summary executions, burning of houses, and widespread looting during the four months that the area was held by the United Front. Several of the executions were reportedly carried out in front of members of the victims' families. Those targeted in the attacks were largely ethnic Pashtuns and, in some cases, Tajiks.

September 20–21, 1998: Several volleys of rockets were fired at the northern part of Kabul, with one hitting a crowded night market. Estimates of the number of people killed ranged from seventy-six to 180. The attacks were generally believed to have been carried out by Massoud's forces, who were then stationed about twenty-five miles north of Kabul. A spokesperson for United Front commander Ahmad Shah Massoud denied targeting civilians. In a September 23, 1998 press statement, the International Committee of the Red Cross described the attacks as indiscriminate and the deadliest that the city had seen in three years.

Late May 1997: Some 3,000 captured Taliban soldiers were summarily executed in and around Mazar-i Sharif by Junbish forces under the command of Gen. Abdul Malik Pahlawan. The killings followed Malik's withdrawal from a brief alliance with the Taliban and the capture of the Taliban forces who were trapped in the city. Some of the Taliban troops were taken to the desert and shot, while others were thrown down wells and then blown up with grenades.

January 5, 1997: Junbish planes dropped cluster munitions on residential areas of Kabul. Several civilians were killed and others wounded in the indiscriminate air raid, which also involved the use of conventional bombs.

March 1995: Forces of the faction operating under Commander Massoud, the Jamiat-i Islami, were responsible for rape and looting after they captured Kabul's predominantly Hazara neighborhood of Karte Seh from other factions. According to the U.S. State Department's 1996 report on human rights practices in 1995, 'Massood's troops went on a rampage, systematically looting whole streets and raping women.'

On the night of February 11, 1993, Jamiat-i Islami forces and those of another faction, Abdul Rasul Sayyaf's Ittihad-i Islami, conducted a raid in West Kabul, killing and 'disappearing' ethnic Hazara civilians, and committing widespread rape. Estimates of those killed range from about seventy to more than one hundred.

In addition, the parties that constitute the United Front have committed other serious violations of internationally recognized human rights. In the years before the Taliban took control of most of Afghanistan, these parties had divided much of the country among themselves while battling for control of Kabul. In 1994 alone, an estimated 25,000 were killed in Kabul, most of them civilians killed in rocket and artillery attacks. One-third of the city was reduced to rubble, and much of the remainder sustained serious damage. There was virtually no rule of law in any of the areas under the factions' control. In Kabul, Jamiat-i Islami, Ittihad, and Hizb-i Wahdat forces all engaged in rape, summary executions, arbitrary arrest, torture, and 'disappearances.' In Bamiyan, Hizb-i Wahdat commanders routinely tortured detainees for extortion purposes."[19]

The Rise of the Taliban

Control of Afghanistan by the warlords of the Northern Alliance was, however, increasingly curbed by the Taliban forces backed by Pakistan and Saudi Arabia. When the Taliban took control of Kabul in 1996, signaling the faction's domination of Afghanistan, respected French observer Oliver Roy noted that: "When the Taleban took power in Afghanistan (1996), it was largely orchestrated by the Pakistani secret service [ISI] and the oil company Unocal, with its Saudi ally Delta." Furthermore, it appears that at this time Pakistan's support for the Taliban drew the approval of public and private Saudi authorities, the CIA, and the American oil company UNOCAL.[20]

The Taliban's brutal policies were particularly exemplified when its forces captured Mazar-e Sharif in 1998. Following this military takeover on 8 August, Taliban guards systematically killed 8,000 civilians. The vast majority of those killed were from the Hazara ethnic group, who are mostly Shi'a Muslims. They were killed deliberately in their homes and in the streets, where their bodies were left for several days, or in locations between Mazar-e Sharif and Hairatan.

Victims of these acts of genocide included women, children and the elderly—many of whom were shot trying to flee. Furthermore, 11 Iranian nationals (ten diplomats and one journalist) were killed when Taliban guards entered the Iranian Consulate in Mazar-e Sharif. According to eyewitnesses, their bodies were left in the consulate for two days before being buried in a mass grave at the Sultan Razieh girls' school.[21]

Having sealed their military capture of Mazar-e Sharif, Taliban guards imposed a curfew in the city. In the Uzbek populated areas, people were ordered to hand in their weapons, while in the Hazara area people were ordered to stay in their homes. Taliban forces subsequently entered Hazara houses, killing older men and children, and taking away young men without explanation. In some houses, they also abducted young women, this time with explanation: they would be married off, whether they liked it or not, to the Taliban militia.[22]

Thousands of detainees were reportedly transferred in military vehicles to detention centres in Mazar-e Sharif and Shebarghan and interrogated to identify their ethnic identity. Non-Hazaras were released after a few days. Amnesty International reports that former detainees were beaten during their detention, sometimes severely. Moreover, hundreds were reportedly taken by air to Kandahar, while many others were taken during the night to fields in the surrounding areas of Mazar-e Sharif and Shebarghan to be executed.[23]

Severe restrictions were imposed on the movement of Afghan people in and out of Mazar-e Sharif—again, for apparently genocidal purposes. Amnesty reports that families who managed to leave the area were stopped at many checkpoints on the way. At each checkpoint, Taliban guards would ask them whether Hazaras were among them. Anyone whom the guards suspected of being a Hazara was abducted. Hazara men, and boys younger than 12 years old, were taken to Jalalabad prison, while women and girls were sent to Sarshahi camp.

Such reports reveal the simple but horrifying fact that the Taliban was implementing a two-pronged programme of ethnic cleansing and genocide. As Amnesty International observes, "A new pattern in Afghanistan's human rights tragedy is the targeting of people on the basis of their group identity." AI confirms that "The Taleban," which is composed of the largest ethnic group in Afghanistan, "is targeting minorities such as Tajiks and Hazaras." By May 1999, brutal treatment of civilians continued as territory around the city of Bamiyam was captured and recaptured by the Taliban and another faction, Hezb-e Wahdat. While the majority of people fled after the Taliban recaptured the city on 9 May, many civilians who stayed behind were later systematically slaughtered by arriving Taliban guards.[24]

In continuation of such policies of terror and repression, in August, 1999, tens of thousands of people were violently evicted from their homes by Taliban forces who were attempting to uproot rebels in northern Afghanistan. The Taliban was undertaking a 'scorched earth' policy, involving the burning of homes, villages and crops, to prevent residents from returning to their homes in the Shomali Valley north of Kabul.

After the massive expulsion, long lines of men, women and children reportedly trudged toward Kabul. According to a UN statement from officials in Pakistan, "Families speak of whole villages being burned to the ground and crops set on fire to deter them from moving back to this once-fertile valley."

At this time, Kabul was already hosting a refugee population of 400,000. Thanks to the Taliban-sponsored 'cleansing' of the Shomali Valley, tens of thousands more refugees arrived. Additionally, as many as 150,000 reportedly fled the region towards rebel bases northeast of Kabul.[25]

Humanitarian Catastrophe Under Factional War

It is, of course, important to remember that systematic human rights abuses were routinely perpetrated by all major factions in the ongoing conflict in Afghanistan, not just by the Taliban. These have included:

"... the killing of tens of thousands of civilians in deliberate or indiscriminate attacks on residential areas, deliberate and arbitrary killing of thousands of men, women and children by armed guards during raids on their homes, unacknowledged detention of several thousand people after being abducted by the various armed political groups, torture of civilians including rape of women, routine beating and ill-treatment of civilians suspected of belonging to rival political groups or because of their ethnic identity."[26]

More than 25,000 people were killed from 1992 to 1997 in deliberate or indiscriminate attacks against civilian areas, with killings often occurring on a daily basis after severe battles for control of territory. With the war for territory between the Taliban and other factions escalating, civilians increasingly became the victims of indiscriminate attacks. Air raids on residential areas, ongoing fighting, landmines, gunfire, unreported massacres and the uncovering of mass graves illustrate the extent to which warring factions have dragged the country into a downward spiral of devastation.[27]

As Human Rights Watch reported at the end of the year 2000 in a succinct overview of the tragedy plaguing Afghanistan:

"Afghanistan has been at war for more than twenty years. During that time it has lost a third of its population. Some 1.5 million people are estimated to have died as a direct result of the conflict. Another 5 million fled as refugees to Iran and Pakistan; others became exiles elsewhere abroad. A large part of its population is internally displaced... Throughout the war, all of the major factions have been guilty of grave breaches of international humanitarian law. Their warmaking is supported and perpetuated by the involvement of Afghanistan's neighbors and other states in providing weapons, ammunition, fuel, and other logistical support. State and non-state actors across the region and beyond continue to provide new arms and other materiel, as well as training and advisory assistance. The arms provided have been directly implicated in serious violations of international humanitarian law. These include aerial bombardments of civilian targets, indiscriminate bombings, rocketing and other artillery attacks on civilian-populated areas, reprisal killings of civilians, summary executions of prisoners, rape, and torture."[28]

Due to the ravages of such ongoing war, Kabul has been without municipal water and electricity since 1994. This state of affairs had not improved by the beginning of 2002. Trade is frequently blockaded and subjected to extortionate 'taxes' by local power holders. Nearly everywhere, a new generation has emerged with minimal education in a land infested with landmines, due to which thousands of civilians continue to be killed or maimed. U.N. reports repeatedly show that the socio-economic conditions of the population are amongst the worst in the world.

The investment of previous governments in schools, roads and hospitals has been reduced to near insignificance. Literacy rates are extremely low, with nationwide literacy rates for women plunging to 4 per cent, the level in rural areas before the war. Healthcare is rudimentary at best, with many people lacking access to even the basics. Every year, thousands of children die from malnutrition and respiratory infections, while maternal mortality rates are among the highest in the world. Irrigation systems and the agricultural sector are neglected and destroyed.

Afghanistan has been plagued by a perpetual orgy of destruction, impoverishment and repression. One to two million Afghans have been killed. Before 11th September 2001, there were already over 2 million Afghan refugees in Iran and Pakistan, making Afghans the largest single refugee group in the world. Under the successive rule of Northern Alliance and later Taliban warlords, the majority of the population have been denied their social and human rights. Torture, arbitrary detention, mass killings and ongoing warfare have been the norm. The masses have remained embedded in growing poverty; while the rulers have falsely legitimised their actions under the guise of Islam.[29]

A brief review of certain aspects of this crisis suffices to help us understand its grotesque scale. One may begin with a particularly pertinent indicator, poverty, which has been endemic. According to the U.N. Office for the Coordination of Humanitarian Affairs:

"Millions of Afghans have little or no access to food through commercial markets, just as their access to food through self-production has been severely undermined by drought. The purchasing power of most Afghans has been seriously eroded by the absence of employment. About 85 percent of Afghanistan's estimated 21.9 million people are directly dependent on agriculture... The agricultural infrastructure has been severely damaged due to war and irrigation facilities are in urgent need of rehabilitation."[30]

Afghanistan also has one of the worst records on education in the world. According to UNICEF estimates, only 4-5 per cent of primary aged children received a broad based schooling—for secondary and higher education, the picture was worse. As Kate Clark reported:

"Twenty years of war has meant the collapse of everything. Both sides in the long running civil war prefer to spend money on fighting... However, the desire for schooling runs deep in Afghanistan, even among the uneducated. But the chances of getting a decent education are very slim. A whole generation of children is losing out, prompting questions about where this leaves the future of this devastated country."[31]

Then, of course, there has been the notorious repression of women. It should be noted that, as the international Muslim newsmagazine *Crescent International* rightly observed, "Criticism of the Taliban, whether it comes from non-Muslims or Muslims, is often heavily overlaid with prejudices or political interests." It is therefore important to ensure that facts are separated from propaganda. Nevertheless, *Crescent* admits that the Taliban regime has undoubtedly been highly repressive, to the extent that therein "the phrase 'Islamic justice' [is] used as a synonym for tyranny." Numerous reports of "draconian restrictions on women" being enforced in the name of Islam unfortunately reveal harsh realities.

"Men responsible for enforcing public decency are said to beat women in the streets who show their faces or ankles. Most women are 'not allowed to work.' They are forbidden to see male doctors, yet there are few female doctors available [to compensate]. Most girls' schools have been closed, and the only religious instruction is for girls who have not reached puberty."[32]

When the Taliban marched into Kabul in 1996, its policies of repression were highlighted. Political opponents were executed without trial. Females were barred from schools and employment; the ban including up to 50,000 war widows who were the sole support of their families.[33] Indeed, there have been endless reports concerning the mass oppression of women in Afghanistan by the Taliban.

While an increasing number of women were having to beg to survive and support their families, there were many reported cases of forced marriages and prostitution; of women being forcefully taken from their homes, or forcefully separated from their husbands and moved to camps; of huge numbers of women throughout the country suffering from clinical depression due to unceasing confinement; and even of sexual assaults. Radhika Coomaraswamy, the U.N. Special Rapporteur on Violence Against Women concluded: "Never have I seen a people suffering as much as in Afghanistan... The situation looks very bleak in terms of poverty, in terms of war, in terms of the rights of women." Coomaraswamy has concluded that discrimination against females is official Taliban policy, a veritable war on women which is "widespread, systematic and officially sanctioned."[34]

Misogynism Under Taliban Rule

The facts have been documented extensively by numerous independent human rights organisations that have directly witnessed the impact of the Taliban and undertaken meticulous grassroots research. It is worth quoting copiously from a survey conducted by the international Physicians for Human Rights (PHR) in 1998 to comprehend the scale of the crisis in Afghanistan under Taliban rule, utilising direct interviews with Afghan citizens and investigations on the ground. PHR reports that:

"One of the first edicts issued by the regime when it rose to power was to prohibit girls and women from attending school. Humanitarian groups initiated projects to replace through philanthropy what prior governments had afforded as a right to both sexes... On June 16, 1998, the Taliban ordered the closing of more than 100 privately funded schools where thousands of young women and girls were receiving training in skills that would have helped them support their families. The Taliban issued new rules for nongovernmental organizations providing the schooling: education must be limited to girls up to the age of eight, and restricted to the Qur'an... PHR's researcher when visiting Kabul in 1998, saw a city of beggars—women who had once been teachers and nurses now moving in the streets like ghosts... selling every possession and begging so as to feed their children."

The Taliban had thus:

"... deliberately created such poverty by arbitrarily depriving half the population under its control of jobs, schooling, mobility, and health care. Such restrictions are literally life threatening to women and to their children. The Taliban's abuses are by no means limited to women. Thousands of men have been taken prisoner, arbitrarily detained, tortured, and many killed and disappeared. Men are beaten and jailed for wearing beards of insufficient length (that of a clenched fist beneath the chin), are subjected to cruel and degrading conditions in jail... Men are also vulnerable to extortion, arrest, gang rape, and abuse in detention because of their ethnicity or presumed political views."[35]

PHR goes on to note that there are "extraordinarily high levels of mental stress and depression" in the country. 81 per cent of participants in the PHR survey "reported a decline in their mental condition...

"A large percentage of respondents met the diagnostic criteria for posttraumatic stress disorder (PTSD) (42%) (based on the Diagnostical and Statistical Manual of Mental Disorders, Fourth Edition) and major depression (97%), and also demonstrated significant symptoms of anxiety (86%) Twenty-one percent of the participants indicated that they had suicidal thoughts 'extremely often' or 'quite often.' It is clear from PHR's forty interviews with Afghan women that the general climate of cruelty, abuse, and tyranny that characterizes Taliban rule has had a profound affect on women's mental health. Ninety-five percent of women interviewed described a decline in their mental condition over the past two years. The denial of education also contributes to Afghan women's deteriorating mental health... The interviews revealed that women attributed the anxiety and depression that affects the vast majority of them to their fear of limited opportunities for their children, specifically denial of education to girl children. Poor and uneducated women spoke with particular urgency of their desire to obtain education for children, and saw health care, schooling, and protection of human rights as a key towards achieving a better future."

PHR notes that the women interviewed "consistently described high levels of poor health...

"... multiple specific symptoms, and a significant decline in women's physical condition since the beginning of the Taliban occupation. Sixty-six percent of women interviewed described a decline in their physical condition over the past two years. An Afghan physician described declining nutrition in children, an increasing rate of tuberculosis, and a high prevalence of other infectious diseases among women and children."

Investigating the Rabia Balkhi Hospital, previously the only facility in Kabul open to women, PHR "found that it lacked basic medical supplies and equipment such as X-ray machines, suction and oxygen, running water, and medications... Yet even these poor facilities are not available to many women who seek treatment for themselves or their children." A massive 87 per cent of women surveyed by PHR "reported a decrease in their access to health services. The reasons given included: no [male] chaperone available

(27%), restrictions on women's mobility (36%), hospital refused to provide care (21%), no female doctor available (48%), do not own a burqa (6%), and economics (61%)." A general environment of constant terror has been instituted.

> "Sixty-eight percent of women interviewed described incidents in which they were detained and physically abused by Taliban officials... Witnessing executions, fleeing religious police with whips who search for women and girls diverging from dress codes or other edicts, having a family member jailed or beaten; such experiences traumatize and retraumatize Afghan women, who have already experienced the horrors of war, rocketing, ever-present landmines and unexploded ordnance, and the loss of friends and immediate family."[36]

Given the historical context of these developments, it is indisputable that a major portion of the responsibility for this escalating humanitarian crisis lies at the door of the leading players in the international community. In other words, not only the then Soviet Union, but principally the United States.

The Distortion of Islam

The U.S. role, in cultivating extremism while establishing the network of Afghan fighters who later went on to form the various warring factions, was particularly crucial and damaging. As already noted, U.S. support of the mujahideen involved inculcating extremist religious 'war values,' garbed with Islamic jargon.[37] Central Asia expert Selig Harrison of the Woodrow Wilson International Center for Scholars recalls that: "I warned them that we were creating a monster. They told me these people were fanatical, and the more fierce they were the more fiercely they would fight the Soviets."[38] The U.S. government was well aware of the monster it had created. As U.S. journalist Ken Silverstein notes:

> "Though Reagan called the rebels 'freedom fighters,' few within the government had any illusions about the forces that the United States was backing. The mujahidin fighters espoused a radical brand of Islam—some commanders were known to have thrown acid in the faces of women who refused to wear the veil—and committed horrific human rights violations in their war against the Red Army."[39]

Indeed, the extremist religious 'jihadi' ideology cultivated in CIA-sponsored training programmes, intertwined with tribal norms and values, combined and gave rise to the distorted 'Islamic' system within Afghanistan under the rule of various factions, including the Taliban. It should thus be noted that the Taliban's status as a genuinely Islamic movement is at the very least highly questionable—there are very few Muslim scholars who would agree that the policies discussed above constitute Islamic policies.

As pointed out by former U.S. Congressman Paul Findley, Chairman Emeritus of the Washington-based Council for National Interest and Chairman of the Illinois-based Human Relations Commission, the Taliban "calls itself 'Islamic,' but its regulations directly violate some of the most cherished principles of the Islamic faith."[40]

Indeed, most Muslim scholars do not ratify or condone Taliban-like repression or atrocities. For instance, the Pakistani newspaper, the *Daily Star*, reports that "Islamic scholars in neighbouring Pakistan say the Taliban's laws reflect tribal traditions more than Islamic tenets."[41] Abdullahi An-Na'im, a Muslim and U.S.-based legal scholar, challenges the Taliban claims that their edicts come from the Qu'ran. He writes, "Unless Muslims [condemn these policies and practices] from an Islamic point of view as well, the Taliban will get away with their false claim that these heinous crimes against humanity are dictated by Islam as a religion."[42]

The Associated Press further reports the little known but important fact that while the "Taliban have imposed their harsh brand of Islamic Laws on the 90 per cent of Afghanistan they rule," in actual fact, "Islamic scholars elsewhere say that the Taliban's laws are based more on tribal traditions than the Koran, Islam's holy book."[43]

In a study of Taliban policies in comparison with a wide-ranging survey of Islamic thought and culture, American journalist Robin Travis points out:

"As to whether the Taliban's practice of Islam is the pure form of Islam, we can see that there is much debate on the interpretation of the Qur'an.... Thus far, we have been able to determine that there are many interpretations of the Qur'an and many definitions of the religious practice of Islam. What we can also see here, is that the majority of those who practice this religion, do not interpret the Qur'an as endorsing oppression and abuse of women."

Travis concludes: "[R]esearch and discussion of the practice of the Islamic faith [shows] that the Taliban are practicing an extreme version of Islam, because other forms and practices do not include the oppression of women... The Taliban has clearly manipulated the Qu'ran to serve its own purposes in causing abuse and hardships on women."[44]

The Muslim Women's League concurs with this analysis, observing that:

"[The] Taliban's insistence on secluding women from public life is a political maneuver disguised as 'Islamic' law. Before seizing power,

Taliban manipulated and used the rights of women as tools to gain control of the country. To secure financial and political support, Taliban emulated authoritarian methods typical of many Middle Eastern countries. The Taliban's stand on the seclusion of women is not derived from Islam, but, rather, from a cultural bias found in suppressive movements throughout the region... The Qur'an and the examples of the first Muslim society give the Muslim Women's League a voice to state that the current manipulation of women to serve geo-political interests, in Afghanistan or elsewhere, is both unIslamic and inhumane."[45]

A representative example of the Taliban's actual contempt for basic Islamic edicts is one of the numerous issues noted by the United Nations Special Rapporteur of the U.N. Commission on Human Rights, in Afghanistan:

"The Special Rapporteur was informed by scholars that it was a religious obligation in Islam to acquire education and that deprivation of education constituted a disobedience of Islamic principles. The view was expressed that the motivations for banning female education on part of the Taliban were neither legal, financial or based on security but were probably politically motivated. One of the most serious consequences of the conflict in Afghanistan was the brain-drain of its educated people."[46]

The U.N. report further confirmed that:

"It should be recalled that the Taliban have a highly idiosyncratic vision of Islam that has been disputed by numerous Sunni Islamic scholars as representing at best a tribal rural code of behaviour applied only in some parts of Afghanistan of which only one aspect is being exploited."[47]

Elsewhere, the report points out again that:

"The Special Rapporteur heard persistent affirmations from qualified sources that the policies applied by the Taliban in the areas under their control did not constitute a correct interpretation of the Shariah (Islamic law) but were at best a narrow tribal and rural code of conduct in limited parts of Afghanistan."[48]

It should also be noted that the repression of women in Afghanistan is not something that was solely introduced by the Taliban, an impression wrongfully propagated by conventional opinion. While Taliban rule certainly led to the exacerbation of this brutal repression, it is a historical fact that such repression had existed long before the concrete establishment of this faction. For example, between 1992 and 1996, under the fragmented rule of Northern

Alliance factions, the same sort of brutal and repressive policies existed. Yet prior to the Taliban's consolidation in Afghanistan—and even during that consolidation—the international community had largely ignored this repression, a fact that at the very least illustrates the extremely fickle nature of the West's promotion of humanitarian principles. Indeed, even when the Taliban had gained power, despite public professions of opposition to the regime's abuses of human rights and repression of women, certain leading members of the international community had approved of—and indeed supported—the Taliban, in a bid to secure their regional strategic and economic interests.

Notes

[5] bifurcation: Dividing into two parts or branches.

[6] Rubin, Barnett R., 'Afghanistan: The Forgotten Crisis,' Writenet (UK), Feb. 1996; Rubin, Barnett R., 'In Focus: Afghanistan,' *Foreign Policy In Focus*, Dec. 1996, Vol. 1, No. 25, www.foreignpolicy-infocus.org; Catalinotto, John, 'Afghan feudal reaction: Washington reaps what it has sown,' Workers World News Service, 3 Sept. 1998; Pentagon report, *Afghanistan: A country study*, 1986, cited in ibid.; Rubin, Barnett R., 'The Political Economy of War and Peace in Afghanistan,' paper presented at Afghan Support Group, Stockholm, Sweden, 21 June 1999, Institute for Afghan Studies. For more detail on the contemporary history of the crisis in Afghanistan see Roy, Oliver, *Islam and Resistance in Afghanistan*, Cambridge University Press, Cambridge, 1990; Rubin, Barnett R., *The Fragmentation of Afghanistan: State Formation and Collapse in the International System*, Yale University Press, New Haven, 1995; Rubin, *The Search for Peace in Afghanistan: From Buffer State to Failed State*, Yale University Press, New Haven, 1995. For further information online, see www.institute-for-afghan-studies.org.

[7] Agence France Presse (AFP), 12 December 2000.

[8] Ibid.

[9] Cited by Agence France Presse, 14 January 1998. Also see Greg Guma, 'Cracks in the Covert Iceberg,' *Toward Freedom*, May 1998, p. 2; Feinberg, Leslie, 'Brezezinski brags, blows cover: U.S. intervened in Afghanistan first,' *Workers World*, 12 March 1998.

[10] *Le Nouvel Observateur*, 15-21 January 1998, p. 76.

[11] Ali, Nour, *US-UN Conspiracy Against the People of Afghanistan*, Online Center for Afghan Studies, now the Institute for Afghan Studies (www.institute-for-afghan-studies.org), 21 February 1998.

[12] Hiro, Dilip, 'Fallout from the Afghan Jihad,' Inter Press Services, 21 November 1995.

[13] Smith, J. W., 'Simultaneously Suppressing the World's Break for Freedom,' in *Economic Democracy: The Political Struggle for the 21st Century*, M. E. Sharpe, New York, Armonk, 2000.

[14] Rubin, Barnett, 'In Focus: Afghanistan,' *Foreign Policy In Focus*, Vol. 1, No. 25., December 1996.

[15] Human Rights Watch, New York, December 1992; *Economist*, 24 July 1993.

[16] Fisk, Robert, 'Just who are our allies in Afghanistan?', *The Independent*, 3 October 2001.

[17] Fisk, Robert, 'What will the Northern Alliance do in our name now?', *The Independent*, 14 November 2001.

[18] HRW Backgrounder, 'Afghanistan: Poor rights record of opposition commanders,' Human Rights Watch, New York, 6 October 2001, www.hrw.org/press/2001/10/afghan1005.htm.

[19] HRW Backgrounder, 'Military Assistance to the Afghan Opposition,' Human Rights Watch, October 2001, www.hrw.org/backgrounder/asia/afghan-bck1005.htm.

[20] Scott, Peter Dale, 'Afghanistan, Turkmenistan Oil and Gas, and the Projected Pipeline,' Online Resource on Al-Qaeda and Osama Bin Laden, 21 October 2001, http://socrates.berkeley.edu/~pdscott/q.html.

[21] AI news release, 'Afghanistan: Thousands of civilians killed following Taliban takeover of Mazar-e Sharif,' Amnesty International, London, 3 September 1998; Sheridan, Michael, 'How the Taliban Slaughtered 8,000,' *Sunday Times*, 1 November 1998.

[22] AI news release, 'Afghanistan: Thousands of civilians killed following Taliban takeover of Mazae-e Sharif,' op. cit.

[23] Ibid.

[24] Ibid.; AI news release, 'Afghanistan: International actors have a special responsibility for ending the human rights catastrophe,' Amnesty International, London, 18 Nov. 1999; AI news release, 'Afghanistan: Civilians in a game of war they have not chosen,' Amnesty International, London, 27 May 1999.

[25] Naji, Kasra, 'UN: Taliban forcing thousands from homes in Afghanistan,' CNN, 15 August 1999. Also see AI report, *Afghanistan: The Human Rights of Minorities*, Amnesty International, London, November 1999.

[26] AI report, *Afghanistan: Grave Abuses in the Name of Religion*, Amnesty International, London, November 1996.

[27] AI report, *Afghanistan: Continuing Atrocities Against Civilians*, Amnesty International, London, September 1997.

[28] HRW Press Backgrounder, 'Fuelling Afghanistan's War,' Human Rights Watch, New York, 15 December 2000.

[29] Rubin, Barnett R., 'Afghanistan: The Forgotten Crisis,' Writenet (UK), Feb. 1996; AI report, *Refugees from Afghanistan: the World's Largest Single Refugee Group*, Amnesty International, London, November 1999; AFP, 'Tuberculosis spreading in Afghanistan killing thousands,' 25 March 2000; Gannon, Kathy, 'Children: the Victims in Afghan War,' Associated Press (AP), 27 Dec. 1998; Dumble, Lynette J., 'Taliban are still brutal villains,' *Green Left Weekly*, Issue 390, 26 Jan. 2000; AI report, *Women in Afghanistan: Pawns in Men's Power Struggles*, Amnesty International, London, Nov. 1999. Also see Catalinotto, John, 'Afghan feudal reaction: Washington reaps what it has sown,' Workers World News Service, 3 Sept. 1998; Griswold, Deirdre, 'Afghanistan: The lynching of a revolution,' Workers World News Service, 10 Oct. 1996.

[30] UN Office for the Coordination of Humanitarian Affairs, 'Hunger threatens millions of poor Afghans,' 9 June 2000.

[31] Clark, Kate, BBC Worldnews Services, 27 April 2000.

[32] Geissinger, Aishah, 'Understanding the Taliban phenomenon – a crucial task for the Islamic movement,' *Crescent International*, 1-15 May 2000, www.muslimedia.org. Geissinger also observes a critical fact that is often missing from the reports on Taliban repression: "Western complicity in and responsibility for the Taliban's excesses is usually ignored." She cites an obvious example: "if the economy is based on opium, what can anyone expect after 22 years of war and upheaval [perpetuated by the West which was supporting various factions throughout the war to secure its strategic interests], to say nothing of the recent imposition of economic sanctions?" For more on how the CIA deliberately encouraged the drugs trade in Afghanistan see Cooley, John K., *Unholy Wars: Afghanistan, America and International Terrorism*, Pluto Press, London, 1999. For an authoritative report on the Taliban from a Muslim perspective see Rashid, Ahmed, 'Afghanistan: Heart of Darkness,' 'Wages of War,' 'Final Offensive?', *Far Eastern Economic Review*, 5 Aug. 1999; Ahmed Rashid is an investigative reporter based in Pakistan. Also see Dumble, Lynette J., 'Taliban are still brutal villains,' *Green Left Weekly*, Issue 390, 26 January 2000.

[33] AI report, *Afghanistan: Grave Abuses in the Name of Religion*, op. cit.; 'Editorial: Who's behind the Taliban?', *Workers World*, 5 June 1997; Catalinotto, John, 'Afghanistan: Battle deepens for Central Asian oil,' *Workers World*, 24 October 1996. See the report by the award-winning investigative journalist and human rights activist Jan Goodwin, 'Buried Alive: Afghan Women Under the Taliban,' *On The Issues*, Vol. 7, No. 3, Summer 1998, www.mosaic.echonyc.com/~onissues/index.html.

[34] CNN, 'UN: Abuse of women in Taliban areas officially sanctioned,' 13 Sept. 1999. Also see AI report, *Afghanistan: Grave Abuses in the Name of Religion*, op. cit.; Dumble, Lynette J., 'Taliban are still brutal villains,' *Green Left Weekly*, Issue 390, 26 Jan. 2000; Goodwin, Jan, 'Buried Alive: Afghan Women Under

the Taliban,' *On The Issues*, Vol. 7, No. 3, Summer 1998; AI report, *Women in Afghanistan: Pawns in Men's Power Struggles*, Amnesty International, London, Nov. 1999.

[35] Afghanistan Campaign, *The Taliban's War on Women: A Health and Human Rights Crisis in Afghanistan Executive Summary*, Physicians for Human Rights, Boston, 1998.

[36] Ibid. Also see the report by Jan Goodwin, 'Buried Alive: Afghan Women Under the Taliban,' op. cit.; AI report, *Women in Afghanistan: Pawns in Men's Power Struggles*, Amnesty International, London, Nov. 1999; AI report, *Human Rights Defenders in Afghanistan: Civil Society Destroyed*, Amnesty International, London, Nov. 1999; AI report, *Children Devastated by War: Afghanistan's Lost Generations*, Amnesty International, London, 1999.

[37] Hiro, Dilip, 'Fallout from the Afghan Jihad,' op. cit.

[38] Suri, Sanjay, 'CIA worked with Pak to create the Taliban,' India Abroad News Service, 6 March 2001.

[39] Silverstein, Ken, 'Blasts from the past,' *Salon*, 22 Sept. 2001, www.salon.com.

[40] Interview with Paul Findley, 'Political Activism By U.S. Muslims,' *American Muslim*, January 2000.

[41] *Daily Star*, Vol. 3, No., 342, 13 August 2000.

[42] PagaNet News, Vol. 4, No., 6, 1998.

[43] Associated Press (AP), 'UN: Abuse of women in Taliban areas officially sanctioned,' 13 September 1999.

[44] Travis-Murphee, Robin C., 'Gender Apartheid: Women and the Taliban – Pure Religion or Purely Oppression?', Essays, 30 April 1999, http://members.aol.com/gracieami/Taleban.htm.

[45] Muslim Women's League, *Perspective on Women's Plight in Afghanistan*, Nov. 1996, www.mwlusa.org/news_afghan.shtml. It is, however, crucial to recall that women in Afghanistan suffered from repression well before the Taliban, as human rights reports prior to 1996 document extensively. In fact, Taliban policies only worsened an already grim situation in this respect.

[46] Paik, Choong-Hyun, *Interim report on the situation of human rights in Afghanistan*, Office of the United Nations High Commissioner for Human Rights, Fifty-second session, Agenda item 112, 16 Oct. 1997, point no. 83.

[47] Ibid., point no. 29.

[48] Ibid., point no. 137.

2. The United States, Afghanistan and the Taliban, 1994-2001

"Life under the Taliban is so hard and repressive, even small displays of joy are outlawed, children aren't allowed to fly kites, their mothers face beatings for laughing out loud. Women cannot work outside the home, or even leave their homes by themselves... The plight of women and children in Afghanistan is a matter of deliberate human cruelty, carried out by those who seek to intimidate and control... Afghan women know, through hard experiences, what the rest of the world is discovering: The brutal oppression of women is a central goal of the terrorists."

Laura Bush, First Lady,
delivering the weekly Presidential Radio Address
(CNN, 17 November 2001)

Throughout the 1990s, urgent calls by human rights organisations for the meaningful intervention of an international body in the escalating Afghan crisis continued, unanswered. This continued despite the fact that two key members of the international community, America and Russia, bear primary responsibility for the state of war that plagues Afghanistan to this day, due to their respective self-interested manipulations of the country. Disregarding their responsibility, these powers refused to undertake a significant intervention, be it diplomatic or otherwise. Meaningful pressure that could have been exerted upon the Taliban to change its policies was simply avoided.

Turning a Blind Eye

BBC foreign correspondent Matt Frei rightly observes that: "Afghanistan today is the product of a war fought by others on its soil...

"The U.S. and its allies plied this country with Stinger missiles and cash to fuel the mujahideen's opposition against Soviet occupation. They encouraged the growth of Islamic fundamentalism to frighten Moscow and of drugs to get Soviet soldiers hooked. The CIA even helped 'Arab Afghans' like Osama bin Laden, now 'America's most wanted,' to fight here."[49]

The responsibility of the U.S. for the ongoing crisis in Afghanistan is therefore not in dispute. But while the U.S. bears principal responsibility, other leading players in the international community cannot be absolved. As Amnesty International (AI) notes: "For two decades, the international community has mostly averted its eyes from the human rights catastrophe in Afghanistan... The United States, its West European allies and the former Soviet Union have failed to bring to an end the very human rights crisis that they helped to create."

The systematic, ethnically-motivated killings of thousands of Hazara Afghans, for example, was not enough to elicit other than a rhetorical response from the Western powers, who thereby illustrated their lack of genuine concern for this tide of genocide. While issuing a statement condemning the killing of Iranian diplomats at Mazar-e-Sharif and calling for investigations into their death, "The UN Security Council... has remained silent about the deaths and arbitrary detention of thousands of 'ordinary' people."

As AI emphasises, public condemnation combined with international pressure "has been shown to be effective in revealing the truth about human rights abuses" and "prevent[ing] further massacres." Yet, Western powers refused to follow through properly with both condemnation and pressure. Twenty years of such ongoing refusal and failure had, quite predictably, signaled effective international consent for the Taliban to continue with its policies. In studiously refraining from implementing even the most simple of such steps, this behaviour by Western powers suggested that there may have been other, more important interests in allowing the Taliban to rise to power and consolidate its control.[50]

The only countries that openly accepted the Taliban as Afghanistan's legitimate government were Pakistan, Saudi Arabia and the United Arab Emirates—all of which happen to be U.S./Western clients.[51] If the United States had exerted political or economic pressure on these countries to cease their well documented financial and military sponsoring of Taliban terrorism, it is highly likely that they would have been forced to acquiesce, simply because of their critical dependence on Western (particularly American) aid.[52]

Indeed, while sometimes condemning atrocious Taliban policies in rhetoric, the West turned a blind eye to the actions of its own regional clients who were actively supporting the same policies. The result was an effective 'green light' to the Taliban to pursue its policies.

Barnett Rubin of the Council on Foreign Relations reports that the professed U.S. policy of promoting peace in Afghanistan has "suffered from a variety of internal contradictions. U.S. policy toward Iran conflicts with

U.S. stated policy toward Afghanistan, and is one of the reasons that many in the region believe the U.S. supports the Taliban." Rubin notes: "If the U.S. is in fact supporting the joint Pakistani-Saudi backing of the Taliban in some way, even if not materially, then it has in effect decided to make Afghanistan the victim of yet another proxy war—this time aimed at Iran rather than the USSR."

America's professed commitment to supporting the UN as the means of creating peace in Afghanistan is similarly highly flawed: "U.S. support of the U.N. as the proper vehicle for a negotiated settlement of the Afghan conflict is undermined by congressional refusal to allocate funds for U.N. dues or the U.S. share of peacekeeping expenses."

Moreover, "The U.S. has not described and criticized in a straightforward manner the specific types of external interference occurring in Afghanistan," from Pakistan and Saudi Arabia, for instance. "Public statements by the State Department condemn such interference but never specify who is undertaking it," annulling the whole purpose of condemnation.[53]

Indeed, expressing the conclusions of the majority of Afghan analysts on U.S.-U.N. policy in the late 1990s, former Afghan Minister of Finance (1965-69) Dr. Nour Ali, an expert on Afghan affairs, noted other vast internal contradictions in the approach. Highlighting the U.N.'s claim to have "mediated the withdrawal of foreign (Soviet) forces from Afghanistan," Nour Ali observed that the policy only succeeded in "planting and strengthening the warring factions and factionalism in Afghanistan...

"For in connection with this mediation there is a question: mediation between who and who? Normally, logically, and legally, it should be conducted between Afghanistan and the former Soviet Union, and the Geneva Accords should be concluded accordingly. Scandalously and shamefully, the mediation took place among all the interested parties, but in the sheer exclusion of Afghanistan. And the accords were signed between the delegate of the Soviet-installed government in Kabul representing the former Soviet Union and that of the Government of Pakistan representing somehow the Government of the United States."

This peculiar form of "mediation," which deliberately excluded Afghanistan, indicated the "U.S. Administration's policy—implemented by the United Nations—to deny Afghanistan its right for a national government representing its people in its relations with foreign nations, letting other powers decide its fate." Furthermore, this state of affairs had been exacerbated by the ongoing funding of various Afghan factions by foreign powers attempting to secure their own regional interests:

"There is no doubt that the presaging has been confirmed by the subsequent development: No national Afghan government has yet emerged; the country is fragmented and no longer independent; its fate is in the hands of alien powers; all its social, political, and administrative services are abolished; the warring factions and factionalism—introduced by the U.S. Administration and maintained by the United Nations—are prevailing."[54]

The Western powers had thus primarily ignored Afghanistan's humanitarian catastrophe, refraining from implementing any significant action to alleviate it. Indeed, one is led to wonder why the NATO powers were so willing to impose massive pressure on a country such as Serbia for its alleged human rights abuses against Kosovars, although they refused for so long to impose a comparable kind of pressure on the Taliban—despite the fact that the Taliban implemented the same brand of mass abuses, yet on a much more brutal and extensive scale.

This sort of comparative analysis of Western foreign policy under U.S. leadership illustrates the selectivity of alleged Western commitment to the promotion of democracy and the protection of human rights. Such Western indifference is probably linked to the fact that, as Ben C. Vidgen remarks: "In Afghanistan and Pakistan, fundamentalism could not have bloomed without the CIA's covert assistance—a fact that is apparent when one examines the history of the area."[55]

America and the Taliban: *Dancing with the Devil*

In this connection, there is considerable evidence that the anti-Taliban stance of the United States constitutes a shift in policy. From 1994 to 1998, the United States supported the Taliban while attempting to secure a variety of strategic and economic interests. U.S. support of the Taliban was envisaged to be a vehicle of sustained and directed American involvement in the region. Between 1999 and 2000, this support continued, but began to wane.

Amnesty International (AI) reports that although the "United States has denied any links with the Taleban," according to then U.S. Assistant Secretary of State Robin Raphel, Afghanistan was a "crucible of strategic interest" during the Cold War, though she denies any U.S. influence or support of factions in Afghanistan today, dismissing any possible ongoing strategic interests. However, former Department of Defense official Elie Krakowski, who worked on the Afghan issue in the 1980s, points out that Afghanistan remains important because:

"[It] is the crossroads between what Halford MacKinder called the world's Heartland and the Indian sub continent. It owes its importance to its location at the confluence of major routes. A boundary between land power and sea power, it is the meeting point between opposing forces larger than itself. Alexander the Great used it as a path to conquest. So did the Moghuls. An object of competition between the British and Russian empires in the 19th century, Afghanistan became a source of controversy between the American and Soviet superpowers in the 20th. With the collapse of the Soviet Union, it has become an important potential opening to the sea for the landlocked new states of Central Asia. The presence of large oil and gas deposits in that area has attracted countries and multinational corporations... Because Afghanistan is a major strategic pivot what happens there affects the rest of the world."[56]

Raphel's denial of U.S. interests in the region also stands in contradiction to the fact that, as Amnesty reports, "many Afghanistan analysts believe that the United States has had close political links with the Taleban militia. They refer to visits by Taleban representatives to the United States in recent months and several visits by senior U.S. State Department officials to Kandahur, including one immediately before the Taleban took over Jalalabad."

AI further refers to a comment by *The Guardian*: "Senior Taleban leaders attended a conference in Washington in mid-1996 and U.S. diplomats regularly traveled to Taleban headquarters." *The Guardian* points out that although such "visits can be explained," "the timing raises doubts as does the generally approving line which U.S. officials take towards the Taleban."[57] Raphel's denial also stands in contradiction to her own behaviour. Agence France Presse reported that:

"In the months before the Taliban took power, former U.S. Assistant Secretary of State for South Asia Robin Raphel waged an intense round of shuttle diplomacy between the powers with possible stakes in the [UNOCAL] project. 'Robin Raphel was the face of the Unocal pipeline,' said an official of the former Afghan government who was present at some of the meetings with her... In addition to tapping new sources of energy, the [project] also suited a major U.S. strategic aim in the region: isolating its nemesis Iran and stifling a frequently mooted rival pipeline backed by Tehran, experts said."[58]

Amnesty goes on to confirm that recent "accounts of the madrasas (religious schools) which the Taleban attended in Pakistan indicate that these [Western] links [with the Taleban] may have been established at the very inception of the Taleban movement...

"In an interview broadcast by the BBC World Service on 4 October 1996, Pakistan's then Prime Minister Benazir Bhutto affirmed that the madrasas had been set up by Britain, the United States, Saudi Arabia and Pakistan during the Jihad, the Islamic resistance against Soviet occupation of Afghanistan."[59]

The CIA's sponsoring of the Taliban movement through Pakistan and Saudi Arabia has been documented extensively by Michel Chossudovsky, Professor of Economics at the University of Ottawa, Canada.[60] According to Selig Harrison, an expert on U.S. relations with Asia, the creation of the Taliban was "actively encouraged by the [Pakistani] ISI and the CIA."[61] As former Pakistani Interior Minister, retired Major General Naseerullah Babar commented: "[The] CIA itself introduced terrorism in the region and is only shedding crocodiles tears to absolve itself of the responsibility."[62] Thus, when the Taliban succeeded in consolidating its power in 1996, U.S. State Department spokesperson Glyn Davies explained that the U.S. found "nothing objectionable" in the event.

Indeed, Chairman of the Senate Foreign Relations Subcommittee on the Near East and South East, Senator Hank Brown, announced gleefully that: "The good part of what has happened is that one of the factions at last seems capable of developing a new government in Afghanistan."[63] After a visit by the head of Saudi intelligence, Prince Turki, to Islamabad and Kandahar, U.S. ally Saudi Arabia funded and equipped the Taliban march on Kabul.[64] U.S. Afghan experts, including Radha Kumar of the Council on Foreign Relations, now admit that the U.S. supported the rise of the Taliban. Agence France Press reported in early October 2001 that: "Afghanistan's Taliban regime, now bracing for punitive U.S. military strikes, was brought to power with Washington's silent blessing as it dallied in an abortive new 'Great Game' in central Asia...

"Keen to see Afghanistan under strong central rule to allow a U.S.-led group to build a multi-billion-dollar oil and gas pipeline, Washington urged key allies Pakistan and Saudi Arabia to back the militia's bid for power in 1996, analysts said... The United States encouraged Saudi Arabia and Pakistan to support the Taliban, certainly right up to their advance on Kabul... One key reason for U.S. interest in the Taliban was a 4.5-billion-dollar oil and gas pipeline that a U.S.-led oil consortium planned to build across war-ravaged Afghanistan... [The oil] consortium feared there could be no pipeline as long as Afghanistan, battered by war since the Soviet withdrawal in 1989, was split among rival warlords. The Taliban, whose rise to power owed much to their bid to stamp out the drugs trade and install law and order, seemed attractive to Washington."[65]

U.S. support of the Taliban did not end there, but in fact continued throughout most of the 1990s. Professor William O. Beeman, an anthropologist specialising in the Middle East at Brown University, who has conducted extensive research into Islamic Central Asia, points out:

"It is no secret, especially in the region, that the United States, Pakistan and Saudi Arabia have been supporting the fundamentalist Taliban in their war for control of Afghanistan for some time. The U.S. has never openly acknowledged this connection, but it has been confirmed by both intelligence sources and charitable institutions in Pakistan."[66]

Professor Beeman, a long-time observer of Afghan affairs, observes that the U.S.-backed Taliban "are a brutal fundamentalist group that has conducted a cultural scorched-earth policy" in Afghanistan. Extensive documentation shows that the Taliban have "committed atrocities against their enemies and their own citizens... So why would the U.S. support them?"

Beeman concludes that the answer to this question "has nothing to do with religion or ethnicity—but only with the economics of oil. To the north of Afghanistan is one of the world's wealthiest oil fields, on the Eastern Shore of the Caspian Sea in republics formed since the breakup of the Soviet Union." Caspian oil needs to be trans-shipped out of the landlocked region through a warm water port, for the desired profits to be accumulated.

The "simplest and cheapest" pipeline route is through Iran—but Iran is essentially an 'enemy' of the U.S., due to its over-independence. As Beeman notes: "The U.S. government has such antipathy to Iran that it is willing to do anything to prevent this." The alternative route is one that passes through Afghanistan and Pakistan, which "would require securing the agreement of the powers-that-be in Afghanistan"—the Taliban. Such an arrangement would also benefit Pakistani elites, "which is why they are willing to defy the Iranians." Therefore, as far as the U.S. is concerned, the solution is "for the anti-Iranian Taliban to win in Afghanistan and agree to the pipeline through their territory."[67]

Apart from the oil stakes, Afghanistan remains a strategic region for the U.S. in another related respect. The establishment of a strong client state in the country would strengthen U.S. influence in this crucial region, partly by strengthening Pakistan—at that time a prime supporter of the Taliban— which is America's main source of regional leverage. Of course, this also furthers the cause of establishing the required oil and gas pipelines to the Caspian Sea, while bypassing Russia and opening up the Commonwealth of Independent States (CIS)—the Central Asian republics—bordering Russia to the U.S. dominated global market.

"The Taliban will probably develop like the Saudis," commented one U.S. diplomat in 1997. "There will be Aramco [consortium of oil companies controlling Saudi oil], pipelines, an emir, no parliament and lots of Sharia law. We can live with that."[68] Thus, in December 1997, Taliban representatives were invited as guests to the Texas headquarters of UNOCAL, to negotiate their support of the pipeline.

At that time, UNOCAL had already begun training Afghan men in the skills required for pipeline construction, with U.S. government approval: "A senior delegation from the Taleban movement in Afghanistan is in the United States for talks with an international energy company that wants to construct a gas pipeline from Turkmenistan across Afghanistan to Pakistan...

"A spokesman for the company, Unocal, said the Taleban were expected to spend several days at the company's headquarters in Sugarland, Texas... A BBC regional correspondent says the proposal to build a pipeline across Afghanistan is part of an international scramble to profit from developing the rich energy resources of the Caspian Sea... Unocal... has commissioned the University of Nebraska to teach Afghan men the technical skills needed for pipeline construction. Nearly 140 people were enrolled last month in Kandahar and Unocal also plans to hold training courses for women in administrative skills. Although the Taleban authorities only allow women to work in the health sector, organisers of the training say they haven't so far raised any objections."[69]

U.S. Support of the Taliban

Strategic and economic interests, therefore, motivated what *The Guardian* referred to as "the generally approving line that U.S. officials take towards the Taleban." Elaborating, Cable News Network (CNN) reported that the "United States wants good ties [with the Taliban] but can't openly seek them while women are being repressed"—hence they can be sought covertly.[70]

The Inter Press Service (IPS) reported that underscoring "the geopolitical stakes, Afghanistan has appeared prominently in U.S. government and corporate planning about routes for pipelines and roads opening the ex-Soviet republics on Russia's southern border to world markets." Hence, amid the fighting, "some Western businesses are warming up to the Taliban despite the movement's institutionalisation of terror, massacres, abductions, and impoverishment."

"Leili Helms, a spokeswoman for the Taliban in New York, told IPS that one U.S. company, Union Oil of California (Unocal), helped to arrange the visit last week of the movement's acting information, industry and mines ministers. The three officials met lower-level State Department officials before departing for France, Helms said."

"Several U.S. and French firms are interested in developing gas lines through central and southern Afghanistan, where the 23 Taliban-controlled states" just happen to be located, as Helms added, to the 'chance' convenience of American and other Western companies.[71]

Leili Helms was hired by the Taliban to be their PR representative in Washington. She happens to be well versed in the clandestine workings of U.S. intelligence agencies—her uncle, Richard Helms, is a former director of the U.S. Central Intelligence Agency (CIA).[72]

An article appearing in the prestigious German daily *Frankfurter Rundschau*, in early October 1996, reported that UNOCAL "has been given the go-ahead from the new holders of power in Kabul to build a pipeline from Turkmenistan via Afghanistan to Pakistan. It would lead from Krasnovodsk on the Caspian Sea to Karachi on the Indian Ocean coast."

The same article noted that UN diplomats in Geneva believe that the war in Afghanistan is the result of a struggle between Turkey, Iran, Pakistan, Russia and the United States "to secure access to the rich oil and natural gas of the Caspian Sea."[73] Other than UNOCAL, companies that are jubilantly interested in exploiting Caspian oil, apparently at any human expense, include AMOCO, BP, Chevron, EXXON, and Mobile.[74]

It is in this context that Franz Schurmann, Professor Emeritus of History and Sociology at the University of California, commented on "Washington's discreet backing of the Taliban," noting the announcement in May 1996 "by UNOCAL that it was preparing to build a pipeline to transport natural gas from Turkmenistan to Pakistan through Western Afghanistan... UNOCAL's announcement was premised on an imminent Taliban victory."[75] The respected *Pakistan Observer* notes that:

"As for the U.S. government, it wanted UNOCAL to build the oil and gas pipelines from Central Asian states to Pakistan through Afghanistan so that the vast untapped oil and gas reserves in the Central Asian and Caspian region could be transported to markets in South Asia, South-East Asia Far East and the Pacific."[76]

It therefore comes as no surprise to see the *Wall Street Journal* reporting that the main interests of American and other Western elites lie in making Afghanistan "a prime transshipment route for the export of Central Asia's vast oil, gas and other natural resources." "Like them or not," the *Journal* continues, without fear of contradiction, "the Taliban are the players most capable of achieving peace in Afghanistan at this moment in history." The

Journal is referring to the same faction that is responsible for the severe repression of women; massacres of civilians; ethnic cleansing and genocide; arbitrary detention; and the growth of widespread impoverishment and underdevelopment.[77]

Despite all this, as the *New York Times* similarly reported: "The Clinton Administration has taken the view that a Taliban victory... would act as a counterweight to Iran... and would offer the possibility of new trade routes that could weaken Russian and Iranian influence in the region."[78]

In a similar vein, the *International Herald Tribunal* reported that in the summer of 1998, "the Clinton administration was talking with the Taleban about potential pipeline routes to carry oil and natural gas out of Turkmenistan to the Indian Ocean by crossing Afghanistan and Pakistan,"[79] clarifying why the U.S. was approving the consolidation of the Taliban's rule in the country, depriving the indigenous population of the freedom to utilise the region's strategic position for their own benefit. P. Stobdan, Research Fellow at the Institute for Defence Studies and Analysis (IDSA) in New Delhi, reported in the Institute's respected journal *Strategic Analysis* that:

> "Afghanistan figures importantly in the context of American energy security politics. Unocal's project to build oil and gas pipelines from Turkmenistan through Afghanistan for the export of oil and gas to the Indian subcontinent, viewed as the most audacious gambit of the 1990s Central Asian oil rush had generated great euphoria. The U.S. government fully backed the route as a useful option to free the Central Asian states from Russian clutches and prevent them getting close to Iran. The project was also perceived as the quickest and cheapest way to bring out Turkmen gas to the fast growing energy market in South Asia. To help it canvass for the project, Unocal hired the prominent former diplomat and secretary of state, Henry Kissinger, and a former U.S. ambassador to Pakistan, Robert Oakley, as well as an expert on the Caucasus, John Maresca... The president of Unocal even speculated that the cost of the construction would be reduced by half with the success of the Taliban movement and formation of a single government."

Worse still, this corporate endeavour, backed wholeheartedly by the U.S. government, involved direct, material support of the Taliban: "It was reported by the media that the U.S. oil company had even provided covert material support to help push the militia northward against Rabbani's forces." However, as Stobdan also notes, the American corporation UNOCAL indefinitely suspended work on the pipeline in August 1998.[80] It took three months for the oil company to pull out of the CentGas consortium that it had organised to build its proposed pipeline.[81] Since then, the U.S.

grew progressively more hostile towards the Taliban, and began exploring other possibilities to secure its regional supremacy, while maintaining basic ties with the regime, to negotiate a non-military solution.

Even members of the U.S. government have criticised covert U.S. support of the Taliban. One should note, for instance, the authoritative testimony of U.S. Congressman Dana Rohrabacher on American policy toward Afghanistan. Rohrabacher has been involved with Afghanistan since the early 1980s when he worked in the White House as Special Assistant to then U.S. President Ronald Reagan. He is now a Senior Member of the U.S. House International Relations Committee and has been involved in U.S. policy toward Afghanistan for some 20 years. In 1988, he traveled to Afghanistan as a member of the U.S. Congress with mujahideen fighters and participated in the battle of Jalalabad against the Soviets. He testified before a Senate Foreign Relations Subcommittee in April 1999:

"Having been closely involved in U.S. policy toward Afghanistan for some twenty years, I have called into question whether or not this administration has a covert policy that has empowered the Taliban and enabled this brutal movement to hold on to power. Even though the President and the Secretary of State have voiced their disgust at the brutal policies of the Taliban, especially their repression of women, the actual implementation of U.S. policy has repeatedly had the opposite effect."

After documenting a large number of factors indicating a concrete degree of U.S. support of the Taliban, Rohrabacher concludes:

"I am making the claim that there is and has been a covert policy by this administration to support the Taliban movement's control of Afghanistan... [T]his amoral or immoral policy is based on the assumption that the Taliban would bring stability to Afghanistan and permit the building of oil pipelines from Central Asia through Afghanistan to Pakistan... I believe the administration has maintained this covert goal and kept the Congress in the dark about its policy of supporting the Taliban, the most anti-Western, anti-female, anti-human rights regime in the world. It doesn't take a genius to understand that this policy would outrage the American people, especially America's women. Perhaps the most glaring evidence of our government's covert policy to favor the Taliban is that the administration is currently engaged in a major effort to obstruct the Congress from determining the details behind this policy. Last year in August, after several unofficial requests were made of the State Department, I made an official request for all diplomatic documents concerning U.S. policy toward the Taliban, especially those cables and documents from our embassies in Pakistan and Saudi Arabia. As a senior Member of the House International Relations Committee I have oversight responsibility in this area. In November, after months of stonewalling, the Secretary of State herself promised before the International Relations Committee that the documents would be forthcoming. She reconfirmed that promise in February when she testified before our Committee on the State Department budget. The Chairman of the Committee, Ben Gilman, added his voice to the record in support of my document request. To this time, we have received nothing. There can only be two explanations. Either the State Department is totally incompetent, or there is an ongoing cover-up of the State Department's true fundamental policy toward Afghanistan. You probably didn't expect me to praise the State Department at the end of this scathing testimony. But I will. I don't think the State Department is incompetent. They should be held responsible for their policies and the American people should know, through documented proof, what they are doing."[82]

As noted in the *San Francisco Chronicle*, Central Asian specialist Ahmed Rashid has reported in his Yale University study, *Taliban: Militant Islam, Oil and Fundamentalism in Central Asia*, that:

"Impressed by the ruthlessness and willingness of the then-emerging Taliban to cut a pipeline deal, the State Department and Pakistan's Inter-Services Intelligence agency agreed to funnel arms and funding to the Taliban in their war against the ethnically Tajik Northern Alliance. As recently as 1999, U.S. taxpayers paid the entire annual salary of every single Taliban government official."[83]

As late as 2000, hearings in the House of Representatives' International Relations Committee confirmed that U.S. support of the Taliban was secured through the Pakistani ISI (also see Appendix B):

"[T]he United States has been part and parcel to supporting the Taliban all along, and still is let me add... You have a military government [of President Musharraf] in Pakistan now that is arming the Taliban to the teeth.... Let me note; that [U.S.] aid has always gone to Taliban areas... We have been supporting the Taliban, because all our aid goes to the Taliban areas. And when people from the outside try to put aid into areas not controlled by the Taliban, they are thwarted by our own State Department... At that same moment, Pakistan initiated a major resupply effort, which eventually saw the defeat, and caused the defeat, of almost all of the anti-Taliban forces in Afghanistan."[84]

This documentation illustrates that the U.S. was certainly supportive of the Taliban while they were scoring sweeping victories throughout

Afghanistan. As has been noted by Ahmed Rashid, the Pakistan, Afghanistan and Central Asia correspondent for the *Far Eastern Economic Review* and the *Daily Telegraph* (London), from 1994 to 1997 at least, the United States "did support the Taliban, and [the Americans] cannot deny that fact." In his authoritative study of the issue, *Taliban*, Rashid showed that "between 1994-96 the U.S. supported the Taliban politically through its allies Pakistan and Saudi Arabia, essentially because Washington viewed the Taliban as anti-Iranian, anti-Shia and pro-western... [B]etween 1995-97, U.S. support was driven by the UNOCAL oil/gas pipeline project."[85]

Thus, as Afghan scholar Nour Ali accurately points out, by its covert policy "to make of Afghanistan a satellite or a protectorate of Pakistan, the U.S. Administration ignored the very objectives of Afghans themselves to repulse the invader, to recover their independence, to establish the style of government of their choice, and to live in peace... It disregarded the aspirations of the Afghan masses who bore the actual burden of the war and rendered an unparalleled sacrifice to the cause of freedom." Rather than providing genuine help to the Afghan people by making available to them "the necessary facilities to rebuild an independent Afghan state and to reconstruct the Afghan economy, the U.S. Government has shamefully rewarded Pakistan in authorizing it to control Afghanistan as suzerain through the heads of Units—the warring faction's leaders." The U.S. policy is evident in America's failure to condemn the policies of its subservient Pakistani client.

> "The current warfare in Afghanistan is not a civil war. It is rather an international war among the involved regional states, through their respective proxies—Afghan warring factions—using Afghanistan territory as their battle field... the war is between the interfering foreign powers for their expansionist or protectionist objectives within and beyond the region; the warring factions and their leaders are their surrogates and defacto extension of their state organizations."

Summarising the U.S. economic and strategic interests that motivate current policy, Dr. Ali remarks that the Great Game in Central Asia is not ending, but rather "going on briskly." Today however, it is "the United States that is looking North and intended to cross Afghanistan from Pakistan so as to be able (i) to sway Iran; (ii) to expand its power beyond the Amou Daria to control the resources of Central Asia; and (iii) to influence the Federation of Russia from South, and the mainland China from North West, as and when required...

> "The U.S. Government, in complicity with its regional allies, and for want of anything better, is trying to put therein a servile government of its own choice so as to possess the necessary leverage to influence the

overall politics and economics of the region in accordance with its imperialistic objectives. Pending the identification and installation of such a government the country has to endure the state of anarchy and instability accordingly."[86]

The Decline of the U.S.-Taliban Alliance and U.S. War Plans

However, U.S. support of the Taliban continued to decline with the coming of the Bush Administration. The primary reason for this certainly appears to be the fact that the Taliban was incapable of playing the U.S.-friendly role of a "servile government." As Ahmed Rashid points out:

"The UNOCAL project was based on the premise that the Taliban were going to conquer Afghanistan. This premise was fed to them by various countries like Saudi Arabia, Pakistan and elements within the U.S. administration. Essentially it was a premise that was very wrong, because it was based on conquest, and would therefore make it absolutely certain that not only would they not be able to build the pipeline, but they would never be able to have that kind of security in order to build the pipeline."[87]

Once this became absolutely clear to the United States, it also became clear that the Taliban was incapable of providing the security essential for the pipeline to go ahead, as required. This was compounded by the fact that the faction had begun developing an intensifying propensity toward non-subservience in relation to U.S. interests. An increasingly anti-American worldview "appeared to dominate the thinking of senior Taliban leaders...

"Until [Osama Bin Laden's] arrival, the Taliban leadership had not been particularly antagonistic to the USA or the West but demanded recognition for their government. However, after the Africa bombings the Taliban became increasingly vociferous against the Americans, the UN, the Saudis and Muslim regimes around the world. Their statements increasingly reflected the language of defiance Bin Laden had adopted and which was not an original Taliban trait."[88]

Thus, by 1999, the U.S. had begun to see the Taliban as a fundamental obstacle to U.S. interests. Due to this, U.S. policy toward the Taliban took an about-turn. This sequence of events has been described in great detail by the French intelligence analysts, Jean-Charles Brisard and Guillaume Dasquié, who record that the "U.S. government's main objective in Afghanistan was to consolidate the position of the Taliban regime and thereby obtain access to the oil and gas reserves in Central Asia."[89]

In their recently released, widely acclaimed study of the subject, *Bin Laden: the forbidden truth*,[90] they report that until as late as August 2001, the U.S. government hoped, despite a declining relationship with the regime, that the Taliban would be "a source of stability in Central Asia that would enable the construction of an oil pipeline across Central Asia," from the rich oilfields in Turkmenistan, Uzbekistan, and Kazakhstan, through Afghanistan and Pakistan, to the Indian Ocean. From 1999 until 2001, it is clear that U.S. hopes in this respect had grown increasingly skeptical.

It is a matter of record that, corresponding with the growing shift in U.S. policy against the Taliban, a military invasion of Afghanistan was planned long before 11th September. Extensive evidence indicates that in response to the Taliban's failure to meet U.S. requirements, the Bush administration had been planning a war on Afghanistan for October 2001, in concert with several other powers, including Russia, India and Pakistan. Frederick Starr, Chairman of the Central Asia-Caucasus Institute at Johns Hopkins's Nitze School of Advanced International Studies, reported in December 2000 in the *Washington Post* that:

"... the United States has quietly begun to align itself with those in the Russian government calling for military action against Afghanistan and has toyed with the idea of a new raid to wipe out Osama bin Laden. Until it backed off under local pressure, it went so far as to explore whether a Central Asian country would permit the use of its territory for such a purpose."[91]

Starr's insight should not be in question. A specialist in Central Asia, his director at Johns Hopkins was Assistant Secretary of Defense Paul Wolfowitz. In his *Post* report, Starr further noted that meetings between U.S., Russian and Indian government officials occurred at the end of 2000 "to discuss what kind of government should replace the Taliban... [T]he United States is now talking about the overthrow of a regime that controls nearly the entire country, in the hope it can be replaced with a hypothetical government that does not exist even on paper."[92]

The extensive military planning for a war on Afghanistan was also noted by Canadian journalist Eric Margolis, a specialist in Middle East and Central Asian affairs, with firsthand experience of Afghanistan. In a December 2000 edition of the *Toronto Sun*, he reported that the United States was planning to invade Afghanistan to topple the Taliban regime and target Osama bin Laden:

"The United States and Russia may soon launch a joint military assault against Islamic militant, Osama Bin Laden, and against the leadership of the Taliban, Afghanistan's de facto ruling movement. Such an attack would probably include U.S. Delta Force and Navy Seals, who would join up with Russia's elite Spetsnaz and Alpha commandos in Tajikistan, the Central Asian state where Russia has military bases and 25,000 troops. The combined forces would be lifted by helicopters, and backed by air support, deep into neighboring Afghanistan to attack Bin Laden's fortified base in the Hindu Kush mountains."[93]

By March 2001, *Jane's Intelligence Review* confirmed that India had joined "Russia, the USA and Iran in a concerted front against Afghanistan's Taliban regime... Several recent meetings between the newly instituted Indo-U.S. and Indo-Russian joint working groups on terrorism led to this effort to tactically and logistically counter the Taliban." The United States, Russia, India and Iran were already providing military, informational and logistical support to anti-Taliban forces in Afghanistan. "Military sources indicated that Tajikistan and Uzbekistan are being used as bases to launch anti-Taliban operations by India and Russia."[94]

By June 2001, the public affairs magazine *India Reacts* reported the escalation of joint U.S.-Russian plans to conduct a military assault on Afghanistan. According to Indian officials: "India and Iran will only play the role of 'facilitator' while the U.S. and Russia will combat the Taliban from the front with the help of two Central Asian countries, Tajikistan and Uzbekistan." The magazine clarified that: "Tajikistan and Uzbekistan will lead the ground attack with a strong military backup of the U.S. and Russia. Vital Taliban installations and military assets will be targeted. India and Iran will provide logistic support."

In a Moscow meeting in early June, "Russian President Vladimir Putin [had] already hinted of military action against the Taliban to CIS nations." According to diplomats, the formation of this anti-Taliban front "followed a meeting between U.S. Secretary of State Colin Powell and Russian Foreign Minister Igor Ivanov and later between Powell and Indian foreign minister Jaswant Singh in Washington. Russia, Iran and India have also held a series of discussions and more diplomatic activity is expected."[95]

The formulation of U.S. war plans against the Taliban had been accompanied by the imposition of sanctions against Afghanistan. The shift in U.S. policy from pro-Taliban to anti-Taliban had not brought with it any change in the tragic condition of the Afghan people, primarily because the policy shift was rooted in America's attempt to secure its strategic and economic interests. The sanctions on Afghanistan had not only failed to affect the Taliban, but had served primarily to devastate the Afghan population even more. "The U.S. engineered a punishing Iraq-style embargo of war-ravaged Afghanistan at a time when many of its 18 million people are starving and homeless," reported the *Toronto Sun* in December 2000.[96] The London *Guardian* similarly noted a month earlier that:

"When the UN imposed sanctions a year ago on the Taliban because of their refusal to hand over bin Laden, the suffering in Afghanistan increased. The move has not hurt the Taliban. They are well off. It is ordinary Afghans who have suffered. Those in jobs earn a salary of around $4 a month, scarcely enough to live on. The real losers are Afghanistan's women, who have been forbidden by the Taliban from working. Kabul is full of burqa-clad women beggars who congregate every lunchtime outside the city's few functioning restaurants in the hope of getting something to eat."

Indeed, the imposition of sanctions amidst the ongoing famine in Afghanistan quite predictably resulted in the exacerbation of the country's humanitarian crisis. "The country is in the grip of an unreported humanitarian disaster," reported Luke Harding from Kandahar. "In the south and west, there has been virtually no rain for three years. The road from Herat, near the Iranian border, to Kandahar, the southern desert city, winds through half-abandoned villages and swirlingly empty riverbeds. Some 12m people have been affected, of whom 3m are close to starvation."[97] As Pakistani correspondent Arshad Mahmoud observed, the people, particularly the children of Afghanistan, "are facing the grave consequences of the UN sanctions," in tandem with the continuing drought.[98]

Both the threat of war and the economic strangulation of the country appear to have been designed to pressure the Taliban into conforming to U.S. requirements. While establishing its war plans, the Bush administration attempted to save its relationship with the brutal regime, despite the danger of erosion. The methods employed by the administration to cautiously engage the Taliban have been described well by the *Pakistan Observer*:

"As recently as July this year, Christina Rocca, the U.S. Assistant Secretary of State for South Asia met the Taliban officials in Islamabad and announced $43 million in food and shelter aid, bringing to $124 million the U.S. contribution to the IDPs this year alone. Since the humanitarian assistance is spent by the Taliban, without any accountability, the renewed U.S. contacts with the Taliban, including a visit by seven U.S. officials to Kabul in late April preceded by another visit by three U.S. officials earlier in that month, before the terror struck America on September 11, led to media speculations about a shift in the U.S. policy away from a single-focus on the Osama issue towards an approach based on a cautious engagement with Taliban even as they were under stringent sanctions by Washington and the UN Security Council."[99]

Shortly after taking power in January 2001, the Bush administration began to negotiate with the Taliban. U.S. and Taliban diplomatic representatives met several times in February 2001 in Washington, Berlin and Islamabad. The last meeting between U.S. and Taliban representatives took place in August 2001—five weeks before the attacks on New York and Washington. Christina Rocca, then head of Central Asian affairs at the U.S. Department of State, met the Taliban ambassador to Pakistan in Islamabad.[100] These negotiations with the Taliban in 2001 appear to have been conducted by the Bush Administration as a last ditch attempt to salvage a viable relationship with the regime. The recognition that the Taliban would not be capable of maintaining security through "conquest" meant that the U.S. was instead hoping the regime would agree to a joint government in Afghanistan in alliance with the other factions—although the U.S. seemed to be aware that this was exceedingly unlikely.

Until now, observe Brisard and Dasquié, "the oil and gas reserves of Central Asia have been controlled by Russia. The Bush government wanted to change all that." However, confronted with the Taliban's refusal to accept U.S. conditions, "this rationale of energy security changed into a military one." In an interview in Paris, Brisard noted that: "At one moment during the negotiations, the U.S. representatives told the Taliban, either you accept our offer of a carpet of gold, or we bury you under a carpet of bombs."

Describing the key theme of some of the several meetings that occurred in 2001, the intelligence analysts record that:

"Several meetings took place this year under the arbitration of Francesc Vendrell, personal representative of UN Secretary-General Kofi Annan, to discuss the situation in Afghanistan. Representatives of the U.S. government and Russia, and the six countries that border with Afghanistan, were present at these meetings. Sometimes, representatives of the Taliban also sat around the table."[101]

The three Americans at one of these meetings in Berlin in July were Tom Simons, a former U.S. Ambassador to Pakistan, Karl 'Rick' Inderfurth, a former Assistant Secretary of State for South Asian affairs, and Lee Coldren, who headed the office of Pakistan, Afghan and Bangladesh affairs in the State Department until 1997. These meetings, called "6+2" due to the number of states involved (six Central Asian neighbours, plus the new partners, Russia and the U.S.) have also been confirmed by the former Pakistani Minister for Foreign Affairs, Niaz Naik, who was present at the meetings.

In an interview for French television in early November 2001, Naik testified that during one of these "6+2" meetings in Berlin in July 2001, the discussions focused on: "… the formation of a government of national unity. If the Taliban had accepted this coalition, they would have immediately received international economic aid. And the pipelines from Kazakhstan and

Uzbekistan would have come." Naik clarified that one of the U.S. representatives at the meetings, Tom Simons, openly threatened both the Taliban and Pakistan:

"Simons said, 'either the Taliban behave as they ought to, or Pakistan convinces them to do so, or we will use another option.' The words Simons used were 'a military operation.'"[102]

Reporting on this, the London *Guardian* noted that "the Bush team had prepared a new plan to topple the entire Afghan regime...

"[T]here were signs early this year that Washington was moving to threaten Afghanistan militarily from the north, via the wild former Soviet republics. A U.S. department of defence official, Dr. Jeffrey Starr, visited Tajikistan in January. The Guardian's Felicity Lawrence established that U.S. Rangers were also training special troops inside Kyrgyzstan. There were unconfirmed reports that Tajik and Uzbek special troops were training in Alaska and Montana.

And U.S. General Tommy Franks visited Dushanbe on May 16, where he conveyed a message from the Bush administration that the US considered Tajikistan 'a strategically significant country.' On offer was non-lethal military aid. Tajikistan used the occasion to apply to join NATO's Partnership for Peace.

Shortly afterwards the Republican senator from Alabama who is vice-chairman of the Senate intelligence committee, Richard C Shelby, returned from a Gulf tour to bullishly tell the Washington Post that U.S. counterterrorism officials were winning the war against Bin Laden... Reliable western military sources say a U.S. contingency plan existed on paper by the end of the summer to attack Afghanistan from the north... By July 8, the Afghan opposition, Pakistani diplomats, and senior staff from the British Foreign Office, were gathering at Weston Park under UN auspices for private teach-ins on the Afghan situation... And a couple of weeks later, another group gathered in a Berlin hotel. There, former state department official Lee Coldren passed on a message he had got from Bush officials [that]... 'the United States was so disgusted with the Taliban that they might be considering some military action'... The chilling quality of this private warning was that it came—according to one of those present, the Pakistani diplomat Niaz Naik—accompanied by specific details of how Bush would succeed... The hawks in Washington could count on the connivance of Russian troops, and on facilities in such places as Uzbekistan and Tajikistan, already host to US military advisers."[103]

In another, earlier report, *The Guardian* reported that:

"Osama bin Laden and the Taliban received threats of possible American military strikes against them two months before the terrorist assaults on New York and Washington...

The Taliban refused to comply but the serious nature of what they were told raises the possibility that Bin Laden, far from launching the attacks on the World Trade Centre in New York and the Pentagon out of the blue 10 days ago, was launching a pre-emptive strike in response to what he saw as U.S. threats."

Lee Coldren confirmed that: "... there was some discussion of the fact that the United States was so disgusted with the Taliban that they might be considering some military action." Naik, described by Tim Simons himself as "a friend for years" and "an honourable diplomat," testifies that: "The Americans indicated to us that in case the Taliban does not behave and in case Pakistan also doesn't help us to influence the Taliban, then the United States would be left with no option but to take an overt action against Afghanistan. I told the Pakistani government, who informed the Taliban via our foreign office and the Taliban ambassador here."

The warning to the Taliban originated at the four-day Berlin meeting of senior Americans, Russians, Iranians and Pakistanis in mid-July. When asked whether he could be sure that the American officials were passing ideas from the Bush administration rather than their own views, Naik clarified that: "What the Americans indicated to us was perhaps based on official instructions. They were very senior people. Even in 'track two' people are very careful about what they say and don't say." Naik also cited Tim Simons declaring that action against bin Laden was imminent: "This time they were very sure. They had all the intelligence and would not miss him this time. It would be aerial action, maybe helicopter gunships, and not only overt, but from very close proximity to Afghanistan."[104]

In an interview with the British Broadcasting Corporation (BBC), Niaz Naik elaborated on what U.S. officials had informed him in July 2001, specifying that the Bush administration was planning military action against Afghanistan for mid-October. The BBC reported that:

"Niaz Naik, a former Pakistani Foreign Secretary, was told by senior American officials in mid-July that military action against Afghanistan would go ahead by the middle of October... U.S. officials told him of the plan at a UN-sponsored international contact group on Afghanistan which took place in Berlin... [A]t the meeting the U.S. representatives told him that unless Bin Laden was handed over swiftly America would take military action to kill or capture both Bin Laden and the Taleban leader, Mullah Omar. The wider objective, according to Mr. Naik, would be to topple the Taleban regime and install a transitional government of moderate Afghans in its place—possibly under the leadership of the former Afghan King Zahir Shah."

The former Pakistani Minister of Foreign Affairs further stated that, according to information passed on to him by the same U.S. officials in July, "Washington would launch its operation from bases in Tajikistan, where American advisers were already in place," and "Uzbekistan would also participate in the operation... 17,000 Russian troops were on standby." He was also told that "if the military action went ahead it would take place before the snows started falling in Afghanistan, by the middle of October at the latest." He noted that the 11th September attacks provided a convenient trigger for these war plans. "[H]e was in no doubt that after the World Trade Center bombings, this pre-existing U.S. plan had been built upon and would be implemented within two or three weeks," noted the BBC. Indeed, the plans did not even appear to have as their prime motive the capture of Osama bin Laden: "[H]e said it was doubtful that Washington would drop its plan even if Bin Laden were to be surrendered immediately by the Taleban."[105]

The shift in U.S. policy in Afghanistan from pro-Taliban to anti-Taliban was thus rooted in America's attempts to secure its strategic and economic interests. Because the Taliban no longer played a suitably subservient role, U.S. policy grew increasingly hostile to the faction. While establishing extensive war plans, the U.S. continued to conduct negotiations with the regime to ascertain whether it would conform to the latest requirements. Faced with the Taliban's consistent refusals, the shift in policy against the regime—which occurred "without public discussion, without consultation with Congress"[106]—was fully sealed in August, although it had been largely established before then. The war plans for Afghanistan were by then firmly grounded. All that was required was a trigger.

The need for a trigger was particularly exemplified in the fact that the U.S. had backed down from its exploration of a possible war on Afghanistan "under local pressure"—in Central Asia—as the *Washington Post* reported.[107] Some sort of new pretext was thus required to bypass this lack of regional support.

Given that U.S. officials had informed Naik early on in the year 2001 of U.S. plans to invade Afghanistan by mid-October, the U.S. may have envisaged that the trigger that would justify implementation of its war plans would manifest some time between August and October: i.e. September.

It is worth noting the observations of Francis A. Boyle, Professor of International Law at the University of Illinois, in mid-October 2001: "Obviously, the war against Afghanistan was planned for quite some time. We know for a fact that it had been war-gamed by the Pentagon going back to 1997...

"Right around September 11, two U.S. Aircraft carrier task forces conveniently arrived in the Persian Gulf right at the same time on 'rotation.' Obviously, preplanned. Just before September 11, the UK had put together what was billed as the 'largest armada since the Falklands War' and had it steaming towards Oman, where now 23,000 UK troops are on maneuvers. This had been planned for at least 3 years. Also, the U.S. 'Bright Star' operation is currently going on in Egypt. 23,000 U.S. troops plus an additional 17,000 from NATO and its associates. This had been planned at least two years ago. Finally, NATO just landed 12,000 troops into Turkey. This had been planned for at least two years. It is obvious that we are seeing an operational War Plan being executed here that had been in the works for at least the past four years. September 11 is either a pretext or a trigger or both."[108]

Notes

[49] Frei, Matt, 'Hell on earth: Afghanistan,' *Evening Standard*, 20 February 2001.

[50] For example, supporters of the Taliban, such as Pakistan, could have been pressured into withholding support; AI news release, 'Afghanistan: International actors have a special responsibility for ending the human rights catastrophe,' op. cit.; AI news release, 'Afghanistan: Immediate action needed to halt further massacres,' Amnesty International, London, 8 November 1999.

[51] Naji, Kasra, 'UN: Taliban forcing thousands from homes in Afghanistan,' CNN, 15 August 1999.

[52] See Aburish, Said K., *A Brutal Friendship: The West and the Arab Elite*, Indigo, London, 1998.

[53] Rubin, Barnett, 'In Focus: Afghanistan,' *Foreign Policy In Focus*, Vol. 1, No. 25., December 1996.

[54] Ali, Nour, *U.S.-UN Conspiracy Against the People of Afghanistan*, Institute for Afghan Studies, 21 February 1998, www.institute-for-afghan-studies.org. See this paper for a detailed review of the numerous discrepancies in the U.S.-UN policy indicating that the policy is motivated by ominous intentions, and moreover that the policy is resulting—quite predictably—in the entrenchment of factionalism and war in Afghanistan.

[55] Vidgen, Ben C., 'A State of Terror: How many 'terrorist' groups has your government established, sponsored or networked lately,' *Nexus Magazine*, Vol. 3. No. 2, Feb.-March 1996. See especially Cooley, John K., *Unholy Wars: Afghanistan, America and International Terrorism*, Pluto Press, London, 1999.

[56] Krakowski, Elie, 'The Afghan Vortex,' *IASPS Research Papers in Strategy*, Institute for Advanced Strategic and Political Studies, Jerusalem, No. 9, April 2000.

[57] AI report, *Afghanistan: Grave Abuses in the Name of Religion*, Amnesty International, London, November 1996; *Guardian*, 9 October 1996. Also see *Financial Times*, 9 October 1996.

[58] Agence France Presse, 'U.S. gave silent blessing to Taliban rise to power: analysis,' 7 October 2001.

[59] AI report, Afghanistan: Grave Abuses in the Name of Religion, op. cit.

[60] Chossudovsky, Michel, 'Who is Osama Bin Laden?', Centre for Research on Globalisation, Montreal, 12 September 2001, http://globalresearch.ca/articles/CHO109C.html.

[61] Cited in Suri, Sanjay, 'CIA worked with Pakistan to help create Taliban,' India Abroad News Service, 6 March 2001.

[62] 'CIA responsible for terrorism, says Babar,' *Frontier Post*, 5 May 2000.

[63] Cited in Rashid, Ahmed, *Taliban: Militant Islam, Oil and Fundamentalism in Central Asia*, Yale University Press, New Haven, Conn., 2000, p. 166.

[64] Ibid., p. 201.

[65] Agence France-Presse, 'U.S. gave silent blessing to Taliban rise to power: analysts,' 7 October 2001.

[66] Beeman, William O., 'Follow the Oil Trail – Mess in Afghanistan Partly Our Government's Fault,' *Jinn Magazine* (online), Pacific News Service, San Francisco, 24 August 1998, web-site at www.pacificnews.org/jinn. The importance of Pakistan to the U.S., as Brzezinski alluded to, is in its effect on neighbouring countries such as Iran, Afghanistan and India. Pakistan can play a powerful tool of the United States in this respect.

[67] Ibid.

[68] Cited in Rashid, Ahmed, *Taliban*, op. cit., p. 179.

[69] BBC News, 'Taliban in Texas for Talks on Gas Pipeline,' 4 Dec. 1997.

[70] CNN, 'U.S. in a diplomatic hard place in dealing with Afghanistan's Taliban,' 8 October 1996.

[71] Intra Press Service (IPS), 'Politics: UN considers arms embargo on Afghanistan,' IPS, 16 December 1997, website at www.oneworld.org/ips2/dec/afghan.html.

[72] Godoy, Julio, 'U.S. Taliban Policy Influenced by Oil,' Inter Press Service, 16 November 2001.

[73] *Frankfurter Rundschau*, October 1996. Also see Catalinotto, John, 'Afghanistan: Battle deepens for central Asian oil,' Workers World News Service, 24 October 1996.

[74] Goltz, Thomas, 'The Caspian Oil Sweepstakes – A Great Game Replayed,' *Jinn Magazine* (online), Pacific News Service, San Francisco, 15 October 1997, www.pacificnews.org/jinn.

[75] Schurmann, Franz, 'U.S. Changes Flow of History with New Pipeline Deal,' *Jinn Magazine* (online), Pacific News Service, San Francisco, 1 August 1997, www.pacificnews.org/jinn.

[76] Ahmad, Ishtiaq, 'How America Courted the Taliban,' *Pakistan Observer*, 20 October 2001.

[77] *Wall Street Journal*, 23 May 1997.

[78] *New York Times*, 26 May 1997.

[79] Fitchett, Joseph, 'Worries Rise that Taleban May Try to Export Unrest,' *International Herald Tribunal*, 26 September 1998; also see Gall, Carlotta, 'Dagestan Skirmish is a Big Russian Risk,' *New York Times*, 13 Aug. 1999.

[80] Stobdan, P., 'The Afghan Conflict and Regional Security,' *Strategic Analysis* (journal of the Institute for Defence & Strategic Analysis [ISDA]), August 1999, Vol. XXIII, No. 5, p. 719-747.

[81] Ahmad, Ishtiaq, 'How America Courted the Taliban,' op. cit.

[82] Statement of Congressman Dana Rohrabacher, 'U.S. Policy Toward Afghanistan,' Senate Foreign Relations Subcommittee on South Asia, 14 April 1999. Rohrabacher includes the following reasons in his analysis:

"[1] In 1996, the Taliban first emerged as a mysterious force that swept out of so-called religious schools in Pakistan to a blitzkrieg type of conquest of most of Afghanistan against some very seasoned former-mujahideen fighters. As a so-called 'student militia,' the Taliban could not have succeeded without the support, organization and logistics of military professionals, who would not have been faculty in religious schools.

[2] The U.S. has a very close relationship with Saudi Arabia and Pakistan, in matters concerning Afghanistan, but unfortunately, instead of providing leadership, we are letting them lead our policy. This began during the Afghan war against the Soviets. I witnessed this in the White House when U.S. officials in charge of the military aid program to the mujahideen permitted a large percentage of our assistance to be channeled to the most anti-western non-democratic elements of the mujahideen, such as Golbodin Hekmatayar. This was done to placate the Pakistan ISI military intelligence.

[3] In 1997, responding to the pleas of the Afghan-American community and the recognized Afghanistan ambassador, I led an effort to stop the State Department

from permitting the Afghanistan embassy in Washington from being taken under the control of a diplomat loyal to the Taliban. Instead, of permitting a new ambassador who was assigned by the non-Taliban Afghan government that is still recognized at the United Nations, the State Department claimed 'we don't take sides,' and forced the embassy to be closed against the will of the Afghanistan United Nations office.

[4] During late 1997 and early 1998, while the Taliban imposed a blockade on more than two million people of the Hazara ethnic group in central Afghanistan, putting tens of thousands at risk of starving to death or perishing from a lack of medicine during the harsh winter months, the State Department undercut my efforts to send in two plane loads of medicines by the Americares and the Knightsbridge relief agencies. State Department representatives made false statements that the humanitarian crisis was exaggerated and there was already sufficient medical supplies in the blockaded area. When the relief teams risked their lives to go into the area with the medicines – without the support of the State Department they found the hospitals and clinics did not have even aspirins or bandages, no generators for heat in sub-zero weather, a serious lack of blankets and scant amounts of food. The State Department, in effect, was assisting the Taliban's inhuman blockade intended to starve out communities that opposed their dictates.

[5] Perhaps the most glaring evidence of this administration's tacit support of the Taliban was the effort made during a Spring 1998 visit to Afghanistan by Mr. Inderfurth and U.N. Ambassador Bill Richardson. These administration representatives convinced the anti-Taliban Northern Alliance not to go on the offensive against a then-weakened and vulnerable Taliban. And instead convinced these anti-Taliban leaders to accept a cease-fire that was proposed by Pakistan. The cease fire lasted only as long as it took the Paks to resupply and reorganize the Taliban. In fact, within a few months of announcement of the US-backed 'Ulema' process, the Taliban, freshly supplied by the ISI and flush with drug money, went on a major offensive and destroyed the Northern Alliance. This was either incompetence on the part of the State Department and U.S. intelligence agencies or indicative of the real policy of our government to ensure a Taliban victory.

[6] Can anyone believe that with the Taliban, identified by the United Nations and the DEA as one of the two largest producers of opium in the world, that they weren't being closely monitored by our intelligence services, who would have seen every move of the military build up that the Pakistanis and Taliban were undertaking. In addition, at the same time the U.S. was planning its strike against the terrorist camps of Osama bin laden in Afghanistan. How could our intelligence services not have known that Osama bin Laden's forces had moved north to lead the Taliban offensive, where horrendous brutality took place.

[7] In addition, there has been no major effort to end the flow of opium out of Afghanistan, which is the main source of the revenues that enables the Taliban to maintain control of the country, even though the U.S. Government observes by satellite where the opium is grown."

[83] Rall, Ted, 'It's all about oil,' *San Francisco Chronicle*, 2 November 2001.

[84] U.S. House of Representatives, Statement by Representative Dana Rohrabacher, Hearing of the House International Relations Committee on 'Global Terrorism And South Asia,' Washington DC, 12 July 2000.

[85] Interview with Afghanistan specialist Ahmed Rashid by Omar Samad, Azadi Afghan Radio, Washington DC, 15 April 2000.

[86] Ali, Nour, *US-UN Conspiracy Against the People of Afghanistan*, op. cit.

[87] Interview with Ahmed Rashid by Omar Samad, Azadi Afghan Radio, op. cit.

[88] Rashid, Ahmed, 'Special Report – Osama Bin Laden: How the U.S. Helped Midwife a Terrorist,' Center for Public Integrity, Washington D.C., www.public-i.org/excerpts_01_091301.htm.

[89] Godoy, Julio, 'U.S. Taliban Policy influenced by Oil,' op. cit. Brisard and Dasquié both have an extensive record of expertise in their field. Jean-Charles Brisard was until the late 1990s Director of Economic Analysis and Strategy for Vivendi, a French company. Additionally, for several years he worked for French intelligence, writing a 1997 report on the Al-Qaeda network. Guillaume Dasquié is an investigative journalist and the publisher of the highly respected Internet newsletter *Intelligence Online*, which specialises in diplomacy, economic analysis and strategy.

[90] Brisard, Jean-Charles and Dasquié, Guillaume, *Bin Laden, la verité interdite*, Denoel Impacts, Paris, 2001.

[91] Starr, S. Frederick, 'Afghanistan Land Mine,' *Washington Post*, 19 Dec. 2000.

[92] Ibid.

[93] *Toronto Sun*, 4 December 2000.

[94] Bedi, Rahul, 'India joins anti-Taliban coalition,' *Jane's Intelligence Review*, 15 March 2001. The interests of India and Russia in joining the anti-Taliban policy under U.S. leadership is also mentioned in this report: "Oleg Chervov, deputy head of Russia's security council, recently described Taliban-controlled Afghanistan as a base of international terrorism attempting to expand into Central Asia. Radical Islamic groups are also trying to increase their influence across Pakistan, he said at a meeting of Indian and Russian security officials in Moscow. 'All this dictates a pressing need for close co-operation between Russia and India in opposing terrorism,' he said."

[95] Special Report, 'India in anti-Taliban military plan,' *India Reacts*, 26 June 2001.

[96] Margolis, Eric, 'U.S.-Russian Crusade Against Osama Bin Laden,' *Toronto Sun*, 4 December 2000.

[97] Harding, Luke, 'Chasing monsters,' *Guardian*, 24 November 2000.

[98] Mahmoud, Arshad, 'The US/UN Holocaust Against the Children of Afghanistan and Iraq,' *Frontier Post*, 25 Oct. 2000. Also see Institute for Afghan Studies, *Economic, Humanitarian and Political Impact of the UN Imposed Sanctions*, Nov. 1999.

[99] Ahmad, Ishtiaq, 'How America Courted the Taliban,' op. cit.

[100] Godoy, Julio, 'U.S. Taliban Policy influenced by Oil,' op. cit.

[101] Ibid.

[102] Ibid.

[103] Leigh, David, 'Attack and counter-attack,' *The Guardian*, 26 Sept. 2001.

[104] Steele, Jonathan, et. al., 'Threat of U.S. strikes passed to Taliban weeks before NY attack,' *The Guardian*, 22 Sept. 2001. The 'track two' stage of negotiations with the Taliban, reports Steele et. al., "was designed to offer a free and open-ended forum for governments to pass messages and sound out each other's thinking. Participants were experts with long diplomatic experience of the region who were no longer government officials but had close links with their governments."

[105] Arney, George, 'U.S. "planned attack on Taleban",' BBC News, 18 Sept. 2001, http://news.bbc.co.uk/hi/english/world/south_asia/newsid_1550000/1550366.stm.

[106] *Washington Post*, 19 December 2000.

[107] Ibid.

[108] Cited in Ruppert, Michael, 'A Time For Fear,' *From The Wilderness*, Oct. 2001.

3. Strategic Design Behind U.S. War Plans   3

"There is no such hidden agenda. Operation Enduring Freedom is meant to get rid of terrorism in Afghanistan, Central Asia and the surrounding areas."

Bush administration official
(New York Times, 15 December 2001)

The United States, leading an international coalition of powers, began a military invasion of Afghanistan in October 2001. Conventional opinion has it that the U.S. invasion was initiated in response to the 11th September attacks in the United States, and that its sole or principal objective was to find and eliminate the Al-Qaeda terrorist network responsible for the attacks, in particular the Al-Qaeda leader, Osama bin Laden.

However, the facts presented thus far clarify beyond any reasonable doubt that *the U.S. war on Afghanistan that began in October had been planned quite independently of the 11th September attacks.* Rather than being a reaction to those attacks, it seems that the attacks provided a pretext to justify, "build upon" and implement already extant plans for a military invasion. Moreover, those very specific plans were formulated in response to the Taliban's failure to meet U.S. requirements in relation to its regional strategic and economic designs, and were intended for implementation in October 2001.

Contemplating Central Asia

The U.S. military industrial complex has been contemplating a prolonged intervention in Central Asia for at least a decade. As early as 1991, in the aftermath of the Persian Gulf War, *Newsweek* reported in an article titled 'Operation Steppe Shield?', that the U.S. military was preparing an operation in Kazakhstan. Planning for the operation was modeled on the Operation Desert Shield deployment in Saudi Arabia, Kuwait and Iraq, which successfully resulted in the establishment of a network of permanent U.S. military bases in the region.

More specifically, the U.S. war plan to invade Afghanistan has roots in strategic and economic concerns in Central Asia, stretching as far back as 1989. Afghanistan has been widely recognised by U.S. officials as the gateway to Central Asia and the Caspian, and thus to global primacy. Former Department of Defense official Elie Krakowski, who worked on the Afghan issue in the 1980s, records that:

> "With the collapse of the Soviet Union, [Afghanistan] has become an important potential opening to the sea for the landlocked new states of Central Asia. The presence of large oil and gas deposits in that area has attracted countries and multinational corporations... Because Afghanistan is a major strategic pivot what happens there affects the rest of the world."[109]

Afghanistan is thus the primary gateway to Central Asia and the immense energy deposits therein. A September 2001 report, on the results of a May 2001 Brookings Institution conference, shows clearly that the exploitation of Caspian and Asian energy markets was an urgent priority for the Bush administration:

> "[T]he administration's report warned that 'growth in international oil demand will exert increasing pressure on global oil availability' and that developing Asian economies and populations—particularly in China and India—will be major contributors to this increased demand... options for constructing gas pipelines east to Asia from the Caspian have been discussed for the last decade."

Access to Central Asian and Caspian resources has thus been the centerpiece of the Bush energy policy.[110] Indeed, experts agree that both the Caspian Basin and Central Asia are the keys to energy in the 21st century. James Dorian, for instance, observes in the *Oil & Gas Journal*: "Those who control the oil routes out of Central Asia will impact all future direction and quantities of flow and the distribution of revenues from new production."[111]

A 1999 study edited by the leading Central Asian experts Michael Croissant and Bulant Aras, *Oil and Geopolitics in the Caspian Sea Region*, provides further insight. In the book's forward, Pat Clawson of the National Defense University describes the Caspian Sea as a crucial oil region, the target of the ongoing and conflicting interests of surrounding states, as well as the Western powers. The economic and geostrategic issues relate particularly to potential pipeline routes, and attempts by the United States to monopolise them by creating an appropriate international oil regime in the region.[112]

The establishment of such a regime, by nature, requires a combination of economic, political, and military arrangements to support and protect oil production and transportation to markets.[113] U.S. policies, geared toward the creation of an appropriate climate within the region, in accordance with U.S. interests, have thus consisted of a three-pronged programme of economic, political and military penetration into the region. This has included persistent efforts to sideline the intrusion of other powers, particularly Russia and Europe, in attempts to control access to regional resources.[114]

As noted in 1997 by an energy expert at the National Security Council on U.S. policy in Central Asia: "U.S. policy was to promote the rapid development of Caspian energy ... We did so specifically to promote the independence of these oil-rich countries, to in essence break Russia's monopoly control over the transportation of oil from that region, and frankly, to promote Western energy security through diversification of supply."[115]

Former U.S. Energy Secretary Bill Richardson observed in 1998 in relation to the republics of Central Asia:

"We would like these newly independent countries reliant on Western commercial and political interests rather than going another way. We've made a substantial political investment in the Caspian, and it's very important to us that both the pipeline map and the politics come out right."[116]

One year later, the 106th Congress passed the Silk Road Strategy Act of 1999, "...to amend the Foreign Assistance Act of 1961 to target assistance to support the economic and political independence of the countries of the South Caucasus and Central Asia." The U.S. Congress noted that: "The region of the South Caucasus and Central Asia could produce oil and gas in sufficient quantities to reduce the dependence of the United States on energy from the volatile Persian Gulf region." Accordingly, one of the principal objectives of U.S. policy, it was agreed, is "to support United States business interests and investments in the region."[117]

U.S. policy plans in Central Asia are thus rooted in a broad imperialistic context. A 46-page Pentagon draft document, leaked by Pentagon officials in March 1992, clearly reflects the internal planning and strategies produced by the U.S. military in the post-Cold War era. The Pentagon document states that the United States' "first objective is to prevent the re-emergence of a new rival" who may threaten America's domination of global resources in the post-Cold War era. This would naturally involve the U.S. endeavour "to establish and protect a new order that holds the promise of convincing potential competitors that they need not aspire to a greater role or pursue a more aggressive posture to protect their legitimate interests." This world order must "account sufficiently for the interests of the advanced industrial nations to discourage them from seeking to overturn the established political and economic order" under U.S. hegemony. U.S. military dominance must be maintained as "the mechanism for deterring potential competitors from even aspiring to a larger regional or global role."

Such military dominance implicates the preservation of "NATO as the primary instrument of Western defense and security" because NATO extends U.S. hegemony over Western Europe. Thus, the U.S. "must seek to prevent the emergence of European-only security arrangements which would undermine NATO" and thereby U.S. hegemony over Europe. A "dominant consideration underlying the new regional defense strategy" is the necessity for the U.S. to "endeavour to prevent any hostile power from dominating a region whose resources would, under consolidated control, be sufficient to generate global power."

These regions include Western Europe, East Asia, the former Soviet Union and the Middle East, which should, therefore, be integrated into the U.S.-dominated global economic system, and thereby brought under American world domination. What is therefore paramount to maintain is "the sense that the world order is ultimately backed by the U.S. ...The U.S. should be postured to act independently when collective action cannot be orchestrated."

There is no doubt that this Pentagon draft document reflects the fundamental motivations and concerns of U.S. policy planners today.[118]

For these reasons, tension between the United States and Russia still exists in the post-Cold War era, although not with the same degree of intensity and conflict of earlier years. This is primarily due to Russia's weakening since the collapse of the USSR. This weakening has contributed significantly to Russia's willingness to join the U.S. in an alliance dominated by the latter, while attempting to pursue its own goals within a U.S.-dominated framework, challenging that framework only marginally.

As noted by Douglas MacArthur and Professor Stephen Blank, the principal expert on Russia, the Commonwealth of Independent States, and Eastern Europe at the U.S. Army War College's Strategic Studies Institute, "the Transcaspian has become perhaps the most important area of direct Western-Russian contention today."[119] However, Russia is not the only rival to U.S. interests in the Caspian. U.S. policy, with British complicity, also appears to be designed to eventually distance the Balkan and Central Asian countries from German-EU influence, as well as weaken competing Franco-Belgian-Italian oil interests.[120]

Stephen Blank suggests that an ingenious method of imposing U.S. hegemony is now being pursued in the form of peacekeeping missions. Because an open military-backed diplomatic confrontation with U.S. rivals, such as Russia, China and others, remains dangerous and therefore inappropriate, U.S. policy is to find ways of implementing the "functional equivalent... [i.e.] peace operations."[121] Thus, there is good reason to argue that U.S. involvement in Central Asia, undertaken ostensibly as humanitarian peace/security operations, are in fact designed to secure economic and strategic interests.

Indeed, there can be no real disputing the fact that, as matter of policy, military intervention is concerned fundamentally with the protection of Western interests as opposed to human rights, or even domestic security.

Although NATO military expansion is publicly touted as a means of legitimately strengthening the security of NATO members from conflict, and more recently the human rights of peoples around the world thereby, the reality is rather different. The actual objective of NATO, along with NATO's regional programmes, such as Partnership for Peace, can be discerned from NATO's definition of "security" as *any event or entity that challenges the "collective interests" of NATO members.*

For example, former U.S. Secretaries of State and Defense, Christopher and Perry, stated in 1997 that "the danger to security... is not primarily potential aggression to their collective [NATO] territory, but threats to their collective interests beyond their territory... To deal with such threats alliance members need to have a way to rapidly form military coalitions that can accomplish goals beyond NATO territory."[122]

NATO is, therefore, to play the role of military enforcer and protector of regional Western interests. References to "security," therefore, relate to these interests, which are primarily economic in nature. That these interests are primarily orientated around strategic and economic issues, such as access to regional resources and the countering of U.S. rivals, is clear from several examples, such as the fact that U.S. Central Asia experts met at NATO headquarters to discuss, not the threat of conflict, but rather major U.S. interests in Caspian basin energy deposits. It is in this context that Javier Solana, who became NATO Secretary-General during the intervention in Kosovo and later EU Security Affairs chief, stated at a Washington conference on NATO enlargement that Europe cannot be fully secure without bringing the Caucasus into its security zone.[123]

U.S. Ambassador Nathan Nimitz elaborated on how U.S. policy should hence be directed, in no uncertain terms: he concluded that the entirety of Eurasia must be brought under U.S. military-economic hegemony. "Pax NATO is the only logical regime to maintain security in the traditional sense... [and] must recognize a need for expansion of its stabilizing influence in adjacent areas, particularly in Southeastern Europe, the Black Sea region (in concert of course with the regional powers...) and in the Arabian/Persian Gulf. The United States must continue to play the major role in this security system."[124]

As Stephen Blank thus reports, regional military exercises held in 1997 were designed to demonstrate to the world that "U.S. and NATO forces could be deployed anywhere... The obvious implication of current policy is that NATO, under U.S. leadership, will become an international policeman and hegemon in the Transcaspian and define the limits of Russian participation in the region's expected oil boom."[125]

Strategies for Intervention
by the Council on Foreign Relations

In other words, the Great Game of the nineteenth century, which consisted of competition among the powers for control of Central Eurasia, has continued into the twenty-first century with the United States leading the way. While Afghanistan thus constitutes the essential vehicle of control of Central Asia, Central Asia is in turn an essential instrument of global control.

This fact, along with extensive strategic planning for future U.S. intervention in the region, was discussed in a 1997 Council on Foreign Relations (CFR) study, The Grand Chessboard: American Primacy and its Geostrategic Imperatives. Authored by longtime U.S. strategic adviser and former National Security Adviser under the Carter Administration, Zbigniew Brzezinski, the CFR study goes into great detail about U.S. interests in "Eurasia" and the need for a "sustained and directed" U.S. involvement in the Central Asian region to secure these interests.[126]

"Ever since the continents started interacting politically, some five hundred years ago, Eurasia has been the center of world power," he observes.[127] Eurasia consists of all the territory east of Germany and Poland, all the way through Russia and China to the Pacific Ocean, including the Middle East and most of the Indian subcontinent. Brzezinski notes that the key to controlling Eurasia lies in establishing control over the republics of Central Asia.

He further describes Russia and China, both of which border Central Asia, as the two main powers that might threaten U.S. interests in the region, Russia being the more prominent threat. The U.S. must accordingly manage and manipulate the "lesser" surrounding powers, such as Ukraine, Azerbaijan, Iran and Kazakhstan, as counter-actions to Russian and Chinese moves to control the oil, gas and minerals of the republics of Central Asia, namely Turkmenistan, Uzbekistan, Tajikistan, and Kyrgyzstan. He also notes that any nation becoming predominant in Central Asia would thus pose a direct threat to U.S. control of oil resources both within the region and in the Persian Gulf. The Central Asian republics, he records, "are of importance from the standpoint of security and historical ambitions to at least three of their most immediate and more powerful neighbors, namely Russia, Turkey and Iran, with China also signaling an increasing political interest in the region...

"But the Eurasian Balkans are infinitely more important as a potential economic prize: an enormous concentration of natural gas and oil reserves is located in the region, in addition to important minerals, including gold... The world's energy consumption is bound to vastly increase over the next two or three decades. Estimates by the U.S. Department of Energy anticipate that world demand will rise by more than 50 percent between 1993 and 2015, with the most significant increase in consumption occurring in the Far East. The momentum of Asia's economic development is already generating massive pressures for the exploration and exploitation of new sources of energy, and the Central Asian region and the Caspian Sea basin are known to contain reserves of natural gas and oil that dwarf those of Kuwait, the Gulf of Mexico, or the North Sea[128] ... Kazakhstan is the shield and Uzbekistan is the soul for the region's diverse national awakenings ... Uzbekistan is, in fact, the prime candidate for regional leadership in Central Asia.[129] ... Once pipelines to the area have been developed, Turkmenistan's truly vast natural gas reserves augur a prosperous future for the country's people... In fact, an Islamic revival—already abetted from the outside not only by Iran but also by Saudi Arabia—is likely to become the mobilizing impulse for the increasingly pervasive new nationalisms, determined to oppose any reintegration under Russian—and hence infidel—control[130] ... For Pakistan, the primary interest is to gain Geostrategic depth through political influence in Afghanistan—and to deny to Iran the exercise of such influence in Afghanistan and Tajikistan—and to benefit eventually from any pipeline construction linking Central Asia with the Arabian Sea[131] ... Moreover, sensible Russian leaders realize that the demographic explosion underway in the new states means that their failure to sustain economic growth will eventually create an explosive situation along Russia's entire southern frontier.[132] Turkmenistan... has been actively exploring the construction of a new pipeline through Afghanistan and Pakistan to the Arabian Sea."[133]

He then pointed out from the above that: "It follows that America's primary interest is to help ensure that no single power comes to control this geopolitical space and that the global community has unhindered financial and economic access to it."[134]

"...China's growing economic presence in the region and its political stake in the area's independence are also congruent with America's interests[135]... America is now the only global superpower, and Eurasia is the globe's central arena. Hence, what happens to the distribution of power on the Eurasian continent will be of decisive importance to America's global primacy and to America's historical legacy... the Eurasian Balkans threaten to become a cauldron of ethnic conflict and great-power rivalry."

Brzezinski then comes to the crucial conclusion that: "Without sustained and directed American involvement, before long the forces of global disorder could come to dominate the world scene. And the possibility of such a fragmentation is inherent in the geopolitical tensions not only of today's Eurasia but of the world more generally."[136] These observations are rooted indelibly in the Council on Foreign Relations' principal concern—the maintenance of global U.S. dominance:

"The last decade of the twentieth century has witnessed a tectonic shift in world affairs. For the first time ever, a non-Eurasian power has emerged not only as a key arbiter of Eurasian power relations but also as the world's paramount power. The defeat and collapse of the Soviet Union was the final step in the rapid ascendance of a Western Hemisphere power, the United States, as the sole and, indeed, the first truly global power[137]...

But in the meantime, it is imperative that no Eurasian challenger emerges, capable of dominating Eurasia and thus also of challenging America. The formulation of a comprehensive and integrated Eurasian geostrategy is therefore the purpose of this book.[138] ... For America, the chief geopolitical prize is Eurasia... Now a non-Eurasian power is preeminent in Eurasia—and America's global primacy is directly dependent on how long and how effectively its preponderance on the Eurasian continent is sustained[139] ...

In that context, how America 'manages' Eurasia is critical. Eurasia is the globe's largest continent and is geopolitically axial. A power that dominates Eurasia would control two of the world's three most advanced and economically productive regions. A mere glance at the map also suggests that control over Eurasia would almost automatically entail Africa's subordination, rendering the Western Hemisphere and Oceania geopolitically peripheral to the world's central continent. About 75 per cent of the world's people live in Eurasia, and most of the world's physical wealth is there as well, both in its enterprises and underneath its soil. Eurasia accounts for 60 per cent of the world's GNP and about three-fourths of the world's known energy resources[140] ... Two basic steps are thus required: first, to identify the geostrategically dynamic Eurasian states that have the power to cause a potentially important shift in the international distribution of power and to decipher the central external goals of their respective political elites and the likely consequences of their seeking to attain them;... second, to formulate specific U.S. policies to offset, co-opt, and/or control the above ...

To put it in a terminology that harkens back to the more brutal age of ancient empires, the three grand imperatives of imperial geostrategy are to prevent collusion and maintain security dependence among the vassals, to keep tributaries pliant and protected, and to keep the barbarians from coming together[141] ... Henceforth, the United States may have to determine how to cope with regional coalitions that seek to push America out of Eurasia, thereby threatening America's status as a global power[142] ... Hence, support for the new post-Soviet states— for geopolitical pluralism in the space of the former Soviet empire— has to be an integral part of a policy designed to induce Russia to exercise unambiguously its European option. Among these states, three are geopolitically especially important: Azerbaijan, Uzbekistan, and Ukraine... Uzbekistan, nationally the most vital and the most populous of the central Asian states, represents the major obstacle to any renewed Russian control over the region. Its independence is critical to the survival of the other Central Asian states, and it is the least vulnerable to Russian pressures."[143]

Elaborating, Brzezinski observes that:

"With warning signs on the horizon across Europe and Asia, any successful American policy must focus on Eurasia as a whole and be guided by a geostrategic design ... That puts a premium on maneuver and manipulation in order to prevent the emergence of a hostile coalition that could eventually seek to challenge America's primacy ... The most immediate task is to make certain that no state or combination of states gains the capacity to expel the United States from Eurasia or even to diminish significantly its decisive arbitration role[144] ...

In the long run, global politics are bound to become increasingly uncongenial to the concentration of hegemonic power in the hands of a single state. Hence, America is not only the first, as well as the only, truly global superpower, but it is also likely to be the very last."[145]

The next point made by Brzezinski is crucial:

"Moreover, as America becomes an increasingly multi-cultural society, it may find it more difficult to fashion a consensus on foreign policy issues, except in the circumstance of a truly massive and widely perceived direct external threat."[146]

Long-standing U.S. aims to establish hegemony—the "decisive arbitration role" of "America's primacy"—over "Eurasia" through control of Central Asia thus entailed the use of "sustained and directed American involvement," justified through the manufacture of "a truly massive and widely perceived direct external threat." This should also be understood in context with his earlier assertion that: "The attitude of the American public toward the external projection of American power has been much more ambivalent. The public supported America's engagement in World War II largely because of the shock effect of the Japanese attack on Pearl Harbor."[147]

Brzezinski clearly envisaged that the establishment, consolidation and expansion of U.S. military hegemony over Eurasia through Central Asia would require the unprecedented, open-ended militarisation of foreign policy, coupled with an unprecedented manufacture of domestic support and consensus on this militarisation campaign.

He also recognised that this would require the perception of an external threat of hitherto unprecedented proportions.

Given that Afghanistan constitutes the principal opening into Central Asia, it is clear that the CFR's strategic planning for the expansion and consolidation of U.S. global hegemony via control of Eurasia—itself secured through control of Central Asia—would of necessity be initiated through the establishment of U.S. hegemony in Afghanistan.

The Irrelevance of Bin Laden

All this clearly establishes the broad economic and strategic agenda behind the military plans that were in place long before 11th September 2001. This agenda was re-confirmed in February 1998 in U.S. House of Representative hearings held by the Subcommittee on Asia and the Pacific (a subcommittee of the House Committee on International Relations). These meetings revealed the fundamental strategic and economic U.S. interests in Central Asia, and Afghanistan's crucial role in providing a vehicle by which to secure these interests (see Appendix A).

Even in the aftermath of 11th September, contrary to what the public was told, the U.S. General and head of U.S. Central Command directing the operation in Afghanistan revealed that finding Osama bin laden was not actually a mission objective. *USA Today* reported that: "The U.S. combat commander in Afghanistan said Thursday that apprehending Osama bin Laden isn't one of the missions of Operation Enduring Storm...

"'We have not said that Osama bin Laden is a target of this effort,' Franks told reporters at his first Pentagon briefing since the war began a month ago. Usually, Franks, the commander in chief of Central Command and third in the war's chain of command after Bush and Defense Secretary Donald Rumsfeld, is headquartered in Tampa. 'What we are about,' he said, 'is the destruction of the al-Qa'eda network, as well as the... Taliban that provide harbor to bin Laden and al-Qa'eda.' Marine Lt. Col. Dave Lapan, Central Command liaison at the Pentagon, said Franks was trying to reflect the broader nature of the goals in Afghanistan. 'If tomorrow morning someone told us Osama's dead, that doesn't mean we're through in Afghanistan,' Lapan said."[148]

The irrelevance of capturing bin Laden was further revealed when, as London's *Daily Mirror* reported: "... in late September and early October, leaders of Pakistan's two Islamic parties negotiated bin Laden's extradition to Pakistan to stand trial for the September 11 attacks...

"The deal was that he would be held under house arrest in Peshawar. According to reports in Pakistan (and the Daily Telegraph), this had both bin Laden's approval and that of Mullah Omah, the Taliban leader... Later, a U.S. official said that 'casting our objectives too narrowly' risked 'a premature collapse of the international effort if by some luck chance Mr bin Laden was captured'... What the Afghani people got instead was 'American justice'—imposed by a president who, as well as denouncing international agreements on nuclear weapons, biological weapons, torture and global warming, has refused to sign up for an international court to try war criminals: the one place where bin Laden might be put on trial."[149]

As discussed, the war on Afghanistan, planned long before 11th September, thus had as its basis much broader concerns. Capturing and trying bin Laden was a public pretext, not an integral aim of the U.S. mission. Long-standing military plans to invade Afghanistan were rooted in broad strategic and economic concerns related to the consolidation of global U.S. hegemony through control of Eurasia and Central Asia.

Notes

[109] Krakowski, Elie, 'The Afghan Vortex,' *IASPS Research Papers in Strategy*, Institute for Advanced Strategic and Political Studies, Jerusalem, No. 9, April 2000.

[110] Chin, Larry, *Online Journal*, 7 Feb. 2002, www.onlinejournal.com.

[111] Cited in 'How Oil Interests Play Out in the U.S. Bombing of Afghanistan,' *Drillbits and Trailings: Electronic Monthly on the Mining & Oil Industries*,

31 Oct. 2001, Vol. 6, No. 8, www.moles.org/ProjectUnderground/drillbits/6_08/1.html.

[112] Croissant, Michael P. and Aras, Bulent (ed.), *Oil and Geopolitics in the Caspian Sea Region*, Praeger, London, 1999.

[113] Baryiski, Robert V., 'The Caspian Oil Regime: Military Dimensions,' *Caspian Crossroads Magazine*, Volume 1, Issue No. 2, Spring 1995.

[114] Blank, Stephen J., 'The United States: Washington's New Frontier in the Trans-Caspian,' in Croissant, Michael P. and Aras, Bulent (ed.), *Oil and Geopolitics in the Caspian Sea Region*, op. cit.

[115] Cited in Cohn, Marjorie, 'The Deadly Pipeline War: U.S. Afghan Policy Driven By Oil Interests,' Jurist: The Legal Education Network, University of Pittsburgh, 7 December 2001, http://jurist.law.pitt.edu.

[116] Cited in Monbiot, George, 'A Discreet Deal in the Pipeline,' *The Guardian*, 15 February 2001.

[117] Silk Road Strategy Act of 1999, 106th Congress, posted at EurasiaNet, www.eurasianet.org/resource/regional/silkroad.html.

[118] Pentagon draft document cited in *New York Times*, 8 March 1992; *International Herald Tribune*, 9 March 1992; *Washington Post*, 22 March 1992; *The Times*, 25 May 1992. For further discussion of U.S. global strategies see Ahmed, Nafeez M., 'America in Terror–Causes and Context: The Foundational Principles of Western Foreign Policy and the Structure of World Order,' Media Monitors Network, 12 September 2001, mediamonitors.net/mosaddeq12. html.

[119] Blank, Stephen J., 'The United States: Washington's New Frontier in the Trans-Caspian,' op. cit., p.250.

[120] For further discussion see Chossudovsky, Michel, 'America at War in Macedonia,' Transnational Foundation for Future Peace and Research (TFF), TFF Meeting Point, June 2001. Chossudovsky is Professor of Economics at the University of Ottawa.

[121] Blank, Stephen J., 'The United States: Washington's New Frontier in the Trans-Caspian,' op. cit., p. 256.

[122] Cited in ibid., p. 252.

[123] Ibid., p. 250.

[124] Cited in ibid., p. 252.

[125] Ibid., p. 266-267.

[126] Brzezinski, Zbigniew, *The Grand Chessboard: American Primacy and its Geostrategic Imperatives*, Basic Books, 1997. Brzezinski holds a 1953 PhD from Harvard University. His other achievements include: Counselor, Center for Strategic and International Studies; Professor of American Foreign Policy, Johns

Hopkins University; National Security Advisor to President Jimmy Carter (1977-81); Trustee and founder of the Trilateral Commission International; advisor of several major U.S./global corporations; member of National Security Council and Defense Department Commission on Integrated Long-Term Strategy; under Ronald Reagan, member of the President's Foreign Intelligence Advisory Board; past member, Board of Directors, The Council on Foreign Relations; 1988, Co-chairman of the Bush National Security Advisory Task Force. Michael C. Ruppert must be credited for his very useful selection of quotes from Brzezinski's study, in 'A War in the Planning for 4 Years,' From The Wilderness Publications, 7 November 2001.

[127] Brzezinski, Zbigniew, The Grand Chessboard: American Primacy and its Geostrategic Imperatives, op. cit., p. xiii.

[128] Ibid, p. 124-125.

[129] Ibid., p. 130.

[130] Ibid., p. 132-133.

[131] Ibid., p. 139.

[132] Ibid., p. 141.

[133] Ibid., p. 145.

[134] Ibid., p. 148.

[135] Ibid., p. 149.

[136] Ibid., p. 194-195.

[137] Ibid., p. xiii.

[138] Ibid., p. xiv.

[139] Ibid., p. 30.

[140] Ibid., p.31.

[141] Ibid., p. 40.

[142] Ibid., p. 55.

[143] Ibid., p. 121

[144] Ibid., p. 197-198.

[145] Ibid., p. 209.

[146] Ibid., p. 211.

[147] Ibid., p. 24-25

[148] Omicinski, John, 'General: Capturing bin Laden is not part of mission,' *USA Today*, 23 November 2001.

[149] *Daily Mirror*, 16 November 2001.

4. Warning Signs of 9-11 and Intelligence Failures

"What is happening in the United States took me by surprise. I anticipated that in the aftermath of Sept. 11, there would be an enormous hue and cry to find out what went wrong. There has been no hue and cry in the United States. No recriminations, nothing even similar to what happened after Pearl Harbor in 1941... The United States has drawn a veil of silence over the issue of intelligence failure."

Wesley Wark, Canadian Intelligence Expert and Consultant to the Privy Council Office of Canada on Intelligence Policy
(Globe & Mail, 18 December 2001)

"We've been focusing on this perpetrator Osama bin Laden for 3 years, and yet we didn't see this one coming," said Vincent Cannistraro, former chief of CIA counter-terrorism operations. A U.S. Air Force General described the attack as "something we had never seen before, something we had never even thought of." FBI Director Robert Mueller further declared that "there were no warning signs that I'm aware of." Senior FBI officials insisted that in terms of intelligence warnings received prior to 11th September: "The notion of flying a plane into a building or using it as a bomb never came up."[150] According to this official version of events, no one in the Bush administration had the slightest idea of the identities of those who orchestrated the 11th September attacks, the nature of their plans, or their targets.

Contrary to these prolific claims, there is compelling evidence that the U.S. intelligence community had extensive forewarning of the 11th September attacks on New York and Washington. Further evidence suggests that the attacks may, in fact, have been in the interest of certain elements of the Bush administration (see Chapter VII).

Using Planes as Bombs

The Pentagon commissioned an expert panel in 1993 to investigate the possibility of an airplane being used to bomb national landmarks. Retired Air Force Col. Doug Menarchik, who organised the $150,000 study for the Defense Department's Office of Special Operations and Low-Intensity Conflict, recalled: "It was considered radical thinking, a little too scary for the times. After I left, it met a quiet death." Other participants have noted that the decision not to publish detailed scenarios issued to some extent from fear that this may give terrorists ideas. Nevertheless, a draft document detailing the results of the investigation was circulated through the Pentagon, the Justice Department and the Federal Emergency Management Agency. Senior agency officials decided against a public release.[151]

The veracity of the Pentagon's "radical thinking" was confirmed in 1994 when there occurred three attempted attacks on buildings using airplanes. The first, in April of that year, involved a Federal Express flight engineer facing dismissal.

Having boarded a DC-10 as a passenger, he invaded the cockpit, planning to crash the plane into a company building in Memphis. Fortunately, he was overpowered by the crew.

The second attempt occurred in September. A lone pilot crashed a small plane into a tree on the White House grounds, just short of the President's bedroom.

The third incident occurred in December. An Air France flight in Algiers was hijacked by members of the Armed Islamic Group (GIA)— who are linked to Al-Qaeda—aiming to crash it into the Eiffel Tower. French Special Forces stormed the plane on the ground.[152]

Al-Qaeda's Plans: Project Bojinka

Western intelligence had been aware of plans for such terrorist attacks on U.S. soil as early as 1995. Both the Federal Bureau of Investigation (FBI) and the Federal Aviation Administration (FAA) had detailed information about the possible use of hijack/suicide attacks by terrorists connected to Osama bin Laden. The *New York Times* reported that:

> "In 1994, two jetliners were hijacked by people who wanted to crash them into buildings, one of them by an Islamic militant group. And the 2000 edition of the FAA's annual report on Criminal Acts Against Aviation, published this year, said that although Osama bin Laden 'is not known to have attacked civil aviation, he has both the motivation and the wherewithal to do so,' adding, 'Bin Laden's anti-Western and anti-American attitudes make him and his followers a significant threat to civil aviation, particularly to U.S. civil aviation.'"[153]

Moreover, the U.S. intelligence community was aware of bin Laden's specific intentions to use hijacked civilian planes as weapons. In this regard, the *Chicago Sun-Times* reported that:

"The FBI had advance indications of plans to hijack U.S. airliners and use them as weapons, but neither acted on them nor distributed the intelligence to local police agencies. From the moment of the September 11th attacks, high-ranking federal officials insisted that the terrorists' method of operation surprised them. Many stick to that story. Actually, elements of the hijacking plan were known to the FBI as early as 1995 and, if coupled with current information, might have uncovered the plot."[154]

Details of these advanced indications have been noted in a report by the respected German daily, *Die Welt*: "Western secret services knew as far back as 1995 that suspected terror mastermind Osama bin Laden planned to attack civilian sites using commercial passenger planes." Quoting sources "close to western intelligence agencies," the newspaper reported that: "The plan was discovered in January 1995 by Philippine police who were investigating a possible attack against Pope John Paul II on a visit to Manila...

"They found details of the plan in a computer seized in an apartment used by three men who were part of Bin Laden's al-Qaeda network. It provided for 11 planes to be exploded simultaneously by bombs placed on board, but also in an alternative form for several planes flying to the United States to be hijacked and flown into civilian targets. Among targets mentioned was the World Trade Center in New York, which was destroyed in the September 11 terror attacks in the United States that killed thousands."

This plot "re-surfaced during the trial in New York in 1997 of Pakistani Ramsi Yousef, the mastermind of the attack on the World Trade Center in 1993... [The] U.S. Federal Bureau of Investigation and CIA would have known about the plan at the latest at this time."[155] As the Washington DC-based Public Education Center (PEC) observes, "Federal investigative sources have confirmed that Murad"—who was "a close confidant and right-hand man to Yousef, who was convicted of crimes relating to the 1993 bombing of the World Trade Center"—"detailed an entire plot to dive bomb aircraft in the headquarters of the Central Intelligence Agency in Langley, VA." along with other U.S. buildings. "Yousef independently boasted of the plot to U.S. Secret Service agent Brian Parr and FBI agent Charles Stern on an extradition flight from Pakistan to the United States in February 1995," continues the PEC report. "The agents later testified to that fact in court... [T]he plan targeted not only the CIA but other U.S. government buildings in Washington, including the Pentagon."[156]

Rafael M. Garcia III, Chairman/CEO of the Mega Group of Computer Companies in the Philippines, who often works with the National Bureau of Investigation (NBI) in his field of expertise, was involved in the intelligence operation that uncovered Project Bojinka. Garcia was responsible for the decoding of Yousef's computer. "This was how we found out about the various plots being hatched by the cell of Ramzi Yousef. First, there was the plot to assassinate Pope John Paul II," he observes. "Then, we discovered a second, even more sinister plot: Project Bojinka, or a Yugoslav term for loud bang.[157] This was a plot to blow up 11 airlines over the Pacific Ocean, all in a 48-hour period. The planes would have come from Seoul, Hong Kong, Taipei, Tokyo, Bangkok, Singapore, and Manila...

> "Then we found another document that discussed a second alternative to crash the 11 planes into selected targets in the United States instead of just blowing them up in the air. These included the CIA headquarters in Langley, Virginia; the World Trade Center in New York; the Sears Tower in Chicago; the TransAmerica Tower in San Francisco; and the White House in Washington, DC... I submitted my findings to NBI officials, who most certainly turned over the report (and the computer) either to then Senior Superintendent Avelino Razon of the PNP [the Philippine National Police] or to Bob Heafner of the FBI... I have since had meetings with certain U.S. authorities and they have confirmed to me that indeed, many things were done in response to my report."[158]

The *World Tribune* similarly reports, citing an intelligence source involved in the Philippine operation, that: "The hijacked aircraft were to be crashed into structures in the United States, including the World Trade Center, the White House, Pentagon, the Transamerica tower in San Francisco and the Sears Tower in Chicago."[159] Paul Monk, Senior Fellow at the Australian Thinking Skills Institute and a Professor at the Australian Defense University, cites "confidential sources" in Manila and Washington detailing that: "Project Bojinka was an AQ [Al-Qaeda] plan to hijack eleven airliners simultaneously, exploding many of them at various places over the Pacific, but flying at least two of them into major federal government buildings in the United States. The flights to be hijacked were specified. They were all United Airlines, Northwest Airlines and Delta flights...

> "The plan has been masterminded by one Ramzi Yousef, who was arrested in Islamabad in the wake of Murad's interrogation. Both Murad and Yousef were extradited to the United States, tried and convicted for complicity in the 1993 attack on the WTC. The date of Yousef's conviction was 11 September 1996. From that point, given the fascination terrorists have with anniversaries, 11 September should surely have become a watch date."[160]

Detailed elaboration on this matter is provided by the Washington DC-based media watch group, Accuracy In Media (AIM). AIM has harshly criticised the media for largely ignoring the U.S. intelligence community's advanced knowledge of Project Bojinka:

> "In 1995, the CIA and the FBI learned that Osama bin Laden was planning to hijack U.S. airliners and use them as bombs to attack important targets in the U.S. This scheme was called Project Bojinka. It was discovered in the Philippines, where authorities arrested two of bin Laden's agents, Ramzi Yousef and Abdul Hakim Murad. They were involved in planting a bomb on a Philippine airliner. Project Bojinka, which Philippine authorities found outlined on Abdul Murad's laptop, called for planting bombs on eleven U.S. airliners and hijacking others and crashing them into targets like the CIA building…

> It required aviators like Japan's kamikaze pilots who were willing to commit suicide. Bin Laden had no such pilots in 1995, but he set out to train young fanatics willing to die for him to fly airliners. Abdul Murad, whose laptop had revealed the plan, admitted that he was being trained for a suicide mission. Bin Laden began training pilots in Afghanistan with the help of an Afghan pilot and a Pakistani general.

> Project Bojinka was known to the CIA and the FBI. It was described in court documents in the trial in New York of Ramzi Yousef and Abdul Murad for their participation in the bombing of the World Trade Center in 1993. Since the CIA had been mentioned as one of the targets in Project Bojinka, it should have had an especially strong interest in any evidence that bin Laden was preparing to carry it out. The most obvious indicator, and one that should have been watched most carefully, was the recruitment of young, dedicated followers to learn to fly American airliners. That would require keeping a close watch on flight schools where that training is given."[161]

Post-Bojinka Intelligence Gathering

And indeed, the surveillance of flight schools is exactly what subsequently occurred, indicating that the threat posed by Project Bojinka was not dismissed—rather, it was taken seriously and used as the basis for intensive intelligence gathering. As Garcia testifies, in meetings with "certain U.S. authorities… they have confirmed to me that indeed, many things were done in response" to the findings of Project Bojinka.[162] The *Washington Post*, noting the plans outlined in Project Bojinka, reported that: "Since 1996, the FBI had been developing evidence that international terrorists were using flight schools to learn to fly jumbo jets." This evidence began to accumulate shortly after the FBI learned of Project Bojinka. "A foiled plot in Manila to blow up U.S. airliners and later court testimony by an associate of bin Laden had touched off FBI inquiries at several schools, officials say."[163] It should be noted that this report indicates that Al-Qaeda's plans for Project Bojinka were considered by U.S. intelligence to be a credible threat, and thus "touched off" further investigations.

Early in the same year, U.S. officials had identified crop-dusters and suicide flights as potential terrorist weapons. Elaborate steps were adopted to prevent an attack from the air during the Summer Olympic Games in Atlanta. U.S. aircraft were deployed to intercept suspicious aircraft in the skies over Olympic venues, while agents monitored crop-duster flights within hundreds of miles of downtown Atlanta. According to Woody Johnson, head of the FBI's Atlanta office at the time, law enforcement agents fanned out to regional airports throughout northern Georgia "to make sure nobody hijacked a small aircraft and tried to attack one of the venues." From 6th July to 11th August, when the Games ended, the FAA had banned all aviation within a one-mile radius of the Olympic Village where athletes were resident. Aircraft were also ordered to stay at least three miles away from other sites, beginning three hours before each event until three hours after each event ended.[164] These extensive measures in 1996, in response to the general threat of a possible terrorist attack, should be duly noted—there is a stark contrast between these measures and the almost total lack of preventive measures in response to warnings of the 11th September attacks.

By 1999, the Federal Aviation Administration's annual report on Criminal Acts Against Aviation noted the threat posed by bin Laden, recalling that a radical Muslim leader living in British exile had warned in August 1998 that bin Laden "would bring down an airliner, or hijack an airliner to humiliate the United States." The 2000 edition of the annual report, published early in 2001, reiterated concerns that although bin Laden "is not known to have attacked civil aviation, he has both the motivation and the wherewithal to do so... Bin Laden's anti-Western and anti-American attitudes make him and his followers a significant threat to civil aviation, particularly to U.S. civil aviation."[165]

By this time, knowledge of Al-Qaeda's intentions to use planes as missiles to target key U.S. buildings was widespread in the U.S. intelligence community. The *Washington Post* recounts how "a 1999 report prepared for the National Intelligence Council, an affiliate of the CIA, warned that terrorists associated with bin Laden might hijack an airplane and crash it into the Pentagon, White House or CIA headquarters...

"The report recounts well-known case studies of similar plots, including a 1995 plan by al Qaeda operatives to hijack and crash a dozen U.S. airliners in the South Pacific and pilot a light aircraft into Langley. 'Suicide bomber(s) belonging to al-Qaida's Martyrdom Battalion could crash-land an aircraft packed with high explosives (C-4 and semtex) into the Pentagon, the headquarters of the Central Intelligence Agency (CIA), or the White House,' the September 1999 report said."[166]

Meanwhile, the surveillance of Al-Qaeda operatives on U.S. soil continued. Between 2000 and 2001, the CIA had made the FBI aware of the names of about 100 suspected members of bin Laden's terrorist network thought to be headed to, or already in, the United States. A 23rd August 2001 cable specifically referred to Khalid Al-Midhar and Nawaq Alhazmi, who were allegedly aboard the hijacked airplane that crashed into the Pentagon.[167]

Six months before 11th September, U.S. agencies became aware through authoritative intelligence warnings that bin Laden was planning to implement Project Bojinka soon. Three months later, these warnings were repeated. The warnings were, again, not dismissed. On the contrary, the U.S. intelligence community took the reports very seriously. *Newsbytes*, an online division of the *Washington Post*, reported in mid-September that:

"U.S. and Israeli intelligence agencies received warning signals at least three months ago that Middle Eastern terrorists were planning to hijack commercial aircraft to use as weapons to attack important symbols of American and Israeli culture, according to a story in Germany's daily *Frankfurter Allgemeine Zeitung* (FAZ).

The FAZ, quoting unnamed German intelligence sources, said that the Echelon spy network was being used to collect information about the terrorist threats, and that U.K. intelligence services apparently also had advance warning. The FAZ, one of Germany's most respected dailies, said that even as far back as six months ago western and near-east press services were receiving information that such attacks were being planned. Within the American intelligence community, the warnings were taken seriously and surveillance intensified, the FAZ said."[168]

The last comment—"Within the American intelligence community, the warnings were taken seriously"—is crucial. It clearly indicates that in response to the ECHELON warnings, the entire U.S. intelligence community—all U.S. intelligence agencies—were on alert for a Project Bojinka-style attack, and consequently intensified surveillance. The *New Yorker* further reports that according to Richard A. Clarke, U.S. National Coordinator for Counterterrorism in the White House, about ten weeks before 11th September, the U.S. intelligence community was convinced that a terrorist attack by Al-Qaeda on U.S. soil was imminent. Seven to eight weeks prior to the 11th September attacks, all internal U.S. security agencies were warned of an impending Al-Qaeda attack against the Untied States that would likely occur in several weeks time. This warning coincided with the second ECHELON warning cited before:

"Meanwhile, intelligence had been streaming in concerning a likely Al Qaeda attack. 'It all came together in the third week in June,' Clarke said. 'The C.I.A.'s view was that a major terrorist attack was coming in the next several weeks.' On July 5th, Clarke summoned all the domestic security agencies—the Federal Aviation Administration, the Coast Guard, Customs, the Immigration and Naturalization Service, and the F.B.I.—and told them to increase their security in light of an impending attack."[169]

It is apparent then that all U.S. intelligence agencies were fully expecting an impending attack by Al-Qaeda by the beginning of July 2001, and moreover that the U.S. intelligence community was aware that "terrorists were planning to hijack commercial aircraft to use as weapons to attack important symbols of American... culture." In other words, the U.S. intelligence community was anticipating a Project Bojinka-style attack. Among the buildings identified as "symbolic of American culture" in Al-Qaeda's Project Bojinka plans, known by U.S. intelligence, was the World Trade Center. That the WTC was an extremely likely target is further clear from the fact that operatives linked to Osama bin Laden had previously targeted the Twin Towers in a failed bombing attempt. As a consequence, the entire domestic intelligence and security apparatus seems to have been alerted to increase relevant security and surveillance.

Warnings of the impending attack continued to be received thereafter. Approximately 4 weeks prior to 11th September, the CIA received specific information of an attack on U.S. soil. The Associated Press reports that: "Officials also said the CIA had developed general information a month before the attacks that heightened concerns that bin Laden and his followers were increasingly determined to strike on U.S. soil." A CIA official affirmed that: "There was something specific in early August that said to us that he was determined in striking on U.S. soil." AP elaborates that: "The information prompted the CIA to issue a warning to federal agencies."[170]

It was further revealed by a United Press International (UPI) report by U.S. terrorism correspondent Richard Sale on ECHELON's monitoring of bin Laden and other terrorist groups that:

"The targets of Echelon center on the penetration of the major components of most of the world's telephone and telecommunications systems. This could cover conversations NSA targets. Also included are all the telexes carried over the world's telecommunications networks, along with financial dealings: money transfers, airline destinations, stock information, data on demonstrations or international conferences, and much more."

ECHELON's effectiveness against bin Laden's network was further revealed in relation to a case against him in a U.S. District Court in Manhattan, illustrating that the National Security Agency was able to penetrate bin Laden's most secure communications. The case, Sale noted, "is based mainly on National Security Agency intercepts of phone calls between bin Laden and his operatives around the world—Afghanistan to London, from Kenya to the United States."

The technology had been used since at least 1995. Ben Venzke, Director of Intelligence and Special Projects for iDefense, a Virginia information warfare firm, is also quoted: "Since Bin Laden started to encrypt certain calls in 1995, why would they now be part of a court record? 'Codes were broken,' U.S. officials said, and Venzke added that 'you don't use your highest levels of secure communications all the time. It's too burdensome and it exposes it to other types of exploitation..'" The UPI report clarifies that much of the evidence in the case had been obtained in ECHELON intercepts subsequent to the 1998 bombings of U.S. embassies in East Africa.[171] Given that U.S. officials "believe the planning for the Sept. 11 attacks probably began two years ago," information on preparations for the attacks should have been available to, and picked up by, ECHELON.[172]

Confirmation that U.S. intelligence had been successfully monitoring Al-Qaeda's communications right through to the aftermath of 11th September came from Utah Senator Orrin Hatch, a conservative Republican with wide contacts in the national security establishment. On the day of the attacks, Hatch stated that the U.S. government had been monitoring Osama bin Laden's communications electronically, and had thus intercepted two bin Laden aides celebrating the attacks: "They have an intercept of some information that included people associated with bin Laden who acknowledged a couple of targets were hit."[173]

ABC News further reported that shortly before 11th September, the U.S. National Security Agency intercepted "multiple phone calls from Abu Zubaida, bin Laden's chief of operations, to the United States." The information contained in these intercepted phone calls has not been disclosed.[174]

Given that ECHELON was monitoring Osama bin Laden and Al-Qaeda, and even breaking their secure codes, the implications are alarming. As Canadian social philosopher Professor John McMurtry of Guelph University, Ontario, has noted in this connection:

"The pervasive Echelon surveillance apparatus and the most sophisticated intelligence machinery ever built is unlikely not to have eavesdropped on some of the very complicated organisation and plans across states and boundaries for the multi-site hijacking of planes from major security structures across the U.S.—especially since the suicide pilots were trained as pilots in the U.S., and the World Trade Centre had already been bombed in 1993 by Afghan ex-allies of the CIA. Since the prime suspect, Osama bin Laden, is himself an ex-CIA operative in Afghanistan, and his moves presumably under the intensest scrutiny for past successful terrorist attacks on two U.S. embassies in 1998, one has to reflect on the connections."[175]

Air Authorities Were Warned of Bojinka

It is worth noting here that around the time of the first ECHELON warnings, near the end of June 2001, Airjet Airline World News also issued a warning, specifying Project Bojinka: "During the trial a Secret Service agent testified that Yousef boasted during his extradition flight to New York that he would have blown up several jumbo jets within a few weeks if his plan had not been discovered. The government said the defendants even devised a name for their airline terror plot named, 'Project Bojinka'... The airlines are at risk—They need to take all appropriate measures and counter-measures to ensure the safety of their passengers."[176] The White House National Coordinator for Counterterrorism, Richard Clarke, had also given direct warning to the Federal Aviation Administration (FAA) to increase security measures in light of an impending terrorist attack in July 2001.[177] The FAA refused to take such measures.

Former Federal Air Safety Inspector Rodney Stich, who has 50 years of experience in aviation and air safety, had warned the FAA about the danger of skyjacking, specifically highlighting the fact that cockpit doors weren't secure, and further that pilots should be allowed to carry basic weapons. The FAA refused to implement his suggestions, and when it became apparent the threat was real, they blocked efforts to arm pilots, or to place air marshals on planes, among other security measures. In an extensive study of the subject, Stich observes that:

"Federal inspectors... had years earlier reported the hijacking threat and the simple inexpensive measures to prevent hijackers from taking control of the aircraft. Numerous fatal hijackings further proved the need for urgent preventative measures. Instead of taking the legally required corrective actions, arrogant and corrupt FAA management personnel destroyed official reports of the dangers and the need for corrective actions; warned air safety inspectors not to submit reports that would make the office look bad when there is a crash related to the known problems; threatened inspectors who took corrective actions or continued to make reports—even though crashes from these uncorrected safety problems continued to occur."[178]

The *Los Angeles Times* corroborates this assessment: "Federal bureaucracy and airline lobbying slowed and weakened a set of safety improvements recommended by a presidential commission—including one that a top airline industry official now says might have prevented the Sept. 11 terror attacks...

"The White House Commission on Aviation Safety and Security, created in 1996 after TWA Flight 800 crashed off Long Island, N.Y., recommended 31 steps that it said were urgently needed to provide a multilayered security system at the nation's airports... The Federal Aviation Administration expressed support for the proposals, which ranged from security inspections at airports to tighter screening of mail parcels, and the Clinton administration vowed to rigorously monitor the changes. But by Sept. 11, most of the proposals had been watered down by industry lobbying or were bogged down in bureaucracy, a Times review found."[179]

The U.S. government thus bears direct responsibility for this state of affairs, by consistently failing to comply with its avowed responsibility to "rigorously monitor" and enforce the required changes. Larry Klayman, Chairman and General Counsel of Judicial Watch, the Washington-based legal watchdog, comments that: "It is now apparent—given the near total lack of security at U.S. airports and elsewhere—that the U.S. government has not been forthright with the American people...

"During the last eight years of scandal during the Clinton administration, and the first eight months of the Bush Administration, reports this morning confirm that little to nothing was done to secure our nation's airports and transportation systems as a whole—despite warnings. Instead, cosmetic reform of education, social security, taxes, and other less important issues were given precedence. In addition, the American people were led to believe that appropriate anti-terrorist counter measures were being taken. Instead of telling the truth so the problems could be addressed, politicians painted a rosy picture in order to be elected and re-elected."[180]

This is clearly more than a case of incompetence. This systematic inaction, despite escalating warnings of a terrorist threat to the U.S. from the air, indicates wilful and reckless negligence of the highest order on the part of the U.S. government, rooted in sheer indifference to the potential loss in American lives.

Intensification of Surveillance
After Confirmation of Bojinka Plans

It is against this backdrop that the multiple intelligence warnings of an impending terrorist act by bin Laden's operatives should be assessed. Clearly, on the basis of the 1995 revelations about Project Bojinka, coupled with the authoritative warnings in 2001 from America's own ECHELON network among others, "the American intelligence community" was aware that bin Laden was planning imminent attacks on U.S. soil through the hijacking of civilian airliners to be used as bombs against key buildings "symbolic of American culture." Among the buildings in Washington and New York known to be on bin Laden's list of targets was the World Trade Centre.

Project Bojinka, in other words, was underway. U.S. intelligence agencies subsequently intensified their surveillance, and in doing so began tracking suspected terrorists. This indicates that the U.S. intelligence community had intensified surveillance by its various agencies in direct response to fears of a Project Bojinka-style attack on U.S. soil, orchestrated by Osama bin Laden.

It is appropriate then to consider in more detail the findings of this surveillance. *WorldNetDaily*, the Internet news service of the U.S.-based non-profit Western Journalism Center, reports some pertinent revelations in this respect:

"The FBI and other federal law enforcement agencies also knew that two of the hijackers were in the country, according to the Los Angeles Times. They were on a terrorist watch list. But the airlines were not notified... The FBI had several terrorists under surveillance, according to the Oct. 1 issue of Newsweek. They intercepted communications just prior to Sept. 11 that suggested something very big was about to happen... Still, there were more clues. Zacarias Moussaoui was arrested after flight trainers tipped off the feds that he wanted to learn how to fly a 747 but wasn't interested in takeoffs or landings. Zacarias was traveling on a French passport. When contacted, the French government reported that he was a suspected terrorist [linked to Osama Bin Laden]."[181]

Reuters reported in relation to Zacarias that: "The FBI arrested an Islamic militant in Boston last month and received French intelligence reports linking him to Saudi-born dissident Osama bin Laden but apparently did not act on them," a French radio station said on Thursday...

"Europe 1 radio reported that U.S. police arrested a man with dual French and Algerian nationality who had several passports, technical information on Boeing aircraft and flight manuals. The man had been taking flying lessons, it added. Asked for information by the Federal Bureau of Investigation, French security services provided a dossier clearly identifying him as an Islamic militant working with bin Laden."[182]

CBS' investigative documentary programme *60 Minutes II* elaborated that the information provided in the French intelligence report depicted Zacarias as "a dangerous Islamic extremist". Some of the information came from Jean-Louis Brugruiere, a French judge and terrorist hunter who said that the French had given the FBI "everything we had".[183] At the time of his arrest, Zacarias had been in possession of technical information on Boeing aircraft and flight manuals. It was on 26th August that the FBI headquarters was informed by French intelligence that Zacarias had ties to Al-Qaeda and Osama bin Laden. Despite the confirmation of his involvement in bin Laden's terrorist network, a special counterterrorism panel of the FBI and CIA reviewed the information against him, but concluded there was insufficient evidence that he represented a threat. The Minnesota flight school, Pan Am International Flight Academy, where Zacarias had been training, also warned the FBI in no uncertain terms.

As the Minneapolis *Star-Tribune* reported, "Moussaoui raised suspicions at the Pan Am International Flight Academy in Egan [Minnesota]" when he attended the Academy in August 2001 to learn how to fly jumbo jets. He "first raised eyebrows when, during a simple introductory exchange, he said he was from France, but then didn't seem to understand when the instructor spoke French to him... Moussaoui then became belligerent and evasive about his background... In addition, he seemed inept in basic flying procedures, while seeking expensive training on an advanced commercial jet simulator."[184]

Even the flight school's own employees "began whispering that he could be a hijacker." Director of Operations at the Academy John Rosengren recounts how Zacarias' instructor was "concerned and wondered why someone who was not a pilot and had so little experience was trying to pack so much training into such a short time... 'The more he was able to talk to him, the more he decided he was not pilot material... There was discussion about how much fuel was on board a 747-400 and how much damage that could cause if it hit anything.'"[185]

So the instructor contacted the FBI, as the *San Francisco Chronicle* reported:

"An instructor at a Minnesota flight school warned the FBI in August of his suspicion that a student who was later identified as a part of Osama bin Laden's terror network might be planning to use a commercial plane loaded with fuel as a weapon, a member of Congress and other officials said yesterday. The officials, who were briefed by the school, said the instructor warned the FBI in urgent tones about the terrorist threat posed by the student, Zacarias Moussaoui.

According to U.S. Representative James L. Oberstar of Minnesota, the instructor called the bureau several times to find someone in authority who seemed willing to act on the information. His warnings could not have been more blunt. Oberstar noted that: 'He told them, 'Do you realize that a 747 loaded with fuel can be used as a bomb?'

Congressional officials said the account by the school, the Pan Am International Flight Academy in Eagan, outside Minneapolis, raised new questions about why the FBI and other agencies did not prevent the hijackings… [The flight instructor] was a former military pilot who grew suspicious after encounters in which Moussaoui was belligerent and evasive about his background and because he was so adamant about learning to fly a 747 jumbo jet despite his clear incompetence as a pilot. Moussaoui, 33, was arrested in August on immigration charges. But despite the urging of the school and federal agents in Minnesota and despite a warning from the French that Moussaoui was linked to Muslim extremists, FBI headquarters resisted opening a broader investigation until after Sept. 11."[186]

Indeed, the U.S. government actively prevented a further investigation from being conducted. Local FBI investigators in Minneapolis had immediately viewed Zacarias as a terrorist suspect and sought authorisation for a special counterintelligence surveillance warrant in order to search the hard drive of his home computer. The government's Justice Department plus top FBI officials blocked an FBI request for a national security warrant to search Zacarias' computer, claiming that FBI agents lacked sufficient information to meet the legal requirements to justify the warrant. The block remained in place even after the notification from French intelligence that Zacarias was linked to bin Laden.[187]

According to ABC News, however, at the time the Justice Department justified the refusal of a warrant by claiming that there was insufficient evidence connecting Zacarias to any known terrorist group: "Moussaoui was taken into custody on August 16, but to the outrage of FBI agents in the field, headquarters was slow to react and said he could not be connected to any known terror group."[188] This was despite the information from French intelligence demonstrating the latter's links to Osama bin Laden and Al-

Qaeda. While some law enforcement officials justify the block as a legal necessity, others strongly disagree that such justification has any real basis in law. "That decision is being questioned by some FISA experts, who say it's possible a warrant would have been granted," reported Greg Gordon. "The special court that reviews FISA requests has approved more than 12,000 Justice Department applications for covert search warrants and wiretaps and rejected only one since the act was passed in 1978, according to government reports."[189] MS-NBC has similarly reported that:

> "…other law enforcement officials are equally insistent that a more aggressive probe of Moussaoui—when combined with other intelligence in the possession of U.S. agencies—might have yielded sufficient clues about the impending plot. 'The question being asked here is if they put two and two together, they could have gotten a lot more information about the guy—if not stopped the hijacking,' said one investigator."[190]

The *New York Times* comments that the Moussaoui case "raised new questions about why the Federal Bureau of Investigation and other agencies did not prevent the hijackings."[191]

The U.S. response to Mohamed Atta, the alleged lead hijacker, was even more extraordinary. The German public TV channel, ARD, reported on 23rd November, 2001, that Mohamed Atta was subject to telephone monitoring by the Egyptian secret service. The latter had found that Atta had made at least one recent visit to Afghanistan from his home in Hamburg, Germany. The FBI had also been monitoring Atta's movements for several months in 2000, when he traveled several times from Hamburg to Frankfurt and bought large quantities of chemicals potentially usable in making explosives. Atta's name had also been mentioned in a Hamburg phone call between Islamic fundamentalists monitored by the German police in 1999.[192]

In January 2001, Atta was permitted reentry into the United States after a trip to Germany, despite being in violation of his visa status. He had landed in Miami on 10th January on a flight from Madrid on a tourist visa—yet he had told immigration inspectors that he was taking flying lessons in the U.S., for which an M-1 student visa is strictly required. Jeanne Butterfield, Executive Director of the American Immigration Lawyers Association, points out that: "Nine times out of 10, they would have told him to go back and file [for that status] overseas. You're not supposed to come in as a visitor for pleasure and go to work or school."[193]

PBS' Frontlines also takes note of "The failure of the INS to stop the attack's ringleader, Mohamed Atta, from entering the U.S. three times on a tourist visa in 2001, even though officials knew the visa had expired in 2000 and Atta had violated its terms by taking flight lessons."[194]

This failure should be evaluated in context with the fact that Atta had been under FBI surveillance for stockpiling bomb-making materials. Furthermore, Canadian TV reported that Atta had already been implicated in a terrorist bombing in Israel, with the information passed on to the United States before he was first issued his tourist visa.[195]

Yet despite these blatant terrorist connections, Atta was still allowed into the United States freely, and made repeated trips to Europe, each time returning to the U.S., and being admitted by U.S. customs and immigration without obstruction—not because visa regulations were lax, but because they were willfully violated. The London *Observer* notes in surprise that Atta:

"... was under surveillance between January and May last year after he was reportedly observed buying large quantities of chemicals in Frankfurt, apparently for the production of explosives and for biological warfare... The U.S. agents reported to have trailed Atta are said to have failed to inform the German authorities about their investigation. The disclosure that Atta was being trailed by police long before 11 September raises the question why the attacks could not have been prevented with the man's arrest."[196]

Atta also appears to have been under continual surveillance by the FBI. He was among the suspected terrorists linked to bin Laden training at U.S. flight schools, which the FBI had already known about for years. As the BBC observed: "The evidence... reinforces concerns that the international intelligence community may have known more about Atta before September 11 than was previously thought, but had failed to act."[197]

There was a similar lack of response in relation to other suspected terrorists under U.S. surveillance. *Human Events* reported that:

"The FBI and other federal law enforcement agencies knew about the presence of at least two of the terrorists in the United States, but failed to get the information to airlines. Khalid Al-Midhar and Nawaq Alhamzi, who were on Flight 77 that hit the Pentagon, were already on the so-called watch list. But federal officials failed to notify airline officials who might have been able to stop at least one of the terror attacks, reports the Los Angeles Times."[198]

The CIA and FBI knew three weeks before the attacks that these two hijackers, including one with a link to the bombing of the U.S. destroyer Cole in October 2000, were in the United States. Yet despite being on a terrorism watch list, which details individuals banned from entering the country due to their apparent links to terrorist activities, they were neither barred from entry into the U.S. nor apprehended later. The *Washington Post* has further pointed out, incredulously, that more than 50 people were probably involved in preparations for the operation within the U.S.—without agencies doing anything about it:

"The scattered details that have emerged about the plot put this failure in stark relief: More than 50 people were likely involved, Justice Department officials have said, and the plot required extensive communications and planning to pull off. The group's size—not to mention the complexity of its endeavor—should have offered many opportunities for intelligence infiltration. Yet the conspirators proceeded unmolested. What is striking is how safe these people apparently felt, how unthreatened by law enforcement. Some of the terrorists were here for long periods. They left and entered the country unimpeded. Some were reportedly on the so-called 'watch list,' a government catalogue of people who ostensibly are not permitted to enter the country. Yet this apparently caused them no problems."[199]

Further corroborative revelations have surfaced, indicating the extent of the FBI's failure to act. According to reports in *Newsweek*, the *Washington Post* and the *New York Times*, after 11th September U.S. military officials gave the FBI information "suggesting that five of the alleged hijackers received training in the 1990s at secure U.S. military installations."[200] *Newsweek* has further elaborated that U.S. military training of foreign students occurs as a matter of routine, with the authorisation—and payment—of respective governments, clarifying in particular that with respect to training of Saudi pilots, "Training is paid for by Saudi Arabia." The hijackers, we should note, were almost exclusively Saudi; 15 of the 19 hijackers were Saudis, mostly from wealthy families:

"U.S. military sources have given the FBI information that suggests five of the alleged hijackers of the planes that were used in Tuesday's terror attacks received training at secure U.S. military installations in the 1990s. Another of the alleged hijackers may have been trained in strategy and tactics at the Air War College in Montgomery, Ala., said another high-ranking Pentagon official. The fifth man may have received language instruction at Lackland Air Force Base in San Antonio, Tex. Both were former Saudi Air Force pilots who had come to the United States, according to the Pentagon source... NEWSWEEK visited the base early Saturday morning, where military police confirmed that the address housed foreign military flight trainees... It is not unusual for foreign nationals to train at U.S. military facilities. A former Navy pilot told NEWSWEEK that during his years on the base, 'we always, always, always trained other countries' pilots. When I was there two decades ago, it was Iranians. The shah was in power. Whoever the country du jour is, that's whose pilots we train.'

Candidates begin with 'an officer's equivalent of boot camp,' he said. 'Then they would put them through flight training.' The U.S. has a long-standing agreement with Saudi Arabia—a key ally in the 1990-91 gulf war—to train pilots for its National Guard. Candidates are trained in air combat on several Army and Navy bases. Training is paid for by Saudi Arabia."[201]

Knight Ridder news service provided more specific details of the findings. Mohamed Atta had attended International Officers School at Maxwell Air Force Base in Montgomery, Alabama; Abdulaziz Alomari had attended Aerospace Medical School at Brooks Air Force base in Texas; and Saeed Alghamdi had been to the Defense Language Institute in Monterey, California.

The U.S. government has attempted to deny the charges despite the name matches, alleging the existence of biographical discrepancies: "Officials stressed that the name matches may not necessarily mean the students were the hijackers because of discrepancies in ages and other personal data." But measures appear to have been taken to block public scrutiny of these alleged discrepancies. On 16th September, news reports asserted that: "Officials would not release ages, country of origin or any other specific details of the three individuals." This situation seems to have continued up to the time of writing.

Even Senate inquiries into the matter have been studiously ignored by government law enforcement officials, who when pressed, have been unable to deny that the hijackers were training at secure U.S. military installations. When *Newsweek* reported that three of the hijackers were trained at the secure Pensacola Naval Station in Florida, Senator Bill Nelson faxed Attorney General John Ashcroft demanding to know if it was true.

When queried by investigative journalist Daniel Hopsicker about Ashcroft's reply, a spokesman for Senator Nelson explained: "In the wake of those reports we asked about the Pensacola Naval Air Station but we never got a definitive answer from the Justice Department. So we asked the FBI for an answer 'if and when' they could provide us one. Their response to date has been that they are trying to sort through something complicated and difficult."

Hopsicker also queried a major in the U.S. Air Force's Public Affairs Office who "was familiar with the question," and who, unlike U.S. law enforcement, believed that the matter was clear-cut. She explained the Air Force's official 'denial' as follows: "Biographically, they're not the same people. Some of the ages are 20 years off." But when questioned to illustrate the specific discrepancy, she was forced to admit there was none. Hopsicker relates that: "'Some' of the ages? We told her we were only interested in

Atta. Was she saying that the age of the Mohamed Atta who attended the Air Force's International Officer's School at Maxwell Air Force Base was different from the terrorist Atta's age as reported? Um, er, no, the major admitted." Hopsicker asked if he could contact the other alleged "Mohamed Atta" who is supposed to have been confused with the hijacker, who had trained at the International Officer's School at Maxwell Air Force Base, to confirm that they were, in fact, two different individuals. The major declined without explanation, stating that she did not "think you're going to get that information."

By mid-October 2001, the FBI's investigations into these matters were being wrapped up, although no specific answers to this issue, palatable enough to be released to the public, were found. "On Oct. 10, FBI Agents were ordered to curtail their investigation of the Sept. 11 attack in an order describing the investigation of the terrorist hijackings as 'the most exhaustive in its history,'" reported Hopsicker. "'The investigative staff has to be made to understand that we're not trying to solve a crime now,' said one law enforcement official...

> "The order was said to have met with resistance from FBI agents who believed that continued surveillance of suspects might have turned up critical evidence to prove who orchestrated the attacks on the World Trade Center and the Pentagon. Officials said FBI Director Robert Mueller, who was sworn in last month, believed that his agents had a broad understanding of the events of Sept. 11. It was now time to move on."[202]

The simple question brought up by these revelations is, how did terrorists receive clearance for training at secure U.S. military and intelligence facilities, and for what purpose?

As early as three days after the 11th September attacks, FBI Director Robert S. Mueller III claimed that these findings were new and had not been known by the FBI previously. The *Washington Post* noted that he had: "described reports that several of the hijackers had received flight training in the United States as 'news, quite obviously,' adding, 'If we had understood that to be the case, we would have—perhaps one could have averted this.'"[203] But astonishingly, the same *Post* article illustrated that Mueller had lied about the FBI's lack of knowledge. The *Post* reported in the same article that, contrary to the FBI Director's initial testimony, the FBI had in fact known for several years that terrorists were training at U.S. flight schools—yet, absolutely nothing had been done about it:

> "Federal authorities have been aware for years that suspected terrorists with ties to Osama bin Laden were receiving flight training at schools in the United States and abroad, according to interviews and court

testimony... A senior government official yesterday acknowledged law enforcement officials were aware that fewer than a dozen people with links to bin Laden had attended U.S. flight schools."[204]

A report for the *Online Journal* by Daniel Hopsicker, former Executive Producer of a business news show airing internationally on NBC, confirms that:

"Authorities are probing the European business associations of a Venice flight school owner, whose school at the Venice airport trained the nucleus of foreign national terrorist pilots, looking for possible links to international organized crime groups... Three of the airliners involved in the September 11 terrorist attack—two in Manhattan, and one wrested to the ground over Pennsylvania—were piloted by terrorists who had trained at two flight schools at the Venice, Florida airport."[205]

"Almost all of the terrorist pilots," Hopsicker reports, "received their initial training in Venice," at either of two flight schools owned respectively by Arne Kruithof and Rudi Dekkers. "Together, these two schools trained the core cadre of foreign terrorist pilots." But U.S. intelligence allowed this training to continue unimpeded, even amidst escalating warnings of a terrorist attack on U.S. soil through the use of hijacked civilian airplanes, and despite having monitored the terrorists for several years. "The FBI was swarming Huffman Aviation by 2 a.m., just 18 hours following the attack. They removed student files from two schools at the Venice airport: Huffman Aviation and the Florida Flight Training Center just down the street," owned by the above two individuals.

Indeed, it appears that the reason the FBI was able to move so quickly is that "federal authorities have been aware for years that suspected terrorists with ties to Osama bin Laden were receiving flight training at schools in the United States." Hopsicker further observes:

"Experts have been wondering how a conspiracy of such size and duration could have gone unnoticed by U.S. intelligence agencies and law enforcement. At least 15 of the far-flung network of terrorist pilots got their money from the same (so far-unnamed) source. While in the Venice area last year, the terrorist suspects opened checking accounts during the summer.

We called someone who used to work at something like the CIA. 'How could the agency not have known about 15 foreign pilots all paid from one source?' He chose his words carefully. 'I would assume that they did know. It would seem almost impossible for them not to.'"[206]

Hopsicker also points out that the suspicious background and activities of Rudi Dekkers, the owner of Huffman Aviation where most of the terrorists who went on to implement the 11th September attacks were trained, are worthy of a further intelligence inquiry. There are a number of glaring anomalies noted by Hopsicker, a few of which are mentioned here. Dekkers' chronology of his flight training of hijackers Atta and Al-Shehhi, for instance, directly contradicts the testimony of other flight instructors at Jones Aviation Flying Instructors, Inc.

Additionally, "Dekkers had purchased his aviation school at just about the time the terrorist pilots moved into town and began their lessons," according to an aviation employee at Venice Airport. Another observer at the Airport admitted: "I've always had some suspicions about the way he breezed into town out of nowhere. Just too many odd little things. For example, he has absolutely no aviation background as far as anyone can tell. And he evidently had no use for, nor knowledge of, FAA rules and regs." A Special Operations Commando leader from the nearby McDill Air Force Base observed: "Rudi's greedy, and when you're greedy you can be used for something."[207]

According to law enforcement officials, Dekkers has also reportedly been recently indicted in his native country, Holland, on financial charges that may include fraud and money laundering.[208] Yet despite his dubious background, activities and connections, in addition to his role in training most of the terrorists responsible for 11th September, he does not appear to have been investigated by the FBI. Indeed, his innocence seems to have been presumed from the outset: "Forty-eight hours after the Sept. 11 attack, a flight school owner named Rudi Dekkers, known to have trained virtually the entire terrorist pilot cadre… seemed impervious to suspicion."[209]

Most intriguing in this whole affair is the revelation of a Venice Airport executive, as reported by Hopsicker, that Britannia Aviation, which operates from a hangar at Rudi Dekker's Huffman Aviation at Venice Airport, had a "green light" from the Justice Department's Drugs Enforcement Administration (DEA), and that the local Venice Police Department "had been warned to leave them alone." Britannia Aviation had been awarded a five-year contract to run a large regional maintenance facility at the Lynchburg, Virginia, Regional Airport. At the time of the award, virtually nothing was known about the company. When Britannia was chosen over a respected and successful Lynchburg company boasting a multi-million dollar balance sheet and more than 40 employees, aviation executives there began voicing concerns to reporters at the local newspaper.

"… it was discovered that Britannia Aviation is a company with virtually no assets, employees, or corporate history. Moreover, the company did not even possess the necessary FAA license to perform the aircraft maintenance services for which it had just been contracted by the city of Lynchburg... When Britannia Aviation's financial statements were released after prodding by the local aviation community, they revealed Britannia to be a 'company' worth less than $750."

It also emerged that the company had, according to one of its executives Paul Marten, "for some time been successfully providing aviation maintenance services for Caribe Air, a Caribbean carrier," that Hopsicker notes is, in fact, "a notorious CIA proprietary air carrier which, even by the standards of a CIA proprietary, has had a particularly checkered past...

"Caribe Air's history includes 'blemishes' like having its aircraft seized by federal officials at the infamous Mena, Arkansas, airport a decade ago, after the company was accused by government prosecutors of having used as many as 20 planes to ship drugs worth billions of dollars into this country."

Yet as already noted, an executive at Venice Airport informed Hopsicker that a DEA source at the airport "reluctantly told me that Britannia had a 'green light' from the DEA at the Venice airport, whatever that means. He also said the local Venice Police Department (which has mounted round-the-clock patrols at the airport since Sept.11) had been warned to leave them alone."

Why does Britannia—a company reportedly with CIA connections that is operating illegally out of the same flight school which trained Al-Qaeda hijackers—have a "green light" from the Justice Department's DEA, and effective immunity from local police inquiries? Daniel Hopsicker comments that: "The new evidence adds to existing indications that Mohamed Atta and his terrorist cadre's flight training in this country was part of a so-far unacknowledged U.S. government intelligence operation which had ultimately tragic consequences for thousands of civilians on September 11...

"Far from merely being negligent or asleep at the switch... the accumulating evidence suggests the CIA was not just aware of the thousands of Arab student pilots who began pouring into this country several years ago to attend flight training, but was running the operation for still-unexplained reasons...

It was 'Islamic fundamentalist' Osama bin laden who cloaked his covert activities under the cover of religious charities. Were we now discovering that our own government intelligence agencies used the same ruse? What was going on here? ... [W]hy did a transparent dummy front company like Paul Marten's Britannia Aviation have a 'green light' from the DEA? A green light for what?"[210]

The above accounts certainly show that although U.S. intelligence agencies were aware of Al-Qaeda terrorists training in U.S. flight schools, and had apparently been surveilling their activities for years, they did not attempt to apprehend them—despite the escalating warnings of an imminent attack by Osama bin Laden's operatives. This was a consequence of a decision by the FBI command. ABC News reported that only a few weeks before the attacks in early August, the FBI office in Phoenix alerted FBI headquarters to the unusual influx of Arab students with Al-Qaeda connections training at local flight schools. This warning was ignored.[211] It therefore appears that Mueller had attempted to mislead the public about the scope of the FBI's knowledge.

However, his admission that such knowledge could have empowered the U.S. to avert the attacks, taken into account with the fact that the FBI did indeed possess such knowledge, brings up the pertinent question of why the FBI failed to do so, despite being perfectly capable of doing so, according to the FBI Director's own indirect admission. In what seems to be an attempt to explain away the FBI's rather shocking inaction, while Osama bin Laden's terrorist lackeys were undergoing extensive training at U.S. military facilities, financed by Saudi authorities as *Newsweek* reports—and while innumerable credible warnings received by the U.S. intelligence community repeatedly predicted air attacks on "symbols of American culture" by bin Laden-linked terrorists, via the hijacking of civilian planes—the senior U.S. government official cited above claimed that "there was no information to indicate the flight students had been planning suicide hijacking attacks." The *Post* recorded him as follows: "We were unable to marry any information from investigations or the intelligence community that talked to their use of this expertise in the events that we saw unfold on the 11th."[212]

In this context, to interpret the FBI's failure to act as mere incompetence, compounded by bureaucracy, strains the limits of reason. It also flies in the face of the most elementary methods of intelligence gathering. As demonstrated in the preceding documentation, there was abundant intelligence information predicting an imminent attack by Al-Qaeda operatives on U.S. soil. Moreover, this information indicated that Osama bin Laden was orchestrating the hijacking of civilian planes to be used as bombs against key U.S. buildings in Washington and New York. Reports show that this information was "taken seriously" by "the American intelligence community." Hence, U.S. intelligence agencies were already well aware that plans to implement Project Bojinka were in progress—and had accordingly intensified surveillance in direct response.

"SPRINGMANN: Well this is what I was told by reading an article in the Los Angeles Times."[214]

Despite Springmann's prolific warnings and complaints that had alerted the State Department to his opposition to these events, the U.S. government responded not by rolling up the pipeline, but by opening it up even further. This occurred in the face of increasing evidence of Saudi connections to terrorism. The *St. Petersburg Times* reports that: "After the Persian Gulf War in 1991, the visa situation became murkier. FBI agents complained that their Saudi counterparts hampered investigations into terror attacks, including a 1996 bombing on Dhahran that killed 19 U.S. servicemen. The Americans also suspected that the Saudi monarchy was doing little to root out terrorism on Saudi soil and to stop anti-American threats...

"Yet, instead of tightening visa requirements, the U.S. government made it easier for Saudi visitors to come to America. Under a program called U.S. Visa Express, introduced four months before the Sept. 11 attacks, Saudis were allowed to arrange visas through 10 travel agencies—often without coming to the U.S. Embassy or consulate for interviews."[215]

We should recall that these preposterous measures, which are in stark violation of the State Department's mandatory regulations for the issuing of visas, were instituted by the Bush administration at a time when the U.S. intelligence community was on alert for an imminent Al-Qaeda attack. This is not an issue of the supposed need to tighten borders further, but of why existing regulations were ignored and violated. Furthermore, it is a matter of record that U.S. intelligence was already well aware at this time that key figures in the Saudi establishment supported Osama bin Laden's terrorist network (See Chapter VI). Indeed, Springmann himself had warned the State Department repeatedly that unqualified applicants were being issued U.S. visas by the CIA. Yet, the U.S. government apparently allowed the fraudulent visa arrangement to continue, unabated.

High-Level Government Blocks
on Intelligence Investigations

There is good reason to believe that the FBI's failure to apprehend suspected terrorists, who were linked to bin Laden and operating within the U.S., was the result of high-level blocks from the FBI command and Justice Department. Evidence for this comes from the authoritative testimony of U.S. attorney David Philip Schippers, former Chief Investigative Counsel for the U.S. House Judiciary Committee, and head prosecutor responsible for conducting the impeachment against former President Bill Clinton. His long record of impeccable expertise and extensive experience makes him a highly credible source.[216]

Two days after the attacks, Schippers went public in an interview with WRRK in Pittsburgh, PA., stating that he had attempted to warn U.S. Attorney General John Ashcroft, along with other federal officials, about the terrorist attacks weeks before they occurred. He stated that he had received information from U.S. intelligence sources, including FBI agents, that a massive attack was being planned by terrorists, targeting the financial arteries of lower Manhattan. Schippers had attempted to bring this information to the attention of John Ashcroft, six weeks before the tragedy of Black Tuesday.[217] Schippers went public again in October 2001, reiterating that, several months prior to September, impeccable sources in the U.S. intelligence community, including agents of the U.S. government's law enforcement agency, the FBI, had approached him with information about the impending attacks.

According to Schippers, these agents knew, months before the 11th September attacks, the names of the hijackers, the targets of their attacks, the proposed dates, and the sources of their funding, along with other information. At least two weeks prior to 11th September, the FBI agents again confirmed that an attack on lower Manhattan, orchestrated by Osama bin Laden, was imminent. However, the FBI command cut short their investigations into the impending terrorist attacks and those involved, threatening the agents with prosecution under the National Security Act if they publicised information pertaining to their investigations.

The agents subsequently sought the council of David Schippers in order to pressure elements in the U.S. government to take action to prevent the attacks. Schippers warned many Congressmen and Senators, and also attempted to contact U.S. Attorney General John Ashcroft without success, managing only to explain the situation to a lower-ranking Justice Department official who promised a return call from Ashcroft the next day. The Attorney General did not return the call despite the gravity of the situation. Schippers is now legally representing one FBI agent in a suit against the U.S. government in an attempt to subpoena their testimony, so that he can legally speak about the blocked investigations on public record. In a Talk Radio interview on the Alex Jones Show, based in Austin, Texas, Schippers stated:

"Have you ever heard of Yossef Bodansky? ... He is the guy that wrote the book about Bin Laden. He was hooked up with some Congressional leaders in the House—kind of an unofficial, for lack of a better word, a strike force, a task force on terrorism [Bodansky was Director of the U.S. Congress' Task Force on Terrorism and Unconventional Warfare (Ahmed)]. They sent out a warning on February 19, 1995, saying there was going to be a massive attack by the terrorists in the heartland of the

United States and it was going to be a federal facility. Everybody ignored it. By the way, I have seen that warning... I don't have it in front of me so I can't go into the specifics of it too heavily but at the same time, there was in that warning that there was going to be a massive attack in Washington – it took them six years to do it. The targets were going to be Washington, the White House and the Capitol Building – and that they were going to use airliners to attack them."[218]

In an interview with Geoff Metcalf on *WorldNetDaily*, Schippers clarified this as follows:

"I [had] information indicating there was going to be a massive attack in lower Manhattan [from FBI sources]. I couldn't get anybody to listen to me... about a month-and-a-half before Sept. 11. The original thing that I heard—and you might ask Mr. Bodansky about that... He was one of the people behind the warning that came out Feb. 19, 1995, and this was the [original] warning that I saw: that there was going to be an attack on the United States by bin Laden's people, that the original target—and this is the way it reads—the original target was supposed to be the White House and the Capitol building, and they were going to use commercial airliners as bombs."[219]

Alex Jones commented in his interview with the former Chief Counsel: "Now later you got it from FBI agents in Chicago and Minnesota that there was going to be an attack on lower Manhattan." David Schippers responded by explaining how his subsequent warnings were ignored: "Yes—and that's what started me calling...

"I started calling out there. First of all, I tried to see if I could get a Congressman to go to bat for me and at least bring these people out there and listen to them. I sent them information and nobody cared. It was always, 'We'll get back to you,' 'we'll get back to you,' 'we'll get back to you.' Then I reached out and tried to get to the Attorney General, when finally we got an attorney general in there that I would be willing to talk to. And, again, I used people who were personal friends of John Ashcroft to try to get him. One of them called me back and said, 'Alright I have talked to him. He will call you tomorrow morning.' This was like a month before the bombing..."[220]

The call never came. In an interview with the Eagle Forum of Illinois concerning the evidence of a terrorist attack, "this time on the financial district in south Manhattan," Schippers stated: "Five weeks before the September 11 tragedy, I did my best to get a hold of Attorney General John Ashcroft with my concerns. The best that I could do was get in touch with an underling in that office who told me that all investigations start out at lower levels such as his."[221] The Washington DC-based public interest law firm

Judicial Watch which investigates and prosecutes government corruption and abuse, reported in mid-November 2001 that it was joining forces with Schippers to represent his FBI Special Agent against the U.S. Justice Department:

"... an active FBI Special Agent filed a complaint last week concerning FBI/Justice Department interference in and mishandling of terrorist investigations. The FBI Special Agent, who wishes to remain anonymous at this time, alleges that he was retaliated against when he continued to push for and pursue certain terrorist investigations over the objections of his FBI and Justice Department supervisors. The FBI Special Agent, who is represented by Judicial Watch and David Schippers, Esq., filed the complaint last week with the Justice Department's Office of Inspector General (IG) and Office of Professional Responsibility (OPR).

Based on the evidence, the FBI Special Agent believes that if certain investigations had been allowed to run their courses, Osama bin Laden's network might have been prevented from committing the September 11, 2001 terrorist attacks which resulted in the deaths of nearly 5,000 innocents. Judicial Watch is requesting a full scale, independent investigation into its client's concerns and seeks to hold accountable those responsible for preventing the full investigation of terrorist activity here in the United States and abroad."[222]

David Schippers elaborated on these matters towards the end of February 2002 in an interview with this author. He confirmed that U.S. intelligence had "established the sources of the money flow of bin Laden" as early as 1996, but by 1999 intelligence officers began facing fundamental high-level obstructions to their investigations into these matters. Schippers is maintaining the anonymity of his sources to avoid undue pressure on them from elements in government and intelligence agencies.

The earliest warning of attacks was issued by the U.S. Congress' Task Force on Terrorism and Unconventional Warfare in February 1995, which specified in general terms that Al-Qaeda was planning a terrorist attack on lower Manhattan, through the use of hijacked civilian planes as bombs. According to Schippers, the same individuals who issued this authoritative warning had been working ever since on uncovering further information on the same threat. He stated that the warning "had started out just a general threat, but they narrowed it and narrowed it, more and more with time," until the "same people who came out with the first warning" informed him in "May 2002" that "an attack on lower Manhattan is imminent." Schippers elaborates that these U.S. intelligence officers had approached him as a result of "growing frustration" at the higher echelons of the intelligence community who were refusing to take action in response to the imminent threat to U.S. national security.

In addition to the several FBI agents who had spoken to Schippers directly, other U.S. intelligence sources told him that "there are others all over the country who are frustrated, and just waiting to come out." The frustration of these intelligence officers, Schippers explained, was because of the obstructions of a "bureaucratic elite in Washington short-stopping information," with the consequence that they have granted "terrorism a free reign in the United States."

Schippers was also able to confirm the specific nature of some of the FBI investigations, which had been cut short under high-level orders, noting for instance that the agents who had approached him claimed that "they had Atta [the chief hijacker] in their sights." The agents also claimed to have been aware of the names and activities of "very strange characters training at flight schools," which they had attempted to "check out."

Such investigations were blocked from above, to the fury of agents on the trail of individuals who appear to have gone on to perpetrate the atrocities of 11th September—including chief hijacker Mohammed Atta himself. There was simply no adequate justification for these blocks, legal or otherwise, the agents argue, adding that the obstructions came down for no apparent reason. Accordingly, one of them remarked to Schippers that "if they had been permitted to follow through with their investigations, 9-11 would never have happened."[223]

The conservative *New American* magazine has also interviewed several FBI agents who have corroborated Schippers' testimony. In a March 2002 report, the magazine reported that:

> "Three veteran federal law enforcement agents confirmed to THE NEW AMERICAN that the information provided to Schippers was widely known within the Bureau before September 11th. Because these individuals face possible personal or professional retaliation, they agreed to speak with us on condition of anonymity. Two of them, however, have expressed a willingness to testify before Congress regarding the views they have shared with us."

A former FBI official with extensive counterterrorism experience told the magazine: "I don't buy the idea that we didn't know what was coming." He referred to the extraordinary speed with which the FBI had produced detailed information on the attack and the hijackers responsible: "Within 24 hours [of the attack] the Bureau had about 20 people identified, and photos were sent out to the news media. Obviously this information was available in the files and somebody was sitting on it."

Another active FBI counter-terrorism investigator stated that it was widely known "all over the Bureau, how these [warnings] were ignored by Washington... All indications are that this information came from some of [the FBI's] most experienced guys, people who have devoted their lives to this kind of work. But their warnings were placed in a pile in someone's office in Washington... In some cases, these field agents predicted, almost precisely, what happened on September 11th. So we were all holding our breath... hoping that the situation would be remedied."

The first former FBI agent's further damning comments to the *New American* are particularly worth noting:

"This is pretty appalling. The FBI has had access to this information since at least 1997. We're obviously not doing our job. I never expected to see something like this happen in our country, but in a way I wasn't shocked when it did. There's got to be more to this than we can see—high-level people whose careers are at stake, and don't want the truth coming out... What agenda is someone following? Obviously, people had to know— there had to be people who knew this information was being circulated. People like [Al-Qaeda terrorists] don't just move in and out of the country undetected. If somebody in D.C. is taking this information and burying it—and it's very easy to control things from D.C.—then this problem goes much, much deeper... It's terrible to think this, but this must have been allowed to happen as part of some other agenda."[224]

It should be noted here that high-level blocks were also placed on FBI and military intelligence investigations of possible terrorist connections related to members of the bin Laden family and Saudi royals. The London *Guardian* has elaborated that U.S. intelligence had faced high-level blocks in their investigations into bin Laden terrorist connections:

"FBI and military intelligence officials in Washington say they were prevented for political reasons from carrying out full investigations into members of the bin Laden family in the U.S. before the terrorist attacks of September 11...

U.S. intelligence agencies... are complaining that their hands were tied... They said the restrictions became worse after the Bush administration took over this year. The intelligence agencies had been told to 'back off' from investigations involving other members of the Bin Laden family, the Saudi royals, and possible Saudi links to the acquisition of nuclear weapons by Pakistan. 'There were particular investigations that were effectively killed.'"[225]

The documentation provided previously, in tandem with David Schippers' revelations regarding the detailed information possessed by U.S. intelligence on the 11th September terrorist attacks and who was planning them, is damning evidence that, in spite of sufficient information, there was deliberate inaction, in line with high-level Bush administration directives. Indeed, this inference is corroborated by a report in *The Herald* which notes the FBI's arrest of alleged Al-Qaeda conspirator Zacarias Moussaoui "at a Minnesota flight school in August last year, and a July report from the agency's Phoenix, Arizona, office which warned that Middle Eastern students" who "had a connection to Osama bin Laden" were "enrolling for flying lessons in considerable numbers...

"U.S. lawmakers remain astounded that the Phoenix memo and Moussaoui's arrest failed to set alarm bells ringing at FBI headquarters, even after one agent speculated at a high-level meeting that Moussaoui might have been taking lessons to enable him to crash an aircraft into the World Trade Centre in New York."[226]

FBI Director Robert Mueller admitted this in May congressional hearings. The *New York Post* added that: "FBI headquarters ignored its own agent's red-flag warning a month before 9/11 that Zacarias Moussaoui was the kind of person who might 'fly something into the World Trade Center,' FBI Director Robert Mueller admitted yesterday... Mueller's revelation at a congressional hearing showed... that an FBI investigator... actually considered the scenario that occurred Sept. 11" and warned of it at a high-level FBI meeting.[227] We should ask, of course, on what basis did the FBI agent assert at this high-level meeting the possibility that the World Trade Centre in New York would be the target of a hijacking suicide attack by a suspected Al-Qaeda terrorist? Only a few days prior to the 11th September attacks, FBI agents in Minnesota recorded in an official internal FBI document that Zacarias "might be planning on flying something into the World Trade Center."[228]

In context with the documentation discussed previously, it is clear that the agents did not do so randomly in an information vacuum—indeed, this is not how intelligence operates. On the contrary, there was very precise information available to the FBI and other intelligence agencies on Al-Qaeda's Project Bojinka plans, specifying targets in Manhattan, which provided reasonable grounds to believe that the World Trade Centre was the most probable target of an imminent Al-Qaeda attack. *The Herald* report illustrates, however, that although this information was widely known and discussed in the U.S. intelligence community—including the top strata—further investigation and preventive measures were blocked under "high-level" directives.

The response of FBI Headquarters to related urgent internal FBI reports issued around the same time illustrates this. A 10th July 2001 memo from the FBI's Phoenix office "sent to FBI headquarters by a Phoenix FBI agent, warned that bin Laden could have been using U.S. flight schools to train terrorists and suggested a nationwide canvass for Middle Eastern aviation students." This memo was completely ignored by the FBI command, "never acted upon or distributed to outside agencies prior to Sept. 11". Now, at least two names on the list "have been identified by the CIA as having links to al Qaeda." A 6th August presidential briefing handed to George W. Bush had further warned of the danger of a hijacking attempt by Al-Qaeda.[229]

Additionally, as noted above, late in mid-August the FBI command was again alerted to the impending threat of an attack in relation to the arrest of Zacarias. His arrest and interrogation at that time illustrates that proper and routine procedure entailed doing the same with other Al-Qaeda suspects. However both the July and August warnings from local FBI counterterrorist investigators were ignored by FBI Headquarters; indeed, FBI investigations into these increasingly alarming findings and circulation of the relevant memos were simply blocked from above. In other words, the top strata of the FBI unilaterally vetoed routine appeals for action from its own counterterrorist experts.

Multiple Intelligence Warnings
Converged on 11th September

As September neared, multiple authoritative intelligence warnings surfaced with increasing intensity, warning of a terrorist attack against the U.S. We should recall that in response to ECHELON's warnings, U.S. intelligence agencies were already on alert for evidence of a very specific Project Bojinka-style operation, which would target key buildings in Washington and New York. The White House National Coordinator for Counterterrorism, based on CIA confirmation, had alerted all domestic security and intelligence agencies of an impending Al-Qaeda attack, to be implemented in several weeks time, at the beginning of July. According to Chief Investigative Counsel David Schippers, U.S. sources had informed him as early as May that the intelligence community had credible information of an imminent attack targeting the "financial district of lower Manhattan," and that intelligence officers throughout the country were frustrated by high-level blocks on investigations and information. The FBI appears to have had specific information indicating that the World Trade Centre was thus the most probable target. Against this background, the multiple warnings of an impending attack by Osama bin Laden from a variety of credible authorities should have increasingly reinforced the overall intelligence confirmation of the attacks. *USA Today* reports that:

"Since passenger-filled commercial planes slammed into the World Trade Center and the Pentagon 5 weeks ago, a conventional wisdom has emerged that the terrorist attacks were so extraordinary that they couldn't have been predicted...

In fact, a growing mountain of evidence suggests that the hijackings not only were imaginable, they also were foreshadowed. The Bush administration received what Secretary of State Colin Powell describes as a 'lot of signs' throughout the summer that terrorists were plotting U.S. attacks. Among them: al-Qa'eda mentions of an impending 'Hiroshima' on U.S. soil."[230]

The London *Telegraph* reported a few days after the 11th September attacks that:

"Israeli intelligence officials say that they warned their counterparts in the United States last month that large-scale terrorist attacks on highly visible targets on the American mainland were imminent...

The Telegraph has learnt that two senior experts with Mossad, the Israeli military intelligence service, were sent to Washington in August to alert the CIA and FBI to the existence of a cell of as many of 200 terrorists said to be preparing a big operation... [They] linked the plot to Osama bin Laden."[231]

Russian President Vladimir Putin, a leading actor in the new international coalition against terrorism and a close ally of President Bush and Prime Minister Blair, informed interviewers on MS-NBC that the Russian government had warned the U.S. of imminent attacks on airports and government buildings in the strongest possible terms for several weeks prior to the 11th September attacks.[232] These warnings were quite specific in that they indicated the hijacking of airplanes to be used against civilian buildings. According to Russian press reports, Russian intelligence had notified the U.S. government of air attacks against civilian buildings and told them that 25 pilots had been specifically trained for the suicide missions.[233]

French intelligence had also warned their U.S. counterparts of an impending attack in September. The respected French daily *Le Figaro* reported that:

"According to Arab diplomatic sources as well as French intelligence, very specific information was transmitted to the CIA with respect to terrorist attacks against American interests around the world, including on U.S. soil. A DST [French intelligence] report dated 7 September enumerates all the intelligence, and specifies that the order to attack was to come from Afghanistan."[234]

According to the London *Independent*, the U.S. government "was warned repeatedly that a devastating attack on the United States was on its way." The newspaper cited an interview given by Osama bin Laden to a London-based Arabic-language newspaper, *al-Quds al-Arabi*, in late August. At about the same time, tighter security measures were ordered at the World Trade Center, for unexplained reasons.[235]

Further confirmation of the impending attacks came from the occurrence of other very specific warnings. Three days after the terrorist attacks, U.S. Senator Dianne Feinstein pointed out that: "Bin Laden's people had made statements three weeks ago carried in the Arab press in Great Britain that they were preparing to carry out unprecedented attacks in the U.S."[236]

In the summer of 2001, an Iranian man phoned U.S. law enforcement and warned of an imminent attack on the World Trade Center in the week of 9th September. German police confirmed the calls, but further stated that the U.S. Secret Service refused to reveal any further information on the matter. The caller's identity has not been disclosed.[237]

According to MS-NBC, in the week before 11th September, a caller to a Cayman Islands radio talk show gave several warnings of an imminent attack on the U.S. by bin Laden. The identity of the caller has not been disclosed.[238]

The U.S. also received an authoritative warning from the Egyptian President, a U.S. ally and close friend of the Bushes, which was based on the country's intelligence. The Associated Press reported that:

"Egyptian President Hosni Mubarak says he warned the United States that 'something would happen' 12 days before the Sept. 11 terror attacks on New York and Washington... 'We expected that something was going to happen and informed the Americans. We told them,' Mubarak said. He did not mention a U.S. response."[239]

Another authoritative warning came from Garth L. Nicolson, Chief Scientific Officer and Research Professor at the Institute for Molecular Medicine in Huntington Beach, California. Nicolson has been called to testify as an expert before the U.S. Senate in relation to Department of Defense investigations of Gulf War chemical and biological incidents.[240] Professor Nicolson testified that:

"My wife, Dr. Nancy Nicolson and I received at least three warnings of the attack on the Pentagon on Sept. 11, 2001. The nature of these warnings (the specific site, date and source) indicated to us that they were credible. We have many contacts in the retired intelligence community, including Special Forces, and domestic and foreign intelligence services. Mostly these were individuals that we assisted with their health problems from the Gulf War, Vietnam or other conflicts.

The most dramatic source was a Head of State of a North African country. This occurred during a visit to Tunisia in July 2001. This head of state was travelling under cover and met with us at our hotel. He warned us as to the correct date and one of the targets, the Pentagon. We were not given any information as to the method or any other targets.

The information was passed on to the Director of Policy, DoD, the National Security Council, the leadership in the House of Representatives and the Inspector General of the U.S. Army Medical Corps, who happened to be visiting us a month or so before Sept. 11.

To our knowledge no action was ever taken on this information. There has been some mention in the press that others also warned the U.S. Government that on Sept. 11, 2001 there would be a terrorist attack on U.S. soil. I do not know if any of the information from our sources or other sources was ever taken seriously by the National Security Council."[241]

Yet another warning from multiple intelligence agencies just before 11th September put the American intelligence community on alert. The *New York Times* reported:

"One intercept [of bin Laden's communications] before the Sept. 11 attack was, according to two senior intelligence officials, the first early warning of the assault and it set off a scramble by American and other intelligence agencies... That message, which was intercepted by the intelligence services of more than one country, was passed on to the United States, officials from three countries said. '... we assumed it would be soon,' a senior intelligence official said."[242]

On 7th September, the U.S. State Department issued a worldwide alert warning that "American citizens may be the target of a terrorist threat from extremist groups with links to [Osama bin Laden's] al-Qaeda organization." According to ABC News, the "report cited information gathered in May that suggested an attack somewhere was imminent."[243] It is worth reiterating here that Schippers was notified in the same month by key figures in the U.S. intelligence community, who had been working on the Al-Qaeda threat for years, that the attacks would target lower Manhattan. These reports show that U.S. intelligence agencies were on alert for an imminent attack by bin Laden very shortly before 11th September. Moreover, U.S. intelligence had privately anticipated that lower Manhattan would be the target.

Given the previous multiple warnings from various intelligence agencies, compounded and reinforced by the findings of America's own intelligence network, it is clear that bin Laden's Project Bojinka-style plan, to which the U.S. was alerted only a few months earlier, was soon to be implemented. The World Trade Center was among the known targets of Project Bojinka. Additionally, 11th September was the anniversary of the conviction of Ramzi Yousef for the first World Trade Center bombing several years ago.

According to Philippine Chief Superintendent Avelino Razon, "U.S. federal officials were aware of Project Bojinka and… the Philippines' crack terrorist team was continuing to work closely with them… 'I remember that after the first World Trade Center bombing Osama bin Laden made a statement that on the second attempt they would be successful,' Razon stressed. He said they could have chosen to carry out the attack on September 11, to mark the anniversary of Yousef's conviction for the first attack several years ago."[244] As previously noted, Australian analyst Paul Monk points out that 11th September should have been a "watch date."

According to *Newsweek*, the FBI, which as noted previously already had many terrorists under surveillance, were intercepting their communications. Shortly before 11th September they wrote comments such as: "There is a big thing coming," "They're going to pay the price," "We're ready to go."[245]

Just before the attacks, U.S. intelligence received information from Osama bin Laden himself that something "big" would happen on 11th September. NBC News reported at the beginning of October that Osama bin Laden had phoned his mother two days before the World Trade Center attacks and told her: "In two days you're going to hear big news, and you're not going to hear from me for a while." According to NBC, a foreign intelligence service had recorded the call and relayed the information to U.S. intelligence.[246]

The convergence of these multiple warnings would have reinforced earlier warnings, thus clearly indicating that Project Bojinka was to be implemented in September, with some information—including the admission of bin Laden himself—specifying 11th September in no uncertain terms. In particular, we should remind ourselves of the testimony of David Schippers, which was based on information received from FBI agents—that amid these multiple warnings, and on the basis of its own intensive surveillance and intelligence gathering operations, the FBI had specific details of an impending air attack on civilian buildings in lower Manhattan in September 2001. Yet nothing was done.

Further indication of the extent of the American intelligence community's forewarning, particularly in relation to the specific timing of its planned execution, can be found from analysis of financial transactions before 11th September. Only three trading days before 11th September, shares of United Airlines—the company whose planes were hijacked in the attacks on New York and Washington—were massively "sold short" by as yet unknown investors.

This was done by buying dirt-cheap "put" options, which give the owner a short-term right to sell specific shares at a price well below the current market—a long-shot bet. When the stock prices unexpectedly dropped even lower, in response to the terrorist attacks, the options multiplied a hundredfold in value, making millions of dollars in profit. These "short" options plays are a sure sign of investors with foreknowledge of an event that would occur within a few days, and drastically reduce the market price of those shares. The *San Francisco Chronicle* reported that:

"Investors have yet to collect more than $2.5 million in profits they made trading options in the stock of United Airlines before the Sept. 11, terrorist attacks, according to a source familiar with the trades and market data. The uncollected money raises suspicions that the investors—whose identities and nationalities have not been made public—had advance knowledge of the strikes.

... October series options for UAL Corp. were purchased in highly unusual volumes three trading days before the terrorist attacks for a total outlay of $2,070; investors bought the option contracts, each representing 100 shares, for 90 cents each [a price of less than one cent per share, on a total of 230,000 options]. Those options are now selling at more than $12 each. There are still 2,313 so-called 'put' options outstanding [representing 231,300 shares and a profit of $2.77 million] according to the Options Clearinghouse Corp.

...The source familiar with the United trades identified Deutsche Bank Alex. Brown, the American investment banking arm of German giant Deutsche Bank, as the investment bank used to purchase at least some of these options..."[247]

But the United Airlines case was not the only dubious financial transaction indicating, in the *Chronicle's* words, "advanced knowledge of the strikes." The Israeli Herzliyya International Policy Institute for Counterterrorism documented the following transactions related to 11th September, involving American Airlines—whose planes were also used in the attacks—and other companies with offices in the Twin Towers:

"Between September 6 and 7, the Chicago Board Options Exchange saw purchases of 4,744 put options on United Airlines, but only 396 call options... Assuming that 4,000 of the options were bought by people with advance knowledge of the imminent attacks, these 'insiders' would have profited by almost $5 million.

On September 10, 4,516 put options on American Airlines were bought on the Chicago exchange, compared to only 748 calls. Again, there was no news at that point to justify this imbalance;... Again, assuming that 4,000 of these options trades represent 'insiders,' they would represent a gain of about $4 million [the above levels of put options were more than six times higher than normal].

No similar trading in other airlines occurred on the Chicago exchange in the days immediately preceding Black Tuesday.

Morgan Stanley Dean Witter & Co., which occupied 22 floors of the World Trade Center, saw 2,157 of its October $45 put options bought in the three trading days before Black Tuesday; this compares to an average of 27 contracts per day before September 6. Morgan Stanley's share price fell from $48.90 to $42.50 in the aftermath of the attacks. Assuming that 2,000 of these options contracts were bought based upon knowledge of the approaching attacks, their purchasers could have profited by at least $1.2 million.

Merrill Lynch & Co., with headquarters near the Twin Towers, saw 12,215 October $45 put options bought in the four trading days before the attacks; the previous average volume in those shares had been 252 contracts per day [a dramatic increase of 1200%]. When trading resumed, Merrill's shares fell from $46.88 to $41.50; assuming that 11,000 option contracts were bought by 'insiders,' their profit would have been about $5.5 million.

European regulators are examining trades in Germany's Munich Re, Switzerland's Swiss Re, and AXA of France, all major reinsurers with exposure to the Black Tuesday disaster [AXA also owns more than 25% of American Airlines stock]."[248]

These multiple, massive and unprecedented financial transactions point unequivocally to the fact that the investors behind these trades were speculating in anticipation of a mid-September 2001 catastrophe that would involve both United Airlines and American Airlines, and offices in the Twin Towers—a clear demonstration of their foreknowledge or involvement in the 11th September attacks. Ernest Welteke, President of the German Bundesbank, has concluded that it is certain that a group of speculators knew the attack was coming. According to the *New York Times*, he stated: "There have been fundamental movements in these markets [i.e. the airlines], and the oil price rise just ahead of the attacks is otherwise inexplicable."[249]

The London *Times* reports that the U.S. government has a similar perspective: "American authorities are investigating unusually large numbers of shares in airlines, insurance companies and arms manufacturers that were sold off in the days and weeks before the attacks. They believe that the sales were by people who knew about the impending disaster."[250]

But as noted by U.S. investigative journalist and former Los Angeles Police Department (LAPD) narcotics detective Michael C. Ruppert, who rose to fame for uncovering the CIA role in drug-running operations in the 1980s, and who has been interviewed by both the House and the Senate for his expertise on CIA covert operations: "It is well documented that the CIA has long monitored such trades—in real time—as potential warnings of terrorist attacks and other economic moves contrary to U.S. interests."[251] The UPI also reported that the U.S.-sponsored ECHELON intelligence network closely monitors stock trading.[252]

The London *Times* further points out that the UK Financial Services Authority (FSA) is a "stock market watchdog" possessing a "transaction monitoring department that checks suspicious share movements." The FSA, however, has not issued any informative statement on the investigation into the share movements before 11th September: "The FSA would not comment on its instructions from the CIA."[253] In other words, there are both intelligence and civilian monitoring systems that monitor share transactions for the express purpose of tracking suspicious movements, and which, therefore, would have received warning. Elaborating, Ruppert observes that:

"It has been documented that the CIA, the Israeli Mossad and many other intelligence agencies monitor stock trading in real time using highly advanced programs reported to be descended from Promis software. This is to alert national intelligence services of just such kinds of attacks. Promis was reported, as recently as June, 2001 to be in Osama bin Laden's possession and, as a result of recent stories by FOX, both the FBI and the Justice Department have confirmed its use for U.S. intelligence gathering through at least this summer. This would confirm that CIA had additional advance warning of imminent attacks."[254]

Ruppert further describes the CIA's tracking of financial transactions as follows:

"One of the primary functions of the Central Intelligence Agency by virtue of its long and very close history of relationships with Wall Street... the point where the current executive vice president of the New York Stock Exchange is a retired CIA general counsel, has had a mandate to track, monitor, all financial markets worldwide, to look for anomalous trades, indicative of either economic warfare, or insider currency trading or speculation which might affect the U.S. Treasury, or, as in the case of the September 11 attacks, to look for trades which indicated foreknowledge of attacks like we saw.

One of the vehicles that they use to do this is a software called Promis software, which was developed in the 1980s, actually 1979, by Bill Hamilton and a firm called INSLAW, in [the] Washington D.C. area. And Promis is very unique for two reasons: first of all, it had the ability to integrate a wide range of databases using different computer languages and to make them all into one readable format. And secondly, in the years since, Promis has been mated with artificial intelligence to even predict moves in markets and to detect trades that are anomalous, as a result of those projections.

So, as recently as last year, I met with members of the RCMP [Royal Canadian Mounted Police] national security staff, who came down to Los Angeles where I am, who are investigating stolen applications of Promis software and its applications, and we reconfirmed at that time that, not only the U.S., but Israel, Canada, and many other countries use Promis-like software to track real-time trades in the stock markets to warn them of these events."

However, he clarifies that such software is not necessary for intelligence agencies to note the ominous implications of the trades going on shortly before 11th September:

"The key evidence... was the trades themselves, the so-called put options and the short selling of American Airlines, United Airlines, Merrill Lynch, Morgan Stanley, and a couple of reinsurance companies in Europe, which are just really off the maps. You wouldn't need software to look at these trades and say, 'Oh my God, this is directly connected to the World Trade Center.'

Herzliyah, International Policy Institute in Israel which tracks counter-terrorism, also tracks financial trading. That's a clear cut sign about how closely the two are related. And their reports are very clear that between September 6 and 7 the Chicago Board Options Exchange, CBOE, saw purchases of 4,744 put options on UAL, but only 396 call options. On September 10, the day before the attacks, 4,516 put options were placed on American Airlines, against only 748 calls, calls being bets that the stock will go up, puts being that the stock will go down. No similar trading in any other airlines occurred on the Chicago Exchange in the days immediately preceding Black Tuesday. That means that someone had advance knowledge that only the stocks of these two airlines would be adversely impacted. Had it just been an industry-wide slump, then you would have seen the same kind of activity on every airline, not just these two. But what is also very anomalous, very out of whack here, is the fact that the number of put options placed, that the level of these trades was up by 1,200 percent in the three days prior to the World Trade Center attacks."[255]

The *Wall Street Journal* reported some disturbing developments in the investigation into this suspicious share trading at the beginning of October 2001. The ongoing investigation by the Security and Exchange Commission had by then been joined by a U.S. Secret Service probe into purchases of an exceptionally large number of five-year U.S. Treasury notes, just prior to the attacks. Among the Treasury note transactions was a single $5 billion trade. The *Journal* points out that:

> "Five-year Treasury notes are among the best investments in the event of a world crisis, especially one that hits the U.S. The notes are prized for their safety and their backing by the U.S. government, and usually rally when investors flee riskier investments, such as stocks."[256]

The day after the *Journal* report came out, chief of the FBI's financial crimes unit Dennis Lormel attempted to downplay the significance of these trades, claiming in testimony before a Congressional committee that "To date there are no flags or indicators" showing that terrorists used strategies such as "short selling" to profit from the 11th September attacks.[257] However, FOX News cited German central bank president Ernst Welteke, who explained toward the end of September that "a study by his bank strongly points to 'terrorism insider trading' not only in shares of heavily affected industries such as airlines and insurance companies, but also in gold and oil."[258] Admitting that there has been a great deal of "speculation and rumours," Welteke also stated that "there are ever clearer signs that there were activities on international financial markets which must have been carried out with the necessary expert knowledge."[259]

Similarly, *USA Today* cited co-founder of PTI Securities Jon Najarian, described as an "active player" on the Chicago Board Options Exchange, confirming that: "The volumes were exceptional versus the norm."[260] Principal of Broadband Research John Kinnucan commented: "I saw put-call numbers higher than I've ever seen in 10 years of following the markets, particularly the options markets."[261] As CBS *60 Minutes reported*: "Sources tell CBS News that the afternoon before the attack, alarm bells were sounding over unusual trading in the U.S. stock options market."[262]

These trades strongly suggest that certain well-connected and wealthy investors had advance knowledge of the attacks. To date, both the Securities & Exchange Commission (SEC) and the FBI have been tight-lipped about their investigation of the trades. "The SEC and the Federal Bureau of Investigation have said nothing about their investigation into suspect trades," according to the *San Francisco Chronicle*.[263] Indeed, the FBI appears to have taken measures to block public knowledge of the progress of the investigation.

The Investment Dealers Association (IDA), a trade association for the Canadian securities industry, posted on its web site an SEC list of 38 stocks. The SEC had requested Canadian security firms to investigate suspicious trading in these stocks between 27 August and 11 September 2001. But as soon as U.S. officials became aware that the full list of stocks had been posted online, they demanded the removal of the list from the Investment Dealers Association's site. The IDA complied, but reporters were able to copy the list before its removal.[264]

The list of stocks includes the parent companies of American, Continental, Delta, Northwest, Southwest, United and U.S. Airways, as well as Carnival and Royal Caribbean cruise lines, aircraft maker Boeing and defense contractor Lockheed Martin. Several insurance companies are on the list—American International Group, Axa, Chubb, Cigna, CNA Financial, John Hancock and MetLife. Several giant companies that were former tenants in the World Trade Center were also on the list: the largest tenant, investment firms Morgan Stanley; Lehman Brothers; Bank of America; and the financial firm Marsh & McLennan. Other major companies on the list were General Motors, Raytheon, LTV, WR Grace, Lone Star Technologies, American Express, Bank of New York, Bank One, Citigroup and Bear Stearns.[265]

A probe of suspicious stock trading in these companies would attempt to isolate the investors, or group of investors, involved therein, thus uncovering those who had foreknowledge of the attacks.

Why did U.S. officials object to publication of a list of stocks in which suspicious trading occurred? Moreover, why have the results of the investigation so far, and any progress being made, not been made public?

Given that there are both intelligence and civilian systems that monitor share transactions for the express purpose of tracking suspicious movements, and given further that the transactions just prior to 11th September were so unprecedented, massive and specific, these systems would have received advance warning. These monitoring systems would also have clearly pointed to a specified time for the attacks as occurring between early and mid-September. U.S. intelligence would have been alerted as early as 7th September that American and United Airlines, along with the World Trade Center, were potential targets. The question remains, again, as to why nothing was done in response.

The London *Independent* has noted in relation to such events that: "To the embarrassment of investigators, it has also emerged that the firm used to buy many of the 'put' options—where a trader, in effect, bets on a share price fall—on United Airlines stock was headed until 1998 by 'Buzzy' Krongard, now executive director of the CIA."[266]

There is, indeed, abundant evidence discussed by Ruppert that the relationship between Wall Street and the CIA is akin to a 'revolving door.' For instance, elaborating on the *Independent's* observations, Ruppert notes that one of the key firms involved in the put options for United Airlines, Deutsche Bank Alex. Brown, was until 1998 managed by A. B. "Buzzy" Krongard. Before then, until 1997, Krongard was Chairman of the investment bank AB Brown, which was acquired by Banker's Trust in 1997. He then became, as part of the merger, Vice-Chairman of Banker's Trust-AB Brown. He joined the CIA in 1998 as counsel to CIA Director George Tenet, to be later promoted to CIA Executive Director by President Bush in March 2001. BT was acquired by Deutsche Bank in 1999, forming the single largest bank in Europe. Ruppert has also documented other crucial details relating to the interrelationship between the CIA, banks and the brokerage world.[267]

Long-standing links between Western intelligence and finance appear to have been instrumental in the foreknowledge of certain corporations about the attacks. Veteran U.S. journalists Alexander Cockburn and Jeffrey St. Clair reported in their respected current affairs newsletter, *Counterpunch*, that "an internal memo was sent around Goldman Sachs in Tokyo on September 10 advising all employees of a possible terrorist attack. It recommended all employees to avoid any American government buildings."[268]

11th September Warnings
Were Not Ignored by U.S. Authorities

Indeed, there is evidence that the threat was not ignored, at least not in certain selected respects. The *San Francisco Chronicle* reported one day after the attacks that Mayor Willie Brown received a phone call eight hours before the hijackings from what he described as his air security staff, warning him not to travel by air:

"For Mayor Willie Brown, the first signs that something was amiss came late Monday when he got a call from what he described as his airport security—a full eight hours before yesterday's string of terrorist attacks—advising him that Americans should be cautious about their air travel... Exactly where the call came from is a bit of a mystery. The mayor would say only that it came from 'my security people at the airport.'"[269]

San Francisco Mayor Willie Brown was booked to fly from the Bay area to New York City on the morning of September 11.[270] Clearly, it seems that certain high-level U.S. security authorities anticipated some sort of grave danger, and believed it to be urgent, threatening and certainly real enough to inform a U.S. City Mayor about to catch a flight to New York—but not the general public.

The London *Times* reported that the famous novelist, Salman Rushdie, received a similar warning to avoid U.S. and Canadian airlines. According to Rushdie's own testimony, the warning came directly from the U.S. Federal Aviation Administration (FAA). The *Times* reports:

"The author Salman Rushdie believes that U.S. authorities knew of an imminent terrorist strike when they banned him from taking internal flights in Canada and the U.S. only a week before the attacks. On September 3 the Federal Aviation Authority made an emergency ruling to prevent Mr Rushdie from flying."[271]

Another news report records that "the FAA has confirmed it stepped up security levels relating to Rushdie," but "the airlines weren't willing to upgrade their security" in relation to the wider public.[272] It is public knowledge that Rushdie is under 24-hour protection of UK Scotland Yard's Special Branch, and that all his travel plans are approved by the MI5 for domestic travel within the UK, and by the MI6 for international travel. The MI5 and MI6 are the British equivalent of the American CIA. Clearly, it appears that British intelligence anticipated a grave danger, under the guidance of U.S. authorities, and believed it to be urgent, threatening and real enough to inform Rushdie—but once again not the general public.

Another report points to the Pentagon's dubious role. *Newsweek* reported that on 10th September 2001, the day before the attacks, "a group of top Pentagon officials suddenly canceled travel plans for the next morning, apparently because of security concerns."[273] An earlier report by *Newsweek*, published two days after the attacks, referred to the same event in more detail:

"... the state of alert had been high during the past two weeks, and a particularly urgent warning may have been received the night before the attacks, causing some top Pentagon brass to cancel a trip. Why that same information was not available to the 266 people who died aboard the four hijacked commercial aircraft may become a hot topic on the Hill."[274]

Apparently, top Pentagon officials had known not only of an imminent threat to "security" in relation to their "travel plans," but had even anticipated its exact timing and taken measures to protect themselves—but not the general public. Together, these reports strongly suggest that high levels of the U.S. military intelligence community knew something very significant—and took it seriously.

It is noteworthy that these reports also strongly suggest foreknowledge among high-level elements of the U.S. military intelligence community, that attacks would occur mid-September, and even more specifically on the 11th of that month. As *WorldNetDaily* editor and veteran American journalist Joseph Farah rightly observes:

"Now, you're probably wondering why Willie Brown and Salman Rushdie [and senior Pentagon officials] are more important to the U.S. government than you and me and Barbara Olson. I'm wondering the same thing...

These selective warnings—and I have no doubt there were many more we have not yet heard about—suggest strongly that the FBI, CIA and other federal agencies had the information, knew something big was up, something that involved terrorist attacks on airliners, but failed to disclose the information to the airlines and the flying public in general. I think heads should roll at the FBI and CIA. I think there ought to be an investigation into what the FAA knew and when it knew it. I think, once again, the federal government has neglected its main responsibility under the Constitution—protecting the American people from attack."[275]

The U.S. Intelligence Community

As early as 1995, the U.S. had information relating to the plans to launch air attacks on the World Trade Center—information that was repeatedly confirmed by the American intelligence community since then, all the way to the year 2001. Yet these agencies neglected almost entirely to do anything to prevent or prepare for these attacks as far as the general public was concerned.[276] Indeed, all such possible measures were cut short. Such was the case with the investigations by FBI agents confirming the impending 11th September terrorist attacks, whose leads were severed by the FBI command without explanation—a situation apparently maintained with the complicity of the Attorney General, a Presidential appointee. The U.S. government's leading law enforcement agency thus deliberately ignored its own findings, and blocked these findings from being publicised.

We should particularly consider ECHELON's warnings of a Project Bojinka-style attack by Al-Qaeda on U.S. soil, targeting "symbols of American culture," first 6 months and then 3 months prior to September. According to the *Newsbytes* division of the *Washington Post*, "the warnings" that terrorists planned to hijack civilian airplanes and use them as bombs "were taken seriously" by "the American intelligence community", as a consequence of which "surveillance intensified." Furthermore, White House Counter-terrorism chief Richard A. Clarke confirms that the CIA fully anticipated an impending Al-Qaeda attack on U.S. soil in June 2001, and that the entire intelligence community was alerted by the beginning of July, just over six weeks prior to 11th September.

Warnings indicated that Project Bojinka would be implemented in the next several weeks. The World Trade Center was a confirmed target of Project Bojinka. The testimony of David Schippers confirms that knowledge that the impending attack would target key buildings in lower Manhattan, of which the World Trade Center is most prominent as a terrorist target, was fairly widespread among high-levels elements of the U.S. intelligence community. This seems to lead the chain of responsibility for the failure to act right to the top: the Director of Central Intelligence (DCI).

The term "intelligence community" is a specific terminology coined by U.S. intelligence agencies to refer to all the 13 official government agencies that have an "intelligence" role. The *Newsbytes* report on the ECHELON warnings, apart from noting that the entire intelligence community was alerted to an impending Project Bojinka-style terrorist attack, also indicates that surveillance, i.e. intelligence gathering efforts, were increased in direct response to the ECHELON warnings. This means that U.S. intelligence agencies had adequate information with which to marry their specific findings, e.g. the FBI's surveillance and investigations of Al-Qaeda operatives training at U.S. flight schools.

The official line has been that intelligence agencies had no reason to believe that these people with links to bin Laden were about to use their training to perform a terrorist act—but the documentation presented here shows that this is entirely false: the intelligence community already knew what Al-Qaeda was planning—it was just a matter of who and when.

Indeed, as a direct consequence of the intensification of surveillance, U.S. intelligence began finding out who. And as a direct consequence of the convergence of urgent warnings from multiple credible sources, including the interception of communications by Osama bin Laden himself, the probable date of the attacks also grew increasingly evident. Yet when FBI agents began finding out who (e.g. Al-Qaeda operatives training at U.S. military and flight facilities), the investigations were blocked by the FBI command and Justice Department. When multiple warnings together pointed clearly to the probability of an imminent attack by bin Laden, likely to occur on 11th September, these warnings were ignored.

The idea that the failure to act was a result of the incompetence resulting from unintentional bureaucratic stumbling blocks within the American intelligence community, fails to address the reality and nature of the multiple warnings received by that community. It is also based on a lack of understanding of the nature of intelligence gathering and the intelligence structure in the United States.

There are 13 official government agencies that constitute the U.S. intelligence community, with a huge budget of $30 billion. The Director of Central Intelligence is charged by law with the coordination and dissemination of intelligence gathered from all U.S. agencies, including the FBI. Additionally, many FBI agents work directly at CIA headquarters. The CIA, in line with its mandate for central managerial oversight of the U.S. intelligence community, produces 'strategic level' intelligence assessments for the U.S. government, drawing upon all available intelligence sources. A discussion follows of the nature and purpose of CIA strategic level intelligence assessments, regularly presented to leading members of the White House Cabinet.[277]

There is also a State Department Working Group set up to accomplish the same task in which the CIA participates.[278] A body of experts known as the Counterterrorism Security Group (CSG) exists, which was effectively chaired by White House Counterterrorism chief Richard Clarke. The CSG constitutes a connecting point for all federal agencies, whose members are "drawn mainly from the C.I.A., the National Security Council, and the upper tiers of the Defense Department, the Justice Department, and the State Department," and who meet "every week in the White House Situation Room." The CSG assesses all reliable intelligence related to counterterrorism received by these agencies and departments.[279]

The regular intelligence assessments produced by the CIA for the top decision-makers of the U.S. government, which draw on all available intelligence sources, are known as 'strategic level' assessments. 'Strategic level' refers to the highest level of decision-making—at the national or alliance level. For example, during the Second World War, when Churchill and Roosevelt met to discuss their long-range plans, they were considering strategic level issues. 'Strategic intelligence' is thus designed to answer the category of questions that arise at the level of strategic decision-making: e.g. is country X about to turn hostile? If so, what would be their overall capability to attack?[280]

The threat of a large-scale terrorist attack orchestrated by operatives located in a particular country (in this case Afghanistan), and harboured/supported by the ruling regime of that country (in this case the Taliban), would certainly come under this "strategic" category. Such a threat, and its various dimensions and implications, should therefore have been passed directly to members of the White House Cabinet, including President Bush himself. According to established procedures by which the CIA keeps U.S. decision-makers informed, President Bush and other key members of his Cabinet would have received CIA intelligence assessments on the imminent Al-Qaeda operation.[281] This seems to lend significant weight to the conclusion that the CIA, the DCI, the State Department, the President, and key figures around him in the White House, were ultimately responsible for doing *nothing* in the face of the mounting evidence of an impending threat to U.S. national security.

Furthermore, since the ECHELON warnings were "taken seriously," this means that the U.S. intelligence community should have been on alert and anticipating a Project Bojinka-style attack. The DCI would consequently have been doing its best to evaluate and coordinate information coming in from all sources to prevent the attack. Given that the U.S. intelligence community anticipated a Project Bojinka-style attack by Al-Qaeda operatives on U.S. soil, and had consequently intensified surveillance, all credible information and warnings that were subsequently collected were reviewed against this backdrop, with the specific intention of gathering further intelligence on bin Laden's plans. This subsequent data, therefore, would have been understood in context with the plans of which the U.S. intelligence community had already become aware—six months and then three months prior to 11th September.

Thus, from both a statutory and an organisational standpoint, the argument of incompetence or bureaucratic blocking is extremely weak. Even to argue that elements of the Bush administration had significant knowledge of what would happen, but not enough detail to take measures to prevent the attacks, is based on a very shallow appraisal of the nature and number of intelligence warnings received. As evidenced on public records, these warnings were not only extremely detailed, but also extremely specific as to probable perpetrators, methods, targets, and dates.[282] As the *Intelligence Note Book* of the Canadian Forces Intelligence Branch Association clarifies in relation to methods of intelligence gathering:

"… one always wants to have as many different sources as possible confirming one's intelligence assessment. When many different sources are combined in this way to produce one final assessment, this is known as 'fused,' 'multi-source' or even 'all-source' intelligence.

Really, the sources used are a technicality, of more concern to the intelligence personnel producing the assessment than to the end-user. The end-users' primary interest in the sources used will simply be to reflect how certain the conclusions are. The more different sources there are indicating a conclusion, the more certain we can be about that conclusion."[283]

Indeed, the numerous warnings received and intercepted by the U.S. intelligence community in regard to 11th September certainly met the four established criteria of what constitutes an intelligence success in strategic warning. Robert K. Betts, Professor of Political Science and Director of the Institute of War and Peace Studies at Columbia University, and Director of National Security Studies at the Council on Foreign Relations,[284] refers to these criteria as follows:

"Intercepted information about the location and timing of attack was so rich as to make the deduction of warning obvious.

The event involved was truly vital to U.S. security rather than just one among many important problems, so leaders had no reason to avoid focusing on the warning.

There was no problem of estimating the enemy's political intent to resort to force, as in pre-war crises.

There was nothing to be lost from prompt and vigorous military reaction to warning..."[285]

Hence, there cannot be any excuse within the U.S. intelligence community for ignoring or blocking further leads and subsequent warnings. When the ECHELON warnings were followed by warning after warning to the U.S. intelligence community from Israel, Russia, France, Egypt, along with numerous leads and warnings within the U.S. itself, according to the established procedures of intelligence gathering, the intelligence community should have grown increasingly certain of what was about to occur, by whom, and when. This is particularly clear given that the ECHELON warnings were taken seriously by the U.S. intelligence community—thus providing the backdrop of credibility against which subsequent reliable warnings could be assessed. Yet, we find that the very opposite happened.

Either pertinent CIA intelligence assessments were not passed on to the Cabinet, in violation of mandatory standard procedures, or they were, and the warnings were deliberately ignored by the nation's top decision-makers. The former scenario is implausible, simply because it is contrary to established procedures. The CIA produces strategic level intelligence assessments, drawing on all sources in the U.S. intelligence community, which are presented to the President and other top decision-makers. These assessments are directly concerned with issues of national security. It is therefore reasonable to believe that the escalating threat to national security posed by Al-Qaeda was, in accordance with routine mandatory procedures, passed on to the President and select members of his Cabinet.

The only other alternative is that the procedures were violated. But, there is no good reason to believe this. If we arbitrarily conjecture that procedure was not followed, and the threat was not passed on to top-decision makers, then one would have to instead conclude that responsibility rests with significant high-level elements of the U.S. military intelligence community, who would bear responsibility for keeping top U.S. decision-makers in the dark. The question would then remain: *why and for what purpose, if any, did they do so?*

Arguably, there is no good reason to accept that this scenario is plausible. On the contrary, there is good reason to accept the probability that, considering their dire gravity, warnings on the impending Al-Qaeda operation did reach the top. According to mandatory procedures, the imminent threat to U.S. national security posed by Al-Qaeda should have been passed on to top decision-makers through CIA intelligence assessments.[286]

If established procedures were followed, as they should have been, and top decision-makers were informed, then the blame lies not only at the highest levels of the DCI, CIA, FBI, the Justice Department, the National Security Agency, and the State Department, but also with the White House Cabinet. According to these procedures, the relevant members of the Cabinet would have received notification of the warnings and subsequent developments in accordance with the CIA's 'strategic level' assessment of the Al-Qaeda threat, as well as related relays of intelligence warnings. This is a more reasonable hypothesis, simply because it is in accordance with the known rules of intelligence warning in relation to issues of U.S. national security.

In the opinion of this author, therefore, the data provided here weighs strongly in favour of the conclusion that significant elements of the Bush administration did indeed receive advance warning of the attacks, but refused to act in the interests of the general public by pursuing measures to prevent the attacks.

Even at the minimal possible level of responsibility on the part of the Bush administration, the evidence on record strongly suggests that the U.S. government had enough advance warning to be at least certain of terrorist attacks on U.S. soil through the hijacking of civilian planes—but despite this, failed to institute even the most minimal of preventive measures.

For instance, the attacks could have been blocked even if the government had ensured that recommended security measures and precautions were pursued by the Federal Aviation Administration at airports, on planes, and so on. Yet the U.S. government, despite longstanding knowledge of the threat of impending suicide attacks from the air—a threat that was about to become a reality in 2001, according to highly credible intelligence warnings—did nothing of the sort. Indeed, the facts on record are sufficient to provide reasonable grounds to believe that the 'intelligence failure' was in fact not a failure at all, but a directive—or rather, the inevitable culmination of carefully imposed high-level directives and blocks that restrained agencies from acting on the very clear intelligence received.

Tyrone Powers, a former FBI Special Agent specialising in counterterrorism—now Professor of Law Enforcement and Criminal Justice at Anne Arundel County Community College and Director of the Institute for Criminal Justice, Legal Studies and Public Service—points out that there was "credible information from the FBI, CIA and foreign intelligence services that an attack was imminent". The information indicated that an Al-Qaeda hijacking attempt was probable. Powers describes this as the "consequentialism" inherent to the decision making process which he has witnessed firsthand in his intelligence and counter-intelligence background: "...on occasion, [damaging] acts are allowed if in the minds of the decision-makers, they will lead to 'greater good'," and as long as the damage is contained within certain limits. Powers further refers pressure on intelligence agencies to vastly reduce their powers; concern over the "blowback" from the controversies of the Presidential election; the desire on the part of elements of the intelligence community to "reconstitute the CIA" after its perceived "emasculation by the Clinton administration;" their belief that such a reconstitution required "a need, a demand and a free hand that would be given by a democratic Congress [only] if there was a National outcry."

He states: "My experience tells me that these incidents would have reached the level at which the 'consequentialism' thought process would have been made a real option"—in other words, that elements of the intelligence community and the administration may have deliberately failed to act in the belief that the resultant damage would contribute to a "greater good," providing a pretext for such policies as the reconstitution of the CIA. However, Powers emphasises that this policy would have been the result of a "miscalculation"—a failure to anticipate the extent of this damage: "But the amount of destruction wrought on a civilian population shocked even the advocates of this policy."[287]

In other words, the U.S. intelligence community had sufficient information of an impending Al-Qaeda hijacking attack, but was probably blocked from undertaking preventive action from above.

Of course, a full-blown inquiry into the causes of the 'intelligence failure' that allowed the 11th September attacks to occur is essential to determine what U.S. government, military and intelligence agencies knew, when they knew it, and why they failed to act. Outside of such an inquiry, it is impossible to conclusively determine the exact degree of advance warning received by particular U.S. government, military and intelligence agencies.

Ongoing attempts by the Bush administration to actively block such an inquiry into the causes of the so-called 9-11 'intelligence failure,' however, only serve to further support the conclusion just outlined. CNN reported at the end of January 2002 that:

> "President Bush personally asked Senate Majority Leader Tom Daschle Tuesday to limit the congressional investigation into the events of September 11, congressional and White House sources told CNN...
>
> The request was made at a private meeting with congressional leaders Tuesday morning. Sources said Bush initiated the conversation... He asked that only the House and Senate intelligence committees look into the potential breakdowns among federal agencies that could have allowed the terrorist attacks to occur, rather than a broader inquiry that some lawmakers have proposed, the sources said. Tuesday's discussion followed a rare call to Daschle from Vice President Dick Cheney last Friday to make the same request... Some Democrats, such as Sens. Joseph Lieberman of Connecticut and Robert Torricelli of New Jersey, have been calling for a broad inquiry looking at various federal government agencies beyond the intelligence community."[288]

The pretext for the administration's proposals, according to Daschle, is that "resources and personnel" would be taken "away from the war on terrorism," in the event of a wider inquiry that is not limited to the assumption that the administration's inaction was solely a consequence of "breakdowns among federal agencies."

Paradoxically, the Bush administration thus justified blocking a wider inquiry into the intelligence failure that allowed the 11th September attacks to occur, by the need to support the administration's attempts to counter terrorism. In other words, the administration suppressed an inquiry into the greatest terror attack in U.S. history—in the name of fighting terrorism.

It is unfortunate that CNN chose not to point out that an integral dimension of any meaningful counterterrorist programme is the gathering of intelligence with the view to avoiding a terrorist attack—which is exactly what Bush's proposals will help prevent. Not only is it clear that the Bush administration was not serious about averting terrorism prior to 11th

September, it also appears that the administration has maintained the same attitude—despite the obvious consequences.

The documentation collated in the previous pages demonstrates beyond doubt that innocent American civilians paid with their lives because high-level elements of the Bush administration engineered blocks on U.S. intelligence agencies in order to fulfil and protect another agenda. Unless a full-blown independent inquiry into this process is mounted soon, there is little doubt that more innocent Americans will pay with their lives again.

Notes

[150] Cited in Public Education Center, www.publicedcenter.org/faaterrorist.htm; *Washington Post*, 2 January 2001.

[151] Warrick, Jo and Stephens, Joe, 'Before Attack, U.S. Expected Different Hit, Chemical, Germ Agents Focus of Preparation,' *Washington Post*, 2 October, 2001.

[152] Wald, Matthew, 'Earlier Hijackings Offered Signals That Were Missed,' *New York Times*, 3 October 2001.

[153] *New York Times*, 3 October 2001.

[154] Novak, Robert, *Chicago Sun-Times*, 27 September 2001.

[155] Agence France Press, 'Western intelligence knew of Laden plan since 1995,' 7 December 2001. Printed in *Hindustan Times*.

[156] PEC Report, 'Terrorist Plans to Use Planes as Weapons Dates to 1995: WTC bomber Yousef confessed to U.S. agents in 1995' Public Education Center, Washington DC, www.publicedcenter.org/faaterrorist.htm.

[157] A dubious etymology. 'Bojin' means 'to be afraid' in Serbo-Croatian, and the suffix -ka is a diminutive. More likely it referred to an act done by or with Boeings.

[158] Garcia, Raphael M., 'Decoding Bojinka,' *Newsbreak Weekly*, 15 November 2001, Vol. 1, No. 43. Also see Cooley, John, *Unholy Wars: Afghanistan, American and International Terrorism*, Pluto Press, London, 1999, p. 247.

[159] Geostrategy-Direct.Com, '1995 plan selected U.S.-bound airliners from East Asia,' *World Tribune*, 19 September 2001, www.worldtribune.com/wta/Archive-2001/me_binladen_09_19.html. Also see Irvine, Reed, 'Letting the Cat Out of the Bag,' *Human Events*, 24 September 2001.

[160] Monk, Paul, 'A Stunning Intelligence Failure,' Australian Thinking Skills Institute, Melbourne, www.austhink.org/monk/index.htm.

[161] AIM Report No. 18, 'Catastrophic Intelligence Failure,' Accuracy In Media, Washington DC, 24 September 2001, www.aim.org/publications/aim_report/2001/18.html.

[162] Garcia, Raphael M., 'Decoding Bojinka,' op. cit.

[163] *Washington Post*, 24 September 2001. The *Post* also discusses Project Bojinka and the plans to hurl civilian jets into key U.S. buildings, including the WTC. Also see Ressa, Maria, 'U.S. warned in 1995 of plot to hijack planes, attack buildings,' CNN, 18 September 2001.

[164] Fineman, Mark and Pasternak, Judy, 'Suicide Flights and Crop Dusters Considered Threats at '96 Olympics,' *Los Angeles Times*, 17 November 2001.

[165] Cited in Grigg, William Norman, 'Could We Have Prevented the Attacks?', *The New American*, 5 November 2001, Vol. 17, No. 23.

[166] Woodward, Bob and Eggen, Dan, 'Aug. Memo Focused on Attacks in U.S.', *Washington Post*, 18 May 2002, http://www.washingtonpost.com/wp-dyn/articles/A35744-2002May17.html.

[167] Grigg, William Norman, 'Could We Have Prevented the Attacks?', op. cit.

[168] Stafford, Ned, 'Newspaper: Echelon Gave Authorities Warning of Attacks,' *Newsbytes*, 13 September 2001, www.newsbytes.com/news/01/170072.html. ECHELON is a vast intelligence information collection system capable of monitoring all the electronic communications in the world. It is operated by the U.S., UK, Canada, Australia and New Zealand. While no government agency has ever confirmed or denied its existence, an EU committee that investigated ECHELON for more than a year confirmed that the system does exist in early September 2001. The EU committee reported that Echelon sucks up electronic transmissions "like a vacuum cleaner", using keyword search techniques to sift through enormous amounts of data. The system covers the whole world's electronic communications with 120 satellites. For more on ECHELON see Bamford, James, *Body of Secrets: Anatomy of the Ultra-Secret National Security Agency*, Doubleday, 2001.

[169] Wright, Lawrence, 'The Counter-Terrorist,' *New Yorker*, 14 January 2002. Under pressure from Congress, the White House has finally officially admitted that the U.S. intelligence community had information that Al-Qaeda was planning an imminent attack through hijacking. However, National Security Adviser Condoleezza Rice has gone on record denying that U.S. intelligence had any other specific information, such as that the planes might be used as missiles (BBC Newsnight, 16 May 2002). This denial, however, is patently false, as demonstrated by the reports on the public record discussed here.

[170] Solomon, John, 'CIA Cited Risk Before Attack,' Associated Press, 3 October 2001.

[171] United Press International (UPI), 13 February 2001. This report provides empirical information disproving an earlier *WorldNetDaily* report alleging that the Clinton administration sold powerful encryption software to Al-Qaeda that would allow the network to encrypt, and thus block U.S. surveillance of, the network's encrypted communications. This report shows that regardless of Osama bin Laden's attempts at encryption, the codes were broken by ECHELON and his communications monitored.

[172] *New York Times*, 14 October 2001.

[173] Associated Press, 'World Trade Center collapses in terrorist attack,' 11 September 2001. In an interview with ABC News the same day, Hatch elaborated that both CIA and FBI officials had informed him of the same. In response, U.S. Defense Secretary Donald Rumsfeld denounced the report as an unauthorised release of classified information. The White House later cited the leak as good reason to withhold information concerning U.S. counterterrorist actions from Congress.

[174] ABC News, 'Missed Opportunities,' World News Tonight, 18-20 February 2001.

[175] *The Record*, 12 September 2001; *Economic Reform*, October 2001.

[176] Airjet Airline World News, Washington DC, 23 June 2001, http://airlinebiz.com/wire.

[177] Wright, Lawrence, 'The Counter-Terrorist,' op. cit.

[178] Stich, Rodney, *The Real Unfriendly Skies*, Diablo Western Press, Reno, Nevada, 2000. Also see www.unfriendlyskies.com.

[179] Pasternak, Judy, 'FAA, Airlines Stalled Major Security Plans,' *Los Angeles Times*, 6 October 2001.

[180] JW Press Release, 'Government Incompetence, Lack of Honesty with American People Lead to Terrorist Disasters of September 11, 2001,' Judicial Watch, Washington DC, 12 September 2001.

[181] Farah, Joseph, 'The failure of government,' *WorldNetDaily* Exclusive Commentary, 19 October 2001, www.wnd.com.

[182] Reuters, 13 September 2001.

[183] CBS, *60 Minutes II*, 8 May 2002.

[184] *Star-Tribune*, 29 December 2001.

[185] *New York Times*, 8 February 2002.

[186] Shenon, Philip, 'FBI ignored attack warning: Flight instructor told agency of terror suspect's plan,' *San Francisco Chronicle*, 22 Dec. 2001.

[187] Seper, Jerry, 'Justice Blocked FBI Warrant,' *Washington Times*, 3 October 2001.

[188] ABC News, 'Missed Opportunities,' World News Tonight, 18-20 February 2001.

[189] Gordon, Greg, 'FAA security took no action against Moussaoui,' *Corpus Christi Caller Times*, 13 January 2002.

[190] Isikoff, Michael and Klaidman, Daniel, 'Access Denied,' MS-NBC, 1 October 2001.

[191] *New York Times*, 22 December 2001.

[192] ARD, 23 November 2001.

[193] *Washington Post*, 28 October 2001.

[194] Smith, Hedrick, 'Inside The Terror Network: should we have spotted the conspiracy?', PBS Frontline, www.pbs.org/wgbh/pages/frontline.

[195] Swain, Diana, Canadian Broadcasting Corporation, 14 Sept. 2001.

[196] *The Observer*, 30 September 2001.

[197] BBC News, 26 November 2001.

[198] Capital Briefs, 'Basic Failure,' *Human Events*, 24 September 2001, Vol. 57, No. 35, p. 2.

[199] AIM Report No. 18, 'Catastrophic Intelligence Failure,' op. cit.

[200] Wheeler, Larry, 'Pensacola NAS link faces more scrutiny,' *Pensacola News Journal*, 17 September 2001.

[201] 'Alleged Hijackers May Have Trained at U.S. Bases,' *Newsweek*, 15 September 2001.

[202] Cited in Hopsicker, Daniel, 'Did terrorists train at U.S. military schools?', *Online Journal*, 30 October 2001.

[203] Fainaru, Steve and Grimaldi, James V., 'FBI Knew Terrorists Were Using Flight Schools,' *Washington Post*, 23 September 2001.

[204] Ibid.

[205] Hopsicker, Daniel, 'Death in Venice (Florida),' *Online Journal*, 28 September 2001.

[206] Hopsicker, Daniel, 'What are they hiding down in Venice, Florida?', *Online Journal*, 9 October 2001.

[207] Hopsicker, Daniel, 'Was the CIA running a terrorist flight school?', *Online Journal*, 7 November 2001.

[208] Hopsicker, Daniel, 'Jackson Stephens active in Venice, FL,' *Online Journal*, 25 November 2001.

[209] Hopsicker, Daniel, 'Rudi Dekkers and the Lone (nut) Cadre,' *Online Journal*, 24 October 2001.

[210] Hopsicker, Daniel, 'Venice, Florida, Flight School Linked to CIA: Firm has 'green light' from local DEA,' *Online Journal*, 2 March 2002.

[211] ABC News, 'Missed Opportunities,' op. cit.

[212] Fainaru, Steve and Grimaldi, James V., 'FBI Knew Terrorists Were Using Flight Schools,' op. cit.

[213] BBC Newsnight, 'Has someone been sitting on the FBI?', 6 November 2001.

[214] Interview with Michael Springmann, 'Dispatches,' CBC Radio One, 16 Jan. 2002, http://radio.cbc.ca/programs/dispatches/audio/020116_springman.rm.

[215] Freedberg, Sydney P., 'Loopholes leave U.S. borders vulnerable,' *St. Petersburg Times*, 25 November 2001.

[216] David P. Schippers served as Chief Counsel to the United States House of Representatives managers for the impeachment trial of President Bill Clinton in the U.S. Senate from 1st Jan. to 28th Feb. 1999. He served as Chief Investigative

Counsel for the United States House of Representatives' Committee on the Judiciary during 1998. From April to September he handled the investigative issues and investigations relating to the committee's oversight investigation of the U.S. Dept. of Justice and all of its sub-agencies. From Sept. to Dec. 1998, he was charged with reviewing and reporting on the Referral of the Office of Independent Counsel concerning possible impeachment offenses committed by President Clinton. He was then responsible for conducting the impeachment inquiry authorised by the House of Representatives and reporting the results to the Committee on the Judiciary. An attorney in private practice since 1967, Schippers is the senior partner in the Chicago law firm, Schippers & Bailey, which specialises in trust law, labour law, trials and appeals in the state and federal courts of Illinois and throughout the country. From 1963 to 1967, Schippers served as a member and later the chief of the Organised Crime and Racketeering Section of the U.S. Department of Justice at Chicago. He prepared and tried many major criminal cases in the federal courts and was also involved in a great number of major grand jury investigations. He previously served in the U.S. Attorney's Office as an assistant United States attorney, trying major criminal cases on behalf of the government and preparing and arguing appeals on behalf of the government. Schippers earned both his undergraduate and J.D. degree from Loyola University in Chicago. He has served as a teacher of trial advocacy and advanced trial advocacy to senior law students at the Loyola University School of Law. He has also taught trial advocacy at the Williamette University School of Law in Salem, Oregon., and at the United States Air Force Air University in Montgomery, Alabama. Schippers served as one of five members of the Illinois State Police Merit Board from 1987 to 1993. He is the recipient of the Loyola University Law Alumni Medal of Excellence, the Loyola University Alumni Association citation for distinguished service to the legal profession and the Award of Appreciation from the Federal Criminal Investigators Association.

[217] Jasper, William F., 'OKC Bombing: Precursor to 9-11?', *New American*, 28 January 2002, Vol. 18, No. 2.

[218] David P. Schippers, 'Government Had Prior Knowledge,' Interview on Alex Jones Show, Talk Radio, Austin, Texas, 10 Oct. 2001, transcript available at www.infowars.com/transcript_schippers.html.

[219] David P. Schippers, 'David Schippers Tells Metcalf Feds ignored warnings of WTC attacks,' WorldNetDaily, 21 October 2001, http://wnd.com/news/article.asp?ARTICLE_ID=25008.

[220] David P. Schippers, 'Government Had Prior Knowledge,' op. cit.

[221] EFI Report, 'What does nationally-renowned attorney David Schippers think of this possibility?' Eagle Forum of Illinois, 30 September 2001, www.ileagles.net/schippers.htm.

[222] JW Press Release, 'Active FBI Special Agent Files Complaint Concerning Obstructed FBI Anti-Terrorist Investigations,' Judicial Watch, Washington DC,

14 November 2001. Also see 'David Schippers Goes Public: The FBI was warned,' *Indianapolis Star*, 13 October 2001.

[223] Telephone interview with Chief Investigative Counsel David P. Schippers by Nafeez M. Ahmed, Institute for Policy Research & Development, Brighton, 26 February 2002.

[224] Grigg, William Norman, 'Did We Know What Was Coming?', *The New American*, Vol. 18, No. 5, 11 March 2002, http://www.thenewamerican.com/tna/2002/03-11-2002/vol18no05_didweknow.htm.

[225] Palast, Gregory and Pallister, David, 'FBI claims Bin Laden inquiry was frustrated,' *The Guardian*, 7 November 2001. For further discussion see Chapter VI.

[226] Bruce, Ian, 'FBI "super flying squad" to combat terror', *The Herald*, 16 May 2002.

[227] Blomquist, Brian, 'FBI Man's Chilling 9/11 Prediction', *New York Post*, 9 May 2002, http://www.nypost.com/news/nationalnews/47581.htm.

[228] Isikoff, Michael, Newsweek, 20 May 2002. See Ruppert, Michael C., 'The Lie Won't Stand', From The Wilderness Publications, 16 May 2002.

[229] *Washington Post*, 18 May 2002.

[230] Editorial, 'Evidence mounts that September 11 was predictable,' *USA Today*, 15 September 2001.

[231] Wastell, David and Jacobson, Philip, 'Israeli security issued warning to CIA of large-scale terror attacks,' *The Telegraph*, 16 September 2001. It has been claimed that the U.S. intelligence community receives numerous warnings such as this which are red-herrings, thus explaining why the latest warning from Israeli intelligence was not taken seriously. This argument fails, however, in light of the fact that the U.S. already knew for certain that Osama Bin Laden was planning to implement Project Bojinka very soon. Given this knowledge, the urgent warnings from other intelligence agencies, including Israel, would have obviously provided increasing confirmation of the plans, not disconfirmation. If not, then one wonders what other sort of criteria would be necessary for U.S. intelligence to take a warning from Mossad seriously!

[232] MS-NBC, 15 September 2001.

[233] Russian press reports translated by a former CIA official, cited in Ruppert, Michael C., 'This Was Not An Intelligence Failure,' From The Wilderness Publications, 24 September 2001. See *Izvestia*, 12 September 2002.

[234] *Le Figaro*, 31 October 2001.

[235] Gumbel, Andrew, 'Bush did not heed several warnings of attack,' *The Independent*, 17September 2001.

[236] *San Francisco Chronicle*, 14 September 2001.

[237] Ananova, 'German police confirm Iranian deportee phoned warnings,' 14 September 2001.

[238] MS-NBC, 16 September 2001.

[239] Associated Press, 'Egypt Leader Says He Warned America,' 7 December 2001. Also see *Atlanta Journal and Constitution*, 8 Dec. 2001.

[240] Nicolson was formally the David Bruton Jr. Chair in Cancer Research and Professor at the University of Texas M. D. Anderson Cancer Center in Houston, and Professor of Internal Medicine and Professor of Pathology and Laboratory Medicine at the University of Texas Medical School at Houston. He was also Adjunct Professor of Comparative Medicine at Texas A & M University. Among the most cited scientists in the world, having published over 480 medical and scientific papers, edited 13 books, served on the Editorial Boards of 12 medical and scientific journals and currently serving as Editor of two (*Clinical & Experimental Metastasis* and the *Journal of Cellular Biochemistry*), Professor Nicolson has active peer-reviewed research grants from the U.S. Army, National Cancer Institute, National Institutes of Health, American Cancer Society and the National Foundation for Cancer Research. In 1998 he received the Stephen Paget Award from the Cancer Metastasis Research Society and the Albert Schweitzer Award in Lisbon, Portugal.

[241] Statement by Professor Garth L. Nicolson to the Institute for Policy Research & Development, 3 January 2002.

[242] Bonner, Raymond and Tagliabue, John, 'Eavesdropping, U.S. Allies See New Terror Attack,' *New York Times*, 21 October 2001.

[243] Ruppe, David, 'Who Did It? U.S. Searches for Terror Clues,' ABC News, 11 September 2001.

[244] AFP, 'Similar plot first uncovered in Philippines, says police chief,' *Sydney Morning Herald*, 13 September 2001.

[245] *Newsweek*, 1 October 2001.

[246] NBC News, 4 October 2001.

[247] *San Francisco Chronicle*, 29 September 2001.

[248] 'Black Tuesday: The World's Largest Insider Trading Scam?', Herzliya International Policy Institute for Counter-terrorism, 21 September 2001.

[249] Eichenwald, Kurt, et al, 'Doubt Intensifies That Advance Knowledge of Attacks Was Used for Profit,' *New York Times*, 28 September 2001.

[250] Doran, James, 'Millions of shares sold before disaster,' *The Times*, 18 September 2001.

[251] Ruppert, Michael C., 'Suppressed Details of Criminal Insider Trading Lead Directly into the CIA's Highest Ranks,' op. cit. The CIA has also confirmed its use of Promis software outside the United States, while not denying its monitoring of stock option trading activity from abroad.
For further discussion see Flocco, Tom, 'Profits of Death—Insider Trading and 9-11,' FTW Publications, 6 December 2001: "In a returned phone call from the

Central Intelligence Agency, press spokesman Tom Crispell denied that the CIA was monitoring 'real-time,' pre-September 11, stock option trading activity *within* United States borders using such software as the Prosecutor's Management Information System (PROMIS). 'That would be illegal. *We only operate outside the United States,*' the intelligence official said..." [emphasis added]

[252] UPI, 13 February 2001.

[253] Doran, James, 'Millions of shares sold before disaster,' op. cit.

[254] Ruppert, Michael C., 'A Timeline Surrounding September 11th,' FTW Publications, 2 November 2001, www.copvcia.com/stories/nov_2001/lucy.html. For further information on Promis, the software descended from it, as well as the use of this new software by the CIA to monitor stock trading, see FTW Publications, 26 October 2001, www.copvcia.com/members/magic_carpet.html; FTW Publications, Vol. IV, No.6, 18 September, 2001, www.copvcia.com/members/sept1801.html; FTW Publications, Vol. 3, No 7, 30 September 2000, www.copvcia.com/stories/may_2001/052401_promis.html. Also see *Washington Times*, 15 June 2001; FOX News, 16 October 2001.

[255] Michael C. Ruppert, 'Guns and Butter: The Economy Watch,' Interview with Kellia Ramares and Bonnie Falkner, KPFA 94.1 FM, Berkeley, CA, 12 October 2001. Available online at 'The CIA's Wall Street Connections,' Centre for Research on Globalisation, Montreal, 3 November 2001, http://globalresearch.ca/articles/RUP111A.html.

[256] *Wall Street Journal*, 2 October 2001.

[257] Hamilton, Walter, *Los Angeles Times*, 18 October 2001.

[258] FOX News, 'EU searches for suspicious trading,' 22 September 2001.

[259] Hooper, John, 'Terror "made fortune for Bin Laden",' *The Observer*, 23 September 2001.

[260] *USA Today*, October 2001.

[261] *Montreal Gazette*, 19 September 2001.

[262] CBS, *60 Minutes*, 19 September 2001.

[263] Pender, Kathleen, 'Terrorism's long, tangled money trail,' *San Francisco Chronicle*, 7 October 2001.

[264] For discussion see for example Grey, Barry, 'Suspicious trading points to advance knowledge by big investors of September 11 attacks,' World Socialist Web Site, 5 October 2001.

[265] Ibid.

[266] *The Independent*, 10 October 2001, www.independent.co.uk/story.jsp?story=99402

[267] Ruppert, Michael C., 'Suppressed Details of Criminal Insider Trading Lead Directly into the CIA's Highest Ranks,' From The Wilderness (FTW) Publications, 9 October 2001, http://copvcia.com. The discussion in this paper on

financial transactions leading up to 11th September is based on Ruppert's analysis. His comments on the CIA-Wall Street alliance are crucial, and have been reproduced here: "Clark Clifford – The National Security Act of 1947 was written by Clark Clifford, a Democratic Party powerhouse, former Secretary of Defense, and one-time advisor to President Harry Truman. In the 1980s, as Chairman of First American Bancshares, Clifford was instrumental in getting the corrupt CIA drug bank BCCI a license to operate on American shores. His profession: Wall Street lawyer and banker. John Foster and Allen Dulles – These two brothers 'designed' the CIA for Clifford. Both were active in intelligence operations during WW II. Allen Dulles was the U.S. Ambassador to Switzerland where he met frequently with Nazi leaders and looked after U.S. investments in Germany. John Foster went on to become Secretary of State under Dwight Eisenhower and Allen went on to serve as CIA Director under Eisenhower and was later fired by JFK. Their professions: partners in the most powerful – to this day – Wall Street law firm of Sullivan, Cromwell. Bill Casey – Ronald Reagan's CIA Director and OSS veteran who served as chief wrangler during the Iran-Contra years was, under President Richard Nixon, Chairman of the Securities and Exchange Commission. His profession: Wall Street lawyer and stockbroker. David Doherty – The current Vice President of the New York Stock Exchange for enforcement is the retired General Counsel of the Central Intelligence Agency. George Herbert Walker Bush – President from 1989 to January 1993, also served as CIA Director for 13 months from 1976-7. He is now a paid consultant to the Carlyle Group, the 11th largest defense contractor in the nation, which also shares joint investments with the bin Laden family. A.B. 'Buzzy' Krongard – The current Executive Director of the Central Intelligence Agency is the former Chairman of the investment bank A.B. Brown and former Vice Chairman of Banker's Trust. John Deutch – This retired CIA Director from the Clinton Administration currently sits on the board at Citigroup, the nation's second largest bank, which has been repeatedly and overtly involved in the documented laundering of drug money. This includes Citigroup's 2001 purchase of a Mexican bank known to launder drug money, Banamex. Nora Slatkin – This retired CIA Executive Director also sits on Citibank's board. Maurice 'Hank' Greenberg – The CEO of AIG insurance, manager of the third largest capital investment pool in the world, was floated as a possible CIA Director in 1995. FTW exposed Greenberg's and AIG's long connection to CIA drug trafficking and covert operations in a two-part series that was interrupted just prior to the attacks of September 11. AIG's stock has bounced back remarkably well since the attacks. To read that story, please go to www.copvcia.com/stories/july_2001/part_2.html."

[268] *Counterpunch*, 14 September 2001.

[269] Matier, Philip, 'Willie Brown got low-key early warning about air travel,' *San Francisco Chronicle*, 12 September 2001.

[270] Cockburn, Alexander and St. Clair, Jeffrey, *Counterpunch*, 14 Sept. 2001.

[271] Doran, James, 'Rushdie's air ban,' *The Times*, 27 September 2001.

[272] Ananova, 'Rushdie "given U.S. air ban week before terrorist attacks",' 27 September 2001.

[273] *Newsweek*, 24 September 2001.

[274] Hirsh, Michael, 'We've hit the targets,' *Newsweek*, 13 Sept. 2001.

[275] Farah, Joseph, 'The failure of government,' op. cit.

[276] For instance, in spite of the multiple dire warnings, the Federal Aviation Administration (FAA) failed to upgrade its security in accordance with repeated recommendations.

[277] CFIBA, 'International Intelligence Agency Links,' Canadian Forces Intelligence Branch, Association, www.intbranch.org/engl/elinks/us.html.

[278] Statement from Michael C. Ruppert, former LAPD narcotics detective and expert on CIA covert operations, to IPRD, 15 January 2001.

[279] Wright, Lawrence, 'The Counter-terrorist Threat,' op. cit.

[280] CFIBA, 'Types of Intelligence,' *Intelligence Note Book*, Canadian Forces Intelligence Branch Association, www.intbranch.org/engl/intntbk/intro.html.

[281] Ibid.

[282] Ibid. Any attempt to claim that intelligence received by the U.S. intelligence community was not sufficient must therefore somehow show that the facts on record, as documented here, are not facts at all.

[283] CFIBA, 'Types of Intelligence,' op. cit.

[284] Betts also served on the staff of the original Senate Select Committee on Intelligence, and has been a consultant in the U.S. intelligence community.

[285] Betts, Richard K., 'Intelligence Warning: Old Problems, New Agendas,' *Parameters* (U.S. Army War College Quarterly), Spring 1998, p. 26-35.

[286] The implausibility of the idea that the CIA failed to pass on the warnings to President Bush Jr. and other top-decision makers in the White House through its regular strategic intelligence assessments, is further clear from the President's strong links to the U.S. intelligence community through his father, former President Bush Sr., who was Director of the CIA. Indeed, the degree to which the current Bush Cabinet is drawn directly from the interlocking U.S. military, intelligence and corporate community, further demonstrates the implausibility of this scenario.

[287] Interview with Tyrone Powers with Bob Slade on Open Line show, 98.7 Kiss FM, New York, 19 May 2002. Cited in Shipman, Dennis, 'The Spook Who Sat Behind The Door: A Modern Day Tale: ', IndyMedia, 20 May 2002, http://portland.indymedia.org/ front.php3?article_id=11188&group=webcast; emailed statement from Powers to the author, 22 May 2002.

[288] CNN, 'Bush asks Daschle to limit Sept. 11 probes,' 29 January 2002. Also see Fineman, Howard, 'The Battle Back Home,' *Newsweek*, 4 February 2002.

5. The Collapse of Standard Operating Procedures on 9-11

"September 11 was not so unprecedented. Passenger jet hijackings have happened before, and the U.S. government has prepared detailed plans to handle them. On September 11 these plans were ignored in their entirety."

George Szamuely
(New York Press, Vol. 15, No. 2)

"For 60 decisive minutes, the military and intelligence agencies let the fighter planes stay on the ground."

Herr von Buelow, former State Secretary
in the German Defence Ministry
(Tagesspiegel, 13 January 2002)

The sequence of events on 11th September 2001 was as follows:

- 8:45 a.m.—American Airlines Flight 11 from Boston smashed into the north tower of the World Trade Center.

- 9:03 a.m.—United Airlines Flight 175 from Boston smashed into the south tower.

- 9:40 a.m.—AA Flight 77 from Dulles hits the Pentagon.

- 10:10 a.m.—United Flight 93 from Newark crashed in Shanksville, Pennsylvania.

"Yet the most amazing feature of the U.S. government's response to these events was the almost complete absence of it," notes American journalist George Szamuely in the *New York Press*, referring to the work of investigative journalist Jared Israel. "Jared Israel on his website www.tenc.net has blazed a trail with fascinating and meticulous research."[289]

Jared Israel, a Colombia and Harvard University educated independent researcher, writing with Illarion Bykov, has indeed conducted a useful investigation of the sequence of events on 11th September:

> "Andrews Air Force Base is a huge military installation about 10 miles from the Pentagon. On 11 September there were two entire squadrons of combat-ready fighter jets at Andrews...

> Their job was to protect the skies over Washington D.C. They failed to do their job. Despite over one hour's advance warning of a terrorist attack in progress, not a single Andrews fighter tried to protect the city. The FAA, NORAD and the military have cooperative procedures by which fighter jets automatically intercept commercial aircraft under emergency conditions. These procedures were not followed."[290]

Standard Operating Procedures for Air Emergencies

Here, we will analyse the responses of the U.S. government and military to the air attacks on 9-11 in context with the normal rules of emergency response employed by air authorities in crisis situations.

Air Traffic Controllers routinely request fighter craft to intercept commercial planes for various reasons when problems faced cannot be solved through radio contact, e.g. to inform commercial pilots when their plane is off course, or simply to assess the situation directly.

The deviation of commercial planes from their designated flight paths is a common problem solved via interception. As a matter of mandatory Standard Operating Procedures, no approval from White House is required for interception. On the contrary, interception occurs on the basis of established flight and emergency response rules.

Military interceptors do not need instructions from the White House to carry out emergency response procedures and other such services—they already have clear "instructions to act," which are followed automatically in relation to varying situations. Detailed FAA and Department of Defense manuals are available online, clarifying that these instructions are exceedingly comprehensive, including issues from minor emergencies to full-blown hijackings. According to these instructions, serious problems are handed over to the National Military Command Center in the Pentagon, if necessary.

Commercial flights must adhere to Instrument Flight Rules (IFR). According to the IFR, before takeoff pilots must file a flight plan with the FAA:

"Commercial flights fly according to predefined flight plans. These flight plans are intended to provide quick routes that take advantage of favorable winds while avoiding the routes traveled by other aircraft. The usual flight plan is a series of three connected routes: a standard instrument departure (SID) route, an en route path, and a standard instrument arrival (STAR). Each route consists of a sequence of geographic points, or fixes, which, when connected, form a trajectory from the point of departure to the point of arrival."[291]

As soon as a plane deviates from its flight plan—for instance, by making a wrong turn at a 'fix'—an Air Traffic Controller contacts the pilot. If the Controller fails to make contact or routine communication becomes impossible, established rules dictate that an aircraft will be requested to scramble and assess the situation by 'interception.'

A clear example of this routine procedure is the FAA's response when the Lear jet chartered by golf professional Payne Stewart deviated from its flight path while the pilot failed to reply by radio. MS-NBC reported that:

"Pilots are supposed to hit each fix with pinpoint accuracy. If a plane deviates by 15 degrees, or two miles from that course, the flight controllers will hit the panic button. They'll call the plane, saying 'American 11, you're deviating from course.' It's considered a real emergency, like a police car screeching down a highway at 100 miles an hour. When golfer Payne Stewart's incapacitated Learjet missed a turn at a fix, heading north instead of west to Texas, F-16 interceptors were quickly dispatched."[292]

The FAA, in other words, immediately contacted the military when it was confirmed that the plane was off course, and communication with the plane was blocked. As CNN reported:

"Several Air Force and Air National Guard fighter jets, plus an AWACS radar control plane, helped the Federal Aviation Administration track the runaway Learjet and estimate when it would run out of fuel."[293]

Once a plane is intercepted by military jets, daytime communications with a commercial plane that fails to respond properly to radio contact are described by the FAA manual as follows: "… [The interceptor military craft communicates by] Rocking wings from a position slightly above and ahead of, and normally to the left of, the intercepted aircraft…" This action conveys the message: "You have been intercepted." The commercial jet is then supposed to respond by rocking its wings to indicate compliance, upon which the interceptor performs a "slow level turn, normally to the left, on to the desired heading [direction]." The commercial plane then responds by following the escort.[294]

The deviation of a plane from its designated flight path obviously creates a hazard in the form of a potential collision with another plane. The FAA thus has a clear definition of what constitutes an emergency situation: "Consider that an aircraft emergency exists... when:... There is unexpected loss of radar contact and radio communications with any... aircraft."[295] Elsewhere, the FAA states: "EMERGENCY DETERMINATIONS: If... you are in doubt that a situation constitutes an emergency or potential emergency, handle it as though it were an emergency."[296]

An FAA Air Defense Liaison Officer stationed in the headquarters of the North American Aerospace Defense Command (NORAD) plays the role of coordinating the FAA with the U.S. military to handle emergencies as efficiently as possible.[297] While NORAD normally scrambles fighter jets, if necessary, other military jets can be scrambled as well: "Normally, NORAD escort aircraft will take the required action. However, for the purpose of these procedures, the term 'escort aircraft' applies to any military aircraft assigned to the escort mission."[298]

Again, the response to the deviation of Payne Stuart's jet from its flight path provides an example. ABC News reported that:

"First, a fighter jet from Tyndall, Fla., was diverted from a routine training flight to check out the Learjet. Two F-16s from another Florida base then picked up the chase, later handing it over to two Air National Guard F-16s from Oklahoma, which handed it over to two F-16s from Fargo, North Dakota."[299]

As a matter of mandatory routine, the established instructions for a serious emergency are followed, and this includes emergencies involving the possibility of a hijacking. In the event of a serious emergency, or if a possible hijacking has occurred: "The escort service will be requested by the FAA hijack coordinator by direct contact with the National Military Command Center (NMCC)."[300]

The Department of Defense affirms the same, adding that once military planes are scrambled in accordance with immediate responses, the Department of Defense will be contacted for approval of special measures: "In the event of a hijacking, the NMCC will be notified by the most expeditious means by the FAA. The NMCC will, with the exception of immediate responses... forward requests for DoD [Department of Defense] assistance to the Secretary of Defense for approval."[301]

An *IEEE Spectrum* Special Report citing an Air Traffic Control expert further emphasises that: "Procedures dictate that controllers alert the U.S.

military when a hijacking is known to be under way. The typical response is for the Air Force to scramble intercept jets."[302]

It should be reiterated that procedures also require controllers to immediately alert the military to scramble fighter craft, if a plane deviates from its flight path and communication between the plane and controllers is blocked. This occurs whether or not the situation consists of a potential hijacking, as was the case with Payne Stuart's Lear jet, which was intercepted by military planes almost immediately, and while communication with the jet was blocked.

Indeed, "The U.S. military has their own radar network …(NORAD). They are tied into the FAA computer in order to get information on incoming flights." If a target is discovered "without flight plan information," or in violation of the same, "they will call on the 'shout' line to the appropriate [Air Traffic Control] Center sector for an ID." If the Center sector "has no datablock or other information on it, the military will usually scramble an intercept flight. Essentially always they turn out to be private pilots… not talking to anybody, who stray too far outside the boundary, then get picked up on their way back in. But, procedures are procedures, and they will likely find two F-18s on their tail within 10 or so minutes."[303] The NMCC can thus tap into radar stations to monitor emergencies and hijackings, as occurred during Payne Stewart's flight when "officers on the Joint Chiefs were monitoring the Learjet on radar screens inside the Pentagon's National Military Command Center."[304]

Indeed, according to the admission of NORAD spokesman Marine Corps Major Mike Snyder recorded in the *Boston Globe*, "its fighters routinely intercept aircraft":

"When planes are intercepted, they typically are handled with a graduated response. The approaching fighter may rock its wingtips to attract the pilot's attention, or make a pass in front of the aircraft. Eventually, it can fire tracer rounds in the airplane's path, or, under certain circumstances, down it with a missile."[305]

The well-known example of Payne Stuart's Learjet also gives an idea of the acceptable time periods of a routine air response. On 11th September, there was virtually no air response at all:

"… from the official National Transportation Safety Board crash report:
9:19 a.m. [of Payne Stewart's plane]:

The flight departs.

9:24: The Learjet's pilot responds to an instruction from air traffic control.

9:33: The controller radios another instruction. No response from the pilot. For 4 ½ minutes the controller tries to establish contact.

9:38: Having failed, the controller calls in the military. Note that he did not seek, nor did he require, the approval of the President of the United States, or indeed anyone. It's standard procedure, followed routinely, to call in the Air Force when radio contact with a commercial passenger jet is lost, or the plane departs from its flight path, or anything along those lines occurs.

9:54: 16 minutes later—the F-16 reaches the Learjet at 46,000 feet and conducts a visual inspection. Total elapsed time: 21 minutes."[306]

Flights 175 and 11

Using the chronology of events compiled by ABC News just after 11th September (timelines vary according to the source), all four commercial planes involved in the attacks took to the air between 7:59 a.m. and 8:14 a.m., 11th September 2001—including American Airlines Flight 11, United Airlines Flight 93, American Airlines Flight 77, and United Airlines Flight 175.

By 8:20 a.m., Flight 11, bound for Los Angeles, had made an unexpected hard turn left and begun heading toward New York. The craft's transponder, which allows the air traffic controller to identify the plane, was disconnected. Within moments, air traffic controllers noticed something was also very wrong with United Flight 175. Instead of heading west to its assigned destination California, it took a U-turn over New Jersey and headed northeast toward Manhattan's World Trade Center.

John Miller of ABC News reported that: "There doesn't seem to have been alarm bells going off, traffic controllers getting on with law enforcement or the military. There's a gap there that will have to be investigated..."[307] Indeed, it appears that the FAA did nothing for 18 minutes: "Boston ATC notifies NORAD that Flight 11 has been hijacked at 8:38."[308] But when radar and cockpit contact is blocked, and/or when planes deviate from their flight plan, standard FAA procedure is to order the scramble of fighter jets immediately in order to regain contact with the pilot. Indeed, the *New York Press* clarifies that:

> "According to The New York Times, air traffic controllers knew at 8:20 a.m. 'that American Airlines Flight 11, bound from Boston to Los Angeles, had probably been hijacked. When the first news report was made at 8:48 a.m. that a plane might have hit the World Trade Center, they knew it was Flight 11.' There was little ambiguity on the matter. The pilot had pushed a button on the aircraft yoke that allowed

controllers to hear the hijacker giving orders... The U.S. is supposed to scramble military aircraft the moment a hijacking is confirmed."[309]

In an earlier report on the subject, the *New York Press* also records that: "Initial reports suggested that no aircraft were scrambled to intercept or shoot down the hijacked jets."[310]

On 13th September, Acting Chairman of the Joint Chiefs of Staff and Air Force General Richard B. Myers stated before the Senate Armed Services Committee: "When it became clear what the threat was, we did scramble fighter aircraft, AWACS, radar aircraft and tanker aircraft to begin to establish orbits in case other aircraft showed up in the FAA system that were hijacked."

Myers was then asked: "Was that order that you just described given before or after the Pentagon was struck? Do you know?" The Air Force General admitted that he did know, replying: "That order, to the best of my knowledge, was after the Pentagon was struck."[311] Myers was asked three times before the Committee about the failure to scramble planes, and each time confirmed the same. At no time in this testimony did Myers indicate that he did not know, had not been in a position to know, or might be mistaken.

A spokesman for NORAD, Marine Corps Major Mike Snyder, corroborated Myers' testimony, explaining that no U.S. fighter jets had been scrambled at all until after the Pentagon crash. Reporting on the NORAD statement, the *Boston Globe* reported on 15th September that: "[T]he command did not immediately scramble any fighters even though it was alerted to a hijacking 10 minutes before the first plane... slammed into the first World Trade Center tower... The spokesman said the fighters remained on the ground until after the Pentagon was hit..." The failure to act was particularly surprising since Snyder had also admitted that "fighters routinely intercept aircraft."[312]

The same was admitted by Vice-President Dick Cheney on 16th September in a 'Meet the Press' session with NBC News correspondent Tim Russert, who observed that: "The first hijacking was confirmed at 8:20, the Pentagon was struck at 9:40, and yet, it seems we were not able to scramble fighter jets in time to protect the Pentagon and perhaps even more than that." Cheney did not dispute Russert's assertion, and further suggested that it was the President who made the decision to allow planes to scramble after the Pentagon crash.[313]

Suddenly, the official story changed. U.S. Air Force and government officials reneged on their own multiple testimonies, attempting to explain away the failure to respond to the attacks. Contradicting the initial reports and testimony of U.S. officials, it was later claimed that fighter jets had in fact been scrambled from Otis Air National Guard Base in Cape Cod, Massachusetts when the first tower was hit. It is in this context that the *New York Press* takes to task the shift in the official explanation:

> "So why were no fighters dispatched to intercept planes on an extraordinary day like Sept. 11? Within days the story changed and it turned out that two F-15 fighters had in fact been scrambled from Otis Air National Guard Base in Cape Cod, MA. Whether this took place before or after the first tower was struck is not clear. In any case it was too late to make a difference."[314]

Thus at 8:45 a.m., Flight 11 slammed into the North Tower of the World Trade Center near the 100th floor of the 110 storey building. According to the modified official version of the sequence of events, hastily propagated a few days later in contradiction to previous confessions, fighters from Otis were indeed ordered to scramble—at 8:44 a.m.. Even if we take these accounts seriously, they only bring up further questions and hardly exonerate the U.S. FAA and military.

Firstly, whenever fighter jets were scrambled, it was a long time after 8:20 a.m., when Flight 11's hijacking was fully confirmed. Secondly, there was a long gap before the fighters from Otis obeyed their already long overdue scrambling orders. Two F-15 Eagles supposedly managed to take off from the Otis ANG Base at 8:52 a.m.—8 minutes after being ordered to do so, which is almost triple the normal time for such aircraft to go from "scramble order" to 29,000 feet. Almost 32 minutes thus passed between the confirmation of the hijackings of Flight 11 and 175 and the scrambling of the intercept fighters—an ominous anomaly that has yet to be investigated.[315]

At 9:03 a.m., eighteen minutes after Flight 11's crash, Flight 175 smashed into the South Tower of the World Trade Centre, near the 90th floor. By this time, as noted by the *New York Press*: "When the second tower was hit the fighters were still 70 miles from Manhattan."[316]

But this should not have been a problem. The U.S. had eighteen minutes after the first plane hit the WTC in which to intercept Flight 175. New York City, where the WTC is based, is only 71 miles from McGuire Air Force Base in New Jersey, a major and active facility. An F-15 strike eagle flies at 1850+ nmph, equivalent to Mach 2.5+.

According to the U.S. Air Force's own website, as a matter of routine the aircraft goes from "scramble order" to 29000 feet in only 2.5 minutes. Even at Mach 2, an F-15 would cover the ground from New Jersey's Air Force Base to New York in under 3 minutes, and thus could have easily intercepted Flight 175. Yet this never happened.

The *New York Press* has also addressed the anomalies in the new 'official' version of events in detail:

"Clearly another, more comforting, story was needed, and on the evening of Sept. 14 CBS launched it by revealing that the FAA had indeed alerted U.S. air defense units of a possible hijacking at 8:38 a.m. on Tuesday, that six minutes later two F-15s received a scramble order at Otis Air National Guard Base on Cape Cod and that by 8:56 the F-15s were racing toward New York. Unfortunately, the fighters were still 70 miles away when the second jet hit the south tower. Meanwhile, at 9:30 a.m., three F-16s were launched from Langley Air Force base, 150 miles south of Washington. But just seven minutes later, at 9:37 a.m., Flight 77 smashed into the Pentagon. The F-16s arrived in Washington just before 10 a.m.

This story, which has now become the 'official' version, raises more questions than it answers. F-15s can travel at speeds of 1875 mph while F-16s can travel at 1500 mph [resp. 31 and 25 miles a *minute*]. If it took the F-16s half an hour to cover 150 miles, they could not have been traveling at more than 300 mph—at 20 percent capability. Boeing 767s and 757s have cruising speeds of 530 mph. Talk about a lack of urgency! Assuming Otis Air National Guard Base is about 180 miles away from Manhattan it should have taken the F-15s less than six minutes to arrive. Moreover, since Washington, DC, is little more than 200 miles from New York, the two F-15 fighters would have had time to get to DC, intercept Flight 77 and grab breakfast on the way.

Ah, but of course the transponders were turned off. So no one could keep track of the planes. If it were true that the moment a transponder is turned off a plane becomes invisible there would be no defense against enemy aircraft. Normal radar echo return from the metal surface of an aircraft would still identify it on the radar scope."[317]

Indeed, according to the Canadian Defense website, 'Canada-United States Defense Regulations:'

"NORAD uses a network of ground-based radars, sensors and fighter jets to detect, intercept and, if necessary, engage any threats to the continent... Through outstanding cooperation and cohesiveness, NORAD has proven itself effective in its roles of watching, warning and responding."[318]

Even if we believe the later version of events espoused by the U.S. government, claiming that planes were scrambled prior to the Pentagon crash, a close analysis of this new official account only confirms the consistent failure to respond in accordance with Standard Operating Procedures.

Flight 77

The *New York Press* continues to analyse the fate of Flight 77:

"We also learned that two F-16 fighters had been scrambled from Langley Air Force Base to try to intercept Flight 77, but they also arrived too late. In fact, they only took off from Langley two minutes before the Boeing 757 smashed into the Pentagon.

There are a number of problems with this story. In the first place, 45 minutes had elapsed from the time the air traffic controllers lost contact with Flight 77 and its crash into the Pentagon. On Sept. 15 The New York Times reported: 'Flight 77... would have been visible on the FAA's radar system as it reversed course in the Midwest...to fly back to Washington. The radars would have observed it even though its tracking beacon had been turned off.'"[319]

Flight 77 had first deviated from its flight plan at about 8:46 a.m. The *New York Times* noted that: "within a few minutes more... [i.e. 8:50] controllers would have known that... Flight 77 had probably been hijacked."[320] This was probably because "controllers at Washington Air Route Traffic Control Center—who handled American Airlines Flight 77, which hit the Pentagon—knew about the hijacking of American Flight 11 even before it crashed."[321]

Indeed, at 9:00 a.m., Flight 77's transponder signal ceased, as the plane flew back straight towards Washington DC. All this would normally have sufficed to compel the FAA to notify the military to scramble fighter craft, and in the extraordinary circumstances which had occurred with the hijacking of Flights 11 and 175 already confirmed, this would have been doubly necessary.

And again, when the first hijacked plane crashed into the World Trade Center, the emergency responses of U.S. air safety and defense systems should have been intensified. Apart from the fact that the Pentagon should already have been monitoring events, the country's emergency services were externally notified almost immediately. According to *Newsday*, at "9:06, Washington notifies all air traffic facilities nationwide of the suspected hijacking of Flight 11."[322] The Pentagon was notified of the emergency simultaneously. New York Police broadcast at 9:06 a.m. that: "This was a terrorist attack. Notify the Pentagon."[323] Flight 77 hit the Pentagon at around 9:40 a.m.

NORAD Commander Gen. Eberhart claimed in testimony before the Senate Armed Services Committee that the FAA had failed to notify

NORAD and the Department of Defense that the flight was heading toward Washington DC and had probably been hijacked, until 9:24 a.m.[324] This implies that there was an inexplicable gap of almost 45 minutes between the time the FAA had lost contact with Flight 77, which was heading directly toward Washington DC, and the time the FAA notified NORAD. This is despite the fact that it was clear at 9:06 a.m. that a terrorist attack was underway.

But anyhow, NORAD would have been monitoring the progress of these flights, including Flight 77, independently, and the Pentagon had already been notified. Indeed, according to the *New York Times*, "military officials in a command center on the east side of the [Pentagon] were urgently talking to law enforcement officials about what to do."[325] Taken into context with the fact that the Pentagon had been externally notified to the national emergency as early as 9:06, this means that military officials refused to scramble fighters for at least 20 minutes.

The implications of this gap are even more ominous given that NORAD apparently chose not to scramble fighter craft that were much closer to Washington DC. Instead, they chose to scramble interceptors from Langley Air Force Base, which is 130 miles from Washington—rather than Andrews Air Force Base, which is 10 miles away. The result was that "the fighter planes that scrambled into protective orbits around Washington did not arrive until 15 minutes after Flight 77 hit the Pentagon."[326]

The U.S. Department of Defense initially issued reports that there were simply no local fighter jets available to intercept Flight 77. According to *USA Today*, attempting to provide an explanation based on U.S. Department of Defense sources: "Andrews Air Force Base, home to Air Force One, is only 15 miles [sic] away from the Pentagon, but it had no fighters assigned to it. Defense officials won't say whether that has changed."

Yet in a report on the same day, *USA Today* stated in contradiction to its other story, that Andrews Air Force Base did actually have fighters present there—but supposedly they were not on alert: "The District of Columbia National Guard maintained fighter planes at Andrews Air Force Base, only about 15 miles [sic] from the Pentagon, but those planes were not on alert and not deployed."[327]

Both these reports amounted to disinformation, as is suggested by their mutual inconsistency. Quoting directly from U.S. National Guard sources, the *San Diego Union-Tribune* clarified the reality of the matter:

> "Air defense around Washington is provided mainly by fighter planes from Andrews Air Force Base in Maryland near the District of Columbia border. The D.C. Air National Guard is also based there and

equipped with F-16 fighter planes, a National Guard spokesman said. 'But the fighters took to the skies over Washington only after the devastating attack on the Pentagon.'"[328]

It is thus clear that combat-ready fighters assigned to the protection of Washington DC did not do anything at all for almost one and a half hours, although it was known that Flight 77 was heading toward DC. Even when NORAD was, according to Gen. Eberhart, notified by the FAA at 9:24 of the danger posed by Flight 77, rather than scrambling Andrews fighter craft 10 miles away from Washington DC, craft from more distant Langley Air Force base were scrambled instead.

Indeed, Andrews Air Force Base houses two combat-ready squadrons served by hundreds of full-time personnel: the 121st Fighter Squadron (FS-121) of the 113th Fighter Wing (FW-113), equipped with F-16 fighters; and the 321st Marine Fighter Attack Squadron (VMFA-321) of the 49th Marine Air Group, Detachment A (MAG-49 Det-A), equipped with F/A-18 fighters. According to the authoritative U.S. military information website, DC Military:

"...as part of its dual mission, the 113th provides capable and ready response forces for the District of Columbia in the event of a natural disaster or civil emergency. Members also assist local and federal law enforcement agencies in combating drug trafficking in the District of Colombia. [They] are full partners with the active Air Force...In the best tradition of the Marine Corps, a 'few good men and women' support two combat-ready reserve units at Andrews AFB. Marine Fighter Attack Squadron (VMFA) 321, a Marine Corps Reserve squadron, flies the sophisticated F/A-18 Hornet. Marine Aviation Logistics Squadron 49, Detachment A, provides maintenance and supply functions necessary to maintain a force in readiness."[329]

In other words, Andrews Air Force Base, an "active" facility, had at least two "combat-ready" squadrons designated for "capable and ready response," whose task was to defend DC in the event of "a natural disaster or civil emergency." These squadrons provide "capable and ready response forces," to maintain a "force in readiness."

These military terms constitute official Air Force jargon, which entail that fighter craft at Andrews are in a constant state of readiness to respond in the event of a disaster or emergency. In other words, they are available to be scrambled on emergencies. Other reports further show that Andrews aircraft were available to be alerted and activated in response to the Pentagon attack.

The *Sunday Telegraph* observed that: "Within minutes of the attack American forces around the world were put on one of their highest states of alert— Defcon 3, just two notches short of all-out war—and F-16s from Andrews Air Force Base were in the air over Washington DC."[330]

The *Denver Post* similarly reported that:

"… an audible gasp went up from the rear of the audience as a large black plume of smoke arose from the Pentagon. Terrorism suddenly was at the doorstep and clearly visible through the big glass windows overlooking the Potomac River. Overhead, fighter jets scrambled from Andrews Air Force Base and other installations and cross-crossed the skies…A thick plume of smoke was climbing out of the hollow center of the Pentagon. Everyone on the train understood what had happened moments before."[331]

NBC similarly clarified that Andrews aircraft were only scrambled after the hijacked plane crashed into the Pentagon, and not at all before this time: "It was after the attack on the Pentagon that the Air Force then decided to scramble F-16s out of the DC National Guard Andrews Air Force Base to fly cover, a protective cover over Washington, DC."[332] As Jared Israel pointedly remarks: "The media should have demanded to know the truth about why fighter jets assigned to protect Washington didn't scramble an hour *before* the Pentagon was hit." He asks:

"… since planes were flying into buildings, and since Washington, DC was the city most likely to be the next target, why would planes be scrambled all the way from Langley Air Force Base, 129 miles from Washington, as late as 9:30? Why wouldn't they be scrambled from Andrews Air Force Base, 10 miles from the Pentagon, at around 8:50, when the military knew that a hijacked plane had hit the World Trade Center?"[333]

An Egyptian military-strategic analyst whose expertise is accredited by both the U.S. Army and the British Ministry of Defence has asked a similar question. Retired Major General Dr. Mahmoud Khalaf—a Fellow at Egypt's Higher Military Academy, Member of the Royal College of Defence Studies in London, Honorary Member of the Association of the United States Army in Fort Benning (Georgia), and a participant in several training courses with the U.S. Army in the United States and Germany—comments:

"The first question [is related to] the air-defense system, the North American aerospace defense command (NORAD). This system is a very sophisticated system, and it is supposed to detect any airplane that takes off...

One pilot did warn. He contacted the Federal Aviation Administration (FAA), and indeed informed it that there was a hijacking, and the air-defense command was informed. We have a surprising case here. The air base in Andrews: this air base, by the way, has its own defense system around the base, which consists of two jet fighters (which can scramble); they would be in the air within 2-3 minutes. The squadron in Andrews received the alert in the same moment but did not fly? This issue disappeared and nobody talked about it. This is noteworthy."[334]

The official U.S. government explanation of this dire failure to protect Washington DC can be found in excerpts from an NBC press conference with U.S. Vice-President Dick Cheney:

"Journalist Mr Russert: What's the most important decision you think he [President Bush] made during the course of the day?

Dick Cheney: Well, the—I suppose the toughest decision was this question of whether or not we would intercept incoming commercial aircraft... We decided to do it. We'd, in effect, put a flying combat air patrol up over the city; F-16s with an AWACS, which is an airborne radar system, and tanker support so they could stay up a long time... It doesn't do any good to put up a combat air patrol if you don't give them instructions to act, if, in fact, they feel it's appropriate."[335]

Cheney had clearly created the impression that the U.S. military required Presidential authorisation to scramble fighter jets to intercept American Airlines Flight 77 before it hit the Pentagon. He seems to have done so on the basis of witnessing actual discussions within the White House related to this issue. He also avoided any discussion of the ominous failure to intercept this flight. Both these actions on his part amounted to disinformation, intended or unintended.

According to Air Force standard operating procedures, Presidential approval is required only for shooting down a civilian aircraft. Therefore, the idea that the interception of the incoming commercial aircraft by fighter planes was "the toughest decision" to be made on Presidential authority is in contradiction to the rules recorded in FAA documents, which establish that fighter jets routinely intercept commercial aircraft under designated circumstances. White House approval is not required for these interceptions.

Contrary to what Cheney implied, and as documented here, fighter jet interceptions of commercial aircraft are followed through automatically (and on a mandatory basis) in emergencies, such as hijackings. The idea inadvertently suggested by Cheney, apparently based on the occurrence of White House discussions in which he was involved, is that the President had somehow intervened in these routine rules, leading to their almost total disruption.

Cheney's testimonial on NBC implied that it was the President who decided to allow planes to scramble one and a half hours too late, thus bearing principal responsibility for the sabotage of systems designed to protect civilians. Cheney further suggested that interception of the commercial flight automatically implied shooting it down. "It doesn't do any good to put up a combat air patrol if you don't give them instructions to act, if, in fact, they feel it's appropriate," he stated.

> **"Journalist Mr Russert:** So if the United States government became aware that a hijacked commercial airline was destined for the White House or the Capitol, we would take the plane down?
>
> **Dick Cheney::** Yes. The president made the decision... that if the plane would not divert... as a last resort, our pilots were authorized to take them out. Now, people say, you know, that's a horrendous decision to make. Well, it is. You've got an airplane full of American citizens, civilians, captured by... terrorists, headed and are you going to, in fact, shoot it down, obviously, and kill all those Americans on board?
>
> ...It's a presidential-level decision, and the president made, I think, exactly the right call in this case, to say, 'I wished we'd had combat air patrol up over New York.'"[336]

The American Heritage Dictionary defines "intercept" as follows: "to stop, deflect or interrupt the progress or intended course of." Interception of a plane is thus aimed at changing its course and does not in itself imply violence. The question as to why no fighter craft were scrambled to intercept Flight 77, as would happen in any routine emergency, thus remains as pertinent as ever, since in this respect there was no burning issue of whether or not a commercial plane should be shot down. Another question also remains—Why did no fighter craft scramble before the Pentagon was hit?

Cheney apparently deflected attention from this issue in the astonishing assertion that: "It doesn't do any good to put up a combat air patrol if you don't give them instructions to act, if, in fact, they feel it's appropriate." Here, Cheney claimed not only that White House approval is necessary to consider whether or not the routine scrambling of fighters should occur— when in fact such scrambling takes place automatically, according to clear FAA rules—but that this was because detailed instructions are needed from White House as to what the craft should perform. Otherwise, Cheney asserted, there is no point in putting up "combat air patrol."

Cheney thus seemed to inadvertently admit that the White House Cabinet was responsible for the failure of combat air patrol to scramble, and thus responsible for the violation of Standard Operating Procedures. It is worth emphasising that Cheney's statements indicate that his understanding of the President's role in determining the response of the U.S. Air Force appears to be based on his direct experience of the decision-making process that occurred among members of his Cabinet.

Evaluating such evidence Jared Israel observes:

"Mr. Cheney's implicit argument—that there is no point in sending up an escort unless the pilot has clearance to shoot down a commercial jet—is absurd. Why would such a decision have to be made in advance of scrambling the escort? Even if an airliner has been taken over by a terrorist with a suicide mission, how could Mr. Cheney, Mr. Bush or anyone else other than God Himself possibly predict how the hijacker would respond to an intercept by military jets? Even if a hijacker were ready to die for the glory of crashing into the Pentagon, does that mean he would also be ready to die for the glory of ignoring a military pilot's order to land? So even if the military had no authority to shoot down Flight 77, why not send up escort planes? Isn't that in fact how police and the military routinely handle hijack situations—by mobilizing a potentially overwhelming force in the hope of getting the hijacker to surrender?"[337]

The question that thus remains is, why did no fighter craft scramble for interception between when Flight 77 was hijacked (between 8:50 and 8:55 AM) and the time the plane smashed into the Pentagon (very close to 9:41 a.m.)? Why were routine emergency response rules violated for so long and so consistently?

A recap of the events of 11th September only exacerbates these concerns. For 35 minutes, from 8:15 a.m. until 9:05 a.m., it was widely known within both the FAA and the U.S. military that planes had been hijacked and had subsequently deviated off their designated flight paths. Despite this, it was not until after Flight 77 smashed into the Pentagon at around 9:40 a.m. that any Washington-based Air Force planes were scrambled to intercept. And according to initial reports, no planes at all were scrambled throughout the U.S. until this time.

In other words, the National Command Authority did virtually nothing for as long as 95 minutes, in systematic violation of its own rules and instructions for dealing with such situations, despite the fact that local 'combat ready' aircraft were available to be scrambled. Astonishingly, it was after over one whole hour and thirty-five minutes—involving three crashes of aircraft into key U.S buildings—that U.S. fighter planes from Andrews finally scrambled and flew over Washington DC. It is noteworthy that this is the first time in history that such a failure has occurred—air authorities respond to problems and emergencies almost immediately on a routine basis.[338]

Flight 93

The travesty did not end there, but continued with the fourth plane, United Airlines Flight 93. Director of the U.S. Air National Guard, Major General Paul Weaver, stated that: "[n]o Air National Guard or other military planes were scrambled to chase the fourth hijacked airliner, United Airlines Flight 93."[339] This is even more astonishing. Three hijacked commercial planes had already crashed consecutively into the World Trade Center and the Pentagon, yet no military craft were scrambled to at least intercept the fourth hijacked plane—a plane which crashed in Pennsylvania almost an hour and a half after the first Tower was hit.

Downplaying the dire implications of the utter absence of interceptors being scrambled in accordance with compulsory FAA and Department of Defense rules, U.S. Deputy Defense Secretary Paul Wolfowitz stated that: "[T]he Air Force was tracking the hijacked plane that crashed in Pennsylvania on Tuesday after other airliners slammed into the Pentagon and World Trade Center and had been in a position to bring it down if necessary."[340]

Wolfowitz also explained that: "any military intervention would have ultimately been the decision of President George W. Bush."[341] But this obscured the facts. The Air Force should have immediately scrambled military craft to intercept the plane, yet the Director of the Air National Guard confirmed that no planes at all were scrambled—in violation of the Guard's own rules governing methods of emergency response.

The issue is not whether the Air Force was monitoring Flight 93, which it certainly should and would have been, but why the mandatory procedure of scrambling fighter jets to at least intercept the plane was not followed. As the *New York Press* commented incredulously: "So why was it not brought down? Or at the very least intercepted? Three key buildings had been attacked. And there is still no emergency!"[342]

An Overview of the Collapse of SOP on 9-11

U.S. military expert Stan Goff has summarised the sequence of events well. Goff is a 26-year U.S. military veteran. A retired U.S. Army Special Forces Master Sergeant who was tactics instructor at the U.S. Army's Jungle Operations Training Center in Panama, Goff taught Military Science and Doctrine at the U.S. Military Academy at West Point, and was involved in operations in eight designated conflict areas from Vietnam to Haiti. He observes:

"I have no idea why people aren't asking some very specific questions about the actions of Bush and company on the day of the attacks...

Four planes get hijacked and deviate from their flight plans, all the while on FAA radar. The planes are all hijacked between 7:45 and 8:10 AM Eastern Daylight Time. Who is notified? This is an event already that is unprecedented. But the President is not notified and going to a Florida elementary school to hear children read.

By around 8:15 AM, it should be very apparent that something is terribly wrong. The President is glad-handing teachers. By 8:45, when American Airlines Flight 11 crashes into the World Trade Center, Bush is settling in with children for his photo ops at Booker Elementary. Four planes have obviously been hijacked simultaneously, an event never before seen in history, and one has just dived into the worlds best know twin towers, and still no one notifies the nominal Commander in Chief.

No one has apparently scrambled any Air Force interceptors either. At 9:03, United Flight 175 crashes into the remaining World Trade Center building. At 9:05, Andrew Card, the Presidential Chief of Staff whispers to George W. Bush. Bush 'briefly turns somber' according to reporters. Does he cancel the school visit and convene an emergency meeting? No. He resumes listening to second graders... and continues this banality even as American Airlines Flight 77 conducts an unscheduled point turn over Ohio and heads in the direction of Washington DC.

Has he instructed Chief of Staff Card to scramble the Air Force? No. An excruciating 25 minutes later, he finally deigns to give a public statement telling the United States what they already have figured out; that there's been an attack by hijacked planes on the World Trade Center. There's a hijacked plane beelining to Washington, but has the Air Force been scrambled to defend anything yet? No.

At 9:30, when he makes his announcement, American Flight 77 is still ten minutes from its target, the Pentagon. The Administration will later claim they had no way of knowing that the Pentagon might be a target, and that they thought Flight 77 was headed to the White House, but the fact is that the plane has already flown South and past the White House no-fly zone, and is in fact tearing through the sky at over 400 nauts.

At 9:35, this plane conducts another turn, 360 degrees over the Pentagon, all the while being tracked by radar, and the Pentagon is not evacuated, and there are still no fast-movers from the Air Force in the sky over Alexandria and DC. Now, the real kicker: A pilot they want us to believe was trained at a Florida puddle-jumper school for Piper Cubs and Cessnas, conducts a well-controlled downward spiral, descending the last 7,000 feet in two-and-a-half minutes, brings the plane in so low and flat that it clips the electrical wires across the street from the Pentagon, and flies it with pinpoint accuracy into the side of this building at 460 nauts.

When the theory about learning to fly this well at the puddle-jumper school began to lose ground, it was added that they received further training on a flight simulator. This is like saying you prepared your teenager for her first drive on I-40 at rush hour by buying her a video driving game... There is a story being constructed about these events."[343]

Stan Goff's observations are very important, and should be duly noted. He testifies that, in his opinion as a U.S. military expert, the official version of events is not the reality, but rather a "story being constructed" by the government. He bases this conclusion on his in-depth understanding of the procedures and capabilities of the U.S. military.

The question that then remains is this: what is the government attempting to deflect attention from, by the construction of false "stories"? As this analysis has demonstrated with certainty, at every step during the escalating crisis on 11th September, clear rules governing the emergency response of U.S. air authorities were systematically broken. The *New York Press* rightly concludes:

"Passenger jet hijackings are not uncommon and the U.S. government has prepared detailed plans to handle them. On Sept. 11 these plans were ignored in their entirety... Here are the FAA regulations concerning hijackings: 'The FAA hijack coordinator...on duty at Washington headquarters will request the military to provide an escort aircraft for a confirmed hijacked aircraft... The escort service will be requested by the FAA hijack coordinator by direct contact with the National Military Command Center (NMCC).' Here are the instructions issued by the Chairman of the Joint Chiefs of Staff on June 1, 2001: 'In the event of a hijacking, the NMCC will be notified by the most expeditious means by the FAA. The NMCC will...forward requests for DOD assistance to the Secretary of Defense for approval.'... The U.S. is supposed to scramble military aircraft the moment a hijacking is confirmed."[344]

But the repeated testimony of the Chairman of the Joint Chiefs of Staff, the Vice-President and NORAD spokesmen confirms that no planes at all were scrambled until after the Pentagon attack. The next crucial question is then: why were these rules, normally adhered to with such routine, suddenly violated on 11th September—especially considering the extensive advance warnings of the attacks that were received by the U.S. military intelligence community?

What occurred on this tragic day was clearly just the sort of emergency that air authorities are fully trained, instructed, experienced, ready and available to deal with. Yet, although four planes were simultaneously hijacked, air authorities did almost nothing about it—in violation of the mandatory rules of response.

It is also an integral aspect of these rules that emergencies are passed on to NORAD and the National Command in the Pentagon, which, if necessary, are backed by government officials in the Department of Defense and other key U.S. leaders with military authority. It is their fundamental duty to monitor and oversee the process of responding to such emergencies. Therefore, these agencies bear ultimate responsibility for violation of the basic instructions, which were designed to deter crises and save lives in emergency situations.

It should also be noted that, on analysis of the official version of events, the FAA failed to contact the military in accordance with standard procedures (the military subsequently also failed to respond in accordance with standard procedures). It also appears that the FAA had "open lines" with the U.S. Secret Service—at least as soon as the first WTC Tower was hit.[345] This suggests that the Secret Service, which was thereafter in constant contact with the FAA, was aware of, and involved in the situation. Therefore, the Secret Service bears additional responsibility for the latter's violations of procedure.

Indeed, it is worth noting the observations of Anatoli Kornukov, the Commander-in-Chief of the Russian Air Force—which of course is closely collaborating with the United States in the 'war on terror'—on the official line of the U.S. government. The Russian current affairs periodical *Pravda Online* reported:

> "'Generally it is impossible to carry out an act of terror on the scenario which was used in the USA yesterday.' This was said by the commander-in-chief of the Russian Air Force, Anatoli Kornukov. 'We had such facts [i.e., events or incidents] too,' said the general straightforwardly. Kornukov did not specify what happened in Russia and when and to what extent it resembled the events in the US. He did not advise what was the end of air terrorists' attempts either. But the fact the general said that means a lot. As it turns out the way the terrorists acted in America is not unique. The notification and control system for the air transport in Russia does not allow uncontrolled flights and leads to immediate reaction of the anti-missile defense,

Kornukov said. 'As soon as something like that happens here, I am reported about that right away and in a minute we are all up,' said the general."[346]

It is, of course, well known that the U.S. Air Force is far superior to Russia's. There are few reasonable inferences one can draw from this analysis. Attempting to explain the absolute negligence of the Air Force on 11th September by alluding to the novelty of the threat, allegedly leading to mistakes as a result of tactical surprise, fails to account for the fact that established procedures are in place to anticipate such threats. As already noted, for instance, there is a manual governing emergency response rules for hijackings. The question that then remains is why Standard Operating Procedures (SOP) were not followed, and in this context, who ensured that SOP was not followed, and for what purpose?

Myers and Bush on 9-11: Negligence Points to Complicity

An inkling of an answer to this question may be found in the shocking inaction of General Richard B. Myers, and of President George W. Bush Jr., on 11th September. According to the *Washington Post*, former NORAD Commander Gen. Richard B. Myers "was deeply involved in the military's response [on 11th September] this week from the outset."[347]

That morning, the *New York Press* reports, the Chairman of the Joint Chiefs of Staff, Gen. Myers, was having a routine meeting on Capitol Hill with Senator Max Cleland.[348] According to the American Forces Press Service (AFPS), just before the meeting began: "While in an outer office, he said, he saw a television report that a plane had hit the World Trade Center. 'They thought it was a small plane or something like that,' Myers said. So the two men went ahead with the office call."[349]

In other words, having been notified of an unprecedented emergency in New York, with a plane for the first time in history ploughing into the World Trade Center, the response of these two officials, and specifically of Gen. Myers, who has specific responsibility to oversee the military response to such emergencies, was to ignore it. This constituted a direct and apparently quite deliberate negligence of his military duty during this obviously unprecedented crisis. While Myers and Cleland chatted away, a "hijacked jet plowed into the World Trade Center's north tower, another one plowed into the south tower and a third one into the Pentagon. And still they went on with their meeting."[350] The AFPS further noted in this connection that:

"Meanwhile, the second World Trade Center tower was hit by another jet. 'Nobody informed us of that,' Myers said. 'But when we came out, that was obvious. Then, right at that time, somebody said the Pentagon had been hit.'

Somebody thrust a cell phone in Myers' hand. Gen. Ralph Eberhart, commander of U.S. Space Command and the North American Aerospace Defense Command [NORAD] was on the other end of the line 'talking about what was happening and the actions he was going to take.'"[351]

In his testimony before the Senate Armed Services Committee, Myers additionally confirmed that the decision to scramble fighter craft was made during his conversation with the current Commander of NORAD, Gen. Eberhart: "I spoke to the commander of NORAD, General Eberhart. And at that point, I think the decision was at that point to start launching aircraft." This statement is particularly damning given that in the same testimony, Myers also confirmed that the Pentagon had been overseeing the crisis at least as soon as the first of the Twin Towers was hit:

"**Senator Levin:** The time that we don't have is when the Pentagon was notified, if they were, by the FAA or the FBI or any other agency, relative to any potential threat or any planes having changed direction or anything like that. And that's the same which you will give us because that's...

Myers: I can answer that. At the time of the first impact on the World Trade Center, we stood up our crisis action team. That was done immediately. So we stood it up. And we started talking to the federal agencies. The time I do not know is when NORAD responded with fighter aircraft. I don't know that time."[352]

These reports indicate, apart from Myers' utter indifference to notification of an air attack on the WTC, and corroborating what has been discussed above, that the U.S. military had been monitoring the crisis at least as soon as the first tower had been hit. Yet Myers also testified that the military only began to consider actions to be taken in response to the attacks, after the Pentagon was hit. The Acting Chairman of the Joint Chiefs Myers was apparently contacted by NORAD Commander Gen. Eberhart about "the actions he was going to take," *after* three hijacked civilian planes had already hit the World Trade Center and the Pentagon, at which time it was finally decided between them to scramble aircraft.

This suggests that both Air Force Gen. Myers and Gen. Eberhart knowingly violated mandatory standard emergency response procedures by considering a response to the hijackings almost one and a half hours later than they should have. Indeed, aircraft should have been scrambled immediately and automatically, as soon as the hijackings were confirmed—

indeed, as soon as the planes had deviated from their flight paths, and communication between them and air control was blocked.

Routine procedures dictate that high-level military approval is required only for special measures and _after_ fighter craft have already scrambled. Yet, it appears that both Myers and Eberhart waited until after the Pentagon was attacked before allowing fighter craft to be scrambled. It is also worth noting that Senator Max Cleland, Chairman of the Personnel Subcommittee of the Armed Services Committee and member of the Senate Governmental Affairs Committee, was also involved in this astonishing process of indifference—he was fully aware of the unfolding crisis, yet like Myers, was quite unmoved.

George Bush Jr.'s response illustrated a similar indifference. The _New York Press_ continues to note that meanwhile, in Florida, "just as President Bush was about to leave his hotel he was told about the attack on the first WTC tower. He was asked by a reporter if he knew what was going on in New York." ABC News has confirmed this. John Cochran, who was covering the President's trip, informed Peter Jennings on ABC TV:

> "He [the President] got out of his hotel suite this morning, was about to leave, reporters saw the White House chief of staff, Andy Card, whisper into his ear. The reporter said to the president, 'Do you know what's going on in New York?' He said he did, and he said he will have something about it [i.e. a statement] later."[353]

As the _Press_ reports, "He said he did, and then went to an elementary school in Sarasota to read to children."[354] Another statement from Vice-President Cheney provides further insight into this: "The Secret Service has an arrangement with the FAA. They had open lines after the World Trade Center was…" Cheney never finished his sentence, but it is obvious that he had meant to say something along the lines of "hit."[355] It is also well known that, as respected Canadian media critic Barry Zwicker points out:

> "The (president of the United States)… travels with an entire staff… (including) the Secret Service, which is responsible for his safety. The members of this support team have the best communications equipment in the world. They maintain contact with, or can easily reach, Bush's cabinet, the national Military Command Center in the Pentagon, the (FAA)…"

But Zwicker also reports that: "By 8:20, according to its own official report, the Federal Aviation Authority, the FAA, is fully aware of the unprecedented emergency in the skies." The implications are duly noted by Zwicker as follows: "In other words, around 8:46 at the absolute latest the Secret Service and the President would have known of all four hijacked airliners and that one had hit the World Trade Center."[356]

Yet only the President, Commander-in-Chief of the U.S. military, had the authority to order the shooting down of a civilian airliner. Additionally, the U.S. military command and Department of Defense—of which Air Force General Myers is a leading figure as Chairman of the Joint Chiefs—are integrally involved in responding and/or approving various measures once planes are scrambled.

But rather than immediately holding an emergency meeting on the situation to consider special instructions for interceptors, Bush continued to the elementary school where he went on to read to children. The sheer indifference of both Myers and Bush at a time when they carried, among other U.S. government and military officials, responsibility for the country's security is both astonishing and revealing: *indicative of a scale of negligence amounting to effective complicity.*

If these individuals had acted sooner, they might have averted the later attacks on the World Trade Center and the Pentagon, saving thousands of lives. Yet by refusing to respond in any way at all to the attacks, and by deliberately continuing with their comparatively mundane activities, they shirked their specific duties to the American people, thereby playing their own role in ensuring that the attacks went ahead unhindered.

The negligence displayed by President Bush indicates a wider, systematic negligence amongst the U.S. Secret Service and military command. Despite his own critical responsibility as Commander-in-Chief, with the sole authority to shoot down a civilian airplane, the President was able to continue on his way to the elementary school in Sarasota, without any apparent protest or advice from the Secret Service and military, which should have called him for an emergency meeting immediately after the first WTC attack occurred.

This broad circle of systematic, top-level U.S. military negligence, despite knowledge of the WTC attack and further impending attacks, since the flight paths of the other planes and their consequent destinations were being monitored by the Pentagon, suggests their complicity through a deliberate, orchestrated failure to act.

Moreover, the damning implications of this sequence of events simply cannot be understood without considering that Standard Operating Procedures (SOP) were completely and inexplicably dropped on 11th September—something that had never occurred before. The question then remains as to who was responsible for ensuring that routine emergency response rules were not adhered to, and why.

In the opinion of this author, the total lack of interest on the part of the Bush administration in the answer to this question, so as to locate the roots of the collapse of SOP on 11th September, incriminates them further.

Jared Israel's conclusions in his work, as featured by the *New York Press*, are disconcerting, but constitute an explanation that follows logically from an analysis of the available data concerning the terrible events of 11th September:

> "Some of what happened on 9-11, such as planes flying into buildings, is unusual. But most of what happened, such as commercial jets flying off-course, transponder failures and possible hijackings, are common emergencies... [T]hese emergencies are routinely handled with expert efficiency based on clear rules...
>
> U.S. air safety and air defense emergency systems are activated in response to problems every day. On 9-11 they failed despite, not because of, the extreme nature of the emergency. This could only happen if individuals in high positions worked in a coordinated way to make them fail."

It is conceivable that this sort of coordinated, high-level collapse could occur—either through deliberate intent on the part of these individuals to cause emergency systems to fail, or through systematic, unintentional incompetence—reaching to the highest levels of the U.S. military command. The latter is an extremely implausible scenario, because if such systematic, unintentional incompetence could occur simultaneously at such high levels, it would have to be the consequence of a grotesque degree of institutional incompetence throughout the emergency response services of the FAA, NORAD, the U.S. Air Force, and other relevant institutions.

If this was the case, however, then evidence of institutional incompetence within these emergency response services should have frequently surfaced during previous responses to routine emergencies, possible hijackings, and so on. *There is no such evidence.*

As Israel rightly pointed out, "commercial jets flying off-course, transponder failures and possible hijackings, are common emergencies... [T]hese emergencies are routinely handled with expert efficiency based on clear rules."

Israel further argues in relation to the coordinated collapse of emergency response systems on 11th September: "Such operatives would almost surely have failed if they tried to disrupt and abort routine protection systems without top-level support. The failure of the emergency systems would be noticed immediately." This would be the case whether these operatives had acted out of intent to cause a collapse, or out of mere incompetence.

"Moreover, given the catastrophic nature of the attacks, the highest military authorities would be alerted. Acting on their own, the operatives could expect that their orders would be countermanded and that they themselves would be arrested [or dealt with in an otherwise appropriate manner]."

Thus, Israel concludes: "The sabotage of routine protective systems, controlled by strict hierarchies, would never have been contemplated let alone attempted absent the involvement of the supreme U.S. military command."

"This includes at least U.S. President George Bush, U.S. Secretary of Defense Donald Rumsfeld and the then-Acting Head of the Joint Chiefs of Staff, Air Force General Richard B. Myers. [This demonstrates] probable cause for charging the above-named persons with treason for complicity in the murders of thousands of people whom they had sworn to protect."[357]

Award-winning Canadian journalist and media analyst Barry Zwicker— former correspondent for the *Toronto Sun* and the *Globe and Mail*, and currently a media critic on *CBC-TV*, *CTV's News1*, and *Vision TV*—boldly dissects the official line:

"Throughout the northeastern United States are many air bases. But that morning no interceptors respond in a timely fashion to the highest alert situation. This includes the Andrews squadrons which have the longest lead time and are 12 miles from the White house.

Whatever the explanation for the huge failure, there have been no reports, to my knowledge, of reprimands. This further weakens the 'Incompetence Theory.' Incompetence usually earns reprimands. This causes me to ask—and other media need to ask—if there were 'stand down' orders."[358]

Elaborating on this in a media commentary for Vision TV, Zwicker concludes:

"The multiple hijackings are unprecedented. The first occurs at 7:45 in the morning. It's a full hour before the first plane hits the World Trade Center. But it's an hour and 20 minutes—and after the second plane hits—that the President allegedly becomes informed. Think about that. Then, he gives no orders. Why? He continues to listen to a student talk about her pet goat. Why?

It's another 25 minutes until he makes a statement, even as flight 77 is making a bee-line for Washington, DC. In the almost two hours of the total drama not a single U.S. Air Force interceptor turns a wheel until it's too late. Why? Was it total incompetence on the part of aircrews trained and equipped to scramble in minutes?

Well, unlike the U.S. Air Force, I'll cut to the chase. Simply to ask these few questions is to find the official narrative frankly implausible. The more questions you pursue, it becomes more plausible that there's a different explanation: namely, that elements within the top U.S. military, intelligence and political leadership—which are closely intertwined—are complicit in what happened on September the 11th."[359]

This conclusion is supported by the behaviour of President Bush, Gen. Myers, Gen. Eberhart, as well as other U.S. officials around them, while planes manned by Al-Qaeda terrorists were ploughing successively into the World Trade Center and Pentagon. In light of what appears to be their studious indifference to the attacks while they occurred, despite their responsibility for the nation's security and their critical role in decisions relating to the behaviour of the Air Force, Israel's inferences, like Zwicker's, become only more pertinent. Indeed, the astonishing responses of Bush and Myers should be understood in context with the revelations contained in this previously discussed statement of U.S. Vice-President Dick Cheney:

"... the toughest decision was this question of whether or not we would intercept incoming commercial aircraft...

We decided to do it. We'd, in effect, put a flying combat air patrol up over the city; F-16s with an AWACS, which is an airborne radar system, and tanker support so they could stay up a long time... It doesn't do any good to put up a combat air patrol if you don't give them instructions to act, if, in fact, they feel it's appropriate... It's a presidential-level decision, and the president made, I think, exactly the right call in this case, to say, 'I wished we'd had combat air patrol up over New York.' "[360]

These observations place the testimony of Myers in context. What is indisputably clear from Cheney's testimonials on NBC's 'Meet the Press,' is that there were certain discussions among the nation's top decision-makers in the White House, including the President, which fundamentally determined the response of the U.S. Air Force on 11th September 2001. Cheney confirms this on the basis of what appears to be his direct experience of, and participation in, these discussions.

Cheney stated that the entire issue of scrambling planes for interception on 11th September was a "presidential-level decision." Cheney also explicitly indicated that the decision to scramble planes was discussed by members of the White House Cabinet, who eventually "decided to do it" with Presidential authorisation. This is highly significant, in that it places direct responsibility for the behaviour of the U.S. Air Force on 11th September on the President and his Cabinet.

Furthermore, according to Cheney, the critical decision that was issued by leading members of the Cabinet, with Presidential authorisation, resulted in planes being scrambled over New York— nearly one and a half hours later than what is required by FAA and Department of Defense manuals.

This is also highly significant, in that it indicates that the failure of the U.S. Air Force to immediately scramble planes, in violation of mandatory standard procedures, was the direct result of a high-level White House decision. At face value then, Cheney's testimony suggests that the blame for the obstruction of mandatory standard procedures lies squarely on the President and members of his Cabinet.

Placing this in context with our above discussion, it thus appears that NORAD's decision to scramble fighter craft, following Gen. Eberhart's consultation with Gen. Myers and after the Pentagon attacks (as opposed to immediately), was the ultimate consequence of a Presidential-level decision from within the White House.

In the opinion of this author, this strongly suggests that significant, high-level elements of the U.S. military and the Bush administration bear direct responsibility for the terrorist acts that occurred on 11th September on U.S. soil, through what appears to be a combination of deliberate action and inaction.

The facts on record weigh strongly in favour of this conclusion, providing reasonable grounds to believe that these officials were complicit in the 11th September attacks, through the active obstruction of routine protective systems, which are designed to automatically deflect the type of emergencies that occurred on 11th September. This appears to have been maintained through the orchestrated prolongation (for up to one and a half hours) of systematic negligence as the attacks occurred, on the part of elements of the FAA, NORAD, the Pentagon, the Secret Service, the White House and the President—despite the clear danger they presented.

Of course, outside of a full-blown independent investigation, it is impossible to provide a conclusive analysis, and one cannot pretend that the documentation gathered here suffices as final proof of these conclusions. A further inquiry is therefore essential, to fully understand the events of 11th September, in the context of the lack of a response by the U.S. Air Force. Nevertheless, pending such an inquiry and its findings, it is the opinion of this author that the inferences made here best explain the documentation presented.

Notes

[289] Szamuely, George, 'Scrambled Messages,' *New York Press*, Vol. 14, No. 50, www.nypress.com/14/50/taki/bunker.cfm.

[290] Israel, Jared and Bykov, Illarion, 'Guilty for 9-11: Bush, Rumsfeld, Myers Part 1,' The Emperor's New Clothes, 14 Nov. 2001, Updated 17 November 2001, http://emperors-clothes.com/indict/indict-1.htm.

[291] See FAA Order 7400.2E, 'Procedures for Handling Airspace Matters,' Effective Date: 7 December 2000 (Includes Change 1, effective 7 July 2001), Chapter 14-1-2. Full text posted at: www.faa.gov/ATpubs/AIR/air1401. html#14-1-2. Also see Dennis, Gregory and Torlak, Emina, 'Direct-To Requirements' http://sdg.lcs.mit.edu/atc/D2Requirements.htm.

[292] MS-NBC, 12 September 2001, www.msnbc.com/news/627524.asp.

[293] CNN, 26 October 1999.

[294] FAA 'Aeronautical Information Manual: Official Guide to Basic Flight Information and Air Traffic Control (ATC) Procedures,' (Includes Change 3 Effective: 12 July 2001) Chapter 5-6-4 'Interception Signals,' Full text posted at: www.faa.gov/ATpubs/AIM/Chap5/aim0506.html#5-6-4.

[295] FAA Order 7110.65M, 'Air Traffic Control,' (Includes Change 3 Effective: 12 July 2001), Chapter 10-2-5 'Emergency Situations,' Full text posted at: www.faa.gov/ATpubs/ATC/Chp10/atc1002.html#10-2-5.

[296] FAA Order 7110.65M, 'Air Traffic Control' (Includes Change 3 Effective: 12 July 2001), Chapter 10-1-1 'Emergency Determinations,' Full text posted at: www.faa.gov/ATpubs/ATC/Chp10/atc1001.html#10-1-1.

[297] FAA Order 7610.4J 'Special Military Operations' (Effective Date: 3 Nov. 1998; Includes: Change 1, effective 3 July 2000; Change 2, effective 12 July 2001), Chapter 4, Section 5, 'Air Defense Liaison Officers.' Full text posted at: www.faa.gov/ATpubs/MIL/Ch4/mil0405.html# Section 5.

[298] Ibid., Chapter 7, Section 1-2, 'Escort of Hijacked Aircraft: Requests for Service.' Full text at: http://faa.gov/ATpubs/MIL/Ch7/mil0701.html#7 1-2.

[299] ABC News, 25 October 1999.

[300] See note 298.

[301] Chairman of the Joint Chiefs of Staff Instruction 3610.01A, 1 June 2001, 'Aircraft Piracy (Hijacking) and Destruction of Derelict Airborne Objects,' 4.Policy (page 1) PDF file available at: www.dtic.mil/doctrine/jel/cjcsd/cjcsi/3610_01a.pdf.

[302] Bretz, Elizabeth A., 'Hard Questions to Answer,' *IEEE Spectrum* Special Report, http://spectrum.ieee.org.

[303] Air Traffic Control Center, 'ATCC Controller's Read Binder,' Xavier Software, Aug. 1998, www.xavius.com/080198.htm. This software is a "fully realistic simulation of actual traffic flows, radar sectors, ATC procedures, and radar equipment currently used throughout the U.S. Designed by a real controller, ATCC is ideal for pilots [and] controller trainees."

[304] CNN, 26 October 1999.

[305] Johnson, Glen, 'Facing Terror Attacks Aftermath: Otis Fighter Jets Scrambled Too Late to Halt the Attacks,' *Boston Globe*, 15 Sep. 2001.

[306] Zwicker, Barry, 'What Really Happened on Sept. 11th? – Part 2,' Straight Goods, 27 Jan. 2002, www.straightgoods.ca/ViewMediaFile.cfm ?REF=138.

[307] ABC News, 'Timeline of Disaster: From Flight School Training to Building Collapse,' 14 September 2001, www.ABCNews.com.

[308] CNN, 16 September 2001.

[309] Szamuely, George, 'Nothing Urgent,' *New York Press*, Vol. 15, No. 2, www.nypress.com/15/2/taki/bunker.cfm

[310] Szamuely, George, 'Scrambled Messages,' *New York Press*, Vol. 14, No. 50, www.nypress.com/14/50/taki/bunker.cfm.

[311] Testimony of General Richard B. Myers, 'U.S. Senator Carl Levin (D-MI) Holds Hearing On Nomination of General Richard Myers to be Chairman of The Joint Chiefs of Staff,' Senate Armed Services Committee, Washington DC, 13 September 2001.

[312] Johnson, Glen, 'Otis Fighter Jets Scrambled Too Late to Halt the Attacks,' *Boston Globe*, 15 September 2001.

[313] NBC News, 'Meet the Press,' 16 September 2001, http://stacks.msnbc.com/news/629714.asp?cp1=1.
Stan Goff, a 26-year U.S. veteran and expert in military science and doctrine, a retired Special Forces Master Sergeant who was tactics instructor at the U.S. Army's Jungle Operations Training Center in Panama, taught Military Science at the U.S. Military Academy at West Point, and was involved in operations in eight designated conflict areas from Vietnam to Haiti, has similarly concluded on analysis of the chronology of the events that no U.S. Air Force jets at all were scrambled until after the Pentagon crash (Goff, Stan, 'The So-called Evidence is a Farce,' Narco News, 10 October 2001, www.narconews.com).

[314] Szamuely, George, 'Scrambled Messages,' op. cit.

[315] See for example, CNN, 'Government failed to react to FAA warning,' 16 September 2001.

[316] Szamuely, George, 'Scrambled Messages,' op. cit.

[317] Szamuely, George, 'Nothing Urgent,' op. cit.

318 Canada-United States Defence Relations, 'NORAD,' www.dnd.ca/menu/
canada-us/bg00.010_e.htm.

319 Szamuely, George, 'Scrambled Messages,' op. cit.

320 *New York Times*, 15 September 2001.

321 *Village Voice*, 13 September 2001.

322 *Newsday*, 23 September 2001, www.newsday.com/ny-
uspent232380681sep23.story.

323 *Daily News* (New York), 12 September 2001.

324 Testimony of Gen. Eberhart, 'Hearing on Role of Defense Department in
Homeland Security,' Senate Armed Services Committee, Washington DC, 25
Oct. 2001, www.ngaus.org/newsroom/HomelandDefense Transcript.doc.

325 *New York Times*, 15 September 2001.

326 *New York Times*, 15 September 2001.

327 *USA Today*, 17 September 2001.

328 *San Diego Union-Tribune*, 12 September 2001.

329 DC Military, private website authorised by U.S. military to provide
information for members of the armed forces, viewed November 2001,
www.dcmilitary.com/baseguides/airforce/andrews/partnerunits.html.

330 *Sunday Telegraph*, 14 September 2001.

331 *Denver Post*, 11 September 2001.

332 NBC Nightly News (6:30 PM ET), 11 September 2001.

333 Israel, Jared. 'Dan Rather's Excellent New Fact,' The Emperor's New
Clothes, 3 January 2001, http://emperors-clothes.com/indict/faq2.htm.

334 Transcript of presentation by Dr. Mahmoud Khalaf at Center for Asian
Studies, University of Cairo, 5 December 2001.

335 NBC, 'Meet the Press' (10:00 AM ET), 16 September 2001.

336 Ibid.

337 Israel, Jared and Bykov, Illarion, 'Mr. Cheney's Cover Story: Guilty for 9-11:
Bush, Rumsfeld, Myers Part 2,' The Emperors New Clothes, 20 Nov. 2001,
Updated 21 Nov. 2001, http://emperors-clothes.com/indict/indict-2.htm.

338 Accounts of the general sequence of events have been published by CNN,
ABC, MS-NBC, the *Los Angeles Times*, the *New York Times* and other sources.

339 *Seattle Times*, 16 September 2001.

340 *Boston Herald*, 15 September 2001.

341 *New York Times*, 15 September 2001.

[342] Szamuely, George, 'Scrambled Messages,' op. cit.

[343] Goff, Stan, 'The So-Called Evidence is a Farce,' op. cit.

[344] Szamuely, George, 'Nothing Urgent,' op. cit.

[345] Testimony of U.S. Vice-President Dick Cheney, 'Meet the Press,' NBC, 16 September 2001.

[346] *Pravda Online*, 13 September 2001, http://pravda.ru.

[347] 'Fighter Response After Attacks Questioned,' *Washington Post*, 14 September 2001.

[348] Szamuely, George, 'Nothing Urgent,' op. cit.

[349] Rhem, Kathleen T. (Sergeant 1st class), 'Myers and Sept. 11: "We Hadn't Thought About This",' American Forces Press Service, 23 Oct. 2001, www.defenselink.mil/news/Oct2001/n10232001_200110236.html

[350] Szamuely, George, 'Nothing Urgent,' op. cit.

[351] Rhem, Kathleen T., 'Myers and Sept. 11: "We Hadn't Thought About This,"' op. cit.

[352] Testimony of General Richard B. Myers, 'U.S. Senator Carl Levin (D-MI) Holds Hearing On Nomination of General Richard Myers to be Chairman of The Joint Chiefs of Staff,' op. cit.

[353] Special Report, 'Planes Crash into World Trade Center,' ABC News, 11 September 2001, 8:53 AM ET.

[354] Szamuely, George, 'Nothing Urgent,' op. cit.

[355] NBC, 'Meet the Press,' 16 September 2001.

[356] Zwicker, Barry, 'The Great Deception,' Vision TV Insight, MediaFile, 18 February 2002.

[357] Israel, Jared and Bykov, Illarion, 'Guilty for 9-11: Bush, Rumsfeld, Myers Part 1,' op. cit.

[358] Zwicker, Barry, 'The Great Deception: What Really Happened on Sept. 11th Part 2,' MediaFile, Vision TV Insight, 28 January 2002, www.visiontv.ca/programs/insight/mediafile_Jan28.htm.

[359] Zwicker, Barry, 'The Great Deception: What Really Happened on Sept. 11th Part 1,' MediaFile, Vision TV Insight, 21 Jan. 2002, www.visiontv.ca/programs/insight/mediafile_Jan21.htm

[360] NBC, 'Meet the Press,' 16 September 2001.

6. American Ties with the Most Wanted Man on Earth

"[It is] a widely circulated but incorrect notion that the CIA once had a relationship with Osama bin Laden. For the record, you should know that the CIA never employed, paid, or maintained any relationship whatsoever with bin Laden."

CIA spokeswoman
(Ananova, 31 October 2001)

The official line of the U.S. government is that Osama bin Laden and his Al-Qaeda network came to power and operate independently of the United States. Accordingly, this view has now become established dogma—Osama bin Laden himself is an outcast from his own family due to his extremist view and actions, while the Saudi establishment with whom he was once close is also vehemently opposed to his activities. This is a dogma that is officially adopted by the White House and, moreover, uncritically accepted—even by purported critics of U.S. policy.

There is, however, abundant evidence that – contrary to the public professions of U.S. officials, Saudi officials, members of the bin Laden family, and even Osama bin Laden himself – Osama continues to maintain relations with his family, rooted in long-standing business activities. There is also considerable evidence that bin Laden maintains long-standing ties with the Saudi establishment. "Bin Laden family members have said they are estranged from their brother, who turned against the Saudi government after joining Muslim fighters following the Soviet Union's 1979 invasion of Afghanistan," reported U.S. correspondent Sig Christenson.[361] Yet, the documentary record contradicts this version of events to a significant extent. The reality of the matter is far more complex.

Osama bin Laden and the CIA: Cold War Allies

Osama bin Laden's father, Sheikh Muhammad bin Laden, was founder of the formidable bin Laden construction dynasty, which soon became "legendary in Arab construction, in the Saudi kingdom, the Gulf emirate of Ras al-Khaimah and in Jordan, for major road, airport and other infrastructure projects," according to ABC News correspondent and Middle East specialist John K. Cooley.

"The firm attracted engineering talent from all over the world and rapidly amassed a huge fortune…

By the time Sheikh Muhammad killed himself by crashing his own aircraft in 1966, the bin Laden conglomerate of companies was the biggest private contractor of its kind in the world… [B]y the late 1970s, one of Sheikh Muhammad's young sons, Usama, was running much of the business. Under his guidance, the group maintained its reputation for professional excellence and 'can do' spirit in large projects. Usama bin Laden's inherited share of the family fortune was soon augmented by huge earnings."[362]

Ahmed Rashid noted in the *Pittsburgh Post-Gazette* that Osama bin Laden's involvement in the U.S.-backed Afghan resistance against Soviet occupation was fully supported by his family: "[His family] backed the Afghan struggle and helped fund it; when Osama bin Laden decided to join the non-Afghan fighters with the Mujaheddin, his family responded enthusiastically."[363]

So did the United States. Cooley reports that Osama bin Laden's activities in Afghanistan occurred "with the full approval of the Saudi regime and the CIA."[364] Under contract with the CIA, he and the family company built the multi-billion dollar caves in which he has apparently been hiding:

"He brought in engineers from his father's company and heavy construction equipment to build roads and warehouses for the Mujaheddin. In 1986, he helped build a CIA-financed tunnel complex, to serve as a major arms storage depot, training facility and medical center for the Mujaheddin, deep under the mountains close to the Pakistan border."[365]

Cooley points out further that:

"Through his own personal reputation as a pious Muslim who favored the cause of Wahabi Islamism, and through involvement of the bin Laden companies in construction and renovation at the holy shrines of Mecca and Medina, he seemed to both Saudi intelligence and the CIA an ideal choice for the leading role he began to play. Bin Laden began to pay, with his own company and funds, for recruitment, transportation and training of the Arab volunteers who flocked, first to Peshawar, and to Afghanistan… By 1985 bin Laden had collected enough millions from his family and company wealth… to organize al-Qaida."[366]

"Delighted by his impeccable Saudi credentials," records Cooley, "the CIA gave Usama free rein in Afghanistan, as did Pakistan's intelligence generals."[367] Former head of the U.S. Visa Bureau in Jeddah, Michael Springmann, further testified as to how the U.S. supported these efforts:

"In Saudi Arabia I was repeatedly ordered by high level State Dept officials to issue visas to unqualified applicants...

These were, essentially, people who had no ties either to Saudi Arabia or to their own country. I complained bitterly at the time there. I returned to the U.S., I complained to the State Department here, to the General Accounting Office, to the Bureau of Diplomatic Security and to the Inspector General's office. I was met with silence. What I was protesting was, in reality, an effort to bring recruits, rounded up by Osama Bin Laden, to the U.S. for terrorist training by the CIA. They would then be returned to Afghanistan to fight against the then-Soviets. The attack on the World Trade Center in 1993 did not shake the State Department's faith in the Saudis, nor did the attack on American barracks at Khobar Towers in Saudi Arabia three years later, in which 19 Americans died. FBI agents began to feel their investigation was being obstructed. Would you be surprised to find out that FBI agents are a bit frustrated that they can't be looking into some Saudi connections?"[368]

Bin Laden's affiliations to the family business did not end there. "After the Soviet withdrawal in 1989 bin Laden returned for a short period to Saudi Arabia to tend to the family construction business at its Jeddah head office."[369] Even after the 1989-91 period, when Saudi security held on to bin Laden's passport, supposedly "hoping to prevent or at least discourage his contact with extremists he had worked with... during the Afghan jihad," he had considerable influence in Saudi royal circles: "After Iraq's invasion of Kuwait he lobbied the Saudi royal family to organize civil defense in the kingdom and to raise a force from among the Afghan war veterans to fight Iraq."[370]

Osama: Not a Black Sheep

Since then, there is good reason to doubt official claims that Osama bin Laden is now an outcast, a "black sheep," from his family due to his extremist views and activities. As already noted, his family was quite "enthusiastic" about Osama's involvement in the "Afghan jihad" against the Soviets during the 1980s.

Additionally, the entire family is well-known for its adherence to the extreme Wahabi interpretation of Islam: "His father is known in these areas as a man with deeply conservative religious and political views and for his profound distaste for non-Islamic influences that have penetrated some of the most remote corners of old Arabia."[371]

Moreover, the origins of the bin Laden family make it highly unlikely that this sort of break would occur between its members.

"Though he grew up in the Saudi Arabian city of Jiddah, about 700 miles away across the Arabian peninsula, those who know him say he retains the characteristics of the people of this remote Yemeni region: extremely clannish and intensely conservative in their adherence to strict forms of Islam."[372]

Credible reports further indicate that, in fact, such a clean break between Osama bin Laden and his family has never occurred, and that the Al-Qaeda leader still maintains close relations with his family. For instance, U.S. national security expert James Bamford cites declassified documents, newly released under the Freedom of Information Act, illustrating that: "In recent years, NSA has regularly listened to bin Laden's unencrypted telephone calls. [National Security] Agency officials have sometimes played tapes of bin Laden talking to his mother to impress members of Congress and select visitors to the agency."[373]

In 1998, another report noted that although members of Osama's family publicly disown him: "[FBI agent] Yossef Bodansky, director of the House Task Force on Terrorism and Unconventional Warfare, said 'Osama maintains connections' with some of his nearly two dozen brothers. He would not elaborate."[374]

Washington DC's public interest law firm, Judicial Watch, observes that: "Other reports have questioned whether members of his Saudi family have truly cut off Osama bin Laden. Osama's sister-in-law, in a recent interview with ABC News, said that she believed that members of her family still supported bin Laden."[375]

The French daily *Le Figaro* reported that: "While he was hospitalised [in the American Hospital in Dubai in July 2001], bin Laden received visits from many members of his family as well as prominent Saudis and Emirates."[376]

Bush and Bin Laden Family Ties

So while there is compelling evidence that Osama bin Laden has not broken away from his family, it is also a matter of record that the Bush administration is in turn very significantly tied to the same family. Reports have emerged that Carlyle Group, the giant U.S. defence contractor that employs former President George W. Bush Sr., has had long-standing financial ties to the bin Laden family.

The Carlyle Group's investments include ownership in at least 164 companies worldwide. As a leading defence contractor, Carlyle has profited immensely from the war on Afghanistan and the corresponding militarisation of U.S. foreign policy. The *Wall Street Journal* records that:

"If the U.S. boosts defense spending in its quest to stop Osama bin Laden's alleged terrorist activities, there may be one unexpected beneficiary: Mr. bin Laden's family...

Among its far-flung business interests, the well-heeled Saudi Arabian clan—which says it is estranged from Osama—is an investor in a fund established by Carlyle Group, a well-connected Washington merchant bank specializing in buyouts of defense and aerospace companies. Through this investment and its ties to Saudi royalty, the bin Laden family has become acquainted with some of the biggest names in the Republican Party. In recent years, former President Bush, ex-Secretary of State James Baker and ex-Secretary of Defense Frank Carlucci have made the pilgrimage to the bin Laden family's headquarters in Jeddah, Saudi Arabia. Mr. Bush makes speeches on behalf of Carlyle Group and is senior adviser to its Asian Partners fund, while Mr. Baker is its senior counselor. Mr. Carlucci is the group's chairman. Osama is one of more than 50 children of Mohammed bin Laden, who built the family's $5 billion business, Saudi Binladin Group, largely with construction contracts from the Saudi government...

A Carlyle executive said the bin Laden family committed $2 million through a London investment arm in 1995 in Carlyle Partners II Fund, which raised $1.3 billion overall. The fund has purchased several aerospace companies among 29 deals. So far, the family has received $1.3 million back in completed investments and should ultimately realize a 40% annualized rate of return, the Carlyle executive said. But a foreign financier with ties to the bin Laden family says the family's overall investment with Carlyle is considerably larger. He called the $2 million merely an initial contribution. 'It's like plowing a field,' this person said. 'You seed it once. You plow it, and then you reseed it again.'"[377]

The same *Wall Street Journal* report notes that there is a history here. U.S. government officials have always been keenly interested in the bin Laden family's views of the U.S., particularly in relation to investment.

"During the past several years, the [bin Laden] family's close ties to the Saudi royal family prompted executives and staff from closely held New York publisher Forbes, Inc. to make two trips to the family headquarters, according to Forbes Chairman Caspar Weinberger, a former U.S. Secretary of Defense in the Reagan administration. 'We would call on them to get their view of the country and what would be of interest to investors.""[378]

Weinberger was pardoned by President George Bush Sr. for his criminal conduct in the Iran-Contra scandal in 1989. The *San Francisco Chronicle* reported that through the Carlyle Group, both George Bush Sr. and the bin Laden family will benefit from the war on Afghanistan. "As America's military involvement abroad deepens, profits are increasing for the Carlyle Group—and, it turns out, for thousands of California civil servants," writes U.S. correspondent David Lazarus.

"The Carlyle Group, as in a secretive Washington, D.C., investment firm managing some $14 billion in assets, including stakes in a number of defense-related companies...

Carlyle counts among its chieftains former Defense Secretary (and deputy CIA Director) Frank Carlucci, former Secretary of State James Baker and, most notably, former President George Bush.

Until October, the Carlyle Group also maintained financial ties with none other than the family of Osama bin Laden... The Carlyle Group has cultivated and enjoyed a decidedly low profile for the past 14 years. Yet it has succeeded in attracting to its ranks not just a who's who of Republican bigwigs but also a dazzling array of international politicos.

John Major, the former British prime minister, is a Carlyle adviser, as are former Philippine President Fidel Ramos and former Thai Premier Anand Panyarachun. So is a former president of Germany's Bundesbank and a former head of the U.S. Securities and Exchange Commission... Critics of the Carlyle Group have grown increasingly vocal in recent weeks, particularly over the perception that a private organization with unmistakable links to the White House is benefiting from America's military action in Afghanistan."[379]

The *Village Voice* observes that the current President, George Bush Jr., also has firm links to Carlyle:

"In a case of 'like father, like son,' President Bush also had connections to the Carlyle Group, the Voice has learned. In the years before his 1994 bid for Texas governor, Bush owned stock in and sat on the board of directors of Caterair, a service company that provided airplane food and was also a component of Carlyle. For his consulting position, Bush was paid $15,000 a year, according to a Texas insider, and a bonus $1000 for every meeting he attended—roughly $75,000 in total. Reports show Carlyle was also a major contributor to his electoral fund."[380]

The Washington DC-based public interest law firm, Judicial Watch, which investigates and prosecutes government corruption and abuse, harshly criticised the Bush-bin Laden connection toward the end of September:

> "George H.W. Bush, the father of President Bush, works for the bin Laden family business in Saudi Arabia through the Carlyle Group, an international consulting firm. The senior Bush had met with the bin Laden family at least twice. (Other top Republicans are also associated with the Carlyle group, such as former Secretary of State James A. Baker.) The terrorist leader Osama bin Laden had supposedly been 'disowned' by his family, which runs a multi-billion dollar business in Saudi Arabia and is a major investor in the senior Bush's firm. Other reports have questioned, though, whether members of his Saudi family have truly cut off Osama bin Laden. Indeed, the Journal also reported yesterday that the FBI has subpoenaed the bin Laden family business' bank records."

Judicial Watch Chairman and General Counsel Larry Klayman commented that: "The idea of the President's father, an ex-president himself, doing business with a company under investigation by the FBI in the terror attacks of September 11 is horrible. President Bush should not ask, but demand, that his father pull out of the Carlyle Group."[381] These concerns were reiterated by Charles Lewis, Executive Director of the Center for Public Integrity:

> "Carlyle is as deeply wired into the current administration as they can possibly be. George Bush is getting money from private interests that have business before the government, while his son is president. And, in a really peculiar way, George W. Bush could, some day, benefit financially from his own administration's decisions, through his father's investments. The average American doesn't know that. To me, that's a jaw-dropper."[382]

That the bin Laden family would have benefited from the Bush administration's decisions is also somewhat of a "jaw-dropper." Given that there are credible reports that Osama bin Laden has not broken away from his family and that he maintains ties with them—and possible financial ties at that—the revelations that the Bush family has long-standing financial ties to the bin Laden family in the defence industry, among other business connections, is a startling indication of the degree of the Bush administration's dubious role in 11th September. The extent to which Carlyle Group is connected to the U.S. government only exacerbates these concerns. Judicial Watch further reported in late September that:

> "[D]ocuments recently uncovered through Judicial Watch's FOIA to the Department of Defense shows that the Carlyle Group has high-level

access to the U.S. government. The documents include a February 15, 2001 letter on Carlyle Group letterhead to Defense Secretary Donald Rumsfeld from former Defense Secretaries Frank Carlucci and William Perry, both now with Carlyle Group. The documents also include Secretary Rumsfeld's April 3 response to Messrs. Carlucci and Perry. The letters seemingly discuss the restructuring of the Defense Department. The Carlyle Group is listed in the documents as Defense Department contractor."[383]

Carlyle, in other words, is so wired into the Bush administration that it has a direct impact on the structure of the administration's Department of Defense. These concerns are further exacerbated in light of the Bush administration's systematic blocking of investigations into the terrorist connections of the bin Laden family. As noted by Agence France Press,

"FBI agents in the United States probing relatives of Saudi-born terror suspect Osama Bin Laden before September 11 were told to back off soon after George W Bush became president...

Bush at one point had a number of connections with Saudi Arabia's prominent Bin Laden family... [T]here was a suspicion that the U.S. strategic interest in Saudi Arabia, which has the world's biggest oil reserve, blunted its inquiries into individuals with suspected terrorist connections—so long as the U.S. was safe... [There are] secret documents from an FBI probe into the September 11 terror attacks that showed that at least two other U.S.-based members of the Bin Laden family are suspected to have links with a possible terrorist organisation."[384]

However, despite the official stance of the Bush administration that the bin Laden family is above suspicion, the latter is currently under investigation by the FBI. The *Wall Street Journal* notes that: "[T]he Federal Bureau of Investigation has issued subpoenas to banks used by the bin Laden family seeking records of family dealings."[385] ABC News further reports that:

"No matter how they try to distance themselves, or denounce Osama, the FBI is very interested in learning more about the family business and has subpoenaed all their records. A recent French Intelligence report reveals a web of bin Laden companies both good and bad. Investigators are trying to make sure no family member is funneling money to the blackest sheep of all. 'They say they don't support anything he is doing, that he is a pariah now in the family,' says Winer. But they have been quite secretive over the years like a number of families in the Middle East about how the financial network actually operates. He adds, 'It is a very tangled web of relationships that needs to be sorted out.'"[386]

The BBC current affairs programme 'Newsnight' has noted other pertinent facts in this connection, reporting that prior to 11th September, the FBI had been ordered to back off from investigating the terrorist connections of bin Laden's relatives:

"In the eight weeks since the attacks, over 1,000 suspects and potential witnesses have been detained. Yet, just days after the hijackers took off from Boston aiming for the Twin Towers, a special charter flight out of the same airport whisked 11 members of Osama Bin Laden's family off to Saudi Arabia. That did not concern the White House. Their official line is that the Bin Ladens are above suspicion—apart from Osama, the black sheep, who they say hijacked the family name. That's fortunate for the Bush family and the Saudi royal household, whose links with the Bin Ladens could otherwise prove embarrassing. But Newsnight has obtained evidence that the FBI was on the trail of other members of the Bin Laden family for links to terrorist organisations before and after September 11th.

This document is marked 'Secret.' Case ID – 199-Eye WF 213 589. 199 is FBI code for case type. 9 would be murder. 65 would be espionage. 199 means national security. WF indicates Washington field office special agents were investigating ABL—because of it's relationship with the World Assembly of Muslim Youth, WAMY—a suspected terrorist organisation. ABL is Abdullah Bin Laden, president and treasurer of WAMY.

This is the sleepy Washington suburb of Falls Church, Virginia where almost every home displays the Stars and Stripes. On this unremarkable street, at 3411 Silver Maple Place, we located the former home of Abdullah and another brother, Omar, also an FBI suspect. It's conveniently close to WAMY. The World Assembly of Muslim Youth is in this building, in a little room in the basement at 5613 Leesburg Pike. And here, just a couple blocks down the road at 5913 Leesburg, is where four of the hijackers that attacked New York and Washington are listed as having lived.

The U.S. Treasury has not frozen WAMY's assets, and when we talked to them, they insisted they are a charity. Yet, just weeks ago, Pakistan expelled WAMY operatives. And India claimed that WAMY was funding an organisation linked to bombings in Kashmir. And the Philippines military has accused WAMY of funding Muslim insurgency. The FBI did look into WAMY, but, for some reason, agents were pulled off the trail."

U.S. national security expert John Trento noted that although the FBI had "wanted to investigate these guys... they weren't permitted to." Yet, he also observes that WAMY have "had connections to Osama bin Laden's people" as well as other "groups that have terrorist connections." Furthermore, they "fit the pattern of groups that the Saudi royal family and Saudi community of princes—the 20,000 princes—have funded who've engaged in terrorist activity. Now, do I know that WAMY has done anything that's illegal? No, I don't know that. Do I know that as far back as 1996 the FBI was very concerned about this organisation? I do."[387] The London *Guardian* observed that the FBI had investigated "two of Osama bin Laden's relatives" as well as WAMY, but closed its files on them due to high-level constraints in 1996 "before any conclusions could be reached."[388]

BBC Newsnight's Gregory Palast further reported other high-level blocks on FBI investigations into bin Laden-related terror connections, based on what appear to be attempts to protect U.S. corporate interests—including the fact that Bush Jr.'s fortune was built on doing business with the bin Laden family:

"The younger Bush made his first million 20 years ago with an oil company partly funded by Salem Bin Laden's chief U.S. representative...

Young George also received fees as director of a subsidiary of Carlyle Corporation, a little known private company which has, in just a few years of its founding, become one of Americas biggest defence contractors. His father, Bush Senior, is also a paid advisor. And what became embarrassing was the revelation that the Bin Ladens held a stake in Carlyle, sold just after September 11... I received a phone call from a high-placed member of a U.S. intelligence agency. He tells me that while there's always been constraints on investigating Saudis, under George Bush it's gotten much worse. After the elections, the agencies were told to 'back off' investigating the Bin Ladens and Saudi royals, and that angered agents... FBI headquarters told us they could not comment on our findings."[389]

Bush Jr.'s latest order to "back off" the bin Laden family and Saudi royals followed previous orders dating back to 1996, frustrating efforts to investigate the latter. The London *Guardian* has elaborated that:

"FBI and military intelligence officials in Washington say they were prevented for political reasons from carrying out full investigations into members of the Bin Laden family in the U.S. before the terrorist attacks of September 11...

U.S. intelligence agencies have come under criticism for their wholesale failure to predict the catastrophe at the World Trade Centre. But some are complaining that their hands were tied... High-placed intelligence sources in Washington told the Guardian this week: 'There were always constraints on investigating the Saudis.' They said the restrictions became worse after the Bush administration took over this year. The intelligence agencies had been told to 'back off' from investigations involving other members of the Bin Laden family, the Saudi royals, and possible Saudi links to the acquisition of nuclear weapons by Pakistan. 'There were particular investigations that were effectively killed.'"[390]

Greg Palast has elaborated on these findings in an interview with the *Green Press*. He stated that he and his team of investigators had "obtained documents from inside the FBI showing that investigations had been shut down on the bin Laden family, the royal family of Saudi Arabia—and that is big, because there are 20,000 princes in the royal family—and their connections to the financing of terrorism...

"Now there is one exception. The FBI, the CIA and all the rest of the agencies are allowed to investigate Osama, the so-called black sheep of the family. But what we were finding was that there was an awful lot of gray sheeps in this family—which is a family of billionaires which is tied in with the Saudi royal household which appears to be involved in the funding of terrorist organizations or organizations linked to terrorism... Now the problem was the investigations were shut down. There were problems that go back to Father Bush—when he was head of the CIA, he tried to stop investigations of the Saudis, continued on under Reagan, Daddy Bush's president, and it continued under Clinton too... I have to add it was also CIA and all the other international agencies... I can say that the sources are not just FBI trying to get even with the other agencies, but in fact other agencies. The information was that they were absolutely prohibited, until Sept. 11, at looking at the Saudi funding of the Al-Qaeda network and other terrorist organizations. There is no question we had what looked like the biggest failure of the intelligence community since Pearl Harbor but what we are learning now is it wasn't a failure, it was a directive."[391]

Palast also refers to a particular example of how this situation had grown so dire that the FBI command refused to even consider investigating the Saudis:

"[T]here was a Saudi diplomat who defected. He had 14,000 documents in his possession showing Saudi royal involvement in everything from assassinations to terror funding...

He offered the 14,000 documents to the FBI but they would not accept them. The low-level agents wanted this stuff because they were tremendous leads. But the upper-level people would not permit this, did not want to touch this material. That is quite extraordinary. We don't even want to look. We don't want to know. Because obviously going through 14,000 documents from the Saudi government files would anger the Saudis. And it seems to be policy number one is we don't get these boys angry."[392]

Increasing press scrutiny of these matters, leading to embarrassing revelations for both the Bush and bin Laden families, appears to have been behind the latter's sudden decision to withdraw their stake in Carlyle in the aftermath of 11th September.[393] The timing of this action only raises further questions about the nature of this Bush-bin Laden financial affair, and whether it really was as innocent as is claimed. If so, why the need for the bin Laden family to pull out, thus preempting further investigations and inquiries?

And finally, it should be noted that among the multiple projects for the establishment of oil pipelines through Afghanistan, there is a joint venture between the construction firm H. P. Price and the bin Laden family.[394] H. P. Price has changed its name to Bredero Shaw, Inc. It now happens to be owned by a subsidiary of the giant Halliburton Corporation, of which current Vice-President Dick Cheney was CEO until the elections in 2000.

The picture that emerges from all this is scandalous. It appears that the Bush family has long-standing financial connections to the bin Laden family. It also appears that Osama bin Laden maintains connections with his family. Moreover, members of his family have been, and are, under investigation by U.S. intelligence for the financial support of terrorism, and specifically for the financial support of Osama.

Prior to 11th September, President Bush Jr. blocked inquiries into the bin Laden family's terrorist connections. Furthermore, both families were set to benefit financially from the war on Afghanistan that was triggered by the 11th September attacks. This appears to indicate a longstanding financial connection, through the bin Laden family, between Osama bin Laden, the Bush family and the current administration.

Osama and the Saudis: a Covert Alliance

There is also specific evidence that Osama bin Laden continues to receive extensive support, not only from members of his own family, but also from members of the Saudi establishment. Martin S. Indyk,[395] former senior

U.S. State Department official and a highly respected commentator on U.S. foreign policy, admits that:

"In the Saudi case, the Clinton administration indulged Riyadh's penchant for buying off trouble as long as the regime also paid its huge arms bills, purchased Boeing aircraft, kept the price of oil within reasonable bounds, and allowed the United States to use Saudi air bases...

The Saudis had protected themselves by co-opting and accommodating the Islamist extremists in their midst, a move they felt was necessary in the uncertain aftermath of the Gulf War... And once Crown Prince Abdullah assumed the regency in 1996, the ruling family set about the determined business of buying off its opposition... The vulnerabilities exposed by the Gulf War, however, created a greater need for shoring up Wahhabi support. The regime accordingly financed the export of Wahhabism through the building of hundreds of mosques and madrassas (religious schools) abroad. The activity was particularly intense in areas affected by the collapse of the Soviet Union—the Balkans, Central Asia, Afghanistan, and Pakistan—where the Saudis engaged in competition with Iranian mullahs for the hearts and minds of local Muslim populations. A public-private partnership was also created in which rich Saudi families would help to fund the enterprise.

While Saudi export of Wahhabism was proceeding apace, the charitable organizations established to funnel the money were being subverted for other purposes. It is now clear that bin Laden, despite being stripped of his Saudi citizenship, was able to take advantage of this system to raise funds and establish his network. Saudi-backed institutions... were used as covers for financing al Qaeda's nefarious activities. And the Sunni fundamentalist Taliban regime in Afghanistan, providers of sanctuary to bin Laden and his cohort, also found itself the direct and indirect beneficiary of Saudi largess..."[396]

Corroborating and expanding on Indyk's observations, the *New Yorker* reports that: "Since 1994 or earlier, the National Security Agency has been collecting electronic intercepts of conversations between members of the Saudi Arabian royal family, which is headed by King Fahd...

"The intercepts depict a regime increasingly corrupt, alienated from the country's religious rank and file, and so weakened and frightened that it has brokered its future by channelling hundreds of millions of dollars in what amounts to protection money to fundamentalist groups that wish to overthrow it."

Furthermore, the NSA intercepts "have demonstrated to analysts that by 1996 Saudi money was supporting Osama bin Laden's Al Qaeda and other extremist groups in Afghanistan, Lebanon, Yemen, and Central Asia, and throughout the Persian Gulf region." According to one senior U.S. intelligence official, the Saudi regime had "gone to the dark side."[397] The Toronto-based newsmagazine *Now* further reports that:

"Generally accepted, too, is the idea that the monarchy boosted al Qaeda through its funding of the Wahhabi movement, a militant Islamist sect... U.S. officials were unwilling to make an issue of al Qaeda's connections to wealthy Saudis... Even after bin Laden turned his wrath on the U.S. in the 1990s, he maintained close contact with key Saudi figures including Prince Turki al-Faisal, the powerful intelligence chief and brother of King Fahd."[398]

Indeed, according to the *Los Angeles Times*:

"[In the 1990s] Taliban authorities also opened the country's airstrips to high-ranking Persian Gulf state officials who routinely flew in for lavish hunting parties... Sometimes joined by Bin Laden and Taliban leaders, the dignitaries, who included several high-ranking officials from Saudi Arabia and the Emirates—left behind money, vehicles and equipment with their hosts, according to U.S. and Afghan accounts... According to U.S. and former Afghan civil air officials, the hunters included Prince Turki al Faisal, son of the late Saudi King Faisal. He headed that nation's intelligence service until late August [2001], maintaining close ties with Bin Laden and the Taliban. Another visitor, officials said, was Sheik Mohammed ibn Rashid al Maktum, the Dubai crown prince and Emirates defense minister."[399]

It should be noted that: "Prince Turki, head of the Saudi Secret Service for more than 20 years, a constrained friend of the CIA, made abundant use of bin Laden's networks," according to Swiss investigative reporter Richard Labeviere.[400] The Prince resigned from his position just two weeks before 11th September.[401]

USA Today has also reported that "prominent businessmen in Saudi Arabia continue to transfer tens of million of dollars to bank accounts linked to Osama Bin Laden." Citing senior U.S. intelligence officials and a Saudi government document, *USA Today* noted that the money transfers had begun five years earlier. One of the businessmen under investigation, Mohammad Hussein al-Amoudi, runs the largest bank in Saudi Arabia, as well as the Capitol Trust Bank in New York. Vernon Jordan, one of Bill Clinton's close friends, is his lawyer.[402] Central Asia specialist Ahmed Rashid, a member of the Center for Public Integrity's International Consortium of Investigative Journalists, further reports that the Saudis prefer "to leave Bin Laden alone in

Afghanistan because his arrest and trial by the Americans could expose the deep relationship that Bin Laden continued to have with sympathetic members of the Royal Family and elements within Saudi intelligence, which could prove deeply embarrassing."[403]

Investigative journalist Greg Palast provides further information on the "deep relationship" between Saudi royals and Osama bin Laden based on sources in U.S. intelligence and elsewhere. He comments in an interview with the *Green Press* that:

"[T]he Saudis say that they have removed Osama bin Laden's citizenship in Saudi Arabia. Of course, there are no citizens of Saudi Arabia, there are only subjects. So he is not allowed to be a subject of the king of Saudi Arabia. What a loss...

And they have frozen his assets, supposedly. But the information I am getting from other sources is that they have given tens of millions of dollars to his networks. This is being done as much as a protection racket as anything else... Osama is often compared to Hitler but he should be seen as John Gotti times one hundred. He is running a massive international protection racket: Pay me or I will blow you up. The fact these payments are made is one of the things the Bush administration is trying very hard to cover-up. Now whether these payments were paid because they want to or it is coercion the Bush administration does not want to make a point of it. I have to tell you the Clinton administration was not exactly wonderful on this either."[404]

High-level U.S. government and intelligence officials, including those in the Bush administration, have therefore long been aware of the financial support of Osama bin Laden by members of the Saudi establishment. Yet, the administration has apparently, quite deliberately, refused to do anything about it, and is moreover attempting to cover up the fact.

In 1998, for example, the CIA ignored warnings from Robert Baer, Case Officer in the CIA's Directorate of Operations, that the Saudi regime was harbouring an Al-Qaeda cell led by two known terrorists. U.S. intelligence offered its Saudi counterpart a more detailed list of known terrorists in the country in August 2001. Saudi intelligence refused to accept it. The *Financial Times* reported that:

"A former U.S. intelligence agent has alleged that the CIA ignored detailed warnings he passed on in 1998 that a Gulf state was harbouring an al-Qaeda cell led by two known terrorists...

When FBI agents attempted to arrest them, the Gulf state's government provided the men with alias passports, the former agent claims... Mr Baer said he [was provided with] a computer record of 'hundreds' of secret al-Qaeda operatives in the Gulf region, many in Saudi Arabia [by a military associate of a prince in a Gulf royal family]. Mr Baer said that in August 2001, at the military officer's request, he offered the list to the Saudi Arabian government. But an aide to the Saudi defence minister, Prince Sultan, refused to look at the list or to pass them (the names) on... The information Mr Baer gave to the CIA was not followed up, he said."[405]

It should be noted that this occurred *after* the U.S. intelligence community received multiple warnings of an impending terrorist attack on U.S. soil by Osama bin Laden's Al-Qaeda. This is the same period during which the U.S. government granted U.S. visas to various Saudis in violation of stringent State Department visa regulations, through the "U.S. Visa Express" programme. This is also the period during which terrorists of Saudi ethnicity were reportedly training at U.S. flight schools and secure U.S. military facilities. Baer explains the context:

"At a time when terrorist threats were compounding globally... Americans were making too much money to bother. Life was good. The White House and the National Security Council became cathedrals of commerce where the interests of big business outweighed the interests of protecting American citizens at home and abroad. Defanged and dispirited, the CIA went along for the ride."[406]

The U.S.-Saudi Alliance

While the Saudi establishment, or significant elements thereof, support Osama bin Laden, in turn, the United States has always protected the Saudi establishment. In this context, we should take note of a *New Statesman* report recording that:

"Bin Laden and his gang are just the tentacles; the head lies safely in Saudi Arabia, protected by U.S. forces...

The hijackers responsible for the 11 September outrage were not illiterate, bearded fanatics from the mountain villages of Afghanistan. They were all educated, highly skilled, middle- class professionals. Of the 19 men involved, 13 were citizens of Saudi Arabia... Regardless of whether Osama Bin Laden gave the order or not, it is indisputable that the bulk of his real cadres (as opposed to foot soldiers) are located in Egypt or Saudi Arabia—America's two principal allies in the region, barring Israel. In Saudi Arabia, support for Bin Laden is strong. He was a close friend of the Saudi intelligence boss Prince Turki Bin Faisal al-Saud, who was dismissed in August apparently because of his failure to curb attacks on U.S. personnel in Riyadh. The real reason, however, was probably his refusal to take sides in the fierce faction fight to determine the succession after the death of the paralysed King Fahd. Both sides are aware that too close an alignment with the U.S. could be explosive. That is why, despite its support for the U.S., the Saudi regime is not 'allowing its bases to be used'...

[T]he state religion... is not an everyday version of Sunni or Shi'a Islam, but a peculiarly virulent, ultra-puritanical strain known as Wahhabism. This is the religion of the Saudi royal family, the state bureaucracy, the army, the air force and Bin Laden—the best-known Saudi citizen in the world, believed currently to reside in Afghanistan... Wahhabism remains the state religion of Saudi Arabia. During the war between Afghanistan and the Soviet Union, Pakistani military intelligence requested the presence of a Saudi prince to lead the jihad. No volunteers were forthcoming, and Saudi leaders recommended the scion of a rich family close to the monarchy. Bin Laden was despatched to the Pakistan border and arrived in time to hear President Jimmy Carter's national security adviser, Zbigniew Brzezinski, turban on head, shout: 'Allah is on your side.'

The religious schools in Pakistan where the Taliban were created were funded by the Saudis, and Wahhabi influence was very strong. Last year, when the Taliban threatened to blow up the old statues of Buddha in Afghanistan, there were appeals from the ancient seminaries of Qom in Iran and al-Azhar in Egypt to desist on the grounds that Islam is tolerant. A Wahhabi delegation from Saudi Arabia advised the Taliban to execute the plan. They did... The expeditionary force being despatched to Pakistan to cut off the tentacles of the Wahhabi octopus may or may not succeed, but its head is safe and sound in Saudi Arabia, guarding the oil wells, growing new arms, and protected by U.S. soldiers and the U.S. air-force base in Dhahran. Washington's failure to disengage its vital interests from the fate of the Saudi monarchy could well lead to further blow-back."[407]

There is an important context to this longstanding political and military alliance between Saudi Arabia and the United States, which has continued despite U.S. knowledge of the former's support of Al-Qaeda. The *Washington Post* observes that the "good fortune" of "a small group of Saudi citizens" who have "accumulated vast personal wealth," "has spilled over to the benefit of American and European money managers, investment banks and the companies in which the money is invested...

"Members of the royal family—there are about 40,000 of them, including 8,000 princes—led the way. The Saudi government has never reported what share of oil income went to the royal family, whose senior princes accumulated fantastic fortunes. According to a credible account, members of the royal family have billions of dollars on deposit in the Banque Pictet in Geneva, for example...

After nearly three decades of accumulating this wealth, the group referred to by bankers as 'high net worth Saudi individuals' holds between $500 billion and $1 trillion abroad, most of it in European and American investments. Brad Bourland, chief economist of the Saudi American Bank (one-quarter owned by Citibank), said in a speech in London last June that his bank's best estimate of the total is about $700 billion, with the possibility that it is as much as $1 trillion.

Raymond Seitz, vice chairman of Lehman Brothers in London and a former U.S. ambassador to Britain, gave a similar estimate. Seitz said Saudis typically put about three-quarters of their money into the United States, the rest in Europe and Asia. That would mean that Saudi nationals have invested perhaps $500 billion to $700 billion in the American economy.

This is a huge sea of fungible assets supporting the American economy and belonging to a relatively small group of people—about 85,000 Saudis, Seitz said, is the estimate of bankers. Managing these hundreds of billions can be a lucrative business for brokers and bankers in London, Geneva and New York."[408]

Indeed, a more in-depth inquiry demonstrates that there are very specific, long-standing financial connections between the White House and leading Saudi figures, who reportedly support Osama bin Laden. One report by the investigative journalist Wayne Madsen, who has been called to testify as an expert witness before U.S. Congressional hearings on covert U.S. foreign policy, is worth quoting extensively:

"Bush's own businesses were once tied to financial figures in Saudi Arabia who currently support bin Laden...

In 1979, Bush's first business, Arbusto Energy, obtained financing from James Bath, a Houstonian and close family friend. One of many investors, Bath gave Bush $50,000 for a 5 percent stake in Arbusto. At the time, Bath was the sole U.S. business representative for Salem bin Laden, head of the wealthy Saudi Arabian family and a brother (one of 17) to Osama bin Laden. It has long been suspected, but never proven, that the Arbusto money came directly from Salem bin Laden. In a statement issued shortly after the September 11 attacks, the White House vehemently denied the connection, insisting that Bath invested his own money, not Salem bin Laden's, in Arbusto.

In conflicting statements, Bush at first denied ever knowing Bath, then acknowledged his stake in Arbusto and that he was aware Bath represented Saudi interests. In fact, Bath has extensive ties, both to the bin Laden family and major players in the scandal-ridden Bank of Commerce and Credit International (BCCI) who have gone on to fund Osama bin Laden. BCCI defrauded depositors of $10 billion in the '80s in what has been called the 'largest bank fraud in world financial history' by former Manhattan District Attorney Robert Morgenthau. During the '80s, BCCI also acted as a main conduit for laundering money intended for clandestine CIA activities, ranging from financial support to the Afghan mujahedin to paying intermediaries in the Iran-Contra affair.

When Salem bin Laden died in 1988, powerful Saudi Arabian banker and BCCI principal Khalid bin Mahfouz inherited his interests in Houston. Bath ran a business for bin Mahfouz in Houston and joined a partnership with bin Mahfouz and Gaith Pharaon, BCCI's frontman in Houston's Main Bank.

The Arbusto deal wasn't the last time Bush looked to highly questionable sources to invest in his oil dealings. After several incarnations, Arbusto emerged in 1986 as Harken Energy Corporation. When Harken ran into trouble a year later, Saudi Sheik Abdullah Taha Bakhsh purchased a 17.6 percent stake in the company. Bakhsh was a business partner with Pharaon in Saudi Arabia; his banker there just happened to be bin Mahfouz.

Though Bush told the Wall Street Journal he had 'no idea' BCCI was involved in Harken's financial dealings, the network of connections between Bush and BCCI is so extensive that the Journal concluded their investigation of the matter in 1991 by stating: 'The number of BCCI-connected people who had dealings with Harken – all since George W. Bush came on board – raises the question of whether they mask an effort to cozy up to a presidential son.' Or even the president: Bath finally came under investigation by the FBI in 1992 for his Saudi business relationships, accused of funneling Saudi money through Houston in order to influence the foreign policies of the Reagan and first Bush administrations.

Worst of all, bin Mahfouz allegedly has been financing the bin Laden terrorist network – making Bush a U.S. citizen who has done business with those who finance and support terrorists. According to USA Today, bin Mahfouz and other Saudis attempted to transfer $3 million to various bin Laden front operations in Saudi Arabia in 1999. ABC News reported the same year that Saudi officials stopped bin Mahfouz from contributing money directly to bin Laden. (Bin Mahfouz's sister is also a wife of Osama bin Laden, a fact that former CIA Director James Woolsey revealed in 1998 Senate testimony.)

When President Bush announced he is hot on the trail of the money used over the years to finance terrorism, he must realize that trail ultimately leads not only to Saudi Arabia, but to some of the same financiers who originally helped propel him into the oil business and later the White House. The ties between bin Laden and the White House may be much closer than he is willing to acknowledge."[409]

But as already noted, early on in his Presidency, Bush Jr. made efforts to prevent investigations of the financial ties between bin Laden and the White House. FBI inquiries into the possible terrorist connections of Saudi royals and other members of the Saudi establishment—along with the bin Laden family—were obstructed.

"[FBI investigators] were pursuing these matters, but were told to back off," noted David Armstrong, an intelligence expert at the Washington DC-based Public Education Center, a nonprofit investigative organisation.[410] The *Boston Herald* elaborates that:

"A steady stream of billion-dollar oil and arms deals between American corporate leaders and the elite of Saudi Arabia may be hindering efforts by the West to defeat international Islamic terrorism...

U.S. business and political leaders are so wedded to preserving the gilded American-Saudi marriage that officials in Washington D.C. continue to give the oil-rich Gulf monarchy a wide berth, despite mounting evidence of support in Saudi Arabia for Osama bin Laden's terrorist network, some experts say... The Saudis have also balked at freezing the assets of organizations linked to bin Laden and international terrorism, some of which are Saudi-run."[411]

And this state of affairs largely continues, even now. Indeed, another *Boston Herald* report records a particularly disconcerting example of this, related to the figure of Bin Mahfouz: "Two billionaire Saudi families scrutinized by authorities for possible financial ties to Osama bin Laden's terrorist network continue to engage in major oil deals with leading U.S. corporations," to the unnerving silence of the Bush administration.

"The bin Mahfouz and Al-Amoudi clans, who control three private Saudi Arabian oil companies, are partners with U.S. firms in a series of ambitious oil development and pipeline projects in central and south Asia, records show...

Working through their companies—Delta Oil, Nimir Petroleum and Corral Petroleum—the Saudi families have formed international consortiums with U. S. oil giants Texaco, Unocal, Amerada Hess and Frontera Resources. These business relationships persist despite evidence that members of the two Saudi families—headed by patriarchs Khalid bin Mahfouz and Mohammed Hussein Al-Amoudi—have had ties to Islamic charities and companies linked financially to bin Laden's al-Qaeda organization."

Curiously, both Mahfouz and Al-Amoudi "have been left untouched by the U.S. Treasury Department." A May 1999 report by the U. S. Embassy in Saudi Arabia records that a Saudi company, Delta Oil was created by 50 prominent Saudi investors in the early 1990s, the prime force behind which "appears to be Mohammed Hussein Al-Amoudi, who is based in Ethiopia and oversees a vast network of companies involved in construction, mining, banking and oil...

"The Al-Amoudis' business interests, meanwhile, are enmeshed with the bin Mahfouz family, which owns the third privately held Saudi oil company, Nimir Petroleum. Nimir was established by the Mahfouz family in Bermuda in 1991, according to the U. S. Embassy report. The closeness of the two clans is underlined by their joint oil venture, Delta-Nimir, as well as by their partnership in the Saudi firm The Marei Bin Mahfouz & Ahmed Al Amoudi Group of Companies & Factories. Meanwhile, information continues to circulate in intelligence circles in the United States and Europe suggesting wealthy Saudi businessmen have provided financial support to bin Laden.

Much of it revolves around a 1999 audit conducted by the Saudi government that reportedly discovered that the bin Mahfouz family's National Commercial Bank had transferred at least $3 million to charitable organizations believed to be fronts for bin Laden's terror network... Some of the Saudi money transferred from National Commercial Bank allegedly went to the Islamic charity Blessed Relief, whose board members included bin Mahfouz's son, Abdul Rahman bin Mahfouz. In October, the U. S. Treasury Department named Blessed Relief as a front organization providing funds to bin Laden. 'Saudi businessmen have been transferring millions of dollars to bin Laden through Blessed Relief,' the agency said."

The *Herald* further notes that: "Despite officials' suspicions, the bin Mahfouz and Al-Amoudi oil companies continue to profit from their working relationship with America's own oil elite."[412] In another report, the *Herald* points out that the bin Laden family has many direct financial ties to bin Mahfouz:

"Public records and intelligence reports show that the Saudi Binladin Group, the international business conglomerate run by some of Osama bin Laden's half-brothers, has numerous business ventures with the bin Mahfouz family... The financial ties between the bin Laden and bin Mahfouz families are many and run the gamut from telecommunications to construction management to high finance."

It is thus worth noting the observation of Paul Michael Wihbey, a Fellow at the Institute for Advanced Strategic and Political Studies in Washington D.C.: "I think we underestimate bin Laden. He comes from the highest levels of Saudi society and he has supporters at all levels of Saudi Arabia. There is no reason to think that every single member of his family has shut him down."[413]

Osamagate?

In his study of Al-Qaeda and U.S. relations, based on four years of intensive research, the leading Swiss television journalist Richard Labeviere, who has written extensively on Arab and African affairs, similarly finds that "Saudi Arabia is bankrolling bin Laden's networks." They have grown in power, he reports, "with the active support of Saudi Arabia, the United Arab Emirates and other oil monarchies and with the benevolence of the American [intelligence] services engaged in these areas."

Labeviere, who draws extensively on European intelligence sources, thus concludes in his book, *Dollars for Terror* (which received favourable reviews in the European press), that the international terrorism networks spawned by Osama bin Laden have been "nurtured and encouraged by elements of the U.S. intelligence community, especially during the Clinton years." Al-Qaeda, he reports, "was protected because the network was designed to serve U.S. foreign policy and military interests."

A former U.S. Army Sergeant, Egyptian-born Ali Mohamed, testified in a New York court that he helped train members of Al-Qaeda after he left the army in 1989. In 2000, he also admitted his involvement in the bombing of the embassies in Africa. Labeviere, however, reports that the former U.S. Army Sergeant "trained Islamic militants in several camps in the New York area and suggests that he was an active U.S. agent."[414]

A native of Egypt, Ali Mohamed rose to the rank of major in the Egyptian Special Forces. In 1984, he was expelled from Egypt's military as a religious extremist. He contacted the CIA, "offering to be a spy," according to a U.S. official who spoke on condition of anonymity. The CIA judged him unreliable and dropped him as a source, the official said. He was later placed on a U.S. government watch list, according to U.S. officials."[415] He should therefore have been banned from entry into the U.S.

A report in the *Wall Street Journal* further indicates that the FBI and the CIA must have been aware of Mohamed's mingling with terrorists. Yet, he was nevertheless able to obtain a U.S. visa, marry an American woman, become a U.S. citizen, settle in California and even become a U.S. Army Sergeant by 1986. Until 1989, he was lecturing on the Middle East at the U.S. Army's John F. Kennedy Special Warfare Center and School at Fort Bragg, North Carolina.

The U.S. Army and the CIA declined to comment when asked by *Journal* reporters about whether Mohamed was working for the CIA in the U.S. proxy war against the Soviets in Afghanistan. San Jose obstetrician Ali Zaki, a close friend of Mohamed, was more forthcoming: "Everyone in the community knew he was working as a liaison between the CIA and the Afghan cause."[416]

Mohamed's relations to the U.S. military and intelligence community thereafter are unclear. According to a report in the *Raleigh News & Observer*:

"Mohamed's relationship with the FBI and intelligence services remains wrapped in secrecy. His plea agreement is sealed, as are many of the court documents and much of the testimony. Mohamed was expected to testify—but did not—at the trial at which the four others were convicted. Mohamed and his lawyer have declined all interview requests."

The same report notes evidence suggesting that the CIA may have continued to use Mohamed as an agent. The *News & Observer* records that, at around the same time he became a major in Egyptian Special Forces, while also joining the extremist group Islamic Jihad:

"... the Egyptian army sent Mohamed to Fort Bragg for special forces training—common for officers from countries the United States regards as friendly...

Training beside U.S. Green Berets, he learned how to command elite soldiers on difficult missions such as special reconnaissance, unconventional warfare and counter-insurgency operations. After four months, he received a diploma with a green beret on it. Returning home, he served in the Egyptian army for three more years. In 1984, he left to work as a security expert for Egypt Air—and started to make contact with the CIA."

He became a regular U.S. Army soldier in 1986. In 1988, while still on active duty, he visited Afghanistan on leave, where he fought the Soviets and made contact with Osama bin Laden, apparently with CIA sponsorship. Honourably discharged in 1989, Mohamed joined the U.S. Army Reserves for another five years. Documents from U.S. court cases prove that while either on active duty or a member of the U.S. Army Reserves, Mohamed continued to travel abroad to meet with Osama bin Laden and his colleagues, as well as train Al-Qaeda members within America:

> "Near the end of his tour at Fort Bragg, Mohamed apparently got busier in his work with terrorist groups. Documents from court cases show that he traveled on weekends to New Jersey, where he trained other Islamic fundamentalists in surveillance, weapons and explosives. He continued this training after he was honorably discharged in 1989 with commendations in his file, including one for 'patriotism, valor, fidelity and professional excellence.'"

Retired Lt. Col. Robert Anderson, who was also at Fort Bragg, testifies that despite informing his superiors of Mohamed's activities in relation to terrorists, nothing was done. In 1988, Mohamed had even openly admitted to Anderson and others that he was to participate in the war against Soviet occupation in Afghanistan. As the *News & Observer* notes, "it was highly irregular, if not illegal, for an active-duty U.S. soldier to fight in a foreign war." Anderson submitted an intelligence report to his superiors two weeks before Mohamed's departure that was completely ignored. The silence of his superiors led him to conclude that Mohamed was indeed "sponsored" by U.S. intelligence.[417]

To this day, there remains a cloud of secrecy maintained by the U.S. government about Mohamed's role, his simultaneous ties with U.S. military intelligence and Al-Qaeda, and how long this continued. Astonishingly, Mohamed was apparently permitted by the U.S. military intelligence community to continue his terrorist activities unhindered through the 1990s—until the U.S. embassy bombings in 1998.

This situation continued even when U.S. Special Forces documents stolen by Mohamed surfaced in the 1995 terror trial in New York, clearly pointing to his terrorist connections and activities in alliance with Al-Qaeda. Even now, Mohamed has not been permitted to testify in the trials over the U.S. embassy bombings, and continues to be held in U.S. custody in a secure, undisclosed location, unsentenced despite his guilty plea. The Associated Press reports that:

> "It remains unclear how Mohamed managed to enter the United States and join the Army in the 1980s, despite the CIA's misgivings. Equally unclear is how he was able to maintain his terror ties in the 1990s without being banished by either side, even after the Special Forces documents he stole turned up in the 1995 New York trial. The State

Department, CIA, and FBI declined to answer questions about Mohamed. Officials have refused to discuss how much he has helped in their investigations as he awaits sentencing, which has been postponed indefinitely."[418]

The question, of course, is this: What is the U.S. government trying to keep under wraps about the former U.S. Army Sergeant who trained Al-Qaeda terrorists, so much so that despite his guilty plea for the 1998 embassy bombings, he has as yet neither been permitted to testify in an open court, nor sentenced for his crime— indefinitely?

Richard Labeviere provides a reasonable answer, drawing on European intelligence sources to record that the CIA blocked the FBI from cracking down on bin Laden's terrorist networks:

"Bin-Ladengate is unfolding, and there is no escape. If it blows up one day, this scandal will reveal exactly how the various American intelligence agencies were involved in the process that led to the Nairobi [Kenya] and Dar es Salaam [Tanzania] bombings."

He further reports that although Clinton and his top aides did not anticipate that Al-Qaeda would turn against the United States, even when they finally did, "they figured the U.S. would gain more from it in the long run."[419] He cites a former CIA analyst on the objectives of this policy, which is clearly motivated by strategic and economic interests rather than concern for American lives. Hinting at a policy involving the ongoing use of Al-Qaeda to secure regional U.S. strategic interests, continuing throughout the 1990s, the CIA analyst stated:

"The policy of guiding the evolution of Islam and of helping them against our adversaries worked marvelously well in Afghanistan against the Red Army. The same doctrines can still be used to destabilize what remains of Russian power, and especially to counter the Chinese influence in Central Asia."

Thus, even after Osama bin Laden was placed on the FBI's Most Wanted List with a reward offered for his capture, the State Department "never exerted any real pressure on the Taliban to apprehend him." A subsequent report in the Associated Press (AP) revealed that the U.S. bombing of Sudan and Afghanistan, in apparent response to the embassy bombings, was not targeted at Osama bin Laden.

AP noted that despite the Clinton administration's "specific intelligence" on bin Laden's location, they had decided not to attempt to capture or kill him—contrary to the public pretext for the bombing. Based on a hundred interviews, numerous journalistic investigations, European intelligence sources, as well as years of archival research and travels, Labeviere's findings should be taken seriously.[420]

Indeed, it is a matter of record that the U.S. government had received advance warning of the Kenya bombing two weeks before it occurred. During the trial in 2000 of four men charged in the bombings, defence lawyers successfully demonstrated that U.S. officials did not pass the received warnings on to the personnel of the threatened embassies, thus establishing a significant degree of U.S. responsibility for the death toll.[421]

Labeviere's book, with meticulous documentation, places all this in the context of an ongoing U.S. policy that aims to selectively foster 'Islamic' militancy to secure various strategic and economic interests around the world. This conclusion is strongly supported by the fact that the U.S. has consciously used Al-Qaeda to support U.S. plans in Central Asia, the Caucasus and the Balkans towards the end of the 1990s. In a succinct overview of this policy, Director of the Centre for Research on Globalisation (CRG) Professor Michel Chossudovsky[422] finds that:

> "Lost in the barrage of recent history, the role of the CIA in supporting and developing international terrorist organisations during the Cold war and its aftermath is casually ignored or downplayed by the Western media...
>
> The 'blowback' thesis[423] is a fabrication. The evidence amply confirms that the CIA never severed its ties to the 'Islamic Militant Network.' Since the end of the Cold War, these covert intelligence links have not only been maintained, they have in fact become increasingly sophisticated. New undercover initiatives financed by the Golden Crescent drug trade were set in motion in Central Asia, the Caucasus and the Balkans. Pakistan's military and intelligence apparatus (controlled by the CIA) essentially 'served as a catalyst for the disintegration of the Soviet Union and the emergence of six new Muslim republics in Central Asia.'"

Chossudovsky refers to, among other reports in the press, a lengthy Congressional report by the Republican Party Committee (RPC) in 1997 confirming that the Clinton administration "helped turn Bosnia into a militant Islamic base," by direct complicity in military support to Bosnian fighters provided through the support of groups "believed to be connected with such fixtures of the Islamic terror network as Sheik Omar Abdel Rahman (the convicted mastermind behind the 1993 World Trade Center bombing) and Osama bin Laden, a wealthy Saudi émigré believed to bankroll numerous militant groups."[424]

It appears that such co-optation of Al-Qaeda to achieve U.S. interests had been tried before, in the inter-Muslim conflict during the early stages of the Bosnia war, when the the U.S. supported the assault by the Izetbegovic regime against local Muslim rival Fikret Adbic.[425]

The "Bosnia pattern" referred to by the RPC was replayed in Kosovo. U.S. Representative John Kasich of the House Armed Services Committee admitted that: "We connected ourselves with the KLA which was the staging point for Bin Laden."[426] In fact, the U.S. government was allied with bin Laden in the war on Yugoslavia through CIA assistance to the Kosovo Liberation Army (KLA). The *Washington Times*, for instance, reported that: "Some members of the Kosovo Liberation Army, which has financed its war effort through the sale of heroin, were trained in terrorist camps run by international fugitive Osama bin Laden...

> "[T]he KLA members, embraced by the Clinton administration in NATO's... bombing campaign to bring Yugoslav President Slobodan Milosevic to the bargaining table, were trained in secret camps in Afghanistan, Bosnia-Herzegovina and elsewhere, according to newly obtained intelligence reports... The reports said bin Laden's organization, known as al-Qaeda, has both trained and financially supported the KLA. Many border crossings into Kosovo by 'foreign fighters' also have been documented and include veterans of the militant group Islamic Jihad from Bosnia, Chechnya and Afghanistan."[427]

In his CRG paper, 'Osamagate,' Chossudovsky refers to authoritative Congressional testimony and press reports confirming the same. These examples—there are others—support the thesis explored by Labeviere: successive U.S. administrations have permitted their allies, Pakistan and Saudi Arabia, among others, to continue to support Al-Qaeda, with the view that the latter would conduct regional operations which ultimately destabilise U.S. rivals, and thus inadvertently secure U.S. interests.

Labeviere documents a "short-sighted" policy that at first did not anticipate the degree to which Al-Qaeda would turn against the U.S., but even after reaping the bloody fruits of its own policy in the 1998 embassy bombings, continued to signal a green light to its allies funneling finances and arms to Al-Qaeda. The maintenance of such a green light signal seems based on the calculation that the policy would ultimately suit U.S. interests far better than the alternative option: pursuing meaningful measures to crack down on bin Laden's network, including intense pressure on its own regional allies. This effective 'harbouring' of Al-Qaeda by successive U.S. administrations through regional allies, including the Bush administration, appears to have continued, even in the aftermath of 11th September 2001.

U.S. Protection of Osama

An examination of U.S. attempts to capture Osama bin Laden only adds weight to the ominous implications of the above facts. According to the authoritative *Jane's Intelligence Review*: "In February 1995, U.S. authorities named bin Laden and his Saudi brother-in-law, Mohammed Jamal Khalifa, among 172 unindicted co-conspirators with the 11 Muslims charged for the World Trade Center bombing and the associated plot to blow up other New York landmarks."[428]

Despite this, the United States has consistently blocked attempts to investigate and capture bin Laden. In March 1996, for example, when bin Laden was present in Sudan after leaving Saudi Arabia, Major General Elfatih Erwa—then Sudanese Minister of State for Defense—offered to extradite bin Laden either to Saudi Arabia or the United States.

"The Sudanese security services, he said, would happily keep close watch on bin Laden for the United States. But if that would not suffice, the government was prepared to place him in custody and hand him over, though to whom was ambiguous. In one formulation, Erwa said Sudan would consider any legitimate proffer of criminal charges against the accused terrorist."[429]

Instead of accepting the offer of extradition and indictment of bin Laden, the U.S. did the opposite:

"[U.S. officials] said, 'Just ask him to leave the country. Just don't let him go to Somalia,' Erwa, the Sudanese general, said in an interview. 'We said he will go to Afghanistan, and they [U.S. officials] said, 'Let him.' On May 15, 1996, Foreign Minister Taha sent a fax to Carney in Nairobi, giving up on the transfer of custody. His government had asked bin Laden to vacate the country, Taha wrote, and he would be free to go."[430]

But this was only one incident out of many in relation to Sudanese intelligence on the Al-Qaeda network.[431] The London *Observer*, for instance, reported that: "Security chiefs on both sides of the Atlantic repeatedly turned down the chance to acquire a vast intelligence database on Osama bin Laden and more than 200 leading members of his al-Qaeda terrorist network in the years leading up to the 11 September attacks...

"They were offered thick files, with photographs and detailed biographies of many of his principal cadres, and vital information about al-Qaeda's financial interests in many parts of the globe. On two separate occasions, they were given an opportunity to extradite or interview key bin Laden operatives who had been arrested in Africa because they appeared to be planning terrorist atrocities.

None of the offers, made regularly from the start of 1995, was taken up... The Observer has evidence that a separate offer made by Sudanese agents in Britain to share intelligence with MI6 has been rejected. This follows four years of similar rebuffs. One U.S. source who has seen the files on bin Laden's men in Khartoum said some were 'an inch and a half thick.' They included photographs, and information on their families, backgrounds and contacts. Most were 'Afghan Arabs.' Saudis, Yemenis and Egyptians who had fought with bin Laden against the Soviets in Afghanistan.

'We know them in detail,' said one Sudanese source. 'We know their leaders, how they implement their policies, how they plan for the future. We have tried to feed this information to American and British intelligence so they can learn how this thing can be tackled.' In 1996, following intense pressure from Saudi Arabia and the U.S., Sudan agreed to expel bin Laden and up to 300 of his associates. Sudanese intelligence believed this to be a great mistake. 'There we could keep track of him, read his mail,' the source went on."

Indeed, instead of agreeing to bin Laden's extradition and indictment, two years later the U.S. launched an attack on Sudan targeting the Al-Shifa pharmaceutical plant, claiming that Sudan was harbouring bin Laden-connected terrorists, in particular by allowing Al-Shifa—alleged by the U.S. to be developing chemical and biological weapons of mass destruction on bin Laden's behalf—to continue operation.

Yet just before the U.S. missile attack, Sudan had made further offers in relation to hunting down members of bin Laden's network, that the U.S. had ignored. According to "a copy of a personal memo sent from Sudan to Louis Freeh, former director of the FBI, after the murderous 1998 attacks on American embassies in Kenya and Tanzania," Sudan had arrested "two named bin Laden operatives held the day after the bombings after they crossed the Sudanese border from Kenya...

"They had cited the manager of a Khartoum leather factory owned by bin Laden as a reference for their visas, and were held after they tried to rent a flat overlooking the U.S. embassy in Khartoum, where they were thought to be planning an attack. U.S. sources have confirmed that the FBI wished to arrange their immediate extradition. However, Clinton's Secretary of State, Madeleine Albright, forbade it. She had classed Sudan as a 'terrorist state,' and three days later U.S. missiles blasted the al-Shifa medicine factory in Khartoum. The U.S. wrongly claimed it was owned by bin Laden and making chemical weapons. In fact, it supplied 60 per cent of Sudan's medicines, and had contracts to make vaccines with the UN."

Despite this illegal bombing perpetrated by the Clinton administration,[432] Sudan continued to hold the suspects for a further three weeks, "hoping the U.S. would both perform their extradition and take up the offer to examine their bin Laden database. Finally, the two men were deported to Pakistan. Their present whereabouts are unknown." Furthermore, U.S. indifference to intelligence information on bin Laden continued into the year 2000:

> "Last year the CIA and FBI, following four years of Sudanese entreaties, sent a joint investigative team to establish whether Sudan was in fact a sponsor of terrorism. Last May, it gave Sudan a clean bill of health. However, even then, it made no effort to examine the voluminous files on bin Laden."[433]

Sudanese intelligence on Osama bin Laden and Al-Qaeda was not the only source of massive information spurned by the U.S. government. *Jane's Intelligence Digest* reports that: "Back in March [2001] Moscow's Permanent Mission at the UN submitted to the UN Security Council an unprecedentedly detailed report on Al-Qaeda's terrorist infrastructure in Afghanistan, but the U.S. government opted not to act." The "extent of intelligence data tabled by the Russians" was "breathtaking." Also uncovered by the report was "the degree of Pakistani military and security involvement in Afghanistan."[434]

The testimony of the late John O'Neill, the Irish-American FBI agent who for several years led U.S. investigations into Osama bin Laden's Al-Qaeda network, is crucial in understanding the real context of such U.S. blockage of attempts to investigate, indict and capture bin Laden. O'Neill, who was Deputy Director and Director of Anti-terrorism for the FBI, investigated the bombings of the World Trade Center in 1993, a U.S. base in Saudi Arabia in 1996, the U.S. embassies in Nairobi and Dar-Es-Salaam in 1998, and the U.S.S. Cole in 2000. According to his FBI associates, John O'Neill "has been regarded as a dedicated, relentless and hard-charging investigator who was one of the FBI's brightest stars." Barry W. Mawn, Assistant Director of the FBI in charge of the New York office described O'Neill as "a tireless worker" in whom he had "complete confidence."[435] The *Irish Times* reported that in interviews with French intelligence analyst Jean-Charles Brisard:

> "He complained bitterly that the U.S. State Department—and behind it the oil lobby who make up President Bush's entourage—blocked attempts to prove bin Laden's guilt. The U.S. ambassador to Yemen, Ms Barbara Bodine, forbade O'Neill and his team of so-called Rambos (as the Yemeni authorities called them) from entering Yemen. In

August 2001, O'Neill resigned in frustration and took up a new job as head of security at the World Trade Centre. He died in the September 11th attack... The FBI agent had told Brisard: 'All the answers, everything needed to dismantle Osama bin Laden's organisation, can be found in Saudi Arabia.'

But U.S. diplomats shrank from offending the Saudi royal family. O'Neill went to Saudi Arabia after 19 U.S. servicemen died in the bombing of a military installation in Dhahran in June 1996. Saudi officials interrogated the suspects, declared them guilty and executed them—without letting the FBI talk to them. 'They were reduced to the role of forensic scientists, collecting material evidence on the bomb site,' Brisard says. O'Neill said there was clear evidence in Yemen of bin Laden's guilt in the bombing of the U.S.S. Cole 'in which 17 U.S. servicemen died,' but that the State Department prevented him from getting it."

We should emphasise here that by deliberately blocking O'Neill's access to the "clear evidence" of bin Laden's guilt—which would have justified his indictment and arrest—the State Department deliberately allowed bin Laden to escape apprehension.

Elaborating on O'Neill's observations on the Saudi role, former French intelligence officer Brisard, who authored a report on Al-Qaeda for the French intelligence agency DST, and his colleague Guillaume Dasquié, Editor of *Intelligence Online*, record that "a significant part of the Saudi royal family supports bin Laden." Pointing out that attacks inside the kingdom have targeted U.S. interests, not the Saudis, Brisard notes that: "Saudi Arabia has always protected bin Laden—or protected itself from him."[436]

The late O'Neill was certainly not alone in his stance. According to Pulitzer prize-winning journalist Seymour Hersh, reporting in the *New Yorker*, "American intelligence officials have been particularly angered by the refusal of the Saudis to help the FBI and the CIA run 'traces'—that is, name checks and other background information—on the nineteen men, more than half of them believed to be from Saudi Arabia, who took part in the attacks on the World Trade Center and the Pentagon...

"'They knew that once we started asking for a few traces the list would grow,' one former official said. 'It's better to shut it down right away.' He pointed out that thousands of disaffected Saudis have joined fundamentalist groups throughout the Middle East. Other officials said that there is a growing worry inside the FBI and the CIA that the actual identities of many of those involved in the attacks may not be known definitively for months, if ever. Last week, a senior intelligence official confirmed the lack of Saudi cooperation and told me, angrily, that the

Saudis 'have only one constant—and it's keeping themselves in power.'"[437]

There is also evidence compounding O'Neill's testimony (discussed previously) that there was direct contact between the CIA and Osama bin Laden as late as the summer of 2001. The respected French daily *Le Figaro*, owned by the U.S. defence contractor Carlyle Group that employs former President George W. Bush Sr., reported in October 2001 that Osama bin Laden underwent treatment in July at the American Hospital in Dubai, where he met a CIA official. Radio France International (RFI) also corroborated the report, which was based on authoritative French intelligence sources as well as "a witness, a professional partner of the administrative management of the hospital." The newspaper recorded:

"Dubai, one of the seven emirates of the Federation of the United Arab Emirates, North-East of Abu-Dhabi. This city, population 350,000, was the backdrop of a secret meeting between Osama bin Laden and the local CIA agent in July. A partner of the administration of the American Hospital in Dubai claims that public enemy number one stayed at this hospital between the 4th and 14th of July...

Each floor of the hospital has two 'VIP' suites and fifteen rooms. The Saudi billionaire was admitted to the well-respected urology department run by Terry Callaway, gallstone and infertility specialist. Dr Callaway declined to respond to our questions despite several phone calls... While he was hospitalised, bin Laden received visits from many members of his family as well as prominent Saudis and Emiratis. During the hospital stay, the local CIA agent, known to many in Dubai, was seen taking the main elevator of the hospital to go to bin Laden's hospital room. A few days later, the CIA man bragged to a few friends about having visited bin Laden. Authorised sources say that on July 15th, the day after bin Laden returned to Quetta, the CIA agent was called back to headquarters...

According to Arab diplomatic sources as well as French intelligence, very specific information was transmitted to the CIA with respect to terrorist attacks against American interests around the world, including on US soil. A DST [French intelligence] report dated 7 September enumerates all the intelligence, and specifies that the order to attack was to come from Afghanistan.

In August, at the U.S. Embassy in Paris, an emergency meeting was called between the DGSE [French foreign intelligence service] and senior U.S. intelligence officials. The Americans were extremely worried, and requested very specific information from the French about Algerian activists, without advising their counterparts about the reasons for their requests. To the question 'what do you fear in the coming days?', the Americans kept a difficult-to-fathom silence. Contacts between the CIA and bin Laden began in 1979 when, as a representative of his family's business, bin Laden began recruiting volunteers for the Afghan resistance against the Red Army. FBI investigators examining the embassy bombing sites in Nairobi and Dar es Salaam discovered that evidence led to military explosives from the US Army, and that these explosives had been delivered three years earlier to Afghan Arabs, the infamous international volunteer brigades involved side by side with bin Laden during the Afghan war against the Red Army. In the pursuit of its investigations, the FBI discovered 'financing agreements' that the CIA had been developing with its 'Arab friends' for years. The Dubai meeting is then within the logic of 'a certain American policy.'"[438]

The London *Guardian* elaborated on the French report, noting that:

"Two months before September 11 Osama bin Laden flew to Dubai for 10 days for treatment at the American hospital, where he was visited by the local CIA agent... The disclosures are known to come from French intelligence... Intelligence sources say that another CIA agent was also present; and that Bin Laden was also visited by Prince Turki al Faisal, then head of Saudi intelligence, who had long had links with the Taliban, and Bin Laden."[439]

Bin Laden's apparent stay at the American hospital in Dubai has also been commented on by the London *Times*.[440] These reports, while now denied by both the CIA and the hospital concerned, must be taken seriously due to the fact that they are based on highly credible sources, namely a partner of the hospital's administrative management along with disclosures from French intelligence—sources that both *Le Figaro* and Radio France International describe as "authoritative."

Arab specialist Antoine Sfeir commented that the ongoing CIA-bin Laden contacts indicated by these reports are not surprising: "The CIA maintained contacts with bin Laden until 1998. Those contacts didn't end after bin Laden moved to Afghanistan. Until the last minute, CIA agents hoped bin Laden would return to U.S. command, as was the case before 1998." Sfeir further noted that the information on the ongoing CIA-bin Laden connection had been in circulation for 15 days before 1st November 2001.[441]

Radio France International followed up its first report with more specific information, identifying the CIA agent as Larry Mitchell, "a connoisseur of the Arab world and specialist of the (Arab) peninsula," whose business card identified him as a "consular agent." According to RFI, Mitchell is "a CIA agent and a prominent fixture in Dubai's expatriate community." RFI also reported that the precise date of the agent's encounter with bin Laden was 12th July, two days before the head of Al-Qaeda left the hospital.[442]

The respected weekly newspaper the *New York Press* has taken these reports seriously.[443] They have also been commented on by Michel Chossudovsky, Professor of Economics at the University of Ottawa and Director of the Centre for Research on Globalisation (CRG) based in Montreal, Canada. He observes that:

> "An article in the French daily Le Figaro confirms that Osama bin Laden underwent surgery in an American Hospital in Dubai in July.

> During his stay in the hospital, he met with a CIA official. While on the World's 'most wanted list,' no attempt was made to arrest him during his two week stay in the hospital, shedding doubt on the Administration's resolve to track down Osama bin Laden.

> Barely a few days ago Defense Secretary Rumsfeld stated that it would be difficult to find him and extradite him. It's like 'searching for a needle in a stack of hay.' But the U.S. could have ordered his arrest and extradition in Dubai last July. But then they would not have had a pretext for waging a war. Meanwhile, innocent civilians are being killed by B-52 Bombers as means 'to go after' Osama bin Laden. According to UN sources, the so-called 'campaign against international terrorism' could lead to the death of several million people from an impending famine."[444]

But the blocking of attempts to apprehend Osama bin Laden does not end there. Judicial Watch has also noted the curious fact that a number of organisations in the U.S., some of which have even received government funding, reportedly support Osama bin Laden financially: "Based on our analysis of publicly available documents, and other published reports, it is clear that this U.S.-based network has also provided financial resources for Osama bin Laden and his terrorist operations."

Judicial Watch accuses America's Internal Revenue Service (IRS) of looking "the other way when it came to investigating and taking action against radical Islamic front groups which reportedly launder money to fund terrorist operations on American soil." The Washington DC law firm further notes that one particular group, the Islamic African Relief Agency (IARA), which has continued to operate unhindered, reportedly "received 2 U.S. State Department grants in 1998 worth $4.2 million dollars" and "transferred money to Mercy International… that purchased the vehicles used by Osama bin Laden to bomb the U.S. embassies in both Kenya and Tanzania on August 8, 1998."[445] The Agency also has reported ties to "an individual who supplied the cell phone Osama bin Laden used to orchestrate the bombing of two U.S. embassies in Africa in 1998."[446]

The conservative U.S. news service, *NewsMax*, elaborated on Judicial Watch's concerns, reporting the legal watchdog's charge that: "Osama bin Laden's al Qaida network, Hamas and others continue to use tax-exempt U.S.-based charities to bankroll terror, unencumbered by even the hint of an audit...

"At least 16 U.S.-based non-profit entities have been linked financially to bin Laden, the legal watchdog group says. The decision not to investigate these groups is especially difficult to understand given that the information in the Judicial Watch complaint is hardly a state secret. On the contrary, the complaint is based largely on reports published over the last three years in venues like the New York Times... One such questionable non-profit, the Islamic African Relief Agency (IARA), has been directly linked to earlier attacks on U.S. interests by bin Laden [in 1998]... Not only did [Internal Revenue Service Commissioner] Rossotti & Co. not investigate, that same year the Clinton State Department showered the IARA with $4.2 million in grants."[447]

In the wake of this dire publicity concerning the Bush administration's continuation of the Clinton 'turn a blind eye to terrorists' legacy, the former's Treasury Department reportedly began investigating two of the alleged "front" organisations, including the IARA. But as Judicial Watch noted in a November update on these developments: "Though now under investigation by the Treasury Department, the organization, based in Columbia Missouri, still operates freely." The law firm's Chairman and General Counsel Larry Klayman, observes:

"It is quite apparent that U.S. charitable dollars have been misused to finance international terrorism and the likes of Osama bin Laden. Given the numerous ties of the Islamic African Relief Agency and other non-profit front groups to terrorism, Judicial Watch does not understand what is holding up law enforcement action against them. Asset seizures must begin immediately, before it is too late."[448]

Jonathan Weiner, former U.S. Deputy Assistant Secretary of State for International Law Enforcement, has pointed out that some of these charities are legitimate enterprises "whose funds have been diverted or taken advantage of or used for terrorist purposes."

Nevertheless, the ongoing lack of a full-blown inquiry is disconcerting, as is the unrestricted freedom with which these organisations continue to operate, despite supposed investigations.[449]

Weiner also confirmed in November 2001 that Bahrain, Kuwait, Saudi Arabia, and the United Arab Emirates have failed to assist federal officials in the disclosure of known terrorist funds moving back and forth between those countries:

> "Since September 11th, all those countries have frozen accounts or have looked in their banking systems for the money of people associated with terrorist finance, [and] have gone through the entire list provided by the United States... country after country has announced, 'We've looked for funds. We've looked diligently. We've been ready to freeze some funds. We just haven't found anything.' No money in the UAE, no money in Kuwait... There is, I can tell, no money announced in Saudi Arabia, none announced in Bahrain. Well, given that we know [that terrorist] funds came out of there and we know [that terrorist] funds went back there, their inability to find funds is pretty astonishing."[450]

The Bush administration has been directly complicit in this. The *New Yorker* notes that even in the aftermath of 11th September, the Saudi establishment has been "shielded from Washington's foreign-policy bureaucracy." According to one U.S. government expert on Saudi affairs, "Only a tiny handful of people inside the government are familiar with U.S.-Saudi relations. And that is purposeful." This cozy relationship appears to be behind the Bush administration's blocking of inquiries into Saudi-bin Laden terrorist connections. "When the Saudis were confronted by press reports that some of the substantial funds that the monarchy routinely gives to Islamic charities may actually have gone to Al Qaeda and other terrorist networks, they denied any knowledge of such transfers. [National Security Agency] intercepts, however, have led many in the intelligence community to conclude otherwise."

Yet despite the U.S. government's longstanding knowledge of the Saudi establishment's financial support of Osama bin Laden and Al-Qaeda, as also corroborated by former State Department official Jonathan Weiner, "The Bush administration has chosen not to confront the Saudi leadership over its financial support of terror organizations and its refusal to help in the investigation. 'As far as the Saudi Arabians go, they've been nothing but cooperative,' President Bush said at a news conference on September 24th."[451]

Two banks located in Bahrain and Kuwait—the Faysal Islamic Bank and the Kuwait Finance House—which had been listed in European reports as having terrorist ties, "were also excluded from Bush Jr.'s financial crackdown after 11th September." Worse still, both of these institutions are correspondent banks with Deutschebank, the German financial giant with links to insider trading in connection with 11th September.

Reuters further reported on 7th November 2001 that the U.S. Treasury Department had added 61 people and organisations to the President's original

Executive Order of 23rd September, purportedly directed at cracking down on the financial arteries of Al-Qaeda—including banks in Somalia and Nassau, the Bahamas. "But mysteriously, no banks in Bahrain, Kuwait, or Saudi Arabia were named in either the original order or its expansion."

More curiously, according to the FBI, Osama bin Laden's personal bank—al Shamal Islamic Bank—which is headquartered in Khartoum, Sudan, and which bin Laden helped capitalize with $50 million in private funds, "is being investigated by U.S. or overseas authorities." Yet the *U.S. News* reported on 8th October 2001 that the FBI refuses to indicate exactly *which* authority, an event that is made all the more ominous by the fact that President Bush has also failed to include Osama bin Laden's al Shamal Islamic Bank in his Executive Order.[452] Yet it is a matter of record that bin Laden's personal bank is used through correspondent transactions with other banks to fund Al-Qaeda projects.

For instance, according to the *Washington Post*, one of bin Laden's associates testified at the U.S. trial on the 1998 African embassy bombings that: "$250,000 was wired from al Shamal Islamic Bank directly into the bin Laden cohort's Texas bank account—where he used it to buy a plane delivered to bin Laden... intended to transport Stinger missiles."

The *Financial Times* elaborated that:

"The money was wired from the Wadi al Aqiq account at al Shamal bank via Bank of New York to a Bank of America account held in Dallas, Texas by Essam al Ridi. Al Ridi, an Egyptian flight instructor who met bin Laden in Pakistan in 1985, flew the plane to Khartoum."[453]

Thus, even now there appears to be an effective unofficial block on U.S. investigations into Saudi and bin Laden terrorist connections, originating from high-level elements of the Bush administration.

As the *Toronto Star* comments: "What are we to make of all of this? One possible conclusion is that the bin Laden terror problem was allowed to get out of hand because bin Laden, himself, had powerful protectors in both Washington and Saudi Arabia."[454]

These facts should be understood in context with Brisard's and Dasquié's revelations in their study, *Bin Laden*, that many members of the Saudi royal family—whom Bush has personally shielded from FBI investigation—actually support Osama bin Laden. Even now, the FBI continues to largely ignore Saudi Arabia. According to the London *Times* reporting at the beginning of November 2001, "FBI arrogance and secrecy dismays the U.S." The FBI has apparently "exhausted most of its leads" and acts as if "convinced that the key to al-Qaeda operations lay in Germany." This is in spite of the fact that FBI arrests made by the security services in Germany and other European countries based on these alleged FBI leads have consistently shown that "in almost every case these cells knew nothing about the September 11 hijacks."[455]

Even more extraordinary is the refusal to apprehend known Al-Qaeda cells currently operating within the U.S. According to the London *Telegraph*: "The real fear for the future since the attacks in New York and Washington is that dozens, perhaps hundreds of operatives loyal to Al'Qaeda are in America and Canada ready to strike again, awaiting a call from Osama Bin Laden...

"In every terrorist act by Al'Qaeda since the early 1990s bin Laden has ensured that the actual suicide bombers were 'sleepers,' long-time residents of the countries they attacked, with ordinary jobs, identity papers and a social and family life. Bin Laden has spent a decade building up such networks of individuals, some of whom have never travelled to Afghanistan to meet him."[456]

Yet as the *Washington Post* reported in late September, the FBI had known "for the last several years" of the existence in the U.S. of such multiple Al-Qaeda groups:

"The FBI has not made any arrests because the group members entered the country legally in recent years and have not been involved in illegal activities since they arrived, the officials said. Government officials say they do not know why the cells are here, what their purpose is or whether their members are planning attacks. One official even described their presence as 'possibly benign,' though others have a more sinister interpretation and give assurances that measures are in place to protect the public."[457]

Firstly, U.S. government officials are issuing contradictory statements to justify their failure to apprehend confirmed 'sleeper' members of the Al-Qaeda terrorist network led by Osama bin Laden within the U.S. This in itself gives good reason to doubt the official explanations.

Secondly, the failure to apprehend these known Al-Qaeda operatives is in stark contrast to official U.S. policy, initiated at the behest of Attorney General John Ashcroft, where hundreds of Arab-Americans, Muslim-Americans and immigrants have been rounded up and questioned based solely on their ethnicity and religion. The result has been that Arabs and other foreigners without any connection to terrorism at all are being detained indefinitely, while known members of bin Laden's terrorist network walk around the U.S. freely.

Thirdly, the idea that known members of the Al-Qaeda terrorist network have not been arrested because they may be "benign," is totally absurd, given that the Al-Qaeda network is responsible for the murder of nearly 3,000 innocent civilians on 11th September, and many others in previous attacks. The U.S. government, in other words, has been knowingly harbouring Al-Qaeda terrorists both before and after 11th September.

The resultant picture is shocking. In tandem with the documentary record briefly discussed before, it strongly suggests a possible combination of U.S. collusion and complicity, rooted in brute strategic and economic interests. The U.S. government has maintained, and continues to maintain, regional alliances with client regimes that it knows full well support Al-Qaeda.

The government has also ensured, and continues to ensure, that the principal sources of Al-Qaeda's support continue to operate unimpeded, thanks to the obstruction and deflection of investigations. The government has also knowingly harboured Al-Qaeda terrorists, and continues to do so. It appears that one of the primary determinants of this policy is the desire on the part of elements of the U.S. government to maintain interests that are secured through these regional alliances.

The U.S.-Pakistan Alliance and the ISI

The missing link in this increasingly sinister web of relationships is the role of Pakistani intelligence in 11th September. To understand this role, it is necessary to understand the historic ties between Pakistan, Al-Qaeda and the United States. Osama bin Laden was recruited during the 1980s in Afghanistan, "ironically under the auspices of the CIA, to fight Soviet invaders."[458]

In 1979, "the largest covert operation in the history of the CIA" was launched in response to the Soviet invasion of Afghanistan.[459] Central Asia specialist Ahmed Rashid records in the leading foreign policy journal *Foreign Affairs* that:

"With the active encouragement of the CIA and Pakistan's ISI [Inter Services Intelligence], who wanted to turn the Afghan jihad into a global war waged by all Muslim states against the Soviet Union, some 35,000 Muslim radicals from 40 Islamic countries joined Afghanistan's fight between 1982 and 1992. Tens of thousands more came to study in Pakistani madrasahs. Eventually more than 100,000 foreign Muslim radicals were directly influenced by the Afghan jihad."[460]

Through the Pakistani ISI, the CIA covertly trained and sponsored the Afghan fighters. In this respect, the ISI served as the intermediary through which the CIA funnelled arms, planning and training to the Afghan rebels. As the *Washington Post* notes:

> "In March 1985, President Reagan signed National Security Decision Directive 166 [authorizing] stepped-up covert military aid to the mujahideen...
>
> [This Directive] made clear that the secret Afghan war had a new goal: to defeat Soviet troops in Afghanistan through covert action and encourage a Soviet withdrawal. The new covert U.S. assistance began with a dramatic increase in arms supplies—a steady rise to 65,000 tons annually by 1987,... as well as a 'ceaseless stream' of CIA and Pentagon specialists who traveled to the secret headquarters of Pakistan's ISI on the main road near Rawalpindi, Pakistan. There the CIA specialists met with Pakistani intelligence officers to help plan operations for the Afghan rebels."[461]

The Pakistani ISI thus became an integral instrument of U.S. foreign policy in the region. Supported by the CIA through intensive military assistance, the ISI became a "parallel structure wielding enormous power over all aspects of government."[462]

The result was not merely a working partnership between the American and Pakistani intelligence agencies, but a subservient relationship, in which the CIA maintained overall directive dominance over an ISI that pursued policies within the strategic framework established by its principal donor, the United States. This can clearly be seen in the impact of the intensification of regional CIA operations through the ISI on General Zia Ul Haq's military regime:

> "'Relations between the CIA and the ISI had grown increasingly warm following Zia's ouster of Bhutto and the advent of the military regime,'... During most of the Afghan war, Pakistan was more aggressively anti-Soviet than even the United States. Soon after the Soviet military invaded Afghanistan in 1980, Zia sent his ISI chief to destabilize the Soviet Central Asian states. The CIA only agreed to this plan in October 1984... 'the CIA was more cautious than the Pakistanis.' Both Pakistan and the United States took the line of deception on Afghanistan with a public posture of negotiating a settlement while privately agreeing that military escalation was the best course."[463]

Jane's Defence Weekly provides a detailed overview of this U.S.-Pakistan-Afghanistan triangle: "The U.S.-led 'proxy war' model was based on the premise that Islamists made good anti-Communist allies. The plan was diabolically simple: to hire, train and control motivated Islamic mercenaries...

> "The trainers were mainly from Pakistan's Inter Services Intelligence (ISI) agency, who learnt their craft from American Green Beret commandos and Navy SEALS in various U.S. training establishments. Mass training of Afghan mujahideen was subsequently conducted by the Pakistan Army under the supervision of the elite Special Services Group (SSG), specialists in covert action behind enemy lines and the ISI... According to intelligence estimates over 10,000 Islamic mercenaries, trained in guerrilla warfare and armed with sophisticated weapons, are unemployed in Pakistan today, waiting to be transported to the next jihad...
>
> In 1988, with U.S. knowledge, Bin Laden created Al Qaeda (The Base): a conglomerate of quasi-independent Islamic terrorist cells in countries spread across at least 26 countries... Washington turned a blind eye to Al-Qaeda."[464]

Thus, without the consistent support of the U.S. government, Pakistan would not possess a powerful military intelligence apparatus in the form of the ISI. Indeed, according to leading U.S. South Asia expert Selig Harrison: "The Taliban are a creation of America's Central Intelligence Agency (CIA) in cooperation with Pakistan's Inter-Services Intelligence Directorate (ISI)...

> "After the Soviet invasion of Afghanistan in 1979, the CIA had encouraged militant Islamic groups from around the world to come to Afghanistan. The U.S.A. and its allies provided 3 billion dollars for building up the largest ever funded 'resistance movement'... Pakistan played a central role in the operation. Not only that most of the militants had been prepared and trained in Pakistani madrassas (Islamic religious schools) and camps, Pakistan provided also money and arms. The CIA had left much of the decision how to use the U.S. funds to Pakistani specialists."

Most crucially, Harrison pointed out as recently as March 2001 that the ISI's role as a regional instrument of the CIA has not ended. The "old association between the intelligence agencies continues." Harrison observes that: "The CIA still has close links with the ISI."[465] Indeed, as noted in previous chapters, multiple official U.S. government sources confirm that, through Pakistani military intelligence, the U.S. had been providing support to the Taliban before the anti-Taliban shift took precedence. The State Department's *Patterns of Global Terrorism* reported in 2000, regarding General Pervez Musharraf's regime, that:

"The United States remains concerned about reports of continued Pakistani support for the Taliban's military operations in Afghanistan. Credible reporting indicates that Pakistan is providing the Taliban with materiel, fuel, funding, technical assistance, and military advisers. Pakistan has not prevented large numbers of Pakistani nationals from moving into Afghanistan to fight for the Taliban. Islamabad also failed to take effective steps to curb the activities of certain madrassas, or religious schools, that serve as recruiting grounds for terrorism."[466]

But behind the public front of concern, Pakistan's support of the Taliban was supported by the United States. We should remind ourselves of the previously noted confirmation of the U.S. House of Representatives' International Relations Committee in mid-2000 that: "[T]he United States has been part and parcel to supporting the Taliban all along, and still is let me add...

"You have a military government in Pakistan now that is arming the Taliban to the teeth... Let me note; that [U.S.] aid has always gone to Taliban areas... We have been supporting the Taliban, because all our aid goes to the Taliban areas. And when people from the outside try to put aid into areas not controlled by the Taliban, they are thwarted by our own State Department... At that same moment, Pakistan initiated a major resupply effort, which eventually saw the defeat, and caused the defeat, of almost all of the anti-Taliban forces in Afghanistan."[467]

Two days after the attacks on the World Trade Centre and the Pentagon, a delegation led by the Director-General of the Pakistani ISI, Lt. Gen. Mahmoud Ahmed, was in Washington. The delegation was holding high-level talks with officials at the U.S. State Department.[468] Reuters reported that the Pakistani ISI chief, in fact, "was in the U.S. when the attacks occurred."[469] The *New York Times* further noted that "he happened to be here on a regular visit of consultations."[470] The London *Daily Telegraph* revealed that he had arrived in the U.S. on 4th September, a week before the 11th September attacks.[471]

One day before the WTC and Pentagon attacks, the Pakistani daily *The News* observed that: "ISI Chief Lt-Gen Mahmood's week-long presence in Washington has triggered speculation about the agenda of his mysterious meetings at the Pentagon and National Security Council...

"Officially, State Department sources say he is on a routine visit in return to CIA Director George Tenet's earlier visit to Islamabad. Official sources confirm that he met Tenet this week. He also held long parleys with unspecified officials at the White House and the Pentagon. But the most important meeting was with Mark Grossman, U.S. Under Secretary of State for Political Affairs. U.S. sources would not furnish any details beyond saying that the two discussed 'matters of mutual interests'...

One can safely guess that the discussions must have centred around Afghanistan, relations with India and China, disarmament of civilian outfits, country's nuclear and missiles programme and, of course, Osama Bin Laden...

What added interest to his visit is the history of such visits. Last time Ziauddin Butt, Mahmood's predecessor, was here during Nawaz Sharif's government domestic politics turned topsy-turvy within days. That this is not the first visit by Mahmood in the last three months shows the urgency of the ongoing parleys."[472]

In the aftermath of these high-level, behind-the-scenes meetings, which continued after 11th September, it was confirmed that under U.S. orders and representing U.S. demands, Lt. Gen. Mahmoud Ahmad would meet with Taliban leaders to negotiate Osama bin Laden's extradition to the U.S. The *Washington Post* reported that: "At American urging, Ahmed traveled... to Kandahar, Afghanistan. There he delivered the bluntest of demands. Turn over bin Laden without conditions, he told Taliban leader Mohammad Omar, or face certain war with the United States and its allies."[473] Once again, this event illustrated the degree to which the ISI represents an instrument of U.S. interests.

Just prior to the commencement of the Anglo-American bombing campaign against Afghanistan, Lt. Gen. Mahmoud Ahmad was dismissed from his position as ISI Director-General. ISI Public Relations stated that he had sought retirement after being superseded on 8th October. But it was soon found that he had actually been dismissed quietly, at U.S. instigation, for far more serious reasons: the alleged leader of the 11th September suicide hijackers, Mohamed Atta, received funding on the General's instructions.

Yet as already discussed, the ISI has had access to considerable military and financial aid from the U.S., for the purpose of supporting operations in Afghanistan by militant groups. Could U.S. aid have been funnelled to Atta, and possibly other Al-Qaeda members, through the ISI? The *Times of India* reported that:

"While the Pakistani Inter Services Public Relations claimed that former ISI director-general Lt-Gen Mahmud Ahmad sought retirement after being superseded on Monday, the truth is more shocking.

Top sources confirmed here on Tuesday, that the general lost his job because of the 'evidence' India produced to show his links to one of the suicide bombers that wrecked the World Trade Centre. The U.S. authorities sought his removal after confirming the fact that $100,000 were wired to WTC hijacker Mohammed Atta from Pakistan by Ahmad Umar Sheikh at the instance of Gen Mahmud.

Senior government sources have confirmed that India contributed significantly to establishing the link between the money transfer and the role played by the dismissed ISI chief. While they did not provide details, they said that Indian inputs, including Sheikh's mobile phone number, helped the FBI in tracing and establishing the link.

A direct link between the ISI and the WTC attack could have enormous repercussions. The U.S. cannot but suspect whether or not there were other senior Pakistani Army commanders who were in the know of things. Evidence of a larger conspiracy could shake U.S. confidence in Pakistan's ability to participate in the anti-terrorism coalition."[474]

This report was based on the official findings of Indian intelligence, which had been promptly passed on to U.S. officials in Washington. Agence France Press confirmed that:

"A highly-placed government source told AFP that the 'damning link' between the General and the transfer of funds to Atta was part of evidence which India has officially sent to the U.S. 'The evidence we have supplied to the U.S. is of a much wider range and depth than just one piece of paper linking a rogue general to some misplaced act of terrorism,' the source said."[475]

These damning revelations were soon further confirmed in the Pakistani and American press. The respected Pakistani newspaper *Dawn*, for instance, reported that the links first uncovered by Indian intelligence had been confirmed by the American FBI. When the FBI traced calls made between General Ahmad and Sheikh's cellular phone, a pattern linking the general with Sheikh clearly emerged:

"Director General of Pakistan's Inter-Services Intelligence (ISI) Lt Gen Mahmud Ahmed has been replaced after the FBI investigators established credible links between him and Umar Sheikh, one of the three militants released in exchange for passengers of the hijacked Indian Airlines plane in 1999. The FBI team, which had sought adequate inputs about various terrorists including Sheikh from the intelligence agencies, was working on the linkages between Sheikh and former ISI chief Gen Mahmud which are believed to have been substantiated... Informed sources said there were enough indications with the U.S. intelligence agencies that it was at Gen Mahmud's instruction that Sheikh had transferred 100,000 U.S. dollars into the account of Mohammed Atta, one of the lead terrorists in strikes at the World Trade Centre on Sept 11."[476]

The *Wall Street Journal* has also confirmed these reports.[477] According to the conservative U.S. news service *WorldNetDaily*, "Dennis M. Lormel, director of FBI's financial crimes unit, confirmed the transaction" between the ISI and the CIA.[478] It is worth noting again the acute observations of the *Times of India* that:

> "A direct link between the ISI and the WTC attack could have enormous repercussions. The U.S. cannot but suspect whether or not there were other senior Pakistani Army commanders who were in the know of things. Evidence of a larger conspiracy could shake U.S. confidence in Pakistan's ability to participate in the anti-terrorism coalition."[479]

This should be understood in context with the observations of Middle East specialist Mohamed Heikal, former Egyptian Foreign Minister and "the Arab world's most respected political commentator." The London *Guardian* reports that Heikal questions whether Osama bin Laden and his Al-Qaeda network were solely responsible for the September 11 attacks. He pointed out in October that:

> "Bin Laden does not have the capabilities for an operation of this magnitude. When I hear Bush talking about al-Qaida as if it was Nazi Germany or the communist party of the Soviet Union, I laugh because I know what is there. Bin Laden has been under surveillance for years: every telephone call was monitored and al-Qaida has been penetrated by American intelligence, Pakistani intelligence, Saudi intelligence, Egyptian intelligence. They could not have kept secret an operation that required such a degree of organisation and sophistication."[480]

Military veteran Stan Goff, a retired U.S. Army Special Forces Master Sergeant and an expert in military science and doctrine, similarly observes that: "One, there is the premise that what this de facto administration is doing now is a 'response' to September 11th. Two, there is the premise that this attack on the World Trade Center and the Pentagon was done by people based in Afghanistan. In my opinion, neither of these is sound...

> "This cartoon heavy they've turned bin Laden into makes no sense, when you begin to appreciate the complexity and synchronicity of the attacks. As a former military person who's been involved in the development of countless operations orders over the years, I can tell you that this was a very sophisticated and costly enterprise that would have left what we call a huge 'signature.' In other words, it would be very hard to effectively conceal."[481]

The testimony of Milton Beardman, the former director of CIA operations in Afghanistan, is also worth noting. In a CBS interview after the

11th September attacks with Dan Rather, Beardman was asked if he thought Osama bin Laden was responsible for the attacks. Beardman virtually snubbed the possibility, observing that on his evaluation of the scale of the attacks, blame should not be automatically laid on bin Laden. Instead, he elaborated that it was more likely that a far more "sophisticated" intelligence operation was behind these precise coordinated attacks. Indeed, when pressed by Rather on the possibility of bin Laden's involvement, Beardman responded: "Look, if they didn't have an Osama bin Laden, they would invent one."[482]

Other intelligence experts have been even more forthright in deriding the idea that Al-Qaeda could perform the 11th September operation alone. Former CIA official Robert Baer, who was Case Officer in the Directorate of Operations for the CIA from 1976 to 1997, and who received the Career Intelligence Medal in 1997, observes: "Did bin Laden act alone, through his own al-Qaida network, in launching the attacks? About that I'm far more certain and emphatic: no."[483]

U.S. military intelligence expert Professor Anthony Cordesman—Senior Fellow in Strategic Assessment at the Washington-based Center for Strategic and International Studies (CSIS) and former senior official in the Office of the Secretary of Defense, the State Department, the Department of Energy, the Defense Advanced Research Projects Agency, and the NATO International Staff—strongly warned against assuming that Osama bin Laden's Al-Qaeda was to blame.

He emphasised the fact that no known terrorist network, including Al-Qaeda, has the capability to carry out the sophisticated 11th September attacks alone: "There is a level of sophistication and co-ordination that no counterterrorism expert had ever previously anticipated, and we don't have a group that we can immediately identify that has this kind of capability."[484]

Eckehardt Werthebach, former President of Germany's domestic intelligence service, Verfassungsschutz, notes that "the deathly precision" and "the magnitude of planning" behind the 11th September attacks would have required "years of planning." An operation of this level of sophistication, would need the "fixed frame" of a state intelligence organisation, something not found in a "loose group" of terrorists like the one allegedly led by Mohammed Atta while he studied in Hamburg, Germany. Werthebach thus argues that the scale of the attacks indicates that they were a product of "state organized actions."[485]

Another former German official has similarly dismissed the conventional explanation. German intelligence expert Herr von Buelow, who was State Secretary in the German Defence Ministry in the 1970s and Social

Democratic Party Speaker in the Schalk-Golodkowski investigation committee in 1993, observed that:

"[T]he planning of the attacks was technically and organizationally a master achievement. To hijack four huge airplanes within a few minutes and within one hour, to drive them into their targets, with complicated flight maneuvers! This is unthinkable, without years-long support from secret apparatuses of the state and industry."[486]

Military-strategic analyst and retired Major General Dr. Mahmoud Khalaf (credentials on p. 156) agrees with this analysis. In a presentation at the Center for Asian Studies in the University of Cairo, he observed: "Military-strategic analysis is an independent branch of science within the strategic sciences, and not mere predictions and speculations. But, it has complete rules that are identical to 'post-mortem tests,' an autopsy process used to find out the causes of the death...

"First, [regarding the September 11 attacks] we are confronted with a technical operation of extremely great dimensions. We estimate that the planning organ for this operation must have consisted of at least 100 specialized technicians, who needed one year for planning... The high level of the operation does not match the level of the evidence presented... Now, the puzzling question is the preparation and training of these people who had the capability to follow up and execute... There is, actually, one question, which is posed here. That is that there is no proportionality between the performance of the operation and the performance of bin Laden and his followers."[487]

Indeed, the picture clears in light of the fact noted by Ahmed Rashid that ISI ties to Osama bin Laden continued throughout the 1990s. Rashid, for example, refers to "The ISI's close contacts with bin Laden, and the fact that he was helping fund and train Kashmiri militants who were using the Khost camps... in December 1998...

"Bin Laden himself pointed to continued support from some elements in the Pakistani intelligence services in an interview. 'As for Pakistan there are some governmental departments, which, by the Grace of God, respond to the Islamic sentiments of the masses in Pakistan. This is reflected in sympathy and co-operation. However, some other governmental departments fell into the trap of the infidels. We pray to God to return them to the right path,' said Bin Laden."

Rashid also notes that "Support for Bin Laden by elements within the Pakistani establishment" has been accompanied by the fact that: "The U.S. was Pakistan's closest ally, with deep links to the military and the ISI."[488] The suggestive implications are that bin Laden derived intensive support for the 11th September operation from a state intelligence organisation. Indeed, a CBS Evening News report by anchorman Dan Rather and foreign correspondent Barry Peterson, citing authoritative Pakistani intelligence sources, reveals that: "the night before the September 11 terrorist attack, Osama bin Laden was in Pakistan. He was getting medical treatment with the support of the very military that days later pledged its backing for the U.S. war on terror in Afghanistan...

> "Pakistan intelligence sources tell CBS News that bin Laden was spirited into this military hospital in Rawalpindi for kidney dialysis treatment. On that night, says this medical worker who wanted her identity protected, they moved out all the regular staff in the urology department and sent in a secret team to replace them. She says it was treatment for a very special person. The special team was obviously up to no good.
>
> 'The military had him surrounded, says this hospital employee who also wanted his identity masked, 'and I saw the mysterious patient helped out of a car. Since that time,' he says, 'I have seen many pictures of the man. He is the man we know as Osama bin Laden. I also heard two army officers talking to each other. They were saying that Osama bin Laden had to be watched carefully and looked after.' Those who know bin Laden say he suffers from numerous ailments, back and stomach problems. Ahmed Rashid, who has written extensively on the Taliban, says the military was often there to help before 9/11."[489]

In light of the *Times* revelations, it seems that Pakistani military intelligence did indeed play a crucial role in the 11th September attacks. But despite the ISI role, it is a matter of record that the U.S. "confidence in Pakistan" has continued all too enthusiastically. It should be noted that Pakistani military headquarters in Rawalpindi are host to numerous resident U.S. military intelligence operatives and advisers. The potential implications are worthy of an urgent inquiry. As *WorldNetDaily* correspondent Paul Sperry observes:

> "The Bush administration has said the money trail is a crucial link in uncovering the support network for the 19 hijackers, and then destroying that network. However, a major hub of that network is in Pakistan, and it's still active... It's become increasingly clear that Pakistan is the epicenter of terrorism, and is most likely sheltering bin Laden. Yet, at least publicly, the Bush administration continues to trust the Pakistani government to help capture bin Laden and other anti-American terrorists."[490]

The U.S., which one would think would be spearheading a full-scale investigation into the role of the ISI, actually prevented one from going ahead by asking from behind the scenes for the ISI chief—whose funding of Mohamed Atta just before 11th September had suddenly been revealed in India (and later in Pakistan)—to quietly resign.

The U.S. has thus studiously obstructed a more in-depth inquiry, preventing further understanding of the ISI's role, and preventing the ISI chief from being arrested, investigated and put on trial for his support of Atta—whom FBI files describe as "the lead hijacker of the first jet airliner to slam into the World Trade Center and, apparently, the lead conspirator."[491]

In an extensive analysis of the sequence of events relating to the ISI's role, University of Ottawa analyst Professor Michel Chossudovsky observes that:

> "[T]he Bush Administration's relations with Pakistan's ISI—including its 'consultations' with General Mahmoud Ahmad in the week prior to September 11—raise the issue of 'cover-up' as well as 'complicity.' While Ahmad was talking to U.S. officials at the CIA and the Pentagon, the ISI allegedly had contacts with the September 11 terrorists. The perpetrators of the September 11 attacks had links to Pakistan's ISI, which in turn has links to agencies of the U.S. government. What this suggests is that key individuals within the U.S. military-intelligence establishment might have known about ISI contacts with the September 11 terrorist 'ring-leader' Mohamed Atta and failed to act. Whether this amounts to the outright complicity of the Bush Administration remains to be firmly established."[492]

With regards to Chossudovsky's last comment, even limited to the available data currently at hand, the implications of these facts suggest the admittedly distasteful possibility of U.S. complicity.

We should reiterate that, with the links between the ISI chief and terrorist ring-leader Mohamed Atta discovered, including the former's authorisation of financial support of the latter, the only U.S. response was to quietly pressure the then Director-General of Pakistani military intelligence, Lt. Gen. Mahmoud Ahmad, to 'request' early retirement after the discovery of his activities in India.

Yet, this amounts to an attempt to cut short a fuller investigation into the ISI's clearly supportive role in the 11th September attacks. As the *Times of India* rightly noted: "A direct link between the ISI and the WTC attack could have enormous repercussions. The U.S. cannot but suspect whether or not there were other senior Pakistani Army commanders who were in the know of things."

By pressuring the then ISI Director-General to resign without scandal on the pretext of routine reshuffling, while avoiding any publicity with respect to his siphoning of funds to alleged lead hijacker Mohamed Atta, the U.S. had effectively blocked any sort of investigation into the matter. It prevented wide publicity of these facts, and allowed the ISI chief, who was clearly complicit in the terrorist attacks of 11th September, to walk away free.

It seems that the U.S. has attempted to protect the former ISI Director-General and the ISI as a whole from any further damaging revelations on what appears to be their complicity in supporting those behind the air attacks. It is certainly conceivable that one consideration by the U.S. administration is the instrumental role played by Musharraf's Pakistan in U.S. regional strategy. An inquiry into ISI complicity in the 11th September attacks could jeopardise beyond repair the close U.S.-Pakistani relations that are so crucial in U.S. strategy.

Yet, one would think that the dire threat to U.S. interests and security supposedly posed by Al-Qaeda and its supporters would be sufficient for the U.S. to temporarily override its regional strategy, to find and hold accountable those responsible for the terrorist attacks. Instead, the U.S. is still supporting those responsible.

There is no valid reason, therefore, to arbitrarily dismiss the possibility that there are additional, broader reasons for the U.S. blocking of an inquiry into ISI complicity in 11th September, as related to U.S. culpability. Indeed, in light of the other documentation presented here, there is evidence suggesting that this is a reasonable, if not probable, possibility that is in need of urgent investigation.

Whatever the motivations behind such a cynical policy, it is indisputable that the U.S. response at least suggests a significant degree of indirect complicity on the part of the U.S. government, which appears more interested in protecting, rather than investigating and prosecuting, a military intelligence agency that funded the lead hijacker in the WTC and Pentagon attacks. The term complicity is being used here in the broad sense of responsibility through aiding and abetting the terrorists involved. And indeed, by continuing to use and promote the Pakistani ISI in relation to its regional U.S. strategy, the U.S. is also promoting a military intelligence agency with confirmed links to terrorism.

When the U.S.' confirmed role in aiding and abetting ISI-backed support of the 11th September terrorist attacks is taken into account, along with longstanding U.S. ties to Osama bin Laden through his family, Saudi royals and Pakistani military intelligence, U.S. complicity arguably becomes a far more plausible and tenable explanation of the facts. It would therefore amount to either extreme foolishness or presumptive prejudice to refuse to consider this explanation.

Given the facts discussed previously, given the U.S.' intimate links with Pakistani intelligence, and given the latter's direct linkage to the terror attacks of 11th September, it is clearly time to bring the leading players of U.S. government, military and intelligence agencies into the witness box. Jared Israel has put the point well:

> "[T]he U.S. pressured the now-retired head of Pakistani Intelligence, Lt-Gen Mahmud Ahmad, to 'request' early retirement... If so, wasn't this an attempt to head off a fuller investigation? And doesn't that mean the U.S. side knows Ahmad is guilty as charged?

> And by demanding early retirement, rather than a trial for terrorism, hasn't the U.S. government acknowledged that a) in sending $100,000 to one of the alleged WTC hijackers, Ahmad was acting in accord with ISI policy and b) the CIA or other U.S. covert forces were also involved?

> If... Lt-Gen Mahmud Ahmad was pushed into retirement to prevent a scandal, and if President Bush really wants to punish the parties behind 9-11, why doesn't he demand a full investigation so that the guilty can be brought to justice, whether they are to be found in Kabul, or Islamabad, or Riyadh, or Langley or Washington, D.C.?... Washington's silence is one more piece of evidence that the 'infinite war' against terrorism is an infinite sham."[493]

Israel is right to bluntly state the possibility of U.S. involvement in Lt. Gen. Ahmad's funding of Mohamed Atta. He is also right in noting that the implications of the known aspects of the U.S. policy clearly illustrate that the war against terror is a "sham." If it were not a sham, then we would expect that, as part and parcel of the war on terror, the U.S. government would mount a full-fledged inquiry into the ISI role. The fact that the Bush administration has blocked such an inquiry proves that the administration is not genuinely concerned with finding the terrorists responsible for 11th September and holding them accountable.

Other interests of the Bush administration, evidently, take precedence. Indeed, it is apparent that such U.S. strategic and economic interests are largely responsible for why the U.S. government's policy continues to promote supporters of terrorism. Exactly what these interests are—whether they are merely regionally strategic or encompass the need to protect a more sinister U.S. complicity—requires a further independent inquiry. A full investigation into these issues is therefore a matter of urgency.

As investigative journalist Wayne Madsen observes in a useful summary of why a further independent inquiry into these events is required:

"The CIA's connections to the ISI in the months before September 11 and the weeks after are also worthy of a full-blown investigation. The CIA continues to maintain an unhealthy alliance with the ISI, the organization that groomed bin Laden and the Taliban...

General Ahmed was in Washington, DC on the morning of September 11 meeting with CIA and State Department officials as the hijacked planes slammed into the World Trade Center and Pentagon... [It was later] confirmed that General Ahmed ordered a Pakistani-born British citizen and known terrorist named Ahmed Umar Sheik to wire $100,000 from Pakistan to the U.S. bank account of Mohammed Atta, the lead hijacker... [N]o move has been made to question General Ahmed or those U.S. government officials, including Deputy Secretary of State Richard Armitage, who met with him in September. Clearly, General Ahmed was a major player in terrorist activities across South Asia, yet still had very close ties to the U.S. government. General Ahmed's terrorist-supporting activities—and the U.S. government officials who tolerated those activities—need to be investigated."[494]

But they have not been investigated, and any such investigation has now been successfully shelved by the Bush administration. The imperialistic agenda, pursued behind the scenes of U.S.-instigated ISI reshuffling – apparently meant to deflect attention from ISI complicity in the attacks – became manifest only a few days after Lt. Gen. Mahmoud Ahmad's early 'retirement,' when the U.S.-led bombardment of Afghanistan began:

The Pakistani newspaper the *Frontier Post* reported that U.S. Ambassador Wendy Chamberlain had contacted the Pakistani Minister of Oil. A previously abandoned UNOCAL pipeline planned to stretch from Turkmenistan, through Afghanistan, and along the Pakistani coast, designed to sell oil and gas to China, was once more ready for construction, "in view of recent geopolitical developments."[495]

Notes

[361] Christenson, Sig, 'Bin Ladens building U.S. troops' housing,' *San Antonio Express-News*, 14 September 1998.

[362] Cooley, John K., *Unholy Wars: Afghanistan, American and International Terrorism*, Pluto Press, London, 1999, p. 117-118.

[363] Rashid, Ahmed, 'How a Holy War against the Soviets turned on U.S.,' *Pittsburgh Post-Gazette*, 23 September 2001.

[364] Cooley, John K., *Unholy Wars: Afghanistan, American and International Terrorism*, op. cit., p. 120.

[365] Rashid, Ahmed, 'How a Holy War against the Soviets turned on U.S.,' op. cit.

[366] Cooley, John K., *Unholy Wars: Afghanistan, American and International Terrorism*, op. cit., p. 119.

[367] Ibid., p. 222.

[368] BBC Newsnight, 'Has Someone Been Sitting On The FBI?', op. cit.

[369] Cooley, John K., *Unholy Wars: Afghanistan, American and International Terrorism*, op. cit., p. 120.

[370] Rashid, Ahmed, 'How a Holy War against the Soviets turned on U.S.,' op. cit.

[371] UPI, cited in www.newsmax.com/archives/articles/2001/1/3/214858.shtml.

[372] Ibid.

[373] Cited in *Baltimore Sun*, 24 April 2001.

[374] *San Antonio Express-News*, 14 September 1998.

[375] JW Press Release, 'Judicial Watch to File FOIA Lawsuit Today Over Carlyle Group Documents,' Judicial Watch, Washington DC, 27 Sept. 2001, www.judicialwatch.org/press_release.asp?pr_id=1892.

[376] *Le Figaro*, 31 October 2001.

[377] Golden, Daniel, et. al., 'Bin Laden Family Could Profit from a Jump in U.S. Defense Spending Due to Ties to U.S. Banks,' *Wall Street Journal*, 27 September 2001.

[378] Ibid.

[379] Lazarus, David, 'Carlyle Profit from Afghan War,' *San Francisco Chronicle*, 2 December 2001.

[380] Gray, Geoffrey, 'Bush Sr. Could Profit From War,' *Village Voice*, 11 October 2001.

[381] JW Press Release, 'Wall Street Journal: Bush Sr. in Business with Bin Laden Family Conglomerate through Carlyle Group,' Judicial Watch, Washington DC, 28 September 2001, http://judicialwatch.org/press_release.asp?pr_id=1624.

[382] Gray, Geoffrey, 'Bush Sr. Could Profit From War,' op. cit.

[383] JW Press Release, 'Judicial Watch to File FOIA Lawsuit Today Over Carlyle Group Documents,' op. cit.

[384] Agence France Press and *Hindustan Times*, 7 November 2001.

[385] Golden, Daniel, et. al., 'Bin Laden Family Could Profit from a Jump in U.S. Defense Spending Due to Ties to U.S. Banks,' op. cit.

[386] ABC News, 'Strained Family Ties,' 1 October 2001.

[387] BBC Newsnight, 'Has Someone Been Sitting On The FBI?', BBC 2, 6 Nov. 2001, http://news.bbc.co.uk/hi/english/events/newsnight/newsid_1645000/1645527.stm.

[388] Palast, Gregory and Pallister, David, 'FBI claims Bin Laden inquiry was frustrated,' op. cit.

[389] BBC Newsnight, 'Has Someone Been Sitting On The FBI?', op. cit.

[390] Palast, Gregory and Pallister, David, 'FBI claims Bin Laden inquiry was frustrated,' op. cit.

[391] 'Above the Law: Bush's Racial Coup d'Etat and Intelligence Shutdown,' *Green Press*, 14 February 2002, www.greenpress.org/html/GPress_2-14-02.html.

[392] Ibid.

[393] Agence France Press and *Hindustan Times*, 7 November 2001.

[394] *Wall Street Journal*, 19 September 2001.

[395] Martin S. Indyk is Senior Fellow of Foreign Policy Studies at the Brookings Institution in Washington DC. His experience in government and international relations include the following: U.S. Ambassador to Israel (1995-97, 2000-01); Assistant Secretary of State for Near East Affairs, U.S. State Department (1997-2000); Special Assistant to the President and Senior Director for Near East and South Asian Affairs, National Security Council (1993-1995); Executive Director, Washington Institute for Near East Policy; Adjunct Professor, Johns Hopkins University.

[396] Indyk, Martin S., 'Back to the Bazaar,' *Foreign Affairs*, January/February 2002.

[397] Hersh, Seymour, M., 'King's ransom: How vulnerable are Saudi royals?', *New Yorker*, 22 October 2001.

[398] Roslin, Alex, 'U.S. Saudi Scandal,' *Now*, 22 November 2001, http://nowtoronto.com.

[399] Braun, Stephen and Pasternak, Judy, 'Long Before Sept. 11, Bin Laden Aircraft Flew Under the Radar,' *Los Angeles Times*, 18 November 2001.

[400] Labeviere, Richard, *Dollars for Terror: The United States and Islam*, Algora Publishing, New York, 2000.

[401] Associated Press, 'Saudi Prince Says Taliban Had Approved Bin Laden Handover,' 3 November 2001.

[402] Kelley, Jack, *USA Today*, 29 October 1999.

[403] Rashid, Ahmed, 'Special Report – Osama Bin Laden: How the U.S. Helped Midwife a Terrorist,' op. cit.

[404] 'Above the Law,' *Green Press*, op. cit.

[405] Robinson, Gwen, 'CIA "ignored warning" on al Qaeda,' *Financial Times*, 12 January 2002; Baer, Robert, *See No Evil: The True Story of a Ground Soldier in the CIA's War on Terrorism*, Random House International, 2002.

[406] Baer, Robert, *See No Evil: The True Story of a Ground Soldier in the CIA's War on Terrorism*, op. cit., Preface.

[407] Ali, Tariq, 'The real Muslim extremists,' *New Statesman*, 1 Oct. 2001.

[408] Kaiser, Robert G., 'Enormous Wealth Spilled Into American Coffers,' *Washington Post*, 11 February 2002.

[409] Madsen, Wayne, 'Questionable Ties,' *In These Times*, Institute for Public Affairs, No. 25, www.inthesetimes.com/issue/25/25/feature3.shtml. Also see *Intelligence Newsletter*, 2 March 2000.

[410] Cited in Roslin, Alex, 'U.S. Saudi Scandal,' op. cit.

[411] Wells, Johnathan, et. al., 'U.S. Ties to Saudi Elite May Be Hurting the War on Terror,' *Boston Herald*, 12 December 2001.

[412] Meyers, Jack, et. al., 'Saudi clans working with U.S. oil firms may be tied to Bin Laden,' *Boston Herald*, 10 December 2001.

[413] Wells, Johnathan, et. al., 'Saudi elite linked to bin Laden financial empire,' *Boston Herald*, 14 October 2001.

[414] Labeviere, Richard, *Dollars for Terror: The United States and Islam*, Algora Publishing, New York, 2000; AIM Report, 'Catastrophic Intelligence Failure,' op. cit.

[415] Hays, Tom and Theimer, Sharon, 'U.S. relying on double agent for details of Al-Qaeda,' Associated Press, 30 December 2001.

[416] 'Ali Mohamed Served In the U.S. Army – And bin Laden's Inner Circle,' *Wall Street Journal*, 26 November 2001.

[417] Neff, Joseph and Sullivan, John, *Raleigh News & Observer*, 24 October 2001.

[418] Hays, Tom and Theimer, Sharon, 'U.S. relying on double agent for details of Al-Qaeda,' op. cit.

[419] "In 1919 Joseph Schumpeter described ancient Rome in a way that sounds eerily like the United States in 2002. 'There was no corner of the known world where some interest was not alleged to be in danger or under actual attack. If the interests were not Roman, they were those of Rome's allies; and if Rome had no allies, the allies would be invented. ... The fight was always invested with an aura of legality. Rome was always being attacked by evil-minded neighbours."

Quoted by Stephen Gowans, 'War in Afghanistan: A $28 Billion Racket,' www.mediamonitors.net/gowans53.html

[420] Labeviere, Richard, *Dollars for Terror: The United States and Islam*, op. cit.; AIM Report, 'Catastrophic Intelligence Failure,' op. cit.

[421] For discussion of this and related issues see Martin, Patrick, 'Was the U.S. government alerted to the September 11 attack? Part 3: The United States and Mideast Terrorism,' WSWS, 22 Jan. 2002, www.wsws.org/articles/2002/jan2002/sept-j22.shtml. It should be noted that the Saudi response to the recent press revelations concerning the regime's support of Osama Bin Laden and Al-Qaeda, have as usual been denied by Saudi spokesmen, who have, however, failed to refute the charges against the regime. The best that has been done is to describe reports from a variety of credible sources as "b**s**." The Australian daily *The Age* (20 Dec. 2001) observes that: "Widespread reports in the U.S. media that Saudi Arabia encourages extremist Islamic violence and is not cooperating in the war on terrorism are 'b**s**,' the country's ambassador to the United States said late Tuesday. Using blunt and decidedly undiplomatic language, an exasperated Prince Bandar bin Sultan rejected reports that Saudi Arabia teaches hatred of non-Muslims in its schools and has paid protection money to Osama bin Laden in order to avoid terrorist attacks on its soil."

[422] Chossudovsky has taught as Visiting Professor at academic institutions in Western Europe, Latin America and Southeast Asia, has acted as economic adviser to governments of developing countries and has worked as a consultant for several international organizations, including the United Nations Development Programme (UNDP), the African Development Bank, the United Nations African Institute for Economic Development and Planning (AIEDEP), the United Nations Population Fund (UNFPA), the International Labour Organization (ILO), the World Health Organisation (WHO), the United Nations Economic Commission for Latin America and the Caribbean (ECLAC).

[423] Blowback: unexpectedly reaping the repercussions of violence sown.

[424] *Washington Post*, 22 Sept. 1996. Cited in Congressional Press Release, Republican Party Committee (RPC), U.S. Congress, 'Clinton-Approved Iranian Arms Transfers Help Turn Bosnia into Militant Islamic Base,' 16 Jan. 1997, www.senate.gov/~rpc/releases/1997/iran.htm.

[425] See Ahmed, Nafeez M., 'Engineering War in Bosnia: A Case Study of the Function of NATO Peacekeeping in the Stabilization of World Order,' Media Monitors Network, Los Angeles, CA, 26 November 2001, www.mediamonitors.net/mosaddeq20.html.

[426] U.S. Congress, Transcripts of the House Armed Services Committee, 5 October 1999.

[427] Seper, Jerry, *Washington Times*, 4 May 1999.

[428] *Jane's Intelligence Review*, 1 October 1995.

[429] *Washington Post*, 3 October 2001.

[430] Ibid.

[431] It is worth noting here that according to the online French intelligence publication *Indigo* (www.indigo-net.com), bin Laden visited London as a guest of British intelligence in 1996–yet Britain is America's leading ally. The possible implications certainly warrant further inquiry into the matter.

[432] For extensive discussion of the U.S. bombing of Al-Shifa in the context of U.S. relations with Sudan, see Ahmed, Nafeez M., 'United States Terrorism in the Sudan: The Bombing of Al-Shifa and its Strategic Role in U.S.-Sudan Relations,' Media Monitors Network, 22 Oct. 2001, www.mediamonitors. net/mosaddeq16.html. The matters raised in this paper were presented to the Policy Committee of the UK's National Union of Journalists in Oct. 2001.

[433] Rose, David, 'Resentful west spurned Sudan's key terror files,' *The Observer*, 30 September 2001.

[434] 'Why was Russia's intelligence on Al-Qaeda ignored?', *Jane's Intelligence Digest*, 5 October 2001.

[435] Johnston, David, *New York Times*, 19 August 2001.

[436] Marlowe, Lara, 'U.S. efforts to make peace summed up by oil,' *Irish Times*, 19 November 2001. O'Neill's charges were also reported on CNN, 'American Morning with Paula Zahn,' 8 January 2001. Richard Butler of the Council on Foreign Relation and U.S. ambassador-in-residence was unable to deny the veracity of the charges, instead promising a further investigation – which has not yet occurred.

[437] Hersh, Seymour M., 'King's ransom: How vulnerable are the Saudis?', op. cit.

[438] Labeviere, Richard, 'CIA Agent Allegedly Met Bin Laden in July,' *Le Figaro*, 31 October 2001.

[439] Sampson, Anthony, 'CIA agent alleged to have met Bin Laden in July,' *The Guardian*, 1 November 2001.

[440] Sage, Adam, 'Ailing bin Laden "treated for kidney disease",' *The Times*, 1 Nov. 2001, www.thetimes.co.uk/article/0,,2001370005-2001380403,00.html.

[441] Bryant, Elizabeth, 'Radio reports new CIA-Bin Laden details,' United Press International, 1 November 2001.

[442] Ibid.

[443] "U.S. benevolence toward bin Laden continued almost up to Sept. 11. A few days ago *Le Figaro* reported that in July bin Laden underwent kidney treatment at an American hospital in Dubai. While there he met with a CIA agent... A

couple of days after the publication of this story, the CIA agent was identified as Larry Mitchell. The CIA vehemently denies the allegation, as does the Dubai hospital, though not, so far as one can gather, Callaway. The story may be nonsense, but it is uncomfortably specific about names and dates. Moreover, *Le Figaro* can hardly be dismissed as a leftist anti-American rag." (Szamuely, George, 'The Neo-Colonialists,' *New York Press*, Vol. 14, No. 46) Indeed, it is worth emphasising that Dr. Terry Callaway, who reportedly treated Bin Laden, is not the only one who has not denied the allegations. The American Embassy in Paris has also not denied the reports (UPI, 31 October, 1 November 2001).

[444] Chossudovsky, Michel, Introduction to *Le Figaro* article, Centre for Research on Globalisation, 2 November 2001, www.globalresearch.ca/articles/RIC111B.html.

[445] Letter to Honourable Charles O. Rossotti, Chairman of Internal Revenue Service, from Judicial Watch, 20 September 2001, www.judicialwatch.org/cases/78/hamascomplaint.htm.

[446] JW Press Release, 'Government Finally Begins to Investigate Alleged Terrorist Front Groups,' Judicial Watch, Washington DC, 5 November 2001, www.judicialwatch.org/1071.shtml.

[447] Limbacher, Carl, 'Judicial Watch: Clinton IRD Turned Blind Eye to Terrorists,' *NewsMax*, 23 September 2001.

[448] JW Press Release, 'Government Finally Begins to Investigate Alleged Terrorist Front Groups,' op. cit.

[449] Perlman, Shirley E., 'Tracking Terror's Money Trail,' *Newsday*, 14 October 2001.

[450] Jonathan Weiner in an interview with Linda Wertheimer, National Public Radio (NPR), 21 November 2001.

[451] Hersh, Seymour M., 'King's ransom: How vulnerable are the Saudi royals?', op. cit.

[452] For sources and further discussion see Flocco, Tom and Ruppert, Michael, 'The Profits of Death, Part III,' FTW Publications, 9 January 2002, www.copvcia.com/stories/dec_2001/death_profits_pt3.html.

[453] *Washington Post*, 29 September 2001; *Financial Times*, 29 November 2001. Cited in ibid. See the Flocco and Ruppert report for further damning revelations.

[454] Walker, Thomas, 'Did bin Laden have help from U.S. friends?', *Toronto Star*, 27 November 2001.

[455] 'FBI arrogance and secrecy dismay U.S.,' *The Times*, 3 November 2001.

[456] Rashid, Ahmed, 'Bin Laden "Has Network of Sleepers Across North America",' *The Telegraph*, 16 September 2001.

[457] Woodward, Bob and Pincus, Walter, 'Investigators Identify 4 to 5 Groups Linked to Bin Laden Operating in US. No Connection Found Between 'Cell' Members and 19 Hijackers, Officials Say,' *Washington Post*, 23 Sept. 2001.

[458] Davies, Hugh, 'Informers point the finger at bin Laden,' *Daily Telegraph*, 24 August 1998.

[459] Halliday, Fred, 'The Un-great game: the Country that lost the Cold War, Afghanistan,' *New Republic*, 25 March 1996.

[460] Rashid, Ahmed, 'The Taliban: Exporting Extremism,' *Foreign Affairs*, November-December 1999.

[461] Coll, Steve, *Washington Post*, 19 July 1992.

[462] Banerjee, Dipankar, 'Possible Connection of ISI With Drug Industry,' *India Abroad*, 2 December 1994.

[463] International Press Services, 22 August 1995. See Cordovez, Diego and Harrison, Selig, *Out of Afghanistan: The Inside Story of the Soviet Withdrawal*, Oxford University Press, Oxford, 1995.

[464] Bedi, Rahul, 'Why? An attempt to explain the unexplainable,' *Jane's Defence Weekly*, 14 September 2001.

[465] 'Creating the Taliban: "CIA Made a Historic Mistake",' *Rationalist International Bulletin*, No. 68, 19 March 2001, http://rationalist international.net.

[466] U.S. State Department, *Patterns of Global Terrorism*, Department of State, Washington DC, 2000, www.state.gov/s/ct/rls/pgtrpt/2000.

[467] See Appendix B.

[468] *The Guardian*, 15 September 2001.

[469] Reuters, 13 September 2001.

[470] *New York Times*, 13 September 2001.

[471] *Daily Telegraph*, 14 September 2001.

[472] Mateen, Amir, 'ISI chief's parleys continue in Washington,' *The News*, 10 September 2001.

[473] *Washington Post*, 23 September 2001.

[474] Joshi, Manoj, 'India helped FBI trace ISI-terrorist links,' *Times of India*, 9 October 2001.

[475] Agence France Presse, 10 October 2001.

[476] Monitoring Desk, 'Gen Mahmud's exit due to links with Umar Sheikh,' *Dawn*, 8 October 2001. Also see Madsen, Wayne, 'Afghanistan, the Taliban and the Bush Oil Team,' Democrats.Com, January 2002.

[477] Taranto, James, 'Our Friends the Pakistanis,' *Wall Street Journal*, 10 October 2001.

[478] Sperry, Paul, 'Did ally Pakistan play role in 9-11?', WorldNetDaily, 30 January 2002, www.worldnetdaily.com/news/article.asp?ARTICLE_ ID=26249.

[479] Joshi, Manoj, 'India helped FBI trace ISI-terrorist links,' op. cit.

[480] Moss, Stephen, 'There isn't a target in Afghanistan worth a $1m missile,' *The Guardian*, 10 October 2001.

[481] Goff, Stan, 'The So-Called Evidence is a Farce,' op. cit.

[482] Interview with Milt Bearden by Dan Rather, Special Report, CBS Evening News, 12 September 2001.

[483] Baer, Robert, *See No Evil*, op. cit. Also see book extracts in *The Guardian*, 12 January 2002, http://books.guardian.co.uk/extracts/story/0,6761,631434,00.html.

[484] Gannon, Kathy, Associated Press, 11 September 2001.

[485] Bollyn, Chris, 'Euro Intel Experts Dismiss 'War on Terrorism' as Deception,' American Free Press, 4 December 2001.

[486] *Tagesspiegel*, 13 January 2001, www2.tagesspiegel.de/archiv/2002/01/12/ak-sn-in-558560.html.

[487] Transcript of presentation by Dr. Mahmoud Khalaf at Center for Asian Studies, University of Cairo, 5 December 2001.

[488] Rashid, Ahmed, 'Special Report – Osama Bin Laden: How the U.S. Helped Midwife a Terrorist,' op. cit.

[489] CBS Evening News, 'Bin Laden Whereabouts Before 9/11,' 28 January 2002.

[490] Sperry, Paul, 'Did ally Pakistan play role in 9-11?', op. cit. [italics added] For further evidence of the likelihood of Pakistan sheltering Bin Laden and Al-Qaeda, see Hersh, Seymour M., 'The Getaway: Questions surround a secret Pakistani airlift,' *New Yorker*, 21 January 2002.

[491] *Weekly Standard*, Vol. 7, No. 7, October 2001.

[492] Chossudovsky, Michel, 'Cover-up or Complicity of the Bush Administration? The Role of Pakistan's Military Intelligence Agency (ISI) in the September 11 Attacks,' Centre for Research on Globalisation (CRG), Montreal, 2 November 2001, http://globalresearch.ca.

[493] 'Did "Our" Allies, Pakistani Intelligence, Fund the WTC Attackers?', The Emperors New Clothes, 15 October 2001, http://emperors-clothes.com/misc/isi.htm.

[494] Madsen, Wayne, 'Afghanistan, the Taliban and the Bush Oil Team,' op. cit.

[495] *Frontier Post*, 10 October 2001.

7. The New War: Power and Profit, at Home and Abroad

"Afghanistan's people have been brutalized – many are starving and many have fled... The United States respects the people of Afghanistan – after all, we are currently its largest source of humanitarian aid – but we condemn the Taliban regime... Our war on terror begins with al Qaeda, but it does not end there. It will not end until every terrorist group of global reach has been found, stopped and defeated."

U.S. President George W. Bush Jr.
(Address to a Joint Session of Congress and the American People, 20 September 2001)

"We're going to protect and honor the Constitution, and I don't have the authority to set it aside. If I had the authority to set it aside, this would be a dangerous government, and I wouldn't respect it. We'll not be driven to abandon our freedoms by those who would seek to destroy them."

U.S. Attorney General John Ashcroft
(Legal Times, 22 October 2001)

The Bush Crisis

Prior to 11th September 2001, the Bush administration was entangled, seemingly inextricably, in a crisis. Revelations in the press concerning the fraudulent nature of George W. Bush Jr.'s rise to Presidency through the suppression of votes, increasingly exacerbated the perception among millions, both in the U.S. and around the world, that his administration was illegitimate.[496]

This perception was further exacerbated by the fact that, as noted by Robert Pollin, Professor of Economics at the University of Massachusetts at Amherst: "U.S. economic policymakers have failed for almost a year to respond adequately to the looming global recession."[497] Indeed, a panel of academic experts announced in November that the U.S. economy had been in recession since March 2001, a recession that was only steadily worsening.[498]

In the face of this deepening recession both within the U.S. and abroad, support for the Bush administration began to rapidly erode. Consequently, the administration began to display signs of internal dissension and disarray, fueled by the inability to solve rocketing unemployment rates, massive losses on the stock market, outrage at the disappearance of the budget surplus—not to mention the government's reneging on its own pledges not to spend Social Security funds.

The *New York Times* reported in August the growing trepidation among world leaders that the global economy was plunging straight into a global recession: "The world economy, which grew at a raging pace just last year, has slowed to a crawl as the United States, Europe, Japan and some major developing countries undergo a rare simultaneous slump...

"The latest economic statistics from around the globe show that many regional economic powers—Italy and Germany, Mexico and Brazil, Japan and Singapore—have become economically stagnant, defying expectations that growth in other countries would help compensate for the slowdown in the United States... [M]any experts say the world is experiencing economic whiplash, with growth rates retreating more quickly and in more of the leading economies than at any time since the oil shock of 1973. And this time there is no single factor to account for the widespread weakness, persuading some economists that recovery may be slow in coming. 'We have gone from boom to bust faster than any time since the oil shock,' said Stephen S. Roach, the chief economist of Morgan Stanley, a New York investment bank. 'When you screech to a halt like that, it feels like getting thrown through the windshield.'"

The Bush administration had attempted to paint an overly optimistic picture of this escalating economic slump, described sceptically by the *New York Times*: "The Bush administration still puts a relatively bright gloss on the picture." While noting the White House projection of a sharp upturn in the U.S. economy later in 2001 or in early 2002, the *Times* went on to report that Ford Motor Co. was preparing to announce more layoffs. CEO Jacques Nasser had observed that: "We don't see any factor that's going to restore the robustness of the economy" in the next 12 to 18 months.[499]

The bleak assessment was corroborated by the *Wall Street Journal*: "Almost a year after the slump in high tech and manufacturing began, many of the other pillars that have been supporting the economy are starting to weaken...

"Businesses that started slashing spending on equipment and software late last year are now doing the same on office and industrial real estate... Automobile sales, which were surprisingly healthy most of this year thanks to generous incentives and low interest rates, have started to slide.... Since April, most industry groups tracked by the Labor Department have been reducing payrolls.... Construction shaved 61,000 jobs between March and July, the clearest example of the spillover from high tech and manufacturing."

Then the U.S. Department of Labor released its August 2001 report, illustrating the sharp rise in the unemployment rate from 4.5 percent to 4.9 percent in a single month. Every sector of the economy was faced with job cuts, leading to almost one million jobs being wiped out in August alone. The prospect of a collapse in consumer spending further meant that investors had rushed to dump their stock holdings. The Dow Jones Industrial Average fell 230 points, ending the day well below the 10,000 mark. Lacking any other economic quick fixes, the Federal Reserve continued to drop interest rates with almost no perceptible results. The Bush tax cut was a failure, succeeding only in rewarded the rich for being rich while further penalising the poor, and accordingly widely criticised.

Abroad, the Bush administration was becoming increasingly isolated due to its foreign policies. In Iraq, the U.S. sanctions policy, along with U.S. plans to intensify its confrontational stance against the country, was met with open opposition from France, Germany, Russia and China. The U.S. was in conflict with most of its nominal allies on a whole host of issues on the Bush foreign policy agenda—including global warming, missile defence, and an international criminal court—and was consequently failing to push through resolutions via the United Nations Security Council and other international bodies.

Along with this, the unprecedented escalation of widespread social protests through a massive wave of 'anti-globalisation' demonstrations, illustrated increasing outrage both in the U.S. and around the world at policies seen as unjust and self-serving. The Bush administration was increasingly perceived to be a leading player in such policies.

Polls showed that Bush approval ratings—both personal and political— were plummeting, and were accompanied by increasing discussion of his administration's illegitimacy, in light of the vote fraud at Florida. In all likelihood, it was going to be extremely difficult for the Bush administration to maintain its already uncomfortably slim majority in the House for the midterm elections in 2002.[500] Indeed, the strategic and military planning outlined in Brzezinski's Council on Foreign Relations study in 1997 would have been impossible to implement at this time.

The 11th September attacks came at a time of severe crisis for the Bush administration. Faced with multiple problems both at home and abroad, with domestic polls plummeting and U.S. allies increasingly aggravated, the Bush administration was confronted with an escalating crisis of legitimacy. As *U.S. News* reports, the Bush administration's "initial, go-it-alone instincts offended even close friends...

"But it was much more than Bush's bluntness that put off friends in Europe and Asia. The administration had championed a treaty-busting missile shield, taken a hard line on China, and rejected pacts to ban nuclear tests, establish a war crimes court, and curb global warming. From abroad, Bush seemed to define U.S. interests narrowly and to act unilaterally. Newspapers caricatured him as a lone cowboy."[501]

Sociologist Walden Bello, Professor at the University of the Philippines and Executive Director of the Bangkok-based research centre Focus on the Global South, further summarises the escalating crisis of legitimacy faced by the Bush administration, as well as the overall structure of world order in general, under U.S. dominance:

"Just a few weeks before, some 300,000 people had marched in Genoa in the biggest show of force yet of an anti-corporate globalization movement that had gone from strength to strength with demonstrations in Seattle, Washington, DC, Chiang Mai, Prague, Nice, Porto Alegre, Honolulu, and Gothenburg. The Genoa protests underlined the fact that the legitimacy of the key institutions of global economic governance— the International Monetary Fund (IMF), World Bank, and the World Trade Organization (WTO)—was at an all time low, as was the whole doctrine of liberalization, deregulation, and privatization that came under the rubric of neoliberal economics or the 'Washington Consensus.' This erosion of credibility had been brought about by a concatenation of disasters including the Asian financial crisis, the slow-motion disaster of structural adjustment in Africa and Latin America, and the spread of the financial crisis, first to Russia and Brazil and now to Argentina. What made the crisis of legitimacy of the key institutions of capitalist globalization so volatile is that it intersected with a profound structural crisis of the global economy.

Before September 11, moreover, an erosion of legitimacy haunted not only the institutions of global economic governance but also the institutions of political governance in the North, particularly the United States. Increasing numbers of Americans had begun to realize that their liberal democracy had been so thoroughly corrupted by corporate money politics that it deserved being designated a plutocracy. In the US presidential campaign of 2000, Senator John McCain ran a popular campaign that was centered on one issue: reforming a system of corporate control of the electoral system that, in scale, was unparalleled in the world. The fact that the candidate most favored by Big Business lost the popular vote—and according to some studies, the electoral vote as well—and still ended up president of the world's most powerful liberal democracy did not help in shoring up the legitimacy of a political system that had been described by many observers as already in a state of being in a state of 'cultural civil war' between conservatives and liberals, a polarization that had roughly half the country on each side of the divide."[502]

Exploiting 9-11

It is thus a matter of record that prior to 11th September, faced with a lack of any significant domestic support and growing resistance from other powerful rivals in Europe and Asia, the U.S. government had become increasingly hampered in implementing its traditional policies. There was increasing opposition even among America's close allies to its interventionist foreign policies. But handed the public mood of shock and revulsion over the shocking tragedy of 11th September, the Bush administration was able to exploit these sentiments to advance long-standing global economic and strategic aims.

Powerful sections of the U.S. elite thus viewed the events of 11th September as a welcome opportunity to implement an agenda designed to secure broad strategic and economic interests through the expansion and consolidation of U.S. military influence. Accordingly, the Bush administration immediately proposed an open-ended expansion of U.S. military action abroad, coupled with the suppression of dissent at home, which conveniently paved the way for just the sort of "sustained and directed American involvement" in Central Asia necessary for domination of Eurasia, and thus the establishment of U.S. "global primacy," as discussed extensively by long-time U.S. strategic adviser Zbigniew Brzezinski.

With U.S. plans to conduct a military invasion of Afghanistan in place, 11th September provided the pretext for the implementation of international policies designed to subjugate the entire country. Under the guise of a response to the terrorist attacks on New York City and the Pentagon on 11th September 2001, the United States has led an international coalition of powers in initiating a bombing campaign on Afghanistan. The campaign was purportedly part of a new "war on terror," an attempt to root out the individuals suspected of having masterminded and arranged the attacks on U.S. soil, and moreover to abolish the regime that harboured them.

But the U.S. response illustrates that this supposed "war on terrorism" is itself guilty of the same category of politically-motivated atrocities that amount to terrorism, making a mockery of the idea that the U.S. has genuinely humanitarian motives. Indeed, the official FBI definition of terrorism states that: "Terrorism is the unlawful use of force or violence against persons or property to intimidate or coerce a government, the civilian population, or any segment thereof, in furtherance of political or social objectives."

Starving to Death, Waiting to be Killed

U.S. and British political leaders promised their public that the intervention in Afghanistan would not target the country's civilian population. U.S. House minority leader Dick Gephardt, for instance, insisted that: "[T]his is not a strike against the people of Afghanistan." But such assurances appear to be contrary to fact. The West's strategy of targeting civilians to achieve regional socio-political objectives in Afghanistan—a strategy falling directly under the FBI definition of terrorism—was perhaps most explicitly outlined in a statement by the Chief of British Defence Staff, Admiral Michael Boyce. Referring to the ongoing bombing campaign, he stated:

> "The squeeze will carry on until the people of the country themselves recognize that this is going to go on until they get the leadership changed."[503]

This admission appears to clearly indicate that Anglo-American strategy includes the punishment of Afghan civilians as an integral objective, designed to secure the final aim of toppling the Taliban regime. In this context, the mass destruction of civilian structures and lives that accompanied the bombing campaign can be understood as part of a deliberate strategy of collective punishment against the Afghan people. That the war against Afghanistan is itself an act of international terrorism thus clarifies the duplicity of the concept of a "war on terrorism" led by the United States.

The *New York Times* reported around mid-September that: "Washington has also demanded [from Pakistan] a cutoff of fuel supplies,... and the elimination of truck convoys that provide much of the food and other supplies to Afghanistan's civilian population."[504] By the end of that month, America's 'newspaper of record' reported that officials in Pakistan "said today that they would not relent in their decision to seal off the country's 1,400-mile border with Afghanistan, a move requested by the Bush administration because, the officials said, they wanted to be sure that none of Mr. Bin Laden's men were hiding among the huge tide of refugees."[505]

The U.S., in other words, effectively called for the mass slaughter of millions of Afghans, most of them already on the brink of starvation, thanks to sanctions imposed under U.S. pressure, by severing the country's last few sources of limited sustenance. Additionally, almost all aid missions withdrew or were expelled from Afghanistan in anticipation of the coming bombing campaign, while several million innocent Afghans fearfully fled to the borders, creating a massive refugee crisis.

With the borders of surrounding countries sealed for several weeks, under U.S. pressure, the refugees were trapped, deprived of sustenance and largely destined to die, with the international community barely batting an eyelid. Indian novelist Arundhati Roy commented aptly on what was at first dubbed Operation Infinite Justice, now euphemistically retitled Operation Enduring Freedom: "Witness the infinite justice of the new century. Civilians starving to death while they're waiting to be killed."[506]

This, indeed, was the assessment of UNICEF, the World Food Programme, the United Nations High Commissioner for Refugees, the United Nations Programme for Humanitarian Affairs, the Office for the Coordination of Development, and the United Nations High Commissioner for Human Rights. A joint statement issued toward the end of September by the above named warns that:

"A humanitarian crisis of stunning proportions is unfolding in Afghanistan... With the eyes of the world on Afghanistan and the neighbouring countries, we call attention to the following indicators of a broad and disastrous humanitarian crisis:

a. More than five million people currently require humanitarian assistance to survive, including more than one million people who have been displaced from their homes.

b. Tens of thousands of people are now on the move in search of safety and assistance and UNHCR believes that many more are unable to move.

c. Already, 3.8 million Afghans rely on UN food aid to survive. By November 1, WFP estimates that 5.5 million people will depend on its food shipments.

d. Nearly 20 per cent of those in need are children under the age of five, according to UNICEF, many of whom are already struggling to survive.

... [L]ack of international humanitarian access is hastening the deterioration of the situation. No additional food supplies can be delivered to Afghanistan at the moment and WFP estimates that food reserves in the country will be exhausted within two to three weeks."[507]

According to UN estimates, about 7-8 million Afghans were at risk of imminent starvation. The *New York Times* noted, for instance, that nearly 6 million people depend on food aid from the UN. Another 3.5 million in refugee camps outside the country, many of whom fled just before the borders were sealed, also face imminent starvation.[508]

The U.S. attempt to absolve itself of responsibility for this predictable humanitarian catastrophe involved the crude public relations exercise of dropping food aid into the country. But this belated response to a genocidal crisis of its own making was condemned almost universally by international aid agencies. Leading British aid agencies have described the U.S. food drops as "virtually useless" as an effective aid strategy.[509]

Thomas Gonnet, head of operations in Afghanistan for the French aid agency Action Against Hunger, observed that: "It's an act of marketing, aimed more at public opinion than saving lives."[510] The propaganda purpose of the food drops has also been noted by the *Christian Science Monitor*: "Experts also urge the United States to improve its image by increasing aid to Afghan refugees."[511]

On the first day of the bombing campaign, the U.S. dropped only 37,500 packaged meals, a number far below the daily needs of even a single large refugee camp. The U.S. had thus been dropping a meagre amount of food aid daily, knowing full well that the aid will leave the vast majority of millions of Afghans facing death through hunger, to appease the public.

The duplicity of the U.S. propaganda campaign was noted by veteran aid worker James Jennings. Jennings, who as President of Conscience International, a humanitarian aid organisation, has been involved in humanitarian aid work for 20 years around the world—and most recently was in Afghan refugee camps in Pakistan in May 2001—observes that:

> "The conditions of the Afghan refugee camps in Pakistan earlier this year were the worst I have ever seen—and I have seen a lot. The camps inside Afghanistan are in even worse shape; for example in Herat there are 600,000 people on the verge of starvation. Food drops from high altitudes alone absolutely cannot provide sufficient and effective relief that is urgently necessary to prevent mass starvation. If you provide one pound of food per day, the minimum for bare survival, it would take 500 planeloads a month to supply the one camp in Herat alone, and Afghanistan is the size of Texas. The administration has stated that two aircraft are being used for food relief so far—for all of Afghanistan. Three weeks ago the head of the United Nations High Commission for Refugees (UNHCR) in Islamabad said that the food would run out—in three weeks."[512]

The international medical aid agency, Doctors Without Borders (Médecins Sans Frontières [MSF]), which has worked in Afghanistan since

1979, condemned the food air drops as "a purely propaganda tool, of real little value to the Afghan people." The agency stated that: "Such action does not answer the needs of the Afghan people and is likely to undermine attempts to deliver substantial aid to the most vulnerable." Dr. Jean-Herve Bradol of MSF elaborated that the real impact of the food drops will be "minimal":

> "How will the Afghan population know in the future if an offer of humanitarian aid does not hide a military operation? We have seen many times before, for example in Somalia, the problems caused for both the vulnerable population and for aid agencies when the military try to both fight a war and deliver aid at the same time. What is needed is large scale convoys of basic foodstuffs, rather than single meals designed for soldiers. Until yesterday the UN and aid agencies such as ourselves were still able to get some food convoys into Afghanistan. Due to the airstrikes the UN have stopped all convoys, and we will find delivering aid also much more difficult. Medical relief is not the same as dropping medicines by plane. Unless they are administered by qualified medical staff, medicines can actually do more harm than good. Dropping a few cases of drugs and food in the middle of the night during air raids, without knowing who is going to collect them, is virtually useless and may even be dangerous."

The military operation can therefore not honestly be cast in any sort of genuinely humanitarian light. MSF "rejects the idea of a humanitarian coalition alongside the military coalition."[513] And to make matters worse, the World Food Programme suspended all food convoys to Afghanistan on 8th October, in response to the Western bombing campaign. Recognising the Holocaust-like proportions of the impending disaster in Afghanistan as a result of the international blockade, a United Nations special investigator called for an end to the bombing in mid-October. Jean Ziegler, Special Rapporteur on the Right to Food to the UN High Commissioner for Human Rights, stated that:

> "The bombing has to stop right now. There is a humanitarian emergency. In winter the lorries cannot go in any more. Millions of Afghans will be unreachable in winter and winter is coming very, very soon. We must give the [humanitarian] organisations a chance to save the millions of people who are internally displaced [inside Afghanistan]."

Unless the bombing campaign is ended, he urged, aid will not get through, and up to 7 million Afghan lives will be at risk from imminent starvation.[514]

The humanitarian crisis largely continued into the New Year. The humanitarian aid organisation Conscience International released a statement from its President on 9th January 2002, emphasizing that:

"It is too early to declare a humanitarian disaster averted in Afghanistan. Early in the Afghan campaign the U.S. recognized that it was necessary to win victories on both the military and humanitarian fronts. Yet while emphasizing that the war is not over, Washington has already hailed an early victory over a looming famine that threatened to kill millions...

World Food Program emergency deliveries, using local Afghan employees, have largely replaced the needed grain tonnage lost or delayed by the war. But merely restoring capacity destroyed by the war hardly constitutes a victory, because the time lost in fighting hunger and malnutrition cannot easily be made up. The main concerns remain security and stability for the whole country—not just the capital; delivery of large-scale food assistance to remote or inaccessible regions; and the scant nutritional value of the food basket. Longer-term worries include the fact that people have eaten their seed grain, the irrigation system remains devastated, and farmers failed to plant winter wheat during October and November because of the war and bombing campaign. I still expect preventable deaths to be very high, perhaps in the lower range predicted earlier, but a deadline of next spring is artificial. I don't think the higher numbers will be reached this winter, but even the lowest previous estimate of up to 1 million deaths is bad enough. What we are likely to see over time is a continuum, a slow ticking of the clock extending far beyond May, with death for many of the most vulnerable, especially children, as a result. Severe malnutrition already exists among a significant percentage of the population.

The food budget for wheat purchases is adequate for the immediate emergency, but a bread-only diet is certainly inadequate for the neediest people. A complex emergency is just that: complex. People die because of malnutrition, disease, inability to reach medical care, enforced migration, exposure, and unhygienic conditions in the refugee camps. Probably triple the amount now being spent by USAID would come nearer to solving the problem. I would spend more on transportation-related items, to make sure food aid reached the people in the mountains, and reached them in time to survive the winter. Then I would double the caloric value of the food basket by diversification, primarily with more legumes and ghee...

[L]ast week USAID administrator Andrew Natsios did some fancy footwork with the numbers. They appear to be impressive, and indeed the December total tonnage is impressive. But in my calculation, it merely makes up for the amounts not delivered during the war. Still, it came a bit late. Put the lack of seed grain together with the inability to plant in October during the heaviest bombing, and the snows on mountain roads and trails, and you can see that, to reach their targets, WFP is delivering grain mostly to four cities: Mazar, Kabul, Jalalabad (which has road access to food supplies anyway and hasn't suffered so much in the drought) and Herat. Secretary Rumsfeld may think things are infinitely better in Afghanistan than before the war, but I doubt if most of the burka-clad beggars I regularly see there would agree."[515]

Indeed, the limited international aid being granted to Afghanistan is not reaching those who need it most. This fact is amply illustrated in a report by London *Guardian* correspondent Suzanne Goldberg, who points to a particularly harrowing example of the extent of poverty and deprivation in the country—a father compelled to sell his daughter to save his family from imminent starvation:

"Rahim Dad had eight mouths to feed and the drought had stolen his crops, his oxen and his goats. So he sold the most valuable asset he had left: his 12-year-old daughter. 'I sold my daughter for money because of the hunger,' he says, shivering with fever in the chill of his mud and chaff house. 'I sold my daughter to save the other people in my family, to save them from dying.' And so Aziz Gul was contracted in marriage to a distant relative on the far side of the gorge that cuts off the village of Siya Sang from the outside world, for a down payment of 2m Afghanis—about £50.

This is Jawand district, a place of majestic red canyons, an awful gnawing poverty and raging tuberculosis, squarely in that swath of Afghanistan that aid agencies call the 'hunger belt.' Villages like Siya Sang will see little or nothing of the $4.5bn (£3.2bn) that America, the EU, Japan and other countries pledged for Afghanistan in Tokyo last month. That money is for the reconstruction of Afghanistan after 23 years of war: rebuilding schools, hospitals and roads, and moulding a civil service and a monetary system. None of these exists in Jawand. There is not a single mile of paved road. Not a single doctor. Not a single school. Not a single medical clinic. Virtually the entire population in the district of 186,000 is illiterate."

Thus, it is this Afghan "hunger belt" that is to be largely excluded from the international 'reconstruction' programme, which in fact is not directed at the most needy among the Afghan population, but most principally at the power-holders in Kabul and the establishment of an infrastructure that benefits them. "But despite such appalling standards in this fourth consecutive year of drought," notes Goldberg, "the international community is focused on bolstering the government in Kabul, solidifying the new Afghanistan built as the U.S. and its allies would wish it...

"It would take a small miracle for the benefits to percolate down to Siya Sang. The village lies about 168 miles from Herat. On a good day it is a nine-hour journey on a dirt track that is only negotiable by four-wheel drive followed by a 90-minute hike up and down two steep and treacherous mountain canyons. Here, as in nearly all the 380-odd villages of Jawand, hunger and disease ravage the population, culling babies, women, and the elderly. The living stagger on, coughing their lungs and their lives out with tuberculosis. People are so weakened by hunger that even flu can kill. Men in their 20s and 30s have the stick-like calves and upper arms of children. New mothers produce no milk. Children are shrunken and listless. Wedding rings slide off skeletal fingers and watch bracelets hang slackly from wasted wrists.

The food aid arriving now may not save them. Many people weigh less than the 50kg sacks of wheat they lug home—on their backs because their donkeys died or were sold. At least four men died on the 24-hour trek to their villages with their sacks of wheat in January. This was the future staring at Rahim Dad when he sold his first-born daughter. He spent the money on flour, rice and tea, and the relative luxuries of soap and sweets. He says he has enough food left for 10 days. At these margins of human existence, the survival instinct rules over sympathy for Aziz Gul. 'She was crying. She was not happy that she was engaged by force. But I could not do anything, and I can't worry about her,' says her grandmother, Yaman. Rahim Dad interrupts: 'If we had not sold her, the whole family would have died of hunger.'"[516]

This example was from the beginning of February. By the end of February, the international aid agency, Doctors Without Borders (MSF), reported its findings of escalating impoverishment despite international intervention.

"There are more children in feeding centres than ever before. The number of severely malnourished have increased. Mortality rates have doubled and the numbers of displaced have increased. Of all the families surveyed, almost half have not received food aid over the past year...

The food crisis in northern Afghanistan is reaching alarming proportions. Medecins Sans Frontieres (MSF) has assessed the condition of populations in Sar-e-Pol displaced camp and in southern

Faryab province (in January, 1,290 families were interviewed, representing 8,680 people) and found a dramatic situation. MSF also sees a constant increase in the number of children admitted to their feeding centers. Prospects are poor for a population that is selling its belongings, leaving their homes in large numbers, and by and large has no land or seeds to prepare for recovery."

The agency's Operational Director, Christopher Stokes, noted the responsibility of the international community, which has stood by in ongoing indifference to the escalating crisis:

"We are getting increasingly frustrated with the promises of the international community. All the talk of world leaders, donor countries and international organizations of their commitment to the Afghan people, translates into little for many people in remote areas. In northern Afghanistan, a new disaster is in the making and can only be averted by immediate and unrestrained action."[517]

The Air War

As for the allegedly "surgical strikes" of the Anglo-American forces, bombarding the major cities of Afghanistan—which purportedly have been "selective" and targeted only at military installations—such claims can hardly have been taken seriously by anyone aware of the West's bloody record. Indeed, Middle East expert Stephen Zunes, Associate Professor of Politics at the University of San Francisco and senior policy analyst at the Foreign Policy in Focus Project, points out that:

"The use of heavy bombers against a country with few hard targets raises serious doubts about the Bush Administration's claim that the attacks are not against the people of Afghanistan. The Taliban has allowed Bin Laden and his followers sanctuary, but there is little evidence that they have provided the kind of direct financial or military support that can be crippled through air strikes."[518]

In the Gulf War, for example, the Western public was informed by military and political leaders of the pinpoint accuracy of the targeting of Iraqi military structures by the Allied forces, with Iraqi civilians rarely in any danger. The fact of the matter was that the West had covertly included the Iraqi civilian population as an official target of the bombing campaign.

A report by the U.S. General Accounting Office, for instance, explicitly affirms that the Desert Storm air campaign of 1991 was aimed at: "Five basic categories of targets—command and control, industrial production, infrastructure, population will, and fielded forces." The bombing of civilian infrastructure—including electricity, water, sanitation and other life-sustaining essentials—was intended, according to the report, to "degrade the will of the civilian population."[519] Middle East Watch (MEW), affiliated to the international U.S.-based rights monitor Human Rights Watch (HRW), has documented numerous cases of the intentional mass destruction of civilian buildings and areas, all of which occurred largely in broad daylight with no governmental or military structures in the vicinity.[520] The Western Allies under U.S. leadership embarked on the purposeful destruction of almost the entirety of Iraq's civilian infrastructure.

Eric Hoskins, a Canadian doctor and Coordinator of a Harvard study team on Iraq, observed that the bombing "effectively terminated everything vital to human survival in Iraq—electricity, water, sewage systems, agriculture, industry, health care. Food, warehouses, hospitals and markets were bombed. Power stations were repeatedly attacked until electricity supplies were at only 4 per cent of prewar levels."[521]

Francis Boyle, Professor of International Law at the University of Illinois, points out that:

"Most of the targets were civilian facilities. The United States intentionally bombed and destroyed centres for civilian life, commercial and business districts, schools, hospitals, mosques, churches, shelters, residential areas, historical sites, private vehicles and civilian government offices. In aerial attacks, including strafing, over cities, towns, the countryside and highways, United States aircraft bombed and strafed indiscriminately. The purpose of these attacks was to destroy life and property, and generally to terrorise the civilian population of Iraq."[522]

To this day, Anglo-American forces operating over the Iraqi no-fly-zones on the pretext of monitoring and protecting the population from Saddam Hussein's atrocities, continue to routinely bomb not only military targets, but civilian targets as well, as recorded in an internal UN Security Sector report for a single five-month period:

"41 per cent of victims of the bombing were civilians in civilian targets: villages, fishing jetties, farmland and vast, treeless valleys where sheep graze. A shepherd, his father, his four children and his sheep were killed by a British or American aircraft, which made two passes at them."[523]

NATO's military intervention in Kosovo under U.S. leadership was similar. In April 1999, the *Washington Times* reported that NATO planned to hit "power generation plants and water systems, taking the war directly to civilians."[524] The *New York Times* similarly reported that: "[T]he destruction of the civilian infrastructure of Yugoslavia has become part of the strategy to end the war on Kosovo... We are bringing down terror on the Serbian people."[525]

In May, NATO Generals admitted that: "Just focussing on field forces is not enough... The [Serbian] people have to get to the point that their lights are turned off, their bridges are blocked so they can't get to work."[526] "NATO officials also have said they believe that putting pressure on the civilian population will undermine the regime," reported the *San Francisco Examiner*.[527]

A British Harrier pilot who had been bombing Serbia in April 1999 was led to remark: "After a while you've got to ignore the collateral damage [i.e. civilian casualties] and start smashing those targets"[528]—in other words, bomb indiscriminately with no regard for the civilian death toll. NATO's attacks were therefore aimed against civilian targets from the outset of the campaign, when a tractor factory was destroyed by cruise missiles. According to an employee of a U.S. intelligence organisation, the CIA had been charged with crafting lists of Yugoslav economic assets—the official testified that "basically, everything in the country's a target unless it's taken off the list."[529] So brutal was the bombing campaign that former U.S. President Jimmy Carter stated:

> "[Our attack] has been counterproductive, and our destruction of civilian life has now become senseless and excessively brutal... The American-led force has expanded targets to inhabited areas and resorted to the use of anti-personnel cluster bombs. The result has been damage to hospitals, offices and residences of a half-dozen ambassadors, and the killing of innocent civilians... [Our] insistence on the use of cluster bombs, designed to kill or maim humans, is condemned almost universally and brings discredit to our nation."[530]

Given this grim record, one could only reasonably expect more of the same in Afghanistan. Indeed, official disregard for civilian life was already perfectly clear in the arbitrary prevention of food aid to the Afghan people, despite the Holocaust-like proportions of the consequences. There could therefore be little doubt that Anglo-American forces were employing the traditional methods of indiscriminate bombardment, methods that also amount to acts of terrorism. An analysis of the sequence of events in the bombing of Afghanistan confirms this.

The first incident widely reported by the mainstream press was the killing of four civilians—and the injuring of another four—when the offices of a United Nations agency, the Afghan Technical Consultants (ATC) in Kabul, were bombed on 9 October 2001. The ATC oversees mine clearing operations in the country.[531] While the Pentagon claimed that the ATC was near a military radio tower, UN officials contradicted the U.S. pretext, pointing out that the tower was a defunct medium and short wave radio station that had been abandoned and out of use for over a decade. Prior to the bombing, the ATC had passed on its address to more senior UN officials to notify the U.S. military of the site so that it would not be bombed.[532]

The second occurrence reported by the press was confirmed by a large number of independent witnesses. In the northern village of Karam, an estimated 100-200 civilians—mostly women, children, and old people—were killed when bombers made repeated passes over the site during early evening prayers, flattening the entire village. The Pentagon claimed that Karam had been a training camp for Osama bin Laden's terrorist network, Al-Qaeda. In fact, the site was used solely to train mujahideen during the Soviet occupation in the 1980s, with CIA support. The camp had been run by Sadiq Bacha to train members of the Hezb-i-Islami faction. The base had never been used by Al-Qaeda, and was closed and abandoned in 1992, long before bin Laden moved to Afghanistan. Since the 1990s, Karam has been inhabited by families living in mud and rock houses, and nomads during the winter.[533]

The bombing of buildings owned by the International Committee of the Red Cross (ICRC), first on 16 October 2001 and again on the 26th, provides further evidence of the systematic targeting of civilian structures in the Anglo-American air raids. The ICRC reported that "two bombs were dropped on an ICRC compound in Kabul, wounding one of the organization's employees who was guarding the facility...

"The compound is located two kilometres from the city's airport. Like all other ICRC facilities in the country, it is clearly distinguishable from the air by the large red cross painted against a white background on the roof of each building. One of the five buildings in the compound suffered a direct hit. It contained blankets, tarpaulins and plastic sheeting and is reported to be completely destroyed. A second building, containing food supplies, caught fire and was partially destroyed before the fire was brought under control."[534]

Only ten days later, clearly visible Red Cross buildings were again destroyed by U.S. bombs in the very same compound. The ICRC reported that "bombs have once again been dropped on its warehouses in Kabul. A large (3X3 m) red cross on a white background was clearly displayed on the roof of each building in the complex...

"At about 11.30 a.m. local time, ICRC staff saw a large, slow-flying aircraft drop two bombs on the compound from low altitude. This is the same compound in which a building was destroyed in similar circumstances on 16 October. In this latest incident, three of the remaining four buildings caught fire. Two are said to have suffered direct hits. Following the incident on 16 October, the ICRC informed the United States authorities once again of the location of its facilities. The buildings contained the bulk of the food and blankets that the ICRC was in the process of distributing to some 55,000 disabled and other particularly vulnerable persons. The U.S. authorities had also been notified of the distribution and the movement of vehicles and gathering of people at distribution points."[535]

The Red Cross incidents in themselves illustrated the United States' flagrant lack of concern for civilian life in relation to the bombing campaign, as well as the Western powers' insistence on punishing the Afghan people as an integral part of their military strategy. A lucid preliminary breakdown of the systematic targeting of civilians since the month of October was recorded by American journalist and peace activist Geov Parrish, based on refugee testimony and reports from Western and Pakistani journalists. Parrish's analysis depicts a bombing campaign that has targeted civilians and civilian infrastructure on a systematic, daily basis. Selections from his breakdown are reproduced here:

- In Jalalabad, the Sultanpur Mosque was hit by a bomb during prayers, with 17 people caught inside. Neighbors rushed into the rubble to help pull out the injured, but as the rescue effort got under way, another bomb fell, killing at least 120 people.

- In the village of Darunta near Jalalabad, a U.S. bomb fell on another mosque. Two people were killed and dozens—perhaps as many as 150 people—were injured. Many of those injured are languishing without medical care in the Sehat-e-Ama hospital in Jalalabad, which lacks resources to treat the wounded...

- In Argandab, north of Kandahar, 10 civilians have died from the bombing and several houses have been destroyed. The same has happened in Karaga, north of Kabul...

- On Oct. 7, the first night of the bombing, at least one private residence in Kabul suffered a direct hit and others were damaged. The U.S. also destroyed the Hotel Continental in the city's center. On the same night, bombs were dropped on the houses of Taliban leaders in Kandahar. Two civilian relatives of Mullah Muhammad Omar were killed: his aged stepfather and his 10-year-old son...

- On Oct. 11, a bomb aimed at the Kabul airport went astray and hit Qala-e-Chaman, a village one mile away, destroying several houses and killing a 12-year-old child. On the same night, another missile hit a house near the Kabul customs building, killing 10 civilians.

- As of Oct. 12, the U.N. had independently reported at least 20 civilian deaths in Mazar-i-Sharif and 10 civilian deaths in Kandahar.

- On Oct. 13, Khushkam Bhat, a residential district between Jalalabad airport and a nearby military area, was accidentally bombed by U.S. planes trying to down a Taliban helicopter. More than 100 houses were flattened. At least 160 people were pulled from the rubble and taken to hospitals. In Kabul, witnesses described a huge fireball over the Kabul airport, indicating either the possible use of fuel-air bombs, which can cause destruction over a wide area, or the bombing of an enormous fuel storage facility, which can have the same effect. Casualties are not yet known...

- On Oct. 17, a bomb scored a 'direct hit' on a boy's school in Kabul, but fortunately didn't explode. A U.S. plane, however, dropped a bomb at Mudad Chowk, a residential area of Kandahar, which did explode, destroying two houses and several shops, and killing at least seven people. In Kabul, four bombs fell near the city center; casualties are still unknown.

- The U.N. reported that Kandahar had fallen into a state of 'pre-Taliban lawlessness,' with gangs taking over homes and looting shops. By the next day, according to the U.N., at least 80 percent of Kandahar's residents had left the city to escape the bombing. They are swamping the surrounding villages, where there are no resources to care for them. Some have moved on to the border and crossed into Pakistan. One refugee said that there are bodies littering the streets of Kandahar and people are dying in the hospitals for lack of drugs. 'We know we will lead a miserable life in Pakistan, in tents,' he said. 'We have come here just to save our children.'

- The civilian death toll is probably in the thousands, and sure to rise with two new developments. U.S. Air Force pilots may now fire 'at will'—at anything they desire, without pre-authorization from strategists peering at satellite and surveillance photos. In fact, there are now regions of the country that have been designated 'kill boxes,' reminiscent of Vietnam's 'free-fire zones' but without benefit of advance warning to Afghanis. Kill boxes are patrolled night and day by low-flying aircraft with the mission to shoot anything that moves within the area.[536]

The testimony of Afghan refugees further demonstrates that the bombing campaign has targeted virtually the entire civilian population. Civilian areas devoid of military structures have been hit with devastating effect. On 22nd October, Reuters reported that:

"Afghan refugees fleeing U.S. air raids said Saturday the strikes destroyed shopping bazaars in the heart of the Taliban stronghold of Kandahar, killing and injuring shoppers and other civilians. The bombs hit the southern city Thursday and Friday, spearing shoppers with shards of shrapnel in attacks apparently targeting government buildings."

Mohammed Ghaus, who crossed into Pakistan with his wife and five children, stated that: "On Thursday night around 10 p.m. and yesterday at 2 p.m. and again last night, there was heavy bombing. The bazaar around the Keptan intersection in the city enter was flattened. My neighbor's house was destroyed. That's why we left." As Reuters added: "There were civilian casualties, he said, but he did not know how many. Other new arrivals, streaming across the Chaman checkpoint in their hundreds Saturday, told similar stories."[537]

Testimonials from many other refugees confirm that American and British forces are indiscriminately inflicting terror on Afghan civilians. The Institute for Health and Social Justice has compiled a sample of such testimony based on reports in the *Boston Globe* and *New York Times*:

Rais Mazloomyar Jabirkhail: 'They are not God. They want to pinpoint every target, but they can't make every missile go after Osama and terrorist training camps.' Clarifying that he is not a supporter of Osama Bin Laden, he asked why, on the pretext of targeting Bin Laden and Al-Qaeda, the U.S. 'is destroying our whole country.'"

Mohammad Akram: 'They should find Osama bin Laden and attack only him. Why did they attack all of Afghanistan? We are just poor people in Afghanistan.'

Mohammad Zahir: 'Everyone wants to eliminate terrorism from the face of the earth, but the way adopted by the U.S. is not fair because masses of ordinary people also live in Afghanistan. The attack was not just on terrorist camps... I know those are residential areas.'

Abdul Malik described the 'great panic among the people' in his village: '[T]hey are running toward hilly areas away from cities... We were telling the women and children that everything will be OK, we will be safe [in the hills], we will pray to God.'

Naseebullah Khan: 'It's not true that the Americans have only been bombing military targets. Many of the bombs are dropping on residential neighborhoods.'"[538]

Testimonials from soldiers of the U.S. Army Special Forces Team 555 that directed 175 aircraft sorties over Afghanistan in 25 days of round-the-clock target-spotting, corroborate the testimony of Afghan refugees. Chief

Warrant Officer Dave Diaz admits that "we started to play this terminology game" to convince "fliers who were reluctant to attack" targets which "did not look like military targets." He informed his nine soldiers and one air force combat controller: "Yes it is a civilian village, mud hut, like everything else in this country. But don't say that. Say it's a military compound. It's a built-up area, barracks, command and control. Just like with the convoys—if it really was a convoy with civilian vehicles they were using for transport, we would just say, 'Hey, military convoy, troop transport.'"

When one pilot expressed reluctance to hit a certain target, members of Team 555 put their case bluntly. One sergeant responded: "Yes, it's a mud hut. We live in mud huts. They live in mud huts. We fight out of mud huts. They fight out of mud huts. There are no good guys there anymore."[539]

The "war on terror" is thus utilising mass terrorism to achieve its alleged objectives. There is clearly nothing humanitarian or moral about this war, which is not a war on terror, but a war *of* terror on America's enemies, conducted to secure strategic and economic interests with a completely racist and xenophobic disregard for the lives of Afghans, and other indigenous peoples. As has been noted in London's *Independent* by British Middle East correspondent, Robert Fisk, "as the Afghan refugees turn up in their thousands at the border, it is palpably evident that they are fleeing not the Taliban but our bombs and missiles...

"The Taliban is not ethnically cleansing its own Pashtun population. The refugees speak vividly of their fear and terror as our bombs fall on their cities. These people are terrified of our 'war on terror,' victims as innocent as those who were slaughtered in the World Trade Centre on 11 September. So where do we stop?... The figure of 6,000 remains as awesome as it did in the days that followed. But what happens when the deaths for which we are responsible begin to approach the same figure?... Once the UN agencies give us details of the starving and the destitute who are dying in their flight from our bombs, it won't take long to reach 6,000. Will that be enough? Will 12,000 dead Afghans appease us, albeit that they have nothing to do with the Taliban or Osama bin Laden? Or 24,000? If we think we know what our aims are in this fraudulent 'war against terror,' have we any idea of proportion?... This particular war is... not going to lead to justice. Or freedom. It's likely to culminate in deaths that will diminish in magnitude even the crime against humanity on 11 September."[540]

Fisk was correct. In a comprehensive study of the civilian victims of the bombing campaign against Afghanistan, Marc W. Herold, Professor of Economics, International Relations and Women's Studies at the University of New Hampshire, found that 3,767 Afghan civilians were killed in eight and a half weeks. His study, based on a detailed analysis of press reports, is furthermore based on conservative estimates of the civilian death toll.

A more realistic figure, Professor Herold noted, would be closer to around 5,000 dead. He notes in his study that: "The explanation [of this massive death toll] is the apparent willingness of U.S military strategists to fire missiles into and drop bombs upon, heavily populated areas of Afghanistan...

"A legacy of the ten years of civil war during the 80s is that many military garrisons and facilities are located in urban areas where the Soviet-backed government had placed them since they could be better protected there from attacks by the rural mujahideen. Successor Afghan governments inherited these emplacements. To suggest that the Taliban used 'human shields' is more revealing of the historical amnesia and racism of those making such claims, than of Taliban deeds. Anti-aircraft emplacements will naturally be placed close by ministries, garrisons, communications facilities, etc... A heavy bombing onslaught must necessarily result in substantial numbers of civilian casualties simply by virtue of proximity to 'military targets,' a reality exacerbated by the admitted occasional poor targeting, human error, equipment malfunction, and the irresponsible use of out-dated Soviet maps. But, the critical element remains the very low value put upon Afghan civilian lives by U.S military planners and the political elite, as clearly revealed by U.S willingness to bomb heavily populated regions. Current Afghan civilian lives must and will be sacrificed in order to (possibly) protect future American lives. Actions speak, and words (can) obscure: the hollowness of pious pronouncements by Rumsfeld, Rice and the servile corporate media about the great care taken to minimize collateral damage is clear for all to see. Other U.S bombing targets hit are impossible to 'explain' in terms other than the U.S seeking to inflict maximum pain upon Afghan society and perceived 'enemies': the targeted bombing of the Kajakai dam power station, the Kabul telephone exchange, the Al Jazeera Kabul office, trucks and buses filled with fleeing refugees, and the numerous attacks upon civilian trucks carrying fuel oil. Indeed, the bombing of Afghan civilian infrastructure parallels that of the Afghan civilian."[541]

By the beginning of January 2002, Professor Herold, continuing to monitor ongoing U.S. bombing raids in Afghanistan, was forced to revise his figures. He estimated that the documented death toll now stands at 4,050—a figure surpassing the number of victims of the 11th September attacks.[542]

Securing Regional U.S. Interests

As soon as the bombing campaign commenced, the Bush administration began pursuing the principal interests that had motivated the war plans against Afghanistan in the first place. Pakistan's *Frontier Post* reported that:

"The U.S. ambassador to Pakistan Wendy Chamberlain paid a courtesy call on the Federal Minister for Petroleum and Natural resources, Usman Aminuddin here Tuesday and discussed with him matters pertaining to Pak-U.S. cooperation in the oil and gas sector... Usman Aminuddin also briefed the Ambassador on the proposed Turkmenistan-Afghanistan-Pakistan gas pipeline project and said that this project opens up new avenues of multi dimensional regional cooperation particularly in view of the recent geo-political developments in the region."[543]

With the removal of the Taliban from power, the U.S. was also ready to establish the unified, friendly government required to ensure the domestic stability and security essential to allow the pipeline to be constructed. The new federal administration of Northern Alliance warlords signaled a return to the pre-Taliban era of barbarism and brutality—although this time with factional war and rivalry limited under the terms of the U.S.-UN brokered agreements.

Ongoing repression and brutalisation of women, children and men, however, does not appear to have been a principal U.S. concern. The concern was merely to establish a federal dictatorship of warlords who will remain in control of their respective Afghan territories, minimise conflict between one another, while remaining free to govern the civilians under their control as they please. Fahima Vorgetts, who headed a women's literacy programme in Kabul before fleeing the country after the 1979 Soviet invasion, observes: "For years we have been trying to raise awareness about the situation of women in Afghanistan and for years we were being ignored. We had to beg people to arrange an event...

"Now people are listening to what we say about the Taliban, but they must listen to what we say about the Northern Alliance to not repeat the same type of tragedy for the country as a whole and especially for the women of Afghanistan. The Taliban are horrible and Afghanistan will be much better off without them, but we must not forget that the Northern Alliance committed so many atrocities, so many crimes during their rule between 1992 and 1996 that they made it easy for the Taliban to come to power. Afghanistan has suffered for 23 years— there is no school, employment, streets, factories or bridges left. The bombing is making it worse, it's causing more damage."[544]

Tahmeena Faryal, spokesperson for the Revolutionary Association of Women in Afghanistan (RAWA, www.rawa.org), the oldest women's humanitarian and political organisation in the country, was even more scathing in her November 2001 comments on both the military and diplomatic dimensions of the U.S. intervention: "Despite the claim of the U.S. that only military and terrorist bases of the Taliban and Al-Qaeda would be struck and that its actions would be accurately targeted and proportionate, what we have witnessed for the past many days leaves no doubt that this invasion will shed the blood of numerous women, men, children, young and old of our country...

"The U.S. and its allies were supporting the policies that helped foster Osama bin Ladin and the Taliban. Today they are sharpening the dagger of the 'Northern Alliance.' So many of those now involved in what has come to be called the Northern Alliance have the blood of our beloved people on their hands, as of course do the Taliban. Their sustained atrocities have been well documented by independent international human rights organizations such as Amnesty International and Human Rights Watch, and others. From 1992 to 1996 in particular, these forces waged a brutal war against women, using rape, torture, abduction and forced marriage as their weapons. Many women committed suicide during this period as their only escape. Any initiative to establish a broad-based government must exclude all Taliban and other criminal Jehadi factions, unless and until a specific faction or person has been absolved of war crimes and crimes against humanity. Otherwise, the people will again be plunged into the living hell that engulfed our country from 1992 to 1996—under elements now involved in the Northern Alliance—and continues to the present under the Taliban."[545]

Former Canadian diplomat Professor Peter Dale Scott, a political scientist at the University of California, Berkeley, thus noted in January 2002 that: "[O]ne has a clear sense that warlordism is returning to Afghanistan. We are seeing a return of the worst features of the pre-Taliban 1990s: unrestricted banditry, looting of food supplies meant for civilians, widespread smuggling of all forms and above all extensive production of opium and heroin."[546]

But the opinion of the Afghan people was irrelevant. What was relevant was the institutionalisation of the rule of various factions implicated in war crimes and human rights abuses, in order to set up a unified federation that could provide a suitable degree of stability, regardless of the ongoing brutalisation of the population. The policy may not be viable in the longrun, but the Bush administration is clearly hoping that it is. Commenting on the disconcerting behind-the-scenes predominance of the oil and gas issue, the *San Francisco Chronicle* observed in late September that:

> "The hidden stakes in the war against terrorism can be summed up in a single word: oil. The map of terrorist sanctuaries and targets in the Middle East and Central Asia is also, to an extraordinary degree, a map of the world's principal energy sources in the 21st century... It is inevitable that the war against terrorism will be seen by many as a war on behalf of America's Chevron, Exxon, and Arco; France's TotalFinaElf; British Petroleum; Royal Dutch Shell and other multinational giants, which have hundreds of billions of dollars of investment in the region."[547]

The *Chronicle's* concerns were confirmed by the end of November when the White House released a statement from Bush Jr. on the opening of the first new pipeline by the Caspian Pipeline Consortium: "The CPC project also advances my Administration's National Energy Policy by developing a network of multiple Caspian pipelines that also includes the Baku-Tbilisi-Ceyhan, Baku-Supsa, and Baku-Novorossiysk oil pipelines and the Baku-Tbilisi-Erzurum gas pipeline."[548] The pipeline is a joint venture of Russia, Kazakhstan, Oman, ChevronTexaco, ExxonMobil and several other oil companies, connecting the Tengiz oilfield in northwestern Kazakhstan to the Russian Black Sea port of Novorossiysk. American companies had put up $1 billion of the $2.65 billion construction cost.

The pipeline consortium involved in the Baku-Ceyhan plan, led by British oil company BP, is represented by the law firm of Baker & Botts, whose principal attorney is James Baker III. Baker III was U.S. Secretary of State under the Bush Sr. Administration. He was also the chief spokesman for Bush Jr.'s year 2000 campaign, during its successful attempt to block the vote recount in Florida.

The *New York Times* reported further developments in December 2001: "There is no oil in Afghanistan, but there are oil politics, and Washington is subtly tending to them, using the promise of energy investments in Central Asia to nurture a budding set of political alliances in the region with Russia, Kazakhstan and, to some extent, Uzbekistan...

> "Since the Sept. 11 attacks, the United States has lauded the region as a stable oil supplier, in a tacit comparison with the Persian Gulf states that have been viewed lately as less cooperative. The State Department is exploring the potential for post-Taliban energy projects in the region, which has more than 6 percent of the world's proven oil reserves and almost 40 percent of its gas reserves... Better ties between Russia and the United States, for example, have accelerated a thaw that began

more than a year ago over pipeline routes from the Caspian Sea to the West."[549]

By New Years Eve, nine days after the U.S.-backed interim government of Hamid Karzai took office in Kabul, President Bush appointed a former aide to the American oil company UNOCAL, Zalmay Khalilzad, as special envoy to Afghanistan. Khalilzad drew up a risk analysis of a proposed gas pipeline from the former Soviet republic of Turkmenistan across Afghanistan and Pakistan to the Indian Ocean, and also participated in talks between UNOCAL and Taliban officials in 1997, aimed at implementing a 1995 agreement to build the pipeline across western Afghanistan. It turns out that the newly appointed Afghani Prime Minister Hamid Karzai is also a former paid consultant for UNOCAL.[550] These nominations illustrate the fundamental interests behind U.S. military intervention in Afghanistan.[551]

Thus, by mid-February, the *Irish Times* reported that: "Pakistani President, Gen Pervez Musharraf, and the Afghan interim leader, Mr Hamid Karzai, agreed yesterday that their two countries should develop 'mutual brotherly relations' and co-operate 'in all spheres of activity'—including a proposed gas pipeline from Central Asia to Pakistan via Afghanistan...

"Mr Karzai, who arrived in Islamabad earlier yesterday for a one-day visit, said he and Gen Musharraf discussed the proposed Central Asian gas pipeline project 'and agreed that it was in the interest of both countries.' Pakistan and several multinational companies, including the California-based Unocal Corp and Bridas S.A. of Argentina, have been toying with the idea of constructing a 1,600-km pipeline from Turkmenistan through Afghanistan to growing natural gas markets in Pakistan and, potentially, India."[552]

The intervention also allowed the U.S. to counter its Russian rival and establish dominance over the Central Asian republics on the country's border. Reuters reported near the end of September that:

"The ex-Soviet republics used the crisis to assert their independence from Moscow, quickly agreeing to open air corridors and possibly airports to the United States, something that was unthinkable only two weeks ago. Once the region's unquestioned master, Moscow found it had little choice but to agree with the Central Asian states and let U.S. forces into the region for the first time."[553]

Thus, new economic programmes have been accompanied by the establishment of a permanent military presence in the region, even whilst the war on Afghanistan was drawing to a close. The *Los Angeles Times* reported that: "Behind a veil of secret agreements, the United States is creating a ring of new and expanded military bases that encircle Afghanistan and enhance the armed forces' ability to strike targets throughout much of the Muslim world...

> "Since Sept. 11, according to Pentagon sources, military tent cities have sprung up at 13 locations in nine countries neighboring Afghanistan, substantially extending the network of bases in the region. All together, from Bulgaria and Uzbekistan to Turkey, Kuwait and beyond, more than 60,000 U.S. military personnel now live and work at these forward bases. Hundreds of aircraft fly in and out of so-called 'expeditionary airfields.'"[554]

There can be no doubt that this presence is intended to be permanent. Radio Free Europe/Liberty further reported developments in the region indicating that the U.S. military has been making itself at home in Central Asia: "Even though the U.S.-led campaign in Afghanistan appears to be drawing to a close, Washington is building up its military presence in Central Asia to protect what it describes as its long-term interests, in an area Russia and China consider part of their sphere of influence...

> "The United States, which has gained a foothold in Central Asia over the course of its antiterrorism campaign in Afghanistan, is now considering ways to consolidate its military buildup there in a bid to raise its political profile in the region. The move is likely to prompt much gnashing of teeth in Russia and China, as the two nations traditionally regard Kazakhstan, Kyrgyzstan, Uzbekistan, and Tajikistan as their backyard...

> [T]he Pentagon and its allies have been using Uzbekistan and Kyrgyzstan as a rear base for military operations and as a corridor for humanitarian aid. Kazakhstan and Tajikistan have no Western troops on their territories, but they have offered their respective airspaces and airfields to U.S. planes for operations in Afghanistan. Allied military experts are currently inspecting Tajik airfields in anticipation of future missions in the region. Some 2,000 U.S. soldiers are already deployed in former Soviet Central Asia, mainly on Uzbekistan's southern Khanabad airfield, near the Afghan border. On 28 December, Uzbek President Islam Karimov said he has set no deadline for U.S. troops to pull out of the base.

> Although the U.S.-led anti-Taliban operation appears near its end, the Pentagon is building military facilities at Manas international airport— some 30 kilometers outside the Kyrgyz capital Bishkek—which could house up to 3,000 troops. And the Kyrgyz parliament last month agreed to let the U.S. military set up a base at Manas for one year. In another sign the U.S. is settling into the region, 'The New York Times' of 10 January reported that U.S. military planners are also considering

rotating troops in the region every six months, increasing technical support for and conducting training exercises with Central Asian countries...

In comments last month to the U.S. Congress's Foreign Affairs Committee, Elizabeth Jones—the assistant secretary of state for European and Eurasian affairs—notably said President George W. Bush's administration hopes a permanent U.S. presence in Central Asia will boost regional economic development... U.S. Deputy Defense Secretary James Wolfowitz said that, by upgrading its military presence in Central Asia, the U.S. wishes to send a clear message to regional countries—especially to Uzbekistan—that it will not forget about them and that it 'has a capacity to come back and will come back in' whenever needed... A report published on 6 January in 'The Washington Post' said that, in addition, the Bush administration is planning to abrogate a Cold War-era bill that places conditions on a number of former Soviet republics' trade relations with the U.S. based on their human rights records... The planned move has already stirred controversy among regional analysts, who believe it could send the message that the U.S. is ready to condone human rights abuses in some of these countries in return for their loyalty."[555]

The expansion of U.S. hegemony is thus to be accompanied by the legitimisation of regional human rights abuses, dictatorship, and general repression. The instrumental role played by 11th September in providing a justification for the anti-humanitarian expansion and consolidation of U.S. hegemony in Central Asia was specifically indicated by U.S. Senator Joseph Lieberman. Speaking on 7th January at Bagram air base near Kabul, he observed: "We learned at a very high and painful price the cost of a lack of involvement in Central Asia on 11 September, and we're not going to let it happen again."[556]

9-11: From Crisis to Silver Lining

The events of 11th September, in other words, allowed the Bush administration to avert the crisis of legitimacy it had previously faced, and re-enter world affairs with a new sense of confidence. In the words of the *U.S. News*: "Then came 9/11. Worldwide revulsion and the shared sense of threat handed Washington a once-in-a-generation chance to shake up international politics. Ten days after the attacks, State Department experts catalogued for Powell a dozen 'silver linings'...

"A flexible wartime foreign policy means the United Nations is back in good graces: The administration is even counting on the oft-maligned international body to lead 'nation building' efforts in postwar Afghanistan. Elsewhere, the new chemistry in foreign affairs continues to transform relationships. Four months ago, U.S.-Russian relations were chilly. But President Vladimir Putin is gambling the counterterrorism campaign will reconnect Russia with the West, bringing economic and diplomatic benefits. Snubbing his military chiefs, Putin accepted a U.S. military presence in Central Asia. That allows unprecedented U.S. ties with states like Uzbekistan...

Almost as unprecedented is Pakistan's shotgun wedding with the United States. Once a Cold War ally, Pakistan was devolving into a consistent source of trouble—nuclear weapons tests, the military overthrow of an elected government, and support for Islamic militants fighting India. Pakistan, of course, propped up the Taliban. But confronted with U.S. demands, Pakistan reinvented itself, at least for now, as an ally. Even China is acquiescing in the U.S.-led war. Not long ago, Bush called it a 'strategic competitor,' and the two sides were arguing over Taiwan and spy planes. Fearful of being left out of a burgeoning U.S.-Russia friendship, China is now eager to talk. Finally, old-line allies are again ascendant going into 2002. British Prime Minister Tony Blair, a Laborite ideologically more in sync with U.S. Democrats than with Bush, stepped into a traditional role: the indispensable ally. France proved a strong supporter. Germany and Japan, where pacifism still runs strong, each dispatched military units. In the coming year, counterterrorism will continue to trump other priorities."[557]

Although the war on Afghanistan is subsiding, the "war on terror" spearheaded by the Bush administration is by no means over. Afghanistan was merely a single stage of a war campaign without borders or limits, thus providing further lucrative opportunities for hegemonic expansion. The online resource, 'The U.S. War on Terror,' outlines the essence of the new developments in U.S. policy in the aftermath of 11th September. "On September 11, 2001, our country was attacked by terrorists. These actions have prompted the U.S. Government to mobilize its forces in a new kind of war."[558] The online military resource StrategyPage further noted that: "The United States and the world have entered into a type of warfare they have never faced before...

"The enemy's loyalties don't lie with a nation-state but with an ideology. An ideology committed to the destruction of all nations and peoples that do not embrace that ideology or threaten it in any way. The war will take years. It will not be limited to one geographic region of the globe. There will be no defined borders. It will be dirty, bloody and at times disheartening. It will be like nothing we have ever seen before in history."[559]

We should refer to Bush Jr.'s own words: "Our response involves far more than instant retaliation and isolated strikes. Americans should not expect one battle, but a lengthy campaign unlike any other we have ever seen." He emphasised that this new war would not be a short and decisive war against any single country. Nor would it simply be an air war without the possibility of substantial American casualties. On the contrary, the war would aim at the "defeat of the global terror network," a "task that does not end... We will direct every resource at our command... and every necessary weapon of war."

Any nation not seen to be in agreement with the U.S., thus posing a potential obstacle to U.S. plans, would constitute a supporter of terrorism. "Every nation in every region now has a decision to make: Either you are with us, or you are with the terrorists." And such nations deemed in any way not to be "with" the U.S., "will be regarded by the United States as a hostile regime." The New York-based Center for Constitutional Rights (CCR) thus reported that:

"Congress has approved resolutions giving the President 40 billion dollars and open-ended authority to use military force. The Senate and House have authorized him to attack any nation, organization or person involved in or that aided the September 11 terrorist attacks. The resolutions name no county or group as targets and contain no time limit. The only positive aspect of these resolutions is the fact that President Bush sought and received the approval of Congress, as the Constitution requires. However the use of unlimited military force that the resolutions allow is dangerous, irresponsible policy... Dangerously this congressional resolution contains no time limit, no congressional oversight and no requirements that the President ever come back to Congress for additional authority. This, unlike prior authorizations of force e.g. authorization to use force in Lebanon, gives the President unlimited power without the checks and balances of the Constitution. It eviscerates congressional control over the use of force and puts the power of war into the hands of one man, leading us quickly from democracy to one-man rule. The resolution permits the use of military force against nations that 'aid[ed]' the September 11 attack. 'Aid' is a vague, broad concept that may permit attacks on nations with only a tenuous relationship to the terrorist acts. This determination will be made with no congressional check and without any requirement of congressional approval."[560]

Indications that these unlimited war powers would be used for chilling purposes, involving provocative interventions in strategic regions, came out in March 2002, when the *Los Angeles Times* retrieved a classified Pentagon document showing that: "The Bush administration has directed the military to prepare contingency plans to use nuclear weapons against at least seven countries and to build smaller nuclear weapons for use in certain battlefield situations...

"The secret report, which was provided to Congress on Jan. 8, says the Pentagon needs to be prepared to use nuclear weapons against China, Russia, Iraq, North Korea, Iran, Libya and Syria. It says the weapons could be used in three types of situations: against targets able to withstand nonnuclear attack; in retaliation for attack with nuclear, biological or chemical weapons; or 'in the event of surprising military developments'... The report says the Pentagon should be prepared to use nuclear weapons in an Arab-Israeli conflict, in a war between China and Taiwan, or in an attack from North Korea on the south. They might also become necessary in an attack by Iraq on Israel or another neighbor, it said."

Joseph Cirincione, a nuclear arms expert at the Carnegie Endowment for International Peace in Washington, observed: "This clearly makes nuclear weapons a tool for fighting a war, rather than deterring them."[561] Defence analyst William Arkin similarly commented:

"In recent months, when Bush administration officials talked about the implications of Sept. 11 for long-term military policy, they have often focused on 'homeland defense' and the need for an anti-missile shield. In truth, what has evolved since last year's terror attacks is an integrated, significantly expanded planning doctrine for nuclear wars."[562]

The New American Police State

The same warmongering sentiments are to apply at home. In an Editorial published three days after the 11th September attacks, the *Washington Post* called for the suppression of democratic and civil rights, and the permanent transformation of U.S. domestic and foreign policy:

"[I]f replying to that attack is truly to become an organizing principle of U.S. policy, as we believe it should—if the United States is to undertake the difficult and sustained campaign against those who threaten it—then neither politics nor diplomacy can return to where they were.... This is most of all true as Congress and others discuss the possible need to sacrifice privacy, freedom of movement or other liberties to the needs of domestic security."[563]

Summarising the wide array of repressive measures being pushed through by the U.S. government to silence domestic dissent, international human rights lawyer Michael Ratner—a U.S. constitutional expert and Skelly Wright Fellow at Yale Law School—records that: "... rights that we thought embedded in the constitution and protected by international law are in serious jeopardy or have already been eliminated...

"It is no exaggeration to say we are moving toward a police state. In this atmosphere, we should take nothing for granted. We will not be protected, nor will the courts, the congress, or the many liberals who are gleefully jumping on the bandwagon of repression guarantee our rights... The domestic consequences of the war on terrorism include massive arrests and interrogation of immigrants, the possible use of torture to obtain information, the creation of a special new cabinet office of Homeland Security and the passage of legislation granting intelligence and law enforcement agencies much broader powers to intrude into the private lives of Americans. Recent new initiatives—the wiretapping of attorney-client conversations and military commissions to try suspected terrorists—undermine core constitutional protections and are reminiscent of inquisitorial practices... the war on terrorism also means pervasive government and media censorship of information, the silencing of dissent, and widespread ethnic and religious profiling of Muslims, Arabs and Asian people. It means creating a climate of fear where one suspects one's neighbors and people are afraid to speak out."[564]

"Since September 11th, we have seen one blow against the Constitution after another," notes Francis A. Boyle, Professor of International Law at the University of Illinois College of Law in Champaigne. "What we've seen, since Sept. 11, if you add up every thing that Ashcroft, Bush and their coterie of federalist society lawyers have done here, is a coup d'etat against the United States Constitution...

"Recently, we've had Ashcroft saying that he had, unilaterally, instituted monitoring of attorney-client communications without even informing anyone—he just went ahead and did it, despite the Fourth Amendment ban on unreasonable searches and seizures without warrant and the Sixth Amendment right to representation by counsel."[565]

About 1,200 people have been detained under the criminal investigations into the attacks. Yet the U.S. Department of Justice has completely failed to build a case against a single prime U.S. suspect. By 15th November 2001, federal authorities had to admit that they had not found any evidence that any of the over 1,200 people facing indefinite detention had any sort of role in the 11th September attacks.

Indeed, numerous legally binding constitutional and international treaties have been sidestepped or worse, completely violated. "We are becoming a banana republic here in the United States, with 'disappeared' people, which was the phenomenon that we all saw down in Latin American dictatorships in the 1970s and 1980s, with the support, by the way, of the United States Government," notes Professor Boyle.

> "We don't know where they are or the conditions under which they are being held. We have no idea whether they have access to attorneys. We do know one of them died, under highly suspicious circumstances, while in custody. There have been reports that he was tortured to death... Clearly aliens here are entitled to the protections of the due process clause of the Fifth Amendment, as well as to the Article III (Section 2, Clause 3) basic constitutional rights in criminal cases, including indictment, trial before a federal district judge or jury, [rights relating to] venue and things of that nature."

Robert B. Reich, Secretary of Labor under the Clinton administration, further commented that:

> "I'm surprised there hasn't been more of an outcry. The president is, by emergency decree, getting rid of rights that we assumed that anyone within our borders legally would have. We can find ourselves in a police state step-by-step without realizing that we have made these compromises along the way."[566]

Meanwhile, the Justice Department has planned to "round up" and interrogate some 5,000 men primarily of Middle Eastern background who entered the U.S. legally in the past two years.

The Department Justice, alongside the FBI, is also considering the use of torture as an approved U.S. policy against detainees who exert their right to remain silent. The *Washington Post* reports that the U.S. government is seriously considering the use of "pressure tactics, such as those employed occasionally by Israeli interrogators, to extract information" from persons in their custody.[567]

Yet a 1998 report by the Israeli human rights organisation, B'Tselem, finds that Israeli interrogators use "routine torture" against Palestinians. Illegal practices included in this are isolation, sleep deprivation, psychological torment and direct physical force including beatings, kickings, violent shaking, painful shackling and use of objects designed or used to inflict extreme pain. Such interrogations usually span months. Human rights groups confirm that Israeli torture against detained Palestinians is often so severe as to result in death during custody.[568]

Boyle observes: "When will the FBI, the CIA and the National Security Agency start to turn these powers, that they have under the Ashcroft police state bill, against American citizens? Clearly, that will be the next step."[569] Indeed, the extent to which the public has been goaded into accepting massive suppression of civil rights was particularly illustrated when U.S. Attorney General John Ashcroft announced that critics of the Bush administration's measures were fear-mongers "who scare peace-loving people with phantoms of lost liberty [and] aid terrorists." Apparently, John Ashcroft believes that people who adhere to the wisdom of U.S. Founding Father Benjamin Franklin, that liberty must not be sacrificed for the sake of security, are supporters of terrorism.

Boyle's concerns are corroborated by the Bush administration's actions. The USA Patriot Act (USAPA), signed by President George W. Bush Jr. on 26th October 2001, has "given sweeping new powers to both domestic law enforcement and international intelligence agencies and have eliminated the checks and balances that previously gave courts the opportunity to ensure that these powers were not abused," as noted by the San Francisco-based Electronic Frontier Foundation (EFF), an organisation which defends civil liberties in the realm of new technologies. "Most of these checks and balances were put into place after previous misuse of surveillance powers by these agencies, including the revelation in 1974 that the FBI and foreign intelligence agencies had spied on over 10,000 U.S. citizens, including Martin Luther King."

The USA Patriot Act will thus pave the way for the abuse of civil liberties at the whims of U.S. agencies. Among the measures the USAPA will impose are the following:

"The government may now spy on web surfing of innocent Americans, including terms entered into search engines, by merely telling a judge anywhere in the U.S. that the spying could lead to information that is 'relevant' to an ongoing criminal investigation. The person spied on does not have to be the target of the investigation. This application must be granted and the government is not obligated to report to the court or tell the person spied upon what it has done.

Nation-wide roving wiretaps. FBI and CIA can now go from phone to phone, computer to computer without demonstrating that each is even being used by a suspect or target of an order. The government may now serve a single wiretap, FISA wiretap or pen/trap order on any person or entity nation-wide, regardless of whether that person or entity is named in the order. The government need not make any showing to a court that the particular information or communication to be acquired is relevant to a criminal investigation. In the pen/trap or FISA situations, they do not even have to report where they served the order or what information they received. The EFF believes that the opportunities for abuse of these broad new powers are immense...

Just as the domestic law enforcement surveillance powers have expanded, the corollary powers under the Foreign Intelligence Surveillance Act have also been greatly expanded, including: General Expansion of FISA Authority. FISA authority to spy on Americans or foreign persons in the US (and those who communicate with them) increased from situations where the suspicion that the person is the agent of a foreign government is 'the' purpose of the surveillance to anytime that this is 'a significant purpose' of the surveillance."[570]

In a detailed point-by-point rebuttal, U.S. Representative Dennis Kucinich harshly criticised the USA Patriot Act as a direct contravention of the U.S. Constitution. "[W]e must challenge the rationale of the Patriot Act," he asserted, before questioning the Act's Constitutional implications:

"We must ask—why should America put aside guarantees of constitutional justice? How can we justify in effect canceling the First Amendment and the right of free speech, the right to peaceably assemble? How can we justify in effect canceling the Fourth Amendment, probable cause, the prohibitions against unreasonable search and seizure? How can we justify in effect canceling the Fifth Amendment, nullifying due process, and allowing for indefinite incarceration without a trial? How can we justify in effect canceling the Sixth Amendment, the right to prompt and public trial? How can we justify in effect canceling the Eighth Amendment which protects against cruel and unusual punishment?

We cannot justify widespread wiretaps and internet surveillance without judicial supervision, let alone with it. We cannot justify secret searches without a warrant. We cannot justify giving the Attorney General the ability to designate domestic terror groups. We cannot justify giving the FBI total access to any type of data which may exist in any system anywhere such as medical records and financial records.

We cannot justify giving the CIA the ability to target people in this country for intelligence surveillance. We cannot justify a government which takes from the people our right to privacy and then assumes for its own operations a right to total secrecy."[571]

It also seems that measures designed to expand the powers of the government over the American people are being pursued in tandem with attempts to decrease public understanding of the uses to which government power is put. At the beginning of November 2001, two members of the U.S. House of Representatives' Committee on Government Reform wrote to Bush expressing their dismay at the President's sudden change to the Executive Order governing the release of Presidential records.

Bush's new Executive Order "contains provisions that could drastically restrict public access to important records." It even goes so far as to allow "the sitting President to withhold the records of a former President, even if that President wants those records released." It further "requires the public to show a specific need for a document before it is released."

The letter from the Congressional Committee of Government Reform goes on to note that:

> "These provisions clearly violate the intent of law. The Presidential Records Act was passed by Congress to assure full public access to Presidential records after a reasonable interval of time. The goal of the law is the orderly and systematic release of records—not the indefinite suppression of these historical documents. We are particularly concerned that the Executive Order tries to rewrite the Act by withholding records that are part of the deliberative process... The Executive Order violates the intent of Congress and keeps the public in the dark."[572]

Exactly why such extraordinary, anti-democratic steps were introduced at this time in a country claiming to be engaged in the defence of democracy and freedom on behalf of civilisation, is hard to imagine, unless one accepts that the President has other ideas concerned with "violating the intent of law," "indefinitely suppressing" Presidential records, bypassing "the intent of Congress" and generally "keeping the public in the dark."

Indeed, discussing the implications of Bush's new Executive Order, the London *Guardian* specifies that:

> "The U.S. president, George Bush, last night signed an executive order that allows either a past or sitting president to block access to White House papers, a move that has angered historians, journalists and former president Bill Clinton... Under the terms of Mr Bush's order, any sitting or former president could veto the release of presidential papers... [T]he order would also mean that Mr Bush's personal papers detailing the decision-making process in the current war on terrorism could remain secret in perpetuity."[573]

The Bush administration's increasing opposition to public understanding of the policies of governmental and intelligence agencies was manifest in its response to a Congressional subpoena exploring abuses in the Boston FBI office around mid-December. President George W. Bush blocked the inquiry, of course bringing up the pertinent question as to what the FBI has to hide. The *Boston Globe* reported that:

"President Bush yesterday invoked executive privilege to block a congressional subpoena exploring abuses in the Boston FBI office, prompting the chairman of a House committee to lambaste his fellow Republicans and triggering what one congressman said is the start of 'a constitutional confrontation.'

'You tell the president there's going to be war between the president and this committee,' Dan Burton, the Indiana Republican who heads the House Government Reform Committee, told a Justice Department official during what was supposed to be a routine prehearing handshake. 'His dad was at a 90 percent approval rating and he lost, and the same thing can happen to him,' Burton added, jabbing his finger and glaring at Carl Thorsen, a deputy assistant attorney general who was attempting to introduce a superior who was testifying. 'We've got a dictatorial president and a Justice Department that does not want Congress involved... Your guy's acting like he's king.' The searing tone continued for more than four hours from Republicans and Democrats, liberals and conservatives. All objected to the order Bush signed Wednesday and made public yesterday. It claimed executive privilege in refusing to hand over prosecutors' memos in criminal cases, including an investigation of campaign-finance abuses, saying doing so 'would be contrary to the national interest.'

Committee members said the order's sweeping language created a shift in presidential policy and practices dating back to the Harding administration. They complained also that it followed a pattern in which the Bush administration has limited access to presidential historical records, refused to give Congress documents about the vice president's energy task force, and unilaterally announced plans for military commissions that would try suspected terrorists in secret. Representative William D. Delahunt, a Quincy Democrat and former district attorney, said: 'This is the beginning of a constitutional confrontation. In a short period of time, this Department of Justice has manifested tendencies that were of concern to Senate members during the confirmation hearings for John Ashcroft as attorney general.'"[574]

Indeed, measures spearheaded by Ashcroft are now in place designed to block access to public records available under the U.S. Freedom of Information Act (FOIA) 1974. The *San Francisco Chronicle* describes the Act as "one of our greatest democratic reforms," allowing "ordinary citizens to hold the government accountable by requesting and scrutinizing public documents and records. Without it, journalists, newspapers, historians and watchdog groups would never be able to keep the government honest." It allows the public "to know what our elected officials do, rather than what they say...

"Yet without fanfare, the attorney general simply quashed the FOIA... rather than asking federal officials to pay special attention when the public's right to know might collide with the government's need to safeguard our security, Ashcroft instead asked them to consider whether 'institutional, commercial and personal privacy interests' could be implicated by disclosure of the information."

Even more disturbing, the *Chronicle* reports the Justice Department's new policy of blocking FOIA requests, citing the Department's official notice to that effect and explaining its implications:

"'When you carefully consider FOIA requests and decide to withhold records, in whole or in part, you can be assured that the Department of Justice will defend your decisions unless they lack a sound legal basis or present an unwarranted risk of adverse impact on the ability of other agencies to protect other important records.'

... When coupled with President Bush's Nov. 1 executive order that allows him to seal all presidential records since 1980, the effect is positively chilling... [H]alf the country is also worried that the government might use the fear of terrorism as a pretext for protecting officials from public scrutiny.

Now we know that they have good reason to worry. For more than a quarter of a century, the Freedom of Information Act has ratified the public's right to know what the government, its agencies and its officials have done. It has substituted transparency for secrecy and we, as a democracy, have benefited from the truths that been extracted from public records... [A] sample of the revelations made possible by recent FOIA requests [shows that]... [n]one of them endanger the national security. It is important to remember that all classified documents are protected from FOIA requests and unavailable to the public.

Yet these secrets have exposed all kinds of official skullduggery, some of which even violated the law. True, such revelations may disgrace public officials or even result in criminal charges, but that is the consequence—or shall we say, the punishment—for violating the public trust.

No one disputes that we must safeguard our national security. All of us want to protect our nation from further acts of terrorism. But we must never allow the public's right to know, enshrined in the Freedom of Information Act, to be suppressed for the sake of official convenience."[575]

Professor Walden Bello has described the resultant situation well: "The war against terror knows no borders, so the war at home must be pursued with equal vigor. Sept 11 was Pearl Harbor II and the Bush administration tells Americans that they are now in the midst of total war like World War II. Not even the Cold War was presented in such totalistic terms as the War against Terror...

> "Laws and executive orders restricting the rights to privacy and free movement have been passed with a speed and in a manner that would have turned Joe McCarthy green with envy. The United States is only nine weeks into this war, observes David Corn in The Nation, but already legislation has been passed and executive orders signed that establish secret military tribunals to try non-U.S. citizens; impose guilt by association on immigrants; authorize the Attorney General to indefinitely lock up aliens on mere suspicion; expand the use of wiretaps and secret searches; allow the use of secret evidence in immigration proceedings that aliens cannot confront or rebut; destroy the secrecy of the client-lawyer relationship by allowing the government to listen in; and institutionalize racial and ethnic profiling."[576]

The 11th September attacks thus provided exactly the sort of "truly massive and widely perceived direct external threat" to "fashion a consensus on foreign policy issues" at home—as envisaged by Brzezinski—that would be essential to justify an open-ended "war on terror" designed more specifically to firmly establish American control over Eurasia, thus consolidating U.S. global hegemony, with Afghanistan constituting the necessary stepping stone.

The ruthlessly jingoistic mood whipped up in the aftermath of 11th September, lending the U.S. a new-found freedom to restructure world order as it wishes, without obstruction or dissent, was captured in *Time Magazine*: "America is no mere international citizen. It is the dominant power in the world, more dominant than any since Rome. Accordingly, America is in a position to reshape norms—How? By unapologetic and implacable demonstrations of will."[577]

This issued from the following background of "rage and retribution," as detailed in an 11th September *Time* Editorial by Lance Morrow:

> "For once, let's have no fatuous rhetoric about 'healing'. Healing is inappropriate now, and dangerous. There will be time later for the tears

of sorrow. A day cannot live in infamy without the nourishment of rage. Let's have rage. What's needed is a unified, unifying Pearl Harbor sort of purple American fury—a ruthless indignation that doesn't leak away in a week or two... Let America explore the rich reciprocal possibilities of the fatwa. A policy of focused brutality does not come easily to a self-conscious, self-indulgent, contradictory, diverse, humane nation... America needs to relearn... why human nature has equipped us all with a weapon... called hatred."[578]

Three months later, the imperialistic, indeed, almost fascist undertone of these sentiments was disclosed by William Pfaff in an article for the *International Herald Tribune*. Pfaff observed that:

"The world begins 2002 in a situation without precedent in human history. A single nation, the United States, enjoys unrivaled military and economic power, and can impose itself virtually anywhere it wants...

Even without nuclear weapons, the United States could destroy the military forces of any other nation on earth. If it should so choose, it could impose complete social and economic breakdown on almost any other state... It seems to many Americans and others that the United States is already potentially head of a modern version of universal empire... The West always took for granted that it provided the universal norm, and that the rest of the world would eventually have to conform to Western standards and beliefs. Its conviction of superiority began in religion... In recent years, even the Americanization of global popular culture has seemed to many to presage a coming Americanization of global political and economic values. Americans themselves have always believed that American society represents what is best and most advanced... The fundamental issue of the next two to three decades will inevitably be how the United States employs the amazing power it now exercises. Before Sept. 11, the country was already close to a universality of influence and even domination of international society that no previous empire ever possessed. It lacked the political will to impose itself. Sept. 11 supplied that will. Intrinsic to the quality of an empire is whether it is imposed culturally, as well as militarily and economically. If it is to succeed, acquiescence, if not conversion, is required on the part of the elites who are potential citizens of the empire."[579]

Imperialism at Home

Empowered by this new-found confidence in the unhindered hegemony of the American Empire, the U.S. government felt free to profit from the aftermath of the 11th September attacks. Under the guise of responding to the recession exacerbated as a result of these attacks, the Bush administration has been able to push forward previously opposed economic programmes of corporate welfare almost completely unnoticed, piling the corporate and military industrial complex with billions of dollars, despite a free-falling economy. Five days before the WTC and Pentagon attacks, President Bush Jr. described his attitude to social security funds: "I have repeatedly said the only time to use Social Security money is in times of war, times of recession, or times of severe emergency. And I mean that. I mean that."[580]

Canadian economist Michel Chossudovsky, in a scathing review of Bush's new policies under the "war on terror," recorded as early as 16th September 2001 that:

"The 'recession' and 'war' buzzwords are being used to mould U.S. public opinion into accepting a massive redirection of the nation's resources towards the military industrial complex... the shift from civilian into military production pours wealth into the hands of defense contractors at the expense of civilian needs... [B]ehind the Bush Administration is the power of the 'big five' defense contractors (Lockheed Martin, Boeing, Raytheon et al), increasingly in partnership with the oil-energy giants... The Big Five defense contractors have been shifting staff and resources from 'civilian' into 'military' production lines. Lockheed Martin (LMT)—America's largest defense contractor—for instance, has implemented major cuts in its satellite division due to 'flat demand' in the commercial satellite market. A company spokesman had reassured Wall Street that Lockheed 'was moving in the right direction' by shifting financial resources out of its troubled commercial (that is, civilian) undertakings into the lucrative production of advanced weapon systems including the F-22 Raptor high tech fighter jet to be assembled at Lockheed Martin Marietta's plant in Georgia."

The new direction of the U.S. economy, Chossudovsky continues, "will generate hundreds of billions of dollars of surplus profits, which will line the pockets of a handful of large corporations. While contributing very marginally to the rehabilitation of the employment of specialised scientific, technical and professional workers laid-off by the civilian economy, this profit bonanza will also be used by the U.S. corporate establishment to finance—in the form of so-called 'foreign investment'—the expansion of the American Empire in different parts of the World."[581]

By touting a so-called "economic stimulus" bill designed quite specifically to cater to corporate interests, the Bush administration has been able to accelerate its corporate agenda on the pretext of trying to boost the economy. While the economy continues to be racked by an ongoing recession regardless, Bush and Co. continue to benefit to a degree that would have been inconceivable in the circumstances prior to 11th September. The *New York Times*, in a piece by leading international economist Paul Krugman, reported in December 2001 that:

> "More than two months ago George W. Bush endorsed a 'stimulus' bill so tilted toward corporate interests that even many conservatives were startled. This left only two ways a bill could pass the Senate: Either the Democratic leadership would collapse, or Mr. Bush would accept something that didn't look like a personal win. It didn't, and he wouldn't."

Indeed, the Bush administration's eagerness to shove through economic programmes from which the majority of the population will only suffer, while rich corporations only get richer, and to an unprecedented degree, was manifest in the fact that: "The struggle really began less than 48 hours after the terrorist attack, when Bill Thomas, chairman of the House Ways and Means Committee, tried to ram through a sharp cut in the capital gains tax...

> "Even opponents of the capital gains tax generally acknowledge that cutting it does little to stimulate the economy in the short run; furthermore, 80 percent of the benefits would go to the wealthiest 2 percent of taxpayers. So Mr. Thomas signaled, literally before the dust had settled, that he was determined to use terrorism as an excuse to pursue a radical right-wing agenda. A month later the House narrowly passed a bill that even The Wall Street Journal admitted 'mainly padded corporate bottom lines.' It was so extreme that when political consultants tried to get reactions from voter focus groups, the voters refused to believe that they were describing the bill accurately. Mr. Bush, according to Ari Fleischer, was 'very pleased' with the bill."[582]

In an earlier report, the *Times* issued a scathing criticism of the Bush "stimulus" project, noting that "it tells you something when Congress votes $15 billion in aid and loan guarantees for airline companies but not a penny for laid-off airline workers...

> "It tells you even more when the House passes a 'stimulus' bill that contains almost nothing for the unemployed but includes $25 billion in retroactive corporate tax cuts—that is, pure lump-sum transfers to

corporations, most of them highly profitable... Since Sept. 11 there has also been a sustained effort, under cover of the national emergency, to open public lands to oil companies and logging interests."[583]

September 11th has thus successfully drawn public attention away from the considerable failings of the Bush administration before the WTC and Pentagon attacks, allowing the government to pursue the same unpopular policies, but this time on a grand scale—without public understanding of what is happening. The *Times* points out that:

"Just before Sept. 11, political debate was dominated by the growing evidence that last spring's tax cut was not, in fact, consistent with George W. Bush's pledge not to raid the projected $2.7 trillion Social Security surplus. After the attack, everyone dropped the subject. At this point, it seems that nobody will complain as long as the budget as a whole doesn't go into persistent deficit... Defending the bill [Dick Armey] and Tom DeLay rammed through the House—the one that gives huge retroactive tax cuts to big corporations—[Armey] asserted that it would create 170,000 jobs next year. That would add a whopping 0.13 percent to employment in this country. So thanks to Mr. Armey's efforts next year's unemployment rate might be 6.4 percent instead of 6.5. Aren't you thrilled? ... This bill has a $100 billion price tag in its first year, more than $200 billion over three years. [W]e're talking about giving at least $600,000 in corporate tax breaks for every job created. That's trickle-down economics without the trickle-down... The dust cloud that rose when the towers fell has certainly helped politicians who don't want you to see what they're up to."[584]

The corporate bailouts have played a similar role. The *Los Angeles Times* observes that: "Bush rushed through a $15-billion bailout to the airlines, promptly proposed ways the government would help shoulder insurers' losses from future terrorist attacks and quickly began promoting a $75-billion pump-priming package." Yet the bailouts and stimulus, like the $1.3 trillion tax cut, amounts to "a handout to big business and the super-rich."

The airline industry is a case in point. A bailout of these companies, which were already facing drastic escalating crises prior to 11th September, was of course to some extent unavoidable. But as the *LA Times* points out, "even as more than 100,000 aviation workers were being laid off, Congress insisted on exactly nothing in return for a hefty taxpayer subsidy...

"Overpaid CEOs were simply left free to slash more jobs and run. The legislation, supported by both Republicans and a Democratic Party leadership enraptured by fiscal austerity, contained no funds for laid off workers stripped of health-care benefits. It allocated no money for job training. Airlines were permitted to disregard the standard severance provisions of their labor contracts. Even expanding unemployment insurance from 26 to 39 weeks—a minimal demand at best—was rejected.

At the same time that the bailout abandons workers, it mollycoddles airline executives. To qualify for the $10 billion in loans available under the bill, airlines must freeze current executive compensation at 2000 levels for two years and limit severance pay to twice that amount. This may sound like some kind of sacrifice. But think of Delta Air Lines Chairman Leo F. Mullin, who got $2.1 million last year in salary and bonuses and as much as $34 million when his stock options are counted. Continental's Gordon Bethune raked in $3 million in salary and bonus, and another $4.8 billion in options. Donald Carty of American Airlines had potential earnings of $15.9 million. James Goodwin, until last week CEO of United Airlines, $10 million. To put this in perspective, it would take 1,365 years for the average American worker, making $25,501 annually, to earn Delta chair Mullin's yearly salary, 623 years to earn Carty's and 392 years to earn Goodwin's. And so it goes. If an airline chooses to skip the loan and go straight for the $5 billion in grants awarded by the bill, the sky's the limit on executive salaries and severance."[585]

The dire reality of this situation, and the sheer duplicity employed to allow it to continue without protest, has been encapsulated well in the remark of Arthur McEwan, Professor of Economics at the University of Massachusetts at Boston: "The administration seems to be using this tragedy to continue its policy of transferring wealth to corporations and ignoring the plight of working people... [L]et us not forget that a recession was already developing before September 11 so we may be bailing out corporations whose troubles did not originate with the tragedy of September 11."[586]

Indeed, the Bush administration has been doing exactly the opposite of what it should be doing to revive the economy. David Swanson of ACORN, an organisation advocating for low and middle income Americans, observes that: "We're headed in exactly the wrong direction with the Bush plan. What's needed both to help the people who are suffering the most and to actually stimulate the economy is to get money into the hands of low income people who need it the most and who are more likely to immediately spend it in a variety of sectors of the economy."[587]

Thus, the *Economic Letter* of the Federal Reserve Bank of San Francisco reports that as far as corporate welfare is concerned, in "the longer run," "the picture is a good deal more positive," largely *because* of 11th September. "Why? Because there are several important sources of stimulus that should make economic activity rebound...The events of September 11 have largely served to reinforce these trends."[588]

9-11: Who Benefits?

The 11th September attacks, in other words, came at an extremely fortuitous time for the Bush administration, the Pentagon, the CIA, the FBI, the weapons industry, and the oil industry, all of which have benefited immensely from this tragedy. In this connection, it is worth noting the acute observations of Canadian social philosopher Professor John McMurtry:

"To begin with, the forensic principle of 'who most benefits from the crime?' clearly points in the direction of the Bush administration. One would be naive to think the Bush Jr. faction and its oil, military-industrial and Wall Street backers who had stolen an election with its man rated in office by the majority of Americans as poor on the economy (a Netscape Poll taken off the screen when the planes hit the towers), and more deplored by the rest of the world as a deep danger to the global environment and the international rule of law, do not benefit astronomically from this mass-kill explosion. If there was a wish-list, it is all granted by this numbing turn of events. Americans are diverted from a free-falling economy to attack another foreign Satan, while the Bush regime's popularity climbs. The military, the CIA and every satellite armed security apparatus have more money and power than ever, and become as dominant as they can over civilians in 'the whole new era' already being declared by the White House. The anti-missile plan to rule the skies is now exonerated (if irrelevantly so), and Israel's apartheid civil war is vindicated at the same time. Even the surgingly popular 'anti world-trade' movement is now associated with foreign terrorists blowing up the World Trade Centre. The more you review the connections and the sweeping lapse of security across so many co-ordinates, the more the lines point backwards."[589]

Professor Walden Bello similarly records that: "The Al Qaeda New York mission was the best possible gift to the U.S. and the global establishment in the pre-September 11 historical conjuncture...

"Arguing that accelerated liberalization was necessary to counter September 11's blow against the world economy, [U.S. Trade Representative Robert Zoellick], European Union Trade Commissioner Pascal Lamy, and World Trade Organization Director General Mike Moore led the charge to stampede the developing countries into approving the launching of a new phase of trade liberalization during the Fourth Ministerial of the WTO in Doha, Qatar, last November. The Doha Declaration set the bicycle of trade liberalization that is the WTO back upright and in motion after its collapse in Seattle.

Horst Kohler, managing director of the IMF, and Jim Wolfensohn, president of the World Bank, also saw the war as an opportunity to reverse the crisis of their institutions. Kohler has cheerfully cooperated in turning the Fund into a key component of Washington's overall program for strategic states such as Pakistan and Indonesia, even as it left a non-strategic country like Argentina, which faces imminent bankruptcy, twisting in the wind. His presidency and his institution threatened by a pincer movement of criticism from the left and the right, Jim Wolfensohn, for his part, has seized on September 11 to project his institution as the key partner of the Pentagon in the war against terrorism, filling the 'soft' role of addressing the poverty that breeds terrorism while the Pentagon plays the 'hard' role of blasting the terrorists.

As for the crisis of political governance in the U.S., September 11 has turned George W. Bush from a minority president whose party lost control of the Senate into arguably the most powerful U.S. president in recent times."[590]

The 11th September attacks thus provided the crucial pretext the Bush administration needed to consolidate its power and pursue a drastic, unlimited militarisation of foreign policy on a massive and unprecedented scale required by long-standing elite planning, while crushing domestic dissent and criminalising legitimate protest. What happened on 11th September constituted exactly what the Bush administration needed, to expand and consolidate America's "global primacy" as the "truly last superpower" by invading Afghanistan, which is a foothold to unrivalled control of Central Asia, and thus Eurasia.

As noted by Karen Talbot, Director of the International Center for Peace and Justice and member of the Executive Committee of the World Peace Council:

"[T]he September 11th terrorist attacks have provided a qualitatively new opportunity for the U.S., acting particularly on behalf of giant oil companies, to permanently entrench its military in the former Soviet Republics of Central Asia, and the Transcaucusus where there are vast oil reserves – the second largest in the world. The way is now open to jump start projects for oil and gas pipelines through Afghanistan and Pakistan to Karachi on the Arabian Sea—the best and cheapest route for transporting those fuels to market. Afghanistan, itself, also has considerable amounts of untapped oil and gas, as does Pakistan… The big payoff for the U.S. is the golden opportunity to establish a permanent military presence in oil-rich Central Asia—which is also wide open to another coveted resource-rich region, Siberia. Thus, realization of another goal could be closer at hand—the further balkanization of Russia and central Asian nations into easily controlled emirate-like entities, lacking any real sovereignty."[591]

And as the *New Statesman* further reports: "The Anglo-American attack on Afghanistan crosses new boundaries. It means that America's economic wars are now backed by the perpetual threat of military attack on any country, without legal pretence...

"It is also the first to endanger populations at home. The ultimate goal is not the capture of a fanatic, which would be no more than a media circus, but the acceleration of western imperial power... The unread news today is that the 'war against terrorism' is being exploited in order to achieve objectives that consolidate American power. These include: the bribing and subjugation of corrupt and vulnerable governments in former Soviet central Asia, crucial for American expansion in the region and exploitation of the last untapped reserves of oil and gas in the world; Nato's occupation of Macedonia, marking a final stage in its colonial odyssey in the Balkans; the expansion of the American arms industry; and the speeding up of trade liberalization."[592]

Joseph Gerson, Director of Programmes at the American Friends Service Committee (AFSC), similarly records that: "The criminal and indiscriminate attacks of September 11, in Colin Powell's words, 'hit the reset button' on U.S. foreign and military policy...

"Reprising Bush the Elder's use of Iraq's attack on Kuwait to reconsolidate U.S. global dominance for the post-Cold War era, the current Bush Administration has used its 'war against terrorism' to consolidate incipient alliances with Russia and India, to disorient and diminish European Union and Chinese challenges to U.S. regional hegemony, to discipline its Saudi, Egyptian, and other Arab clients, to expand its military presence in oil-rich Central Asia, to expand the U.S.-Japan alliance, and to reconsolidate its domination of the Pacific Ocean."[593]

These historic developments are unprecedented in scale. The virtually unhindered expansion of the American Empire is simultaneously and systematically eroding the very values that America claims to stand for. Throughout the West and beyond, civil liberties, basic freedoms and human rights are being curtailed in the name of fighting terrorism, while military interventions with nuclear implications are being planned to pursue brute strategic and economic interests, at the expense of indigenous populations— and for the benefit of corporate elites. Under U.S. leadership, it seems that the entire world is moving towards a situation of global apartheid governed by the Western-based international institutions of what is fast becoming a global police state, administered by the powerful for their own profit.

It is thus fitting to conclude with the observations in October 1967 of Earling Carothers 'Jim' Garrison, District Attorney for New Orleans, who put local businessman Clay Bertrand on trial in connection with the assassination of John F. Kennedy:

"What worries me deeply, and I have seen it exemplified in this case, is that we in America are in great danger of slowly eroding into a proto-fascist state. It will be a different kind of fascist state from the one the Germans evolved; theirs grew out of depression and promised bread and work, while ours, curiously enough, seems to be emerging from prosperity. But in the final analysis, it's based on power and on the inability to put human goals and human conscience above the dictates of the State. Its origins can be traced in the tremendous war machine we've built since 1945, the 'military-industrial complex' that Eisenhower vainly warned us about, which now dominates every aspect of our life. The power of the states and the Congress has gradually been abandoned to the Executive Department, because of war conditions; and we've seen the creation of an arrogant, swollen bureaucratic complex totally unfettered by the checks and balances of the Constitution.

In a very real and terrifying sense, our Government is the CIA and the Pentagon, with Congress reduced to a debating society. Of course, you can't spot this trend to fascism by casually looking around. You can't look for such familiar signs as the swastika, because they won't be there. We won't build Dachaus and Auschwitzes; the clever manipulation of the mass media is creating a concentration camp of the mind that promises to be far more effective in keeping the populace in line. We're not going to wake up one morning and suddenly find ourselves in gray uniforms goose-stepping off to work. But this isn't the test. The test is: What happens to the individual who dissents? In Nazi Germany, he was physically destroyed; here the process is more subtle, but the end results are the same. I've learned enough about the machinations of the CIA in the past year to know that this is no longer the dreamworld America I once believed in... I've always had a kind of knee-jerk trust in my Government's basic integrity, whatever political blunders it may make. But I've come to realize that in Washington, deceiving and manipulating the public are viewed by some as the natural prerogatives of office. Huey Long once said, 'Fascism will come to America in the name of anti-fascism.' I'm afraid, based on my own long experience, that fascism will come to America in the name of national security."[594]

Notes

[496] See for example 'The Wrong Way to Fix the Vote,' *Washington Post*, 10 June 2001; Borger, Julian and Palast, Gregory, 'Inquiry into new claims of poll abuses in Florida,' *The Guardian*, 17 Feb. 2001; BBC Newsnight, 'Theft of the Presidency,' 15 Feb. 2001; 'Florida's "Disappeared Voters": Disenfranchised by the GOP,' *The Nation*, 5 Feb. 2001; 'A Blacklist Burning for Bush,' *The Observer*, 10 Dec. 2000; 'Florida's flawed "voter cleansing" program: Salon.com's politics story of the year,' Salon.com, 4 Dec. 2000, www.salon.com. These reports discuss how the actual vote count means that Gore should have been President. Bush was able to win power through the deliberate disenfranchisement of black voters in Florida. Apart from this, we may note that Bush received just under 49 percent of the total votes cast, in an election in which only 51 percent of those eligible actually participated. This means that only 24 percent of all U.S citizens cast ballots for the man who is now president.

[497] *Los Angeles Times*, 24 September 2001.

[498] IPA Press Release, 'Recession: Now What?', Institute for Public Accuracy, Washington DC, 27 Nov. 2001, www.accuracy.org.

[499] *New York Times*, 20 August 2001.

[500] For extensive references and discussion see the August and September archives of the online Bush Report, www.bushwatch.net/busharchivesaugust01.htm, and www.bushwatch.net/busharchivessept01.htm. The facts mentioned here have also been raised in the Statement of the WSWS Editorial Board, 'Why the Bush Administration Wants War,' World Socialist Web Site, 14 September 2001.

[501] Omestad, Thomas, 'New world order,' *U.S. News*, 31 Dec. 2001.

[502] Bello, Walden, 'The American Way of War,' *Focus on Trade*, December 2001, No. 72.

[503] Cited in Weisbrot, Mark, 'A War Against Civilians?', *Knight Ridder/Tribune*, 2 November 2001. Weisbrot is Co-Director of the Center for Economic and Policy Research in Washington DC.

[504] *New York Times*, 12 September 2001.

[505] *New York Times*, 27 September 2001.

[506] *The Guardian*, 29 September 2001.

[507] Joint Statement, 'In Afghanistan, A Population In Crisis,' Geneva/New York, 24 Sept. 2001. Signed by Carol Bellamy, Executive Director UNICEF; Catherine Bertini, Executive Director World Food Programme; Ruud Lubbers, United Nations High Commissioner for Refugees; Mark Malloch Brown, Administrator United Nations Programme for Humanitarian Affairs; Kenzo Oshim, Emergency Relief Coordinator Office for the Coordination of Development; Mary Robinson United Nations High Commissioner for Human Rights.

[508] *New York Times*, 25 September 2001.

[509] Steele, Johnathan and Lawrence, Felicity, 'Main aid agencies reject U.S. air drops,' *The Guardian*, 8 October 2001.

[510] Cited in Tyler, Patrick E., '4 UN Workers Killed in Initial Strike on Afghanistan,' *New York Times*, 9 October 2001.

[511] Christian Science Monitor, 28 September 2001.

[512] IPA Press Release, 'As Bombing Proceeds: Now What?', Institute for Public Accuracy, 8 October 2001, http://accuracy.org.

[513] MSF Press Release, 'MSF rejects link of humanitarian and military actions,' Médecins Sans Frontières, 8 October 2001.

[514] Zhumatov, Shamil, 'UN investigator condemns bombing of Afghanistan,' Reuters, 15 October 2001.

[515] IPA Press Release, 'Too Early to Declare Hunger Crisis Averted in Afghanistan,' Institute for Public Accuracy, Washington DC, 9 January 2002, http://accuracy.org.

[516] Goldberg, Suzanne, 'Aid packages ignore starving in Afghanistan,' *The Guardian*, 4 February 2002.

[517] MSF Report, 'Alarming Food Crisis in Northern Afghanistan,' Medecins Sans Frontieres (MSF), 21 February 2001.

[518] IPA Press Release, 'As Bombing Proceeds: Now What?', op. cit.

[519] U.S. General Accounting Office, Cruise Missiles: Proven Capability Should Affect Aircraft and Force Structure Requirements. 04/20/95, GAO/NSIAD-95-116. Cited in Abunimah, Ali, letter to National Public Radio News, 25 Jan. 1999, www.abunimah.org/nprletters/nprindex.html.

[520] MER Report, *Needless deaths in the Gulf War: Civilian casualties during the air campaign and violations of the laws of war*, Middle East Watch (Human Rights Watch), New York, 1991.

[521] 'Killing is killing – not kindness,' *New Statesman and Society*, 17 January 1992.

[522] Boyle, Francis A., 'International War Crimes: The Search for Justice,' symposium at Albany Law School, 27 February 1992; reprinted in 'U.S. War Crimes During the Gulf War,' *New Dawn Magazine*, September-October 1992, No. 15.

[523] *The Guardian*, 4 March 2000. It is worth noting John Pilger's exceptional documentary aired on British television, *Paying the Price: The Killing of the Children of Iraq*, ITV Carlton, 6 March 2000, in which the devastating anti-humanitarian Anglo-American war on Iraq was uncompromisingly exposed.

[524] *Washington Times*, 25 April 1999.

[525] *The New York Times*, 9 April 1999.

[526] *Philadelphia Inquirer*, 21 May 1999.

[527] Hundley, Tom, 'NATO bombs Serbs into survival mode,' *San Francisco Examiner*, 26 May 1999.

[528] *Officer*, September 1999.

[529] Hayden, Robert, 'Humanitarian Hypocrisy,' Jurist: The Law Professor's Network, 1999, http://jurist.law.pitt.edu.

[530] Carter, Jimmy, *New York Times*, 27 May 1999.

[531] Tyler, Patrick E., '4 UN Workers Killed in Initial Strike on Afghanistan,' op. cit.

[532] Parrish, Geov, 'Where are the bodies?', Working For Change, 22 October 2001, http://workingforchange.com.

[533] Ibid.

[534] ICRC Press Release, 'ICRC warehouses bombed in Kabul,' International Committee of the Red Cross, 16 October 2001.

[535] ICRC Press Release, 'Bombing and occupation of ICRC facilities in Afghanistan,' International Committee of the Red Cross, 26 Oct. 2001.

[536] Parrish, Geov, 'Where are the bodies?', op. cit.

[537] Reuters, 'Refugees Say U.S. Planes Destroyed Kandahar Bazaars,' 22 October 2001.

[538] Chien, A. J., 'The Civilian Toll,' Institute for Health and Social Justice, 11 October 2001.

[539] Priest, Dana, 'Deadly wordplay: picking Afghan targets,' *Washington Post*, 21 February 2001.

[540] Fisk, Robert, 'As the refugees crowd the borders, we'll be blaming someone else,' *The Independent*, 23 October 2001.

[541] Herold, Marc W., 'A Dossier on Civilian Victims of United States' Aerial Bombing of Afghanistan: A Comprehensive Accounting,' Department of Economics and Women's Studies, Whittemore School of Business and Economics, December 2001. Among some of the feeble attempts to convince the public to ignore this study, such as those made by Mark Steyn in *The Spectator*, is the contention that it relies, partly, on unreliable media sources such as Indian and Pakistani newspapers. The contention fails simply because Herold ensures that he corroborates reports of civilian deaths with several sources for the same

incident, most of which are from reputable Western news services. But it is also worth noting the implicit racism behind the indefensible idea that a non-Western news source such as the *Times of India*, for instance, is more unreliable than, say, *The Times* of London, simply because the former is 'Third World' and not 'Western.' It suggests that the former, for no other reason than being 'Indian,' would either fabricate or distort reports, while the latter, being 'British,' would undoubtedly remain independent and impartial. The implicit racist suggestion is that Indians are less trustworthy than Englishmen. Anyhow, Herold deals quite amply with objections to his findings within the text of his study. For a critical appraisal of Herold's work, and confirmation from other independent investigators such as UN officials, aid workers and U.S. think tanks, that the death toll is certainly in the several thousands, see Traynor, Ian, 'Afghans Still Dying,' *The Guardian*, 12 February 2002.

[542] Campbell, Murray, 'Thousands of Afghans Likely Killed in Afghan Bombing,' *The Globe and Mail*, 3 January 2002.

[543] *Frontier Post*, 10 October 2001.

[544] IPA Press Release, 'Afghan Women Warn of Northern Alliance,' Institute for Public Accuracy, Washington DC, 15 Nov. 2001, http://accuracy.org.

[545] Ibid.

[546] Scott, Peter Dale, 'Many Signs Warlordism Returning to Afghanistan,' Online Resource on Al-Qaeda and Osama Bin Laden, 5 January 2002, http://socrates.berkeley.edu/~pdscott/qfla.html.

[547] Viviano, Frank, *San Francisco Chronicle*, 26 September 2001.

[548] White House Statement, 28 November 2001.

[549] 'As the War Shifts Alliances, Oil Deals Follow,' *New York Times*, 15 December 2001.

[550] *Pravda*, 9 January 2002. *Le Monde*, 25 December 2001.

[551] For discussion see Martin, Patrick, 'Oil company adviser named U.S. representative to Afghanistan,' World Socialist Web Site, www.wsws.org.

[552] Agence France Press and Reuters, 'Musharraf, Karzai agree major oil pipeline in cooperation pact,' *Irish Times*, 9 February 2002.

[553] Reuters, 'Central Asia's Great Game Turned on its Head,' 25 Sept. 2001.

[554] Arkin, William, *Los Angeles Times*, 6 January 2001.

[555] Peuch, Jean-Christophe, 'Central Asia: U.S. Military Build-up Shifts Sphere of Influence,' Radio Free Europe/Liberty, 11 January 2002.

[556] Ibid.

[557] Omestad, Thomas, 'New world order,' op. cit.

[558] 'The U.S. War on Terror,' www.uswaronterror.com.

[559] The StrategyPage, www.strategypage.com/thenewwar/default.asp.

[560] CCR, 'No Time for Cowboy Politics,' Center for Constitutional Rights, New York, 17 September 2001.

[561] Richter, Paul, 'U.S. Works Up Plan for Using Nuclear Arms,' *Los Angeles Times*, 9 March 2002.

[562] Arkin, William, 'Secret Plan Outlines the Unthinkable,' *Los Angeles Times*, 9 March 2002.

[563] Editorial, 'New Rules,' *Washington Post*, 14 September 2001.

[564] Ratner, Michael, 'Moving towards a police state (or have we arrived)?', Centre for Research on Globalisation, Montreal, 30 November 2001, http://globalresearch.ca.

[565] Interview with Francis A. Boyle by Dennis Bernstein, 'Bush's Constitutional Coup: Kangaroo Courts and Disappearances,' Flashpoints on KPFA Radio 94.1 FM, 14 November 2001.

[566] Bollyn, Christopher, 'In the Name of Security, Thousands Denied Constitutional Rights,' American Free Press, 29 November 2001.

[567] *Washington Post*, 21 October 2001.

[568] PCJ Briefing, 'Proposed U.S. Torture Policy?', Partners for Civil Justice, January 2002, www.civil-rights.net.

[569] Interview with Francis A. Boyle by Dennis Bernstein, 'Bush's Constitutional Coup: Kangaroo Courts and Disappearances,' op. cit.

[570] EFF Report, 'EFF Analysis Of The Provisions Of The USA Patriot Act,' Electronic Frontier Foundation, San Francisco, 31 October 2001, www.eff.org/Privacy/Surveillance/Terrorism_militias/20011031_eff_usa_patriot _analysis.html.

[571] AlterNet, 25 February 2002.

[572] Letter from Henry A. Waxman and Janice D. Schakowsky to the President, 6 November 2001, www.house.gov/reform/min/pdfs/pdf_inves/ pdf_admin_records_let.pdf.

[573] Left, Sarah, 'Bush blocks public access to White House papers,' *The Guardian*, 2 November 2001.

[574] Johnson, Glen, 'Bush Halts Inquiry of FBI and Stirs Up Firestorm,' *Boston Globe*, 14 December 2001.

[575] Editorial by Ruth Rosen, 'The day Ashcroft censored Freedom of Information,' *San Francisco Chronicle*, 6 January 2002.

[576] Bello, Walden, 'The American Way of War,' op. cit.

[577] Cited in Lapham, Lewis, 'The American Rome,' *Harper's Magazine*, August 2001, p. 32-3.

[578] Lance Morrow, 'The Case for Rage and Retribution,' *Time Magazine*, 11 September 2001

[579] Pfaff, William, 'Will the New World Order Rest Solely on American Might?', *International Herald Tribune*, 29 December 2001.

[580] U.S. Newswire, Inc, 6 September 2001.

[581] Chossudovsky, Michel, 'War is Good for Business,' Centre for Research on Globalisation, Montreal, 16 September 2001, http://globalresearch.ca.

[582] Krugman, Paul, 'A No Win Outcome,' *New York Times*, 21 Dec. 2001.

[583] Krugman, Paul, 'An Alternate Reality,' *New York Times*, 25 November 2001.

[584] Krugman, Paul, 'Other People's Money,' *New York Times*, 14 Nov. 2001.

[585] Goldin, Greg, 'Bailout—Another Free Lunch for Fat Cats,' *Los Angeles Times*, 4 Nov. 2001. Goldin continues: "The first $24 billion—spread over 10 years—will go to large companies that pay the low-rate 'alternative minimum tax' designed to ensure that profitable corporations paid at least some taxes. Under the plan, such taxes would be retroactively returned. General Electric, the giant defense contractor that stands to benefit from a new military build-up, would receive a rebate of $671 million on past taxes. United Airlines would get back $60 million. IBM a whopping $1.4 billion. The list of megacorporations reaping megabucks includes Enron, General Motors, Chevron, Texaco, Phillips Petroleum and Alaska Air Group. Another $109 billion will go to corporations over the next three years through 'accelerated depreciation,' faster write-offs of equipment costs. So much for some of the nation's most profitable corporations contributing their fair share to Bush's war on terrorism. And that's just the beginning. The president wants to race ahead with the cutbacks in top personal income tax rates he won earlier this year, fully instituting them next year rather than in 2006. If Congress goes along with the administration plan, the richest 1% of all taxpayers would average a $27,000 reduction in 2002. A middle-class family earning $50,000 a year would get just $68. The 37 million individuals and couples who did not get this year's tax rebate because their tax liability was too low would get a one-time $350 payment. This is the same old supply-side agenda, wrapped in the flag. Swaddle the rich and powerful in tax breaks while tossing pennies to the rest of us. As for actually restarting the economy, that burden is reserved for millions shivering at the prospect of a deep recession and, perhaps, already on the brink of personal insolvency. Bush urges these hard-working American households, already saddled with an average of $8,500 in credit card debt, to spend more, as if it were a patriotic duty to go deeper into debt."

[586] IPA Press Release, 'The Economy: Now What?', Institute for Public Accuracy, Washington DC, 24 September 2001, http://accuracy.org.

[587] IPA Press Release, 'United We Stand?', Institute for Public Accuracy, Washington DC, 1 Nov. 2001, http://accuracy.org. For extensive references and discussion on the Bush administration's new economic programmes, see How Dare They, www.howdarethey.org.

[588] FRBSF *Economic Letter*, 'The U.S. Economy After September 11,' Federal Reserve Bank of San Francisco Chronicle, 7 December 2001. "First, the Fed has cut short-term interest rates ten times since January. The federal funds rate now stands at 2%, compared to 6-1/2% back then. The second source of stimulus is fiscal policy, which is coming in three programs: the major tax reduction in June, including the recent tax rebates, the emergency spending bill enacted just after the attacks, and the fiscal stimulus bill currently in the Congress. These fiscal programs add up to a major amount of stimulus—perhaps around $160 billion in fiscal year 2002. Third, energy prices have declined this year. The price of imported oil has fallen by nearly half since last November, and the price of natural gas has fallen even more dramatically.

These price declines give firms and households more purchasing power, and they should help stimulate demand. Fourth, the 'overhang' of capital equipment and software, as well as inventories, that I mentioned earlier is one that will correct itself with time. At some point, the stocks of these assets will get to low enough levels that firms will need to start spending on them again... The events of September 11 have largely served to reinforce these trends."

[589] *The Record*, September 2001; *Economic Reform*, October 2001.

[590] Bello, Walden, 'The American Way of War,' op. cit.

[591] Talbot, Karen, 'Afghanistan is Key to Oil Profits,' Centre for Research on Globalisation, 7 November 2001, http://globalresearch.ca/articles/TAL111A.html.

[592] Pilger, John, 'The ultimate goal of the attacks on Afghanistan is not the capture of a fanatic, but the acceleration of western power,' *New Statesman*, 9 October 2001.

[593] Gerson, Joseph, 'The East Asian Front of World War III,' *Peacework*, December 2001/January2001.

[594] Cited in Dilouie, Craig, *Disinformation*, 29 November 2001, www.disinfo.com. For extensive discussion of the effective annulment of democracy, along with the rise of tendencies towards fascism, in the United States after 11th September, see Stanton, John and Madsen, Wayne, 'The Emergence of the Fascist American Theocratic State,' *Online Journal*, 17 February 2002, at www.onlinejournal.com/Special_Reports/Stanton-Madsen021702/02-17-02_Stanton-Madsen.pdf. Also see Stanton and Madsen, 'The Caligulian American Justice System: UN Intervention is Necessary,' *Online Journal*, 6 March 2002, www.onlinejournal.com.

Conclusions

**"In examining any crime, a central question must be 'who benefits?'
The principal beneficiaries of the destruction of the World Trade
Center are in the United States: the Bush administration, the
Pentagon, the CIA and FBI, the weapons industry, the oil industry. It
is reasonable to ask whether those who have profited to such an
extent from this tragedy contributed to bringing it about."**

Investigative journalist Patrick Martin

As far as the facts on record are concerned, the best explanation of them, in the opinion of this author, is one that points directly to U.S. state responsibility for the events of 11th September 2001. A detailed review of the facts points not only to Kabul, but to Riyadh, Islamabad and most principally, Washington. Furthermore, in the opinion of this author, the documentation presented in this study strongly suggests, though not necessarily conclusively, that significant elements of U.S. government, military and intelligence agencies had extensive advance warning of the 11th September attacks, and were in various ways complicit in those attacks. This is certainly not a desirable inference, but it is one that best explains the available data.

This examination has found that a specific war on Afghanistan to be launched in October 2001 had been planned for at least a year, and in general terms related to regional strategic and economic interests, had actually been rooted in at least four years of strategic planning. This planning, in turn, is the culmination of a decade of regional strategising. All that was required was a trigger for these war plans, which was amply provided by the tragic events of 11th September.

We have also discussed compelling evidence that not only did U.S. government, military and intelligence agencies anticipate what was going to happen on 11th September, no public warnings were given and no appropriate measures were taken. It is a fact that the American intelligence community received multiple authoritative warnings, both general and specific, of a terrorist attack on the U.S. using civilian airliners as bombs, targeting key buildings located in the nation's capital and New York City, and likely to occur around early to mid-September.

It is also a recorded fact that emergency response systems suffered consistently inexplicable failures on that day, allowing the attacks on the World Trade Center and Pentagon to continue without an effective air response. A detailed investigation of the actual chronology of events on 11th September strongly suggests that this sort of massive systematic failure was possible only through wilful obstructions from key U.S. government and military officials.

It is a documented fact that the Bush administration furthermore systematically blocked investigations of terrorists involved or strongly suspected of being involved—including Osama bin Laden, his family and suspect Saudi royals who support him—prior to 11th September. Even after 11th September, the Bush administration has continued to misdirect investigations and block pertinent inquiries, with the FBI concentrating futile efforts on Germany rather than Saudi Arabia, where according to the late former FBI Deputy Director, John O'Neill, the real source of bin Laden's network lies. In particular, it is a documented fact that the Bush administration has sealed any inquiry into the complicity of the ISI in the 11th September attacks.

Indeed, there is reason to believe that through the ISI, which has "close links" to the CIA and plays the role of a regional instrument of U.S. interests, elements of U.S. military intelligence may have been directly complicit in funding and supporting the terrorists who undertook the air attacks on 11th September. This notion is supported by the fact that the ISI chief, who siphoned $100,000 to the alleged lead hijacker Mohamed Atta, resigned quietly under U.S. pressure, thus avoiding a scandal produced by undue publicity, along with any accompanying demands for an investigation into the full extent of the ISI role in 11th September. It is a documented fact that in doing so, the Bush administration has successfully protected the ISI from any further damaging revelations on its complicity in supporting those behind the air attacks, while also protecting the ex-chief of ISI himself.

By obstructing investigations of terrorists, and by maintaining what effectively amounts to a covert financial, political and even military alliance with them, the Bush administration has effectively supported their activities. The objective of U.S. policy has, furthermore, been focused principally on securing elite strategic and economic interests abroad, while deterring public understanding at home. As shocking and horrifying as these conclusions are, they are based on an extensive analysis of events leading up to, during and after 11th September 2001.

However, it is not the intent of this author to pretend that the conclusions outlined here are final. On the contrary, in the opinion of this author, these conclusions are merely the best available inferences from the available facts that have been so far unearthed. It is up to the reader to decide whether or not to agree with this assessment. Ultimately, this study is not concerned with providing a conclusive account, but rather is intended to clarify the dire need for an in-depth investigation into the events of 11th September, by documenting the facts.

A summary of the facts on record as documented in this study is presented here:

- Both the U.S. and the USSR are responsible for the rise of religious extremism, terrorism and civil war within Afghanistan since the 1980s. The U.S., however, is directly responsible for the cultivation of a distorted 'jihadi' ideology that fuelled, along with U.S. arms and training, the ongoing war and acts of terrorism within the country after the withdrawal of Soviet forces.

- The U.S. approved of the rise of the Taliban, and went on to at least tacitly support the movement, despite its egregious human rights abuses against Afghan civilians, to secure regional strategic and economic interests.

- The U.S. government and military planned a war on Afghanistan prior to 11th September for at least a year, a plan rooted in broad strategic and economic considerations related to control of Eurasia, and thus the consolidation of unrivalled global U.S. hegemony.

- The U.S. government has consistently blocked investigations and inquiries of Saudi royals, Saudi businessmen, and members of the bin Laden family, implicated in supporting Osama bin Laden and terrorist operatives linked to him. This amounts in effect to protecting leading figures residing in Saudi Arabia who possess ties with Osama bin Laden.

- The U.S. government has consistently blocked attempts to indict and apprehend Osama bin Laden, thus effectively protecting him directly.

- The U.S. government has allowed suspected terrorists linked to Osama bin Laden to train at U.S. military facilities, financed by Saudi Arabia, as well as U.S. flight schools, for years.

- High-level elements of the U.S. government, military, intelligence and law enforcement agencies received numerous credible and urgent warnings of the 11th September attacks, which were of such a nature as to successively reinforce one another. Only a full-fledged inquiry would suffice to clarify in a definite manner why the American intelligence community failed to act on the warnings received. However, the nature of the multiple warnings received, along with the false claims by U.S. intelligence agencies that they had no specific warnings of what was about to occur, suggests that they indeed had extensive foreknowledge of the attacks, but are now attempting to prevent public recognition of this.

- In spite of extensive forewarnings, the U.S. Air Force emergency response systems collapsed systematically on 11th September, in violation of the clear rules that are normally and routinely followed on a strict basis. This is an event that could only conceivably occur as a result of deliberate obstructions to the following of Standard Operating Procedures for emergency response.

- To succeed, such systematic obstructions could only be set in place by key U.S. government and military officials. Both President Bush and Chairman of the Joint Chiefs of Staff Myers displayed sheer indifference to the 11th September attacks as they were occurring, which further suggests their particular responsibility. Once again, a full-fledged inquiry is required into this matter.

- Independent journalists revealed that Mahmoud Ahmed, as ISI Director-General, had channeled U.S. government funding to Mohamed Atta, described as the "lead hijacker" by the FBI. The U.S. government protected him, and itself, by asking him to resign quietly after the discovery, thus blocking a further inquiry and a potential scandal.

- The events of 11th September have in fact been of crucial benefit to the Bush administration, justifying the consolidation of elite power and profit both within the U.S. and throughout the world. The tragic events that involved the murder of thousands of innocent civilians were exploited by the U.S. government to crack down on domestic freedoms, while launching a ruthless bombing campaign on the largely helpless people of Afghanistan, directly resulting in the further killing of almost double the number of civilians who died on 9-11.

There are a variety of possible scenarios regarding the role of the U.S. government that explain these facts. All of these possibilities, however, strongly suggest a significant degree of U.S. complicity in the events of 11th September. This does not imply that the U.S. was involved in orchestrating the events of 11th September from start to finish, or that the attacks on the World Trade Center and Pentagon were 'staged' by the U.S, or that those responsible were on a direct U.S. payroll in receipt of direct U.S. orders.

What it does mean, is that the U.S. government, through its actions and inactions, effectively facilitated the attacks, protected those responsible, blocked attempts to prevent the attacks, and maintained close political, financial, military and intelligence ties to key figures who supported those responsible. Whether or not every stage of these policies was a result of deliberation, the role that the U.S. government has played both historically and currently in key events leading up to, and after, 11th September, strongly suggests U.S. responsibility for those events.

At the very least, this amounts to complicity through negligence or omission, for the simple reason that the U.S. government has systematically behaved with wilful recklessness, with sheer indifference as to the probable consequences in terms of loss of American lives, in the pursuit of strategic and economic interests. Furthermore, the consistent and indeed systematic manner in which these policies have been implemented, even in the aftermath of 11th September, also suggests deliberate complicity.[595]

There is, of course, a context to this complicity, which establishes that the U.S. relationship with Osama bin Laden is far more complex than conventional opinion would have us believe. The Saudi establishment appears to have been supporting bin Laden largely as a form of bribery, payment of which secures the regime from being targeted by his network. In the words of the *New Yorker* (22 October 2001), the regime is "so weakened and frightened that it has brokered its future by channelling hundreds of millions of dollars in what amounts to protection money to fundamentalist groups that wish to overthrow it." As a result, it has been specifically U.S. interests, rather than those of the Saudi establishment, that have come under fire from such groups.

While the U.S. seems to have been aware for many years of the Saudi establishment's involvement in funding Al-Qaeda, successive administrations have deliberately allowed this to continue, motivated by concern for oil profits as secured through U.S. hegemony over the Saudi regime, whose 'stability'—meaning ongoing rule—must be preserved at any cost. It appears that this stability is worth preserving even if the cost be the lives of American soldiers and civilians, abroad and at home.

Corporate elite interests, in other words, far outweigh alleged concerns for American lives. A documented precedent for this sort of policy is Al-Qaeda's bombing of the U.S. embassies in Kenya and Tanzania, which as Richard Labeviere reports, did not interrupt the Clinton administration's indirect support of bin Laden's network, since "they figured the U.S. would gain more from it in the long run." The same brand of considerations seem to have motivated the continuation and promotion of U.S. ties with those responsible for supporting Al-Qaeda even in the aftermath of 11th September—namely Pakistan and Saudi Arabia.

Simultaneously, it is also clear that U.S. intelligence had anticipated Al-Qaeda's terrorist plans for 11th September (at least to a general extent, but most probably to a highly specific degree), but continued to facilitate and support—from behind-the-scenes through its regional allies—the build-up to the implementation of those plans, while ensuring the lack of preventive measures at home, both prior to and on 11th September. The reason for this appears to be that those attacks were about to occur at a fortuitous time for the Bush administration, which was facing both a domestic and an international crisis of legitimacy, accompanied by growing cracks in world order under U.S. hegemony in the form of escalating world-wide dissent and protest.

By allowing these terrorist acts to occur, and by apparently pushing a few necessary buttons while closing a few important doors, thus ensuring their occurrence, the Bush administration effectively permitted and supported Al-Qaeda through its key allies in its 11th September assault (whether the terrorist network knew it or not), thus establishing the trigger so desperately needed to re-assert its power politics world-wide.

Indeed, the measures taken by the Bush administration in the aftermath of 11th September appear to have been specifically tailored to ensure that the increasingly fatal cracks in world order that had begun to appear both at home and abroad before 11th September, do not appear again.

The domestic crackdown on basic civil rights, combined with the demonisation of dissent, has come part and parcel with the granting of unlimited war powers—lending the Bush administration a free hand to embark on a new unlimited war against any regime that challenges U.S. interests.

The protection of a stable dictatorship within Saudi Arabia is also an integral part of this programme of hegemonic consolidation and expansion. The Bush administration apparently feels that as long as the Saudi establishment continues to pour protection money into Al-Qaeda pockets, the required modicum of regional stability will be maintained, thus protecting unimpeded U.S. access to Middle East oil reserves. Whether or not this policy is viable is another matter, although it seems to have 'worked' so far, which probably explains why the Bush administration believes it can continue in this manner, at least for some time further.[596]

Meanwhile, the scattered continued existence of Al-Qaeda plays a functional role within world order, at least for the next few years. The London *Guardian* noted this functional role played by Osama bin Laden within the matrix of U.S. foreign policy objectives in an 18th September report:

"If Osama bin Laden did not exist, it would be necessary to invent him. For the past four years, his name has been invoked whenever a U.S. president has sought to increase the defence budget or wriggle out of arms control treaties. He has been used to justify even President Bush's missile defence programme, though neither he nor his associates are known to possess anything approaching ballistic missile technology. Now he has become the personification of evil required to launch a crusade for good: the face behind the faceless terror... [H]is usefulness to western governments lies in his power to terrify. When billions of pounds of military spending are at stake, rogue states and terrorist warlords become assets precisely because they are liabilities."[597]

To consolidate and expand U.S. hegemony, and to fully counter its Russian, Chinese and European rivals, a massive threat is required, to establish domestic consensus on the unrelentingly interventionist character of U.S. foreign policy in the new and unlimited "war on terror."

The bogeyman of Osama bin Laden's international terrorist network thus plays, in the view of the Bush administration, a functional role within the matrix of U.S. plans to increasingly subject the world order to its military, political, strategic, and economic influence. This explains the Bush administration's systematic failure to investigate known supporters of Al-Qaeda in Saudi Arabia and Pakistan—and even Al-Qaeda cells operating within the borders of the U.S. itself. Whether or not Al-Qaeda members, including bin Laden himself, are aware of this is another matter.

Until Al-Qaeda loses this functional role within a U.S.-dominated world order, this state of affairs is likely to continue. At the least, the U.S. government has clearly adopted this array of policies on the basis of a cold, but meticulous 'cost-benefit' analysis, weighing up the potential gains and losses of the following possible policies:

- Taking meaningful action against Al-Qaeda, while damaging U.S. regional interests tied to allies who support bin Laden

- Allowing allies to continue their support of Al-Qaeda, and refraining from action against it, in order to protect perceived U.S. interests

The second policy appears to be the one currently adopted by the Bush administration, for the reasons discussed above. It is a policy that amounts, at the very least, to indirect complicity in the 11th September attacks, through ongoing U.S. protection of leading allies supporting those who carried out the attacks. On this basis, it is evident that in the near future, on the pretext of targeting scattered terrorist cells connected to Al-Qaeda, various countries around the world that are of strategic value to the United States will fall victim to Bush's 'new war' for U.S. hegemony.

The escalating and contrived 'clash of civilisations' that may result from this cynical U.S. policy, and the corresponding chaos and destruction, bear ominous implications for the future of humanity.

Indeed, the new pretexts are already being conjured up. President Bush Jr. virtually declared war on any country deemed by the U.S. to be a threat, in his State of the Union address on Tuesday, 29th January 2002. Bush warned of "thousands of dangerous killers, schooled in the methods of murder, often supported by outlaw regimes," and openly threatened an attack on Iran, Iraq and North Korea in particular. Both the U.S. government and media have made concerted efforts to allege some sort of connection between Al-Qaeda and the countries of Iran and Iraq. "By seeking weapons of mass destruction, these regimes pose a grave and growing danger. States like these and their terrorist allies constitute an axis of evil, arming to threaten the peace of the world." Bush added that: "The United States of America will not permit the world's most dangerous regimes to threaten us with the world's most destructive weapons."

The horrid irony of these statements is clear in light of the documentation presented here concerning the Bush administration's role in the events of 11th September, its conscious use of massive terror against the Afghan population, and the accompanying policies of imperialism at home and abroad.

The Middle East and Central Asia together hold over two-thirds of the world's reserves of oil and natural gas. After Saudi Arabia, Iran and Iraq are respectively the second and third largest oil-producers in the region. Both Iran and Iraq, in accordance with their local interests, are fundamentally opposed to the U.S. drive to secure unimpeded access to regional resources.

Iran, for instance, has been attempting to secure its own interests in Afghanistan and Central Asia, thus coming into direct conflict with regional U.S. interests, Iraq has for a decade now been tolerated only because the U.S. has been unable to replace Saddam Hussein's regime with a viable alternative.[598] In light of the results of the apparently successful 'test case' provided by the war on Afghanistan, the U.S. seems intent on attempting a replay in Iraq by eliminating Saddam, and enlisting the opposition to establish a compliant new regime. Similar plans may be in the pipeline for Iran.

As for North Korea, this country borders China, and is thus strategically located in terms of longstanding U.S. policy planning. China has long been viewed by U.S. policy planners as its principal rival in north and east Asia. The military network being installed by the United States in the wake of 11th September systematically encircles China—Uzbekistan, Tajikistan, Kyrgyzstan, Pakistan, India, the Philippines, and now Korea.

The Guardian has also commented on these developments and their military-strategic context: "Every twist in the war on terrorism seems to leave a new Pentagon outpost in the Asia-Pacific region, from the former USSR to the Philippines. One of the lasting consequences of the war could be what amounts to a military encirclement of China." In explanation, the London daily cites the Pentagon's *Quadrennial Defense Review* warning of the danger that "a military competitor with a formidable resource base will emerge in the region." The journal recommended a U.S. policy that "places a premium on securing additional access and infrastructure agreements."[599] The expansion of the misnamed 'war on terror' is thus specifically tailored to target regions of strategic and economic interest to the United States, and thus to consolidate unrivalled U.S. hegemony in these regions.

It is worth emphasising here that even the lowest possible level of involvement on the part of the Bush administration fails to absolve this administration of scandalous responsibility for the events of 11th September. At the very least, the facts on record demonstrate with certainty that the U.S. government is fully aware that its regional allies, Saudi Arabia, Pakistan and some others, have funded and supported Al-Qaeda for years. Yet despite this, the U.S. government has permitted this support to continue, actively obstructing intelligence investigations into the matter, and funneling U.S. aid to the same allies. This policy has continued with the objective of maintaining these lucrative alliances, through which regional U.S. economic and strategic interests are secured.

At the same time, the U.S. government has long been aware of the threat posed by Al-Qaeda to U.S. national security, and in particular was certainly aware that some sort of devastating attack by Al-Qaeda on U.S. soil was imminent in the later half of 2001. Despite this, the U.S. government refused to reverse its policy of maintaining regional alliances with the principal supporters of Al-Qaeda, including the funneling of financial and military aid—and continues to do the same, even after the 11th September.

At the very least then, the facts on record demonstrate with certainty an ongoing U.S. policy of wilful and reckless indifference to American lives, motivated fundamentally by strategic and economic interests. This policy has been relentlessly pursued, regardless of the dangers to American lives, of which the U.S. policy-making establishment is fully aware. This policy therefore amounts, even at the lowest possible level of involvement, to deliberate if indirect complicity in the 11th September attacks, on the part of the Bush administration.

Although it is the opinion of this author that the documentation gathered strongly indicates the conscious complicity of the Bush administration in the 11th September attacks, it should once again be emphasised that this study does not aim to provide a conclusive or exhaustive analysis. It is primarily intended to collate the innumerable facts surrounding the events of 11th September, of which the public is largely unaware, and clarify them with extensive documentation.

These facts have simply not been addressed in an adequate fashion in the media, and the conventional version of events officially espoused by the

Bush administration, and slavishly repeated by the media and academia, fails to account for or explain them. Most commentators, including supposed critics of U.S. policy, are content to arbitrarily dismiss any discussion of the role of the U.S. government in 11th September as irrelevant. But as this study demonstrates, the facts on record are far too important in their implications to be dismissed by anyone who is serious about understanding the events of 11th September.

In the final analysis, then, this study points to a host of unanswered questions and blatant anomalies that U.S. government, military and intelligence agencies must be forced to answer through a public inquiry. Such an inquiry is clearly a matter of the greatest urgency, and must be demanded as such by all sectors of society.

> The U.S. government's actions should be transparent, justifiable, and reasonable. And in the event of a failure to meet these criteria, the U.S. government should be accountable to the American people. This is a public right, and an elementary aspect of democracy. Whether key U.S. figures and institutions have been guilty of complicity or sheer incompetence, the public has a right to know—this is the least that could be done in memory of those who died on 11th September. Thus, a full-scale, independent public inquiry must be launched as soon as possible. Unless this occurs, the truth of what happened on 11th September – and thereafter – will remain indefinitely suppressed.

---

[595] A typical objection to these conclusions, which attempts to imply that from the outset there is no point in even considering evidence of U.S. complicity in 9-11, posits that the government's allowing—or deliberately provoking—the destruction of the World Trade Center, the Pentagon and potentially the White House, is *a priori* an impossible scenario, due to the potentially uncontrollable ramifications for the world economy and the U.S. as such. This, however, is a disingenuous position based on unwarranted assumptions that the side effect of 9-11 might be uncontrollable.

Assuming that the conclusions of this study are correct: It is perfectly conceivable that the government, while anticipating an attack on the WTC, did not at all anticipate that the towers would actually collapse as a consequence. The architects and engineers who designed the Twin Towers, for instance, have stated that they had been designed to withstand nightmare scenarios, such as being hit by a plane (although hindsight proves they had not accounted for certain developments related to such scenarios).

Prior to the WTC attacks, the architects' assurances would probably have been taken for granted. It is a fact that no top WTC executives were killed in the attacks. It is a fact that the thousands of victims who were killed in the attacks constitute a fraction of the total number of employees who work at the WTC. It is a fact that none of the Pentagon employees who died were members of the top military establishment. It is a fact that the main hub of the Pentagon can survive even a nuclear attack—the maximum damage caused, and that could have been caused, by the impacting plane was the destruction of a few walls and segments of the building's outer structure, along with the loss of lower-level Pentagon staff who can be, and have been, easily replaced.

It is a fact that even the total destruction of the White House as a building (unlikely as a consequence of a plane crash, due to its broad and more sturdy structure) would not in reality damage the control and economic wealth of the Bush administration, the oil industry, the defence industry, and so on. It is a fact that all key high-level U.S. political officials had their own safety ensured throughout the proceedings of the attacks. It is a fact that the bombing of civilian buildings does not in itself damage the economy. It is a fact that the increasingly recessive world economy, while badly damaged and freefalling, was already in recession long before 11th September, and set to recede much further regardless of the latter.

It is a fact that the economic freefall has come to an end, largely thanks to the indirect impact of 11th September, such as the corporate bail-out, among other policies, it permitted. It is a fact that the attacks provided an opportunity for the corporate elite to escape the worst effects of this recession, and that as a consequence the recession has not had any adverse impact on Bush & Co. Finally, it is also therefore a fact that if high-level U.S. policy planners had considered allowing or provoking the occurrence of 9-11, they would have certainly taken all this into account, and projected that no fundamental damage to the interests of Bush & Co. would occur, as long as certain safeguards were taken on their behalf.

[596] Other ways of securing U.S. interests in the region in the event that the policy loses its viability, however, are no doubt being explored by U.S. policy planners. See for instance Peters, Ralph, 'The Saudi Threat,' *Wall Street Journal*, 4 Jan. 2002. Indeed, both the U.S. and Saudi governments are certainly cognisant of the dangers inherent in the current arrangement. This appears to be why they have both agreed to visibly discuss the reduction of the U.S. military presence in Saudi Arabia, with the aim of reducing pressure on the Saudi regime from groups, particularly those sympathetic to bin Laden, calling for an end to U.S. occupation there.

White House Chief of Staff Andrew Card, affirming that the Saudis are "wonderful allies in this war against terrorists," admitted that: "Ever since the Gulf War ended, we've been working to try to minimize the amount of time and the size of the footprint that U.S. forces have in Saudi Arabia... They've been asking a long time, and we've been working with them for a long time—not just during this administration but during previous administrations—to reduce the footprint. I think it's been a long-term interest of both countries... It will happen over time... There is a valuable reason for us to be in that region, but we are

looking to reduce the footprint within Saudi Arabia, consistent with America's interests and consistent with the interests of Saudi Arabia." (CNN, 'Saudis ask U.S. to reduce forces, W. House admits,' 27 Jan. 2002)
The reduction of the U.S. military presence is designed quite specifically to meet the mutual interests of both the U.S. and the Saudi regime—in terms of the latter's internal stability and continuing rule, and in terms of thereby maintaining the former's regional oil interests. This all ties in with the fact noted by former Saudi Oil Minister, Ahmad Zaki al-Yamani, that the "U.S. has a strategic objective, which is to control the oil of the Caspian sea and to end dependence on the oil of the Gulf." (ArabicNews, 'Yamani: importance of Gulf oil collapses in the interests of the Caspian Sea,' 1 Feb. 2002, www.arabicnews.com/ansub/Daily/Day/020201/2002020118.html)

[597] Monbiot, George, 'The need for dissent,' *The Guardian*, 18 Sept. 2001.

[598] See Ahmed, Nafeez M., 'The 1991 Gulf Massacre: The Historical and Strategic Context of Western Terrorism in the Gulf,' Media Monitors Network, Los Angeles, CA, 2 October 2001, www.mediamonitors.net/mosaddeq14.html.

[599] *The Guardian*, 29th January 2002.

Appendix A: Excerpts from Hearings on U.S. Interests in the Central Asian Republics

Excerpts from transcript, House of Representatives, 'Hearings on U.S. Interests in the Central Asian Republics,' Subcommittee on Asia and the Pacific, House Committee on International Relations, Washington DC, 12 February 1998

Chairman of Subcommittee: Hon. Doug Bereuter

Mr. BEREUTER. I would like to proceed to the subject of the hearing for today, U.S. interests in the Central Asian Republics. I do have a statement. One hundred years ago, Central Asia was the arena for a great game played by Czarist Russia, Colonial Britain, Napoleon's France, and the Persian and the Ottoman Empires. Allegiances meant little during this struggle for empire building, where no single empire could gain the upper hand. One hundred years later, the collapse of the Soviet Union has unleashed a new great game, where the interests of the East India Trading Company have been replaced by those of Unocal and Total, and many other organizations and firms.

302 The War on Freedom

Today the Subcommittee examines the interests of a new contestant in this new great game, the United States. The five countries which make up Central Asia, Kazakhstan, Kyrgyzstan, Tajikistan, Turkmenistan, and Uzbekistan, attained their independence in 1991, and have once again captured worldwide attention due to the phenomenal reserves of oil and natural gas located in the region. In their desire for political stability as well as economic independence and prosperity, these nations are anxious to establish relations with the United States.

Kazakhstan and Turkmenistan possess large reserves of oil and natural gas, both on-shore and off-shore in the Caspian Sea, which they urgently seek to exploit. Uzbekistan has oil and gas reserves that may permit it to be self-sufficient in energy and gain revenue through exports. Estimates of Central Asian oil reserves vary widely, but are usually said to rival those of the North Sea or Alaska. More accurate estimates of oil and gas resources await wider exploration and the drilling of test wells.

Stated U.S. policy goals regarding energy resources in this region include fostering the independence of the States and their ties to the West; breaking Russia's monopoly over oil and gas transport routes; promoting Western energy security through diversified suppliers; encouraging the construction of east-west pipelines that do not transit Iran; and denying Iran dangerous leverage over the Central Asian economies. (...)

Central Asia would seem to offer significant new investment opportunities for a broad range of American companies which, in turn, will serve as a valuable stimulus to the economic development of the region. Japan, Turkey, Iran, Western Europe, and China are all pursuing economic development opportunities and challenging Russian dominance in the region. It is essential that U.S. policymakers understand the stakes involved in Central Asia as we seek to craft a policy that serves the interests of the United States and U.S. business.

On the other hand, some question the importance of the region to U.S. interests, and dispute the significance of its resources to U.S. national security interests. Others caution that it will take a great deal of time and money to bring these resources to world markets. Still others point to civil and ethnic conflicts in Tajikistan and Afghanistan as a reason to avoid involvement beyond a minimal diplomatic presence in the area. (...)

Statement of Robert W. Gee, Assistant Secretary for Political and International Affairs, Department of Energy

Mr. GEE. Thank you, Mr. Chairman. Good afternoon, Mr. Chairman and Members of the Committee. My name is Robert Gee, Assistant Secretary for the Office of Policy and International Affairs at the Department of Energy. I am pleased and honored to appear before this Committee today to report on the U.S. energy policy in the Caspian region. I welcome the opportunity to discuss our government's strategic and economic interests in this important region, our policy to advance those interests, and how we can achieve our goals.

I also appreciate the opportunity to appear before you as you begin consideration of H.R. 2867, the House version of the Silk Road Strategy Act. While the Administration does not yet have a formal position on the bill, the underlying theme of the proposed legislation is consistent with our policy objectives and strategic goals in the region.

To begin, you may ask why is the United States active in the region? The United States has energy security, strategic, and commercial interests in promoting Caspian region energy development. We have an interest in strengthening global energy security through diversification, and the development of these new sources of supply. Caspian export routes would diversify rather than concentrate world energy supplies, while avoiding over-reliance on the Persian Gulf.

We have strategic interests in supporting the independence, sovereignty, and prosperity of the Newly Independent States of the Caspian Basin. We want to assist the development of these States into democratic, sovereign members of the world community of nations, enjoying unfettered access to world markets without pressure or undue influence from regional powers.

We also have an interest in maximizing commercial opportunities for U.S. firms and for U.S. and other foreign investment in the region's energy development. In short, our interests are rooted in achieving multiple objectives. Rapid development of the region's energy resources and trade linkages are critical to the independence, prosperity, democracy, and stability of all of the countries of that region.

Four factors frame our policy. First, promoting multiple export routes. The Administration's policy is centered on rapid development of the region's resources and the transportation and sale of those resources to hard-currency markets to secure the independence of these new countries. Accordingly, our government has promoted the development of multiple pipelines and diversified infrastructure networks to open and integrate these countries into the global market and to foster regional cooperation. (...)

Second, emphasizing commerciality. While we recognize the influence regional politics will play on the development of export routes, we have always maintained that commercial considerations will principally determine the outcome. These massive infrastructure projects must be commercially competitive before the private sector and the international financial community can move forward. Our support of specific pipelines, such as the Baku-Ceyhan oil pipeline and trans-Caspian oil and gas lines, is not driven by any desire to intervene in private commercial decisions. Rather, it derives from our conclusion that it is not in the commercial interest of companies operating in the Caspian States, nor in the strategic interests of those host States, to rely on a major competitor for transit rights.

In general, we support those transportation solutions that are commercially viable and address our environmental concerns and policy objectives. Based on discussions with the companies involved, a Baku-Ceyhan pipeline appears to be the most viable option. We have urged the Turks to take steps to make Baku-Ceyhan a commercially attractive option. For our part, we are also looking at steps the United States can take to provide political risk guarantees and to foster cooperation among the regional States on an approach that can lead to a regional solution for the longer term. (...)

The United States supports regional approaches to Caspian energy development. The Eurasian corridor will enhance Turkey's energy security through diversification, and will ensure that Kazakhstan, Uzbekistan, Turkmenistan and Azerbaijan have reliable and diversified outlets for their resources. (...)

Fourth, isolating Iran. Our policy on Iran is unchanged. The U.S. Government opposes pipelines through Iran. Development of Iran's oil and gas industry and pipelines from the Caspian Basin south through Iran will seriously undercut the development of east-west infrastructure, and give Iran improper leverage over the economies of the Caucasus and Central Asian States. Moreover, from an energy security standpoint, it makes no sense to move yet more energy resources through the Persian Gulf, a potential major hot spot or chokepoint. From an economic standpoint, Iran competes with Turkmenistan for the lucrative Turkish gas market. Turkmenistan could provide the gas to build the pipeline, only to see itself displaced ultimately by Iran's own gas exports.

How are we implementing U.S. policy? First, we have stepped up our engagement with the regional governments through Cabinet level and senior level visits to the region, and have established formal government-to-government dialogs (...)

Second, we are pursuing an aggressive strategy with the regional governments. The Eurasian energy transport corridor, spanning at least six countries and disputed regions, presents complicated problems for even the most efficient governments. The number of potential players ensures that negotiations and equity structures will be enormously complicated. The

United States has stressed the importance of achieving agreement on concrete project proposals among the relevant countries as early as possible. Along these lines, we have encouraged the regional governments to accelerate multilateral discussions with their neighboring States and with the private sector shippers through the establishment of national working groups. These groups have a critical role in resolving regulatory, legal, tariff, and other issues that will make the Eurasian corridor most commercially attractive. (...)

Mr. BEREUTER. Switching geography slightly, what is the status of proposals by Unocal and others to build a gas pipeline through Afghanistan to Pakistan?

Mr. GEE. Perhaps the Unocal witness can give you more detail. I do understand that they do have an agreement with the government of Turkmenistan. They have also been in discussions with the various factions within Afghanistan through which that proposed pipeline would be routed.

The U.S. Government's position is that we support multiple pipelines with the exception of the southern pipeline that would transit Iran. The Unocal pipeline is among those pipelines that would receive our support under that policy.

I would caution that while we do support the project, the U.S. Government has not at this point recognized any governing regime of the transit country, one of the transit countries, Afghanistan, through which that pipeline would be routed. But we do support the project. (...)

Next we would like to hear from Mr. John J. Maresca, vice president of international relations, Unocal Corporation. You may proceed as you wish.

Statement of John J. Maresca, Vice President of International Relations, Unocal Corporation

Mr. MARESCA. Thank you, Mr. Chairman. It's nice to see you again. I am John Maresca, vice president for international relations of the Unocal Corporation. Unocal, as you know, is one of the world's leading energy resource and project development companies. I appreciate your invitation to speak here today. I believe these hearings are important and timely. I congratulate you for focusing on Central Asia oil and gas reserves and the role they play in shaping U.S. policy.

I would like to focus today on three issues. First, the need for multiple pipeline routes for Central Asian oil and gas resources. Second, the need for U.S. support for international and regional efforts to achieve balanced and lasting political settlements to the conflicts in the region, including Afghanistan. Third, the need for structured assistance to encourage economic reforms and the development of appropriate investment climates in the region. In this regard, we specifically support repeal or removal of section 907 of the Freedom Support Act.

Mr. Chairman, the Caspian region contains tremendous untapped hydrocarbon reserves. Just to give an idea of the scale, proven natural gas reserves equal more than 236 trillion cubic feet. The region's total oil reserves may well reach more than 60 billion barrels of oil. Some estimates are as high as 200 billion barrels. In 1995, the region was producing only 870,000 barrels per day. By 2010, western companies could increase production to about 4.5 million barrels a day, an increase of more than 500 percent in only 15 years. If this occurs, the region would represent about 5 percent of the world's total oil production.

One major problem has yet to be resolved: how to get the region's vast energy resources to the markets where they are needed. Central Asia is isolated. Their natural resources are landlocked, both geographically and politically. Each of the countries in the Caucasus and Central Asia faces difficult political challenges. Some have unsettled wars or latent conflicts. Others have evolving systems where the laws and even the courts are dynamic and changing. In addition, a chief technical obstacle which we in the industry face in transporting oil is the region's existing pipeline infrastructure.

Because the region's pipelines were constructed during the Moscow-centered Soviet period, they tend to head north and west toward Russia. There are no connections to the south and east. But Russia is currently unlikely to absorb large new quantities of foreign oil. It's unlikely to be a significant market for new energy in the next decade. It lacks the capacity to deliver it to other markets.

Two major infrastructure projects are seeking to meet the need for additional export capacity. One, under the aegis of the Caspian Pipeline Consortium, plans to build a pipeline west from the northern Caspian to the Russian Black Sea port of Novorossiysk. Oil would then go by tanker through the Bosporus to the Mediterranean and world markets.

The other project is sponsored by the Azerbaijan International Operating Company, a consortium of 11 foreign oil companies, including four American companies, Unocal, Amoco, Exxon and Pennzoil. This consortium conceives of two possible routes, one line would angle north and cross the north Caucasus to Novorossiysk. The other route would cross Georgia to a shipping terminal on the Black Sea. This second route could be extended west and south across Turkey to the Mediterranean port of Ceyhan.

But even if both pipelines were built, they would not have enough total capacity to transport all the oil expected to flow from the region in the future. Nor would they have the capability to move it to the right markets. Other export pipelines must be built.

At Unocal, we believe that the central factor in planning these pipelines should be the location of the future energy markets that are most likely to need these new supplies. Western Europe, Central and Eastern Europe, and the Newly Independent States of the former Soviet Union are all slow growth markets where demand will grow at only a half a percent to perhaps 1.2 percent per year during the period 1995 to 2010.

Asia is a different story all together. It will have a rapidly increasing energy consumption need. Prior to the recent turbulence in the Asian Pacific economies, we at Unocal anticipated that this region's demand for oil would almost double by 2010. Although the short-term increase in demand will probably not meet these expectations, we stand behind our long-term estimates.

I should note that it is in everyone's interest that there be adequate supplies for Asia's increasing energy requirements. If Asia's energy needs are not satisfied, they will simply put pressure on all world markets, driving prices upwards everywhere.

The key question then is how the energy resources of Central Asia can be made available to nearby Asian markets. There are two possible solutions, with several variations. One option is to go east across China, but this would mean constructing a pipeline of more than 3,000 kilometers just to reach Central China. In addition, there would have to be a 2,000-kilometer connection to reach the main population centers along the coast.   The question then is what will be the cost of transporting oil through this pipeline, and what would be the netback which the producers would receive.

For those who are not familiar with the terminology, the netback is the price which the producer receives for his oil or gas at the wellhead after all the transportation costs have been deducted. So it's the price he receives for the oil he produces at the wellhead.

The second option is to build a pipeline south from Central Asia to the Indian Ocean. One obvious route south would cross Iran, but this is foreclosed for American companies because of U.S. sanctions legislation. The only other possible route is across Afghanistan, which has of course its own unique challenges. The country has been involved in bitter warfare for almost two decades, and is still divided by civil war. From the outset, we have made it clear that construction of the pipeline we have proposed across

Afghanistan could not begin until a recognized government is in place that
has the confidence of governments, lenders, and our company.

Mr. Chairman, as you know, we have worked very closely with the
University of Nebraska at Omaha in developing a training program for
Afghanistan which will be open to both men and women, and which will
operate in both parts of the country, the north and south.

Unocal foresees a pipeline which would become part of a regional
system that will gather oil from existing pipeline infrastructure in
Turkmenistan, Uzbekistan, Kazakhstan and Russia. The 1,040-mile long oil
pipeline would extend south through Afghanistan to an export terminal that
would be constructed on the Pakistan coast. This 42-inch diameter pipeline
will have a shipping capacity of one million barrels of oil per day. The
estimated cost of the project, which is similar in scope to the trans-Alaska
pipeline, is about $2.5 billion.

Given the plentiful natural gas supplies of Central Asia, our aim is to link
gas resources with the nearest viable markets. This is basic for the
commercial viability of any gas project. But these projects also face
geopolitical challenges. Unocal and the Turkish company Koc Holding are
interested in bringing competitive gas supplies to Turkey. The proposed
Eurasia natural gas pipeline would transport gas from Turkmenistan directly
across the Caspian Sea through Azerbaijan and Georgia to Turkey. Of course
the demarcation of the Caspian remains an issue.

Last October, the Central Asia Gas Pipeline Consortium, called CentGas,
in which Unocal holds an interest, was formed to develop a gas pipeline
which will link Turkmenistan's vast Dauletabad gas field with markets in
Pakistan and possibly India. The proposed 790-mile pipeline will open up
new markets for this gas, traveling from Turkmenistan through Afghanistan
to Multan in Pakistan. The proposed extension would move gas on to New
Delhi, where it would connect with an existing pipeline. As with the
proposed Central Asia oil pipeline, CentGas cannot begin construction until
an internationally recognized Afghanistan Government is in place.

The Central Asia and Caspian region is blessed with abundant oil and gas
that can enhance the lives of the region's residents, and provide energy for
growth in both Europe and Asia. The impact of these resources on U.S.
commercial interests and U.S. foreign policy is also significant. Without
peaceful settlement of the conflicts in the region, cross-border oil and gas
pipelines are not likely to be built. We urge the Administration and the
Congress to give strong support to the U.N.-led peace process in
Afghanistan. The U.S. Government should use its influence to help find
solutions to all of the region's conflicts.

U.S. assistance in developing these new economies will be crucial to business success. We thus also encourage strong technical assistance programs throughout the region. Specifically, we urge repeal or removal of section 907 of the Freedom Support Act. This section unfairly restricts U.S. Government assistance to the government of Azerbaijan and limits U.S. influence in the region.

Developing cost-effective export routes for Central Asian resources is a formidable task, but not an impossible one. Unocal and other American companies like it are fully prepared to undertake the job and to make Central Asia once again into the crossroads it has been in the past. Thank you, Mr. Chairman.

Mr. BEREUTER. Thank you, Mr. Maresca. In light of what you just said, I thought you might be interested to know I actually have a draft resolution on Afghanistan we have been looking at up here today which does indeed weigh in strongly in behalf of the U.N. peace process. (...)

Mr. MARESCA. First, on the question about Afghanistan, of course we're not in a phase where we are negotiating on a contract because there is no recognized government really to negotiate with. However, we have had talks and briefings with all the factions. It is clear that they all understand the significance for their country of this pipeline project, and they all support it, all of them. They all want it. They would like it to start tomorrow. All of the factions would like it to start tomorrow if we could do it.

So I believe that over time, if it's built, it would be secure. I believe that the Afghans will see it as a national asset once it's built. It will provide them with many millions of dollars in transit fees. It will provide them with real jobs and technology and a lot of other things.

Mr. BEREUTER. Mr. Maresca, if I could just interrupt here. Why wouldn't you have the situation whereby whoever is in power drawing resources from that pipeline would find that their adversaries would decide to damage their resource base and stop the flow?

Mr. MARESCA. It's not going to be built until there is a single Afghan Government. That's the simple answer. We would not want to be in the situation where we became the target of the other faction. In any case, because of the financing situation, credits are not going to be available until there is a recognized government of Afghanistan.

Mr. BEREUTER. So you are not making any suggestions about the prospects of that or timing of that. It's just you are not going to move or it's not going to be moved from another source until that happens. That would be your judgment?

Mr. MARESCA. That's my judgment. We do of course follow very closely the negotiations which have been going on. We are hopeful that they will lead somewhere. All wars end. I think that's a universal rule. So one of these days this war too will end. Then I believe the pipeline will be secure. (...)

Mr. BEREUTER. Thank you very much, Mr. Maresca. I want to recognize the fact that Secretary Gee is remaining. I very much appreciate that. That does not always happen. You are listening to the witnesses and our questions to them. I think that is very helpful for you, I hope, and certainly for us to know that you are also having this information.

It's my pleasure now to turn to my colleague from California, Mr. Rohrabacher, for any questions he may have.

Mr. ROHRABACHER. I am reminded of a joke where God is asked when peace will come to the Middle East. He says, "Not in my lifetime." I am afraid that this may well be true of Afghanistan as well. In fact, I am more hopeful right now, having just returned from one trip to the Middle East and another trip to Central Asia that there is a greater chance for peace between Israel and its neighbors than there is for peace in Afghanistan. And I know Afghanistan probably better than anyone else in the Congress. I hate to tell you that.

But let me ask a few questions. So there will be no pipeline until there is an internationally recognized government and a government that is recognized by the people of Afghanistan too, I would imagine that you wanted to put that caveat on it. Right? It's not just internationally recognized, but it has to be accepted by the people of the country. Right?

Mr. MARESCA. It depends on who you mean by the people. I assume that no matter what government is put in place, there will be some people who are opposed to it.

Mr. ROHRABACHER. I found something here. There seems to be a little attachment onto there that may be a little more controversial than people understood when they first heard what you were saying. So the government doesn't necessarily have to be acceptable to the people of Afghanistan as long as it's internationally recognized?

Mr. MARESCA. Of course it has to be accepted by the people. What I mean is that there will always be factions in Afghanistan. There certainly will be factions even when a single government is formed. But when a government is formed that is recognized internationally, it will certainly have to be recognized by the people, yes.

Mr. ROHRABACHER. The current government of Afghanistan or the current group of people who hold Kabul, I guess is the best way to say that, and about 60 percent of the country are known as the Taliban. What type of relationship does your company have to the Taliban?

Mr. MARESCA. We have the same relationship as we have with the other factions, which is that we have talked with them, we have briefed them, we have invited them to our headquarters to see what our projects are.

Mr. ROHRABACHER. Right.

Mr. MARESCA. These are exactly the same things we have done with the other factions.

Mr. ROHRABACHER. However, the Taliban, who are now in control of 60 percent of Afghanistan, could you give me an estimate of where the opium that's being produced in Afghanistan is being produced? Is it in the Taliban areas or is it in the northern areas of Afghanistan?

Mr. MARESCA. I can't tell you precisely, but I think it's being produced all over Afghanistan.

Mr. ROHRABACHER. Yes. To be precise, it's being produced in the Taliban areas. You are talking to someone who has studied it. Whether there is some minor amount of heroin and opium being produced in the other areas is debatable. There is some obviously being produced everywhere, but the major fields that are being produced are in the Taliban-controlled areas.

What about the haven for international terrorists? There is a Saudi terrorist who is infamous for financing terrorism around the world. Is he in the Taliban area or is he up there with the northern people?

Mr. MARESCA. If it is the person I am thinking of, he is there in the Taliban area. (...)

Mr. MARESCA. Congressman, I am not here to defend the Taliban. That is not my role. We are a company that is trying to build a pipeline across this country.

Mr. ROHRABACHER. I sympathize with that. By the way, you are right. All factions agree that the pipeline will be something that's good. But let me warn you that if the pipeline is constructed before there is a government that is acceptable at a general level to the population of Afghanistan and not just to international, other international entities, other governments, that your pipeline will be blown up. There is no doubt about that. I have been in and out of Afghanistan for 15 years. These are very brave, courageous people. If they think they are being stepped on, just like the Soviets found out, they are going to kick somebody back. They are not going to lay down and let somebody put the boot in their face. If the government that is receiving the funds that you are talking about is a government that is not accepted by a large number of people in Afghanistan, there will continue to be problems. You say you have had a positive relationship with all the factions. That is what you are presenting to us today.

Appendix B: Excerpts from Hearings on Global Terrorism and South Asia

Excerpts from transcript, House of Representatives, 'Hearings on Global Terrorism and South Asia,' House Committee on International Relations, Washington DC, 12 July 2000

Chaired by: Representative Benjamin Gilman. Witnesses: Michael Sheehan, State Department Coordinator For Counterterrorism; Alan Eastham, Jr., Deputy Assistant Secretary Of State For South Asian Affairs

REP. DANA ROHRABACHER: Mr. Chairman, thank you very much, and thank you very much for holding this hearing.

As we discuss terrorism in South Asia, I think it is important to renew the members of this committee's and the public's acquaintance with the request that I have made for the last three years concerning American policy toward the Taliban, because as we examine -- as we examine terrorism in South Asia, one can't help but recognize that if it weren't for the fact that the Taliban are in power, there would be a different equation going on.

It would be whole different situation in South Asia.

After a year of requesting to see State Department documents on Afghan policy – and I would remind the committee that I have – I have stated that I believe that there is a covert policy by this administration, a shameful covert policy of supporting the Taliban – the State Department, after many, many months – actually, years – of prodding, finally began giving me documents, Mr. Chairman. And I have, in the assessment of those documents, I have found nothing to persuade me that I was wrong in my criticism. And I might add, however, that there has been no documents provided to me, even after all of these years of requesting it, there have been no documents concerning the time period of the formation of the Taliban. And I would, again, I would hope that the State Department gets the message that I expect to see all those documents. And the documents that I have read, Mr. Chairman, indicate that the State Department, time and again, has had as its position that they have no quarrel, or that it would give them no heartburn, to have the Taliban in power. This, during the time period when the Taliban was struggling to take over Afghanistan.

And although the administration has denied supporting the Taliban, it is clear that they discouraged all of the anti-Taliban supporters from supporting the efforts in Afghanistan to defeat the Taliban. Even so much as when the Taliban was ripe for being defeated on the ground in Afghanistan, Bill Richardson and Rick Inderfurth, high-ranking members of this administration, personally visited the region in order to discourage the Taliban's opposition from attacking the Taliban when they were vulnerable, and then going to neighboring countries to cut off any type of military assistance to the [opponents of the] Taliban. This, at a time when Pakistan was heavily resupplying and rearming the Taliban.

What did this lead to? It led to the defeat of all of the Taliban's major enemies except for one, Commander Massoud, in the north, and left the Taliban the supreme power in Afghanistan.

So what we hear today about terrorism and crocodile tears from this administration, let us remember this administration is responsible for the Taliban. This administration has acted in a way that has kept the Taliban in power.

One last note. Many people here understand that I have been in Afghanistan on numerous occasions and have close ties to people there. And let me just say that some of my sources of information informed me of where bin Laden was, they told me they knew and could tell people where bin Laden could be located. And it took me three times before this administration responded to someone who obviously has personal contacts in Afghanistan, to even investigate that there might be someone who could give them the information. And when my contact was actually contacted, they said that the people who contacted them were half-hearted, did not follow through, did not appear to be all that interested, appeared to be forced to be talking to him.(...)

[U.S. Representative David E. Bonior denies Rohrabacher's charges, but fails to do so, addressing the matter in only the most general terms without discussing Rohrabacher's specific charges]

REP. DAVID E. BONIOR (D-MI): On earlier occasions, the administration has expressed the importance of working with Pakistan in addressing terrorism in South Asia. I also believe that cooperation with Pakistan continues to be very much in our national interest. Combating and preventing global terrorism is one of the most serious challenges facing America's foreign policy in this new era.

It is my belief, Mr. Chairman, that Pakistan, as a long-standing ally of the United States, is committed to cooperating with the United States on terrorism. Its record shows that. Sanctioning Pakistan will serve no purpose other than to isolate them and aggravate the social and economic and political challenges in the region.

I also strongly believe that the Taliban support for terrorism, and its harboring of Osama bin Laden, must be condemned in the strongest possible terms. We must also respond to the threat, and I believe that is where Pakistan plays a very critical role. We must remember that it is not in Pakistan's interest to have the Taliban on its border. It is also not in Pakistan's interest to have terrorist groups operating within its borders. And it is clearly not in India's interest to have Pakistan isolated, thereby producing a greater threat to peace and stability in South Asia....

I know from my talks with General Musharraf, when I visited Pakistan and India in April, that he is committed to dealing with the Taliban. He has met with one leader of the Taliban and is prepared to meet with others in Afghanistan. Throughout my trip, I gained a new appreciation of the new challenges facing the region. I also came away, more convinced than ever, that the United States must play a proactive role in helping to meet those challenges.

There are serious challenges and threats, which exist in Pakistan. But I also know that General Musharraf and General Aziz (sp), in Pakistan, are well aware of what needs to be done. (...)

[State Department officials Michael Sheehan and Alan Eastham Jr. then speak, once again denying the charges in only general terms]

REP. GEJDENSON: ...One last thing. Are there any countries supplying weapons to the Taliban at this point?

MR. SHEEHAN: I think I'll have to go in closed session on that as well, Mr. Congressman. I'm not – what I know about that is from classified sources. I'll be glad to talk to you about it after this.

REP. GEJDENSON: Thank you. You might check with Mr. Rohrabacher for any other information you need on Afghanistan – (laughter). He seems to be very knowledgeable about the military situation there.

REP. GILMAN: Thank you, Mr. Gejdenson. Mr. Rohrabacher?

REP. ROHRABACHER: (Laughing.) This is a joke! I mean, you have to go to closed session to tell us where the weapons are coming from? Well, how about let's make a choice. There's Pakistan or Pakistan or Pakistan. (Laughs.) Where do you think the Taliban – right as we speak – I haven't read any classified documents. Everybody in the region knows that Pakistan is involved with a massive supply of military weapons and has been since the very beginning of the Taliban.

Let me just state for the record, here, before I get into my questions, that I think there's -- and it's not just you, Mr. Ambassador, but it is this administration and, perhaps, other administrations as well. I do not believe that terrorism flows from a lack of state control. A breakdown of state control, all of sudden you have terrorism. That's not what causes terrorism. What causes terrorism is a lack of freedom and democracy, a lack of a means to solve one's problems through a democratic process.

Afghanistan, from the very beginning, we have been – when the Reagan administration was involved with helping the Afghans fight the Russians, which was engaged in trying to put a totalitarian government there – because of Pakistan's insistence, a lion's share of our support went to a guy named Hekmatyar Gulbuddin, who had no democratic tendencies whatsoever. And since the Russians lost, we have not been supporting, the United States has not been supporting any type of somewhat free, somewhat democratic alternatives in Afghanistan, and there are such alternatives, and we all – those of us who have been involved know that.

So there's no democracy or freedom in Afghanistan, where people who are good and decent and courageous people, have a chance to cleanse their society of the drug dealers and the fanatics that torture and repress, especially the women of Afghanistan. But the men of Afghanistan are not fanatics like the Taliban, either. They would like to have a different regime. Only the United States has given – and I again make this charge – the United States has been part and parcel to supporting the Taliban all along, and still is let me add. But you don't have any type of democracy in Afghanistan. (...)

Let me note that, three years ago, I tried to arrange support, aid, humanitarian aid, to a non-Taliban-controlled section of Afghanistan, the Bamian area. Mr. Chairman, the State Department did everything they could to thwart these humanitarian medical supplies from going into Bamian. And we heard today that we are very proud that we are still giving aid to Afghanistan. Let me note; that aid has always gone to Taliban areas. So what message does that send to the people of Afghanistan? We have been supporting the Taliban, because all our aid goes to the Taliban areas. And when people from the outside try to put aid into areas not controlled by the Taliban, they are thwarted by our own State Department.

And let me just note that that same area, Bamian, where I tried to help those people who are opposed to the Taliban; Bamian now is the headquarters of Mr. Bin Laden. Surprise, surprise! Everyone in this committee has heard me, time and again over the years, say, unless we did something, Afghanistan was going to become a base for terrorism and drug dealing. And, Mr. Chairman, how many times did you hear me say that this administration either ignored that or – a part of the problem, rather than part of the solution?

Again, let me just – I am sorry Mr. Inderfurth is not here to defend himself – but let me state for the record: At a time when the Taliban were vulnerable, the top person of this administration, Mr. Inderfurth, and Bill

Richardson, personally went to Afghanistan and convinced the anti-Taliban forces not to go on the offensive and, furthermore, convinced all of the anti-Taliban forces, their supporters, to disarm them and to cease their flow of support for the anti-Taliban forces. At that same moment, Pakistan initiated a major resupply effort, which eventually saw the defeat, and caused the defeat, of almost all of the anti-Taliban forces in Afghanistan.

Now, with a history like that, it's very hard, Mr. Ambassador, for me to sit here and listen to someone say, "Our main goal is to drain the swamp" – and the swamp is Afghanistan – because the United States created that swamp in Afghanistan. And the United States' policies have undercut those efforts to create a freer and more open society in Afghanistan, which is consistent with the beliefs of the Afghan people. (...)

REP. GILMAN: Did the panelists want to respond at all?

MR. SHEEHAN: I would, Mr. Congressman.

REP. GILMAN: Ambassador Sheehan.

MR. SHEEHAN: First of all, Mr. Congressman, I'm sorry that you think it's a joke that I won't respond on the issue of support for the arms for the Taliban, but the information that I have, which is – I cannot respond by public source – is based on intelligence methods, and I don't have the authority to speak about that in this session. But I'll be glad to talk to you or anybody else afterwards.

Secondly, regarding the responsibility the United States government has for Afghanistan and the situation there, I don't accept that conclusion at all. The United States did help participate in helping the mujaheddin reject the Soviet occupation in the mid-'80s, and that was a policy that I think was a correct one at that time. The situation in Afghanistan, the deterioration of that state since 1979, has primarily to do with the situation in Afghanistan. Certainly there were those responsible, whether it was the Soviet occupiers or those who were involved in a civil war that has waged there for 20 years. But the idea that the United States government is responsible for everything in Afghanistan I think is not true.

And the idea that we support the Taliban I also reject as well completely. I have spent 18 months in this job leading the effort within the United States government and around the world to bring pressure on the Taliban. After the bombing of the embassies in East Africa, when I got hired for this job, I have made it my sole effort, my primary effort in this job to bring pressure on that regime. And the United States government leads that effort in providing pressure on that regime. My office leads that effort within the United States government. We started with an executive order in August of 1999 that brought sanctions to bear on the Taliban. We've led the effort in the U.N. to bring international sanctions against them. We're also leading the effort internationally right now to look at further measures against the Taliban. It's the United States government that is leading that effort – we're ahead of everybody else – to bring pressure on the Taliban. And the Taliban knows it, and those other member states within the U.N. and other – the other community knows our efforts to bring pressure to bear on that organization because of its support for state – for terrorism.

REP. GILMAN: Thank you.

Mr. Eastham, did you want to comment?

MR. EASTHAM: Yes, sir, I would. I would be happy to defend Mr. Inderfurth, if you'd like, Mr. Rohrabacher, even if he's not here in person.

I would just note that I have spent nearly 15 years of my life working on this part of the world. I was with the mujaheddin in Peshar [Pakistan] from 1984 to 1987. I was in the consulate in Peshar at that time. I've been back on this account now for – I began my sixth year on the South Asia account this time, around this week. I was in Pakistan when you were trying your effort to put – the airdrop assistance into Bamian. So I'm quite familiar with the history of the whole episode. And I can say that at no point – at no point – in the last six years has the United States of America offered its support to the Taliban.

This is why I think that despite the fact we've provided you nearly a thousand documents in response to the request of the chairman, that you haven't been able to find the support for the Taliban, because it isn't there.

REP. ROHRABACHER: That is incorrect, by the way. And I will say that for the record. That is incorrect. I have found several references. And documents have been kept from me indicating what our policy formation about the Taliban has been. So that is not accurate.

MR. EASTHAM: Well, we have a fundamental difference of opinion, then, about the record of what this administration has done with respect to the Taliban.

But I will say that we have – that our goals with respect to the Taliban have shifted over the past two years, almost, since the East Africa bombings. When the Taliban first came into power in Afghanistan, we had an agenda which addressed terrorism, narcotics, human rights, including the rights of women, and bringing peace to Afghanistan. We tried to address all of those at the same time.

After the East Africa bombing, the terrorism problem became much more acute and a much higher priority in terms of our – in terms of what we were doing. But we've been addressing all these issues since the first day the Taliban came into being, and particularly since they came to power in Kabul.

Thank you very much, Mr. Chairman. (...)

REP. ROHRABACHER: All right.

Let me just say that, in your denials to the charges that I made, you were very good at general denials. But there was no denial of some specific charges, so I'd like to ask you about them now.

I charged that the aid that the United States has been giving has been going to the Taliban-controlled territories, especially during that time period when one-third of Afghanistan was being controlled by non- and anti-Taliban forces. Specifically, I used the example of the Bamian effort in which we tried to help the folks down there, who my sources said were in great deprivation and starving, and the State Department undermined that effort.

And we mentioned earlier there is an aid program going on to Afghanistan. Ten percent of Afghanistan is still controlled by anti-Taliban forces. Is any of the aid that we are giving going to this anti-Taliban area? (...)

MR. EASTHAM: The answer to the question is, yes, there is aid flowing to all areas in Afghanistan. That is a function, however, of accessibility, of how you get it to them. There is assistance, which flows through the United Nations who are the implementers of the program, into the North, via Tajikistan, and also through the Chitral area of Pakistan –

REP. ROHRABACHER: Okay. Okay. So –

MR. EASTHAM: – as well as to the 80 percent of the country.

REP. ROHRABACHER: – okay. So your answer is yes, that currently that one area in the Panjshir Valley, now controlled by Commander Massoud, that does – they do receive humanitarian supplies?

MR. EASTHAM: I can't take you specifically to the Panjshir Valley because access to the Panjshir Valley is blocked from the south by the Taliban.

REP. ROHRABACHER: But of course, it's not blocked from Tajikistan, right?

MR. EASTHAM: Yeah. But there is assistance, which flows into all areas of Afghanistan, through these U.N. programs.

REP. ROHRABACHER: All right. Okay. So you're on the record. Thank you very much.

MR. EASTHAM: Okay. But –

REP. ROHRABACHER: That's not what my sources say.

MR. EASTHAM: – with respect to Bamian, I want to take you back to the period two, three years ago that you are referring to. In fact, I have – at around that same time, I made a trip myself from Pakistan to Kandahar, to talk to the Taliban about the blockade, which they had imposed at the time, upon assistance to Bamian, because at the time Bamian was controlled by non-Taliban forces, from the Hazara people, there.

One of the main effects of the trip by Mr. Richardson and Mr. Inderfurth that you have so criticised was to attempt to persuade the Taliban in fact to lift that very blockade of Bamian, which was – and we followed it up with discussions in Islamabad, in which the Taliban did, in fact, agree to a partial lifting to enable foodstuffs to go into Bamian.

REP. ROHRABACHER: So we traded off with the Taliban that they were going to lift their blockade and we were going to disarm all of their opponents.

MR. EASTHAM: No, sir, that's not the case.

REP. ROHRABACHER: Okay. Well, let's go back – go to disarming the Taliban's opponents. And by the way, this has been reconfirmed in everything that I've read, both official and unofficial. Are you trying to tell us now that the State Department's policy was not, at that crucial moment when the Taliban was vulnerable, to disarm the Taliban's opponents? Did not Mr. Inderfurth and the State Department contact all of the support groups that were helping the anti-Taliban forces and ask them to cease their flow of military supplies to the anti-Taliban forces?

MR. EASTHAM: At that time we were trying to – we were trying to construct a coalition which would cut off support for all forces in Afghanistan from the outside.

REP. ROHRABACHER: Oh, and I take it – so I take it that's a yes to my question. But the –

MR. EASTHAM: No, sir; you've left out the cutting off the Taliban part.

REP. ROHRABACHER: – but the Taliban were – but the Taliban were included; except what happened right after all of those other support systems that had been dismantled because of Mr. Inderfurth's and Mr. Richardson's appeal, and the State Department's appeal? What happened immediately – not only immediately after, even while you were making that appeal, what happened in Pakistan? Was there an airlift of supplies, military supplies, between Pakistan and Kabul and the forward elements of the Taliban forces?

REP. ROHRABACHER: The answer is yes. I know.

MR. EASTHAM: The answer is –

REP. ROHRABACHER: You can't tell me because –

MR. EASTHAM: The answer is –

REP. ROHRABACHER: – it's secret information.

MR. EASTHAM: The answer is closed session, if you would like to dredge up that record.

REP. ROHRABACHER: Right. Okay.

MR. EASTHAM: That would be fine.

REP. ROHRABACHER: Well, I don't have to go into closed session because I didn't get that information from any classified document. That information is available to anybody watching the scene up there. They know exactly what happened. Mr. Inderfurth, Mr. Bill Richardson, a good friend of mine, doing the bidding of this administration, basically convinced the anti-Talibans' mentors to quit providing them the weapons they needed, with some scheme that the Taliban were then going to lay down their arms. And immediately thereafter, Pakistan started a massive shift of military supplies which resulted in the total defeat of the anti-Taliban forces.

This is – now, this is either collusion or incompetence on the part of the State Department, as far as this congressman is concerned...

Why haven't I been provided any documents about State Department analysis of – during the formation period of the Taliban, about whether or not the Taliban was a good force or a bad force? Why have none of those documents reached my desk after two years?

MR. EASTHAM: Congressman, we were responding to a specific request dealing with a specific time period, which I believe the commencing period of the request for documents was after the time period you're talking about. We were asked to provide documents, by the chairman of this committee, from 1996 to 1999.

REP. ROHRABACHER: I see. You found a loophole in the chairman's wording –

MR. EASTHAM: No, sir. We were responding to the chairman's request.

REP. ROHRABACHER: You found a loophole in the chairman's wording of his request as to not to provide me those documents. You know, I am the only one here. I am not the chairman of the committee. I would never get the opportunity to have a back and forth with you, except in times like this.

The State Department has taken full advantage of its use of words in order not to get this information out. I am looking forward to more documents. I will say this, I have spent hours overlooking those documents, and there's been nothing in those documents to persuade me that my charges that this administration has been covertly supporting the Taliban is not accurate. Feel free to respond to that.

MR. EASTHAM: It's not true.

REP. ROHRABACHER: Okay.

MR. EASTHAM: I have to negate the whole thesis that you're operating under, sir.

REP. ROHRABACHER: All right. Then – okay, the other option is the State Department is so incompetent that we have done things that helped the Taliban and have put them in a position of having hundreds of millions of dollars of drug money, and had power in Afghanistan, and undercutting the anti-Taliban forces. This is just – this isn't intent, this is just incompetence?

MR. EASTHAM: That's a judgment you can make.

REP. ROHRABACHER: All right.

MR. EASTHAM: And if you want to make that judgment, that's up to you, Congressman.

REP. ROHRABACHER: Okay.

MR. EASTHAM: I would just observe that it's considerably more complex than that to deal with people over whom we have so little influence as with Taliban. I have spent – I have been myself, by my count, six times into Afghanistan on both the northern side and the southern side. I have met innumerable times with Taliban officials to attempt to achieve U.S. objectives, and I have to tell you that it's a tough job.

REP. ROHRABACHER: I believe it is a tough job –

MR. EASTHAM: I'd like to introduce you to some of them sometime.

REP. ROHRABACHER: Oh, I've met many Taliban, thank you. And as you are aware, I have met many Taliban and talked to them. Especially when you disarm their opponents, and you participate in an effort to disarm their opponents at a time when they're being supplied -- resupplied militarily, I guess it is very hard for them to take us seriously when we say we're going to get tough with them.

MR. EASTHAM: You keep saying that, but it's not true.

REP. ROHRABACHER: Well – oh –

MR. EASTHAM: The effort –

REP. ROHRABACHER: You're just saying – no, you're just –

MR. EASTHAM: The effort was to stop the support for all the factions.

REP. ROHRABACHER: That's correct. You didn't deny that we disarmed their opponents, you just said we were doing it with the Taliban as well. But as I pointed out, which you did not deny, the Taliban were immediately resupplied. Which means that we are part and parcel to disarming a victim against this hostile, totalitarian, anti-Western, drug-dealing force in their society, and we were part and parcel of disarming the victim, thinking that the aggressor was going to be disarmed as well, but it just didn't work out – at the moment when Pakistan was arming them, I might add.

Appendix C: Pearl Harbor and Operation Northwoods

While many would consider the harsh conclusions of this study to be contrary to the general course of U.S. policy, the fact remains that there is historical precedent for the current policy. Indeed, it is a matter of public record that the U.S. government and military intelligence apparatus has in the past deliberately provoked acts of terrorism against itself, anticipating massive civilian and military casualties, in order to justify American military action.

The example under consideration here is Pearl Harbor. The History Channel (U.S.A.) recently aired a BBC-produced documentary, *Betrayal at Pearl Harbor*, which demonstrated using, among other historical records declassified U.S. documents, that then U.S. President Franklin Roosevelt and his chief military advisers knew full well that Japan was about to spring a 'surprise attack' on the U.S. under the latter's provocation, but allowed the attack to occur to justify U.S. entry into war.[600] Detailed documentation of this fact has been provided by Robert Stinnett in his authoritative study, *Day of Deceit: The Truth About FDR and Pearl Harbor*. Stinnett served in the U.S. Navy from 1942-46 where he earned ten battle stars and a Presidential Unit Citation. Examining recently declassified American documents, he concludes that far more than merely knowing of the Japanese plan to bomb Pearl Harbor, Roosevelt deliberately steered Japan into war with America.[601]

"Lieutenant Commander Arthur McCollum, a U.S. Naval officer in the Office of Naval Intelligence, saw an opportunity to counter the U.S. anti-war movement by provoking Japan into a state of war with the U.S., and triggering the mutual assistance provisions of the Tripartite Pact. Memorialized in a secret memo dated October 7, 1940, McCollum's proposal called for eight provocations aimed at Japan. President Roosevelt acted swiftly, and throughout 1941, implemented the remaining seven provocations. The island nation's militarists used the provocations to seize control of Japan and organize their military forces for war against the U.S., Great Britain, and the Netherlands. During the next 11 months, the White House followed the Japanese war plans through the intercepted and decoded diplomatic and military communications intelligence. At least 1,000 Japanese radio messages per day were intercepted by monitoring stations operated by the U.S. and her Allies, and the message contents were summarized for the White House. The intercept summaries from Station CAST on Corregidor Island were current—contrary to the assertions of some who claim that the messages were not decoded and translated until years later—and they were clear: Pearl Harbor would be attacked on

December 7, 1941, by Japanese forces advancing through the Central and North Pacific Oceans."[602]

The case has also been put well by Daryl S. Borgquist, a U.S. Naval Reserve Public Affairs Officer and a Media Affairs Officer for the Community Relations Service Headquarters at the U.S. Department of Justice: "President Franklin D. Roosevelt requested the national office of the American Red Cross to send medical supplies secretly to Pearl Harbor in advance of the 7 December 1941 Japanese attack...

"Don C. Smith, who directed the War Service for the Red Cross before World War II and was deputy administrator of services to the armed forces from 1942 to 1946, when he became administrator, apparently knew about the timing of the Pearl Harbor attack in advance. Unfortunately, Smith died in 1990 at age 98. But when his daughter, Helen E. Hamman, saw news coverage of efforts by the families of Husband Kimmel and Walter Short to restore the two Pearl Harbor commanders posthumously to what the families contend to be their deserved ranks, she wrote a letter to President Bill Clinton on 5 September 1995. Recalling a conversation with her father, Hamman wrote:

'... Shortly before the attack in 1941 President Roosevelt called him [Smith] to the White House for a meeting concerning a Top Secret matter. At this meeting the President advised my father that his intelligence staff had informed him of a pending attack on Pearl Harbor, by the Japanese. He anticipated many casualties and much loss, he instructed my father to send workers and supplies to a holding area at a P.O.E. [port of entry] on the West Coast where they would await further orders to ship out, no destination was to be revealed. He left no doubt in my father's mind that none of the Naval and Military officials in Hawaii were to be informed and he was not to advise the Red Cross officers who were already stationed in the area. When he protested to the President, President Roosevelt told him that the American people would never agree to enter the war in Europe unless they were attack [sic] within their own borders...

'He [Smith] was privy to Top Secret operations and worked directly with all of our outstanding leaders. He followed the orders of his President and spent many later years contemplating this action which he considered ethically and morally wrong. I do not know the Kimmel family, therefore would gain nothing by fabricating this situation, however, I do feel the time has come for this conspiracy to be exposed and Admiral Kimmel be vindicated of all charges. In this manner perhaps both he and my father may rest in peace.'"

In a detailed historical account published by the respected *Naval History* journal of the U.S. Naval Institute, Borgquist documents the U.S. government's foreknowledge and provocation of Japan's attack on Pearl Harbor, through analysis of the relationship between the government and the Red Cross alone.[603]

There are other even more pertinent indications of the extent to which the U.S. military is willing to go in its pursuit of its interests. Declassified secret U.S. documents reveal that top levels of the U.S. military proposed carrying out acts of terrorism against U.S. citizens in the early 1960s, in order to drag the United States into a war against Cuba. These revelations have been extensively documented in a study by U.S. national security expert James Bamford, a former investigative reporter for ABC News. In his book, *Body of Secrets: Anatomy of the Ultra-Secret National Security Agency*, Bamford records that the U.S. Joint Chiefs of Staff "proposed launching a secret and bloody war of terrorism against their own country in order to trick the American public into supporting an ill-conceived war they intended to launch against Cuba... [T]he Joint Chiefs of Staff drew up and approved plans for what may be the most corrupt plan ever created by the U.S. government." This account is based on documents that were ordered declassified by the Assassination Records Review Board, and subsequently released by the National Archives within the past few years.

The terrorism plan was called Operation Northwoods, and is laid out in documents signed by the five Joint Chiefs but never carried out. Citing a White House document, Bamford notes that the idea of creating a pretext for the invasion of Cuba appears to have began with President Dwight D. Eisenhower in the last weeks of his administration. The plans were drawn up after President John F. Kennedy had shifted responsibility for dealing with Cuba, in late 1961, from the CIA to the Department of Defense (DOD), in the aftermath of the Bay of Pigs. The overall Pentagon project was known as Operation Mongoose, and was the responsibility of Edward Lansdale, Deputy Director of the Pentagon's Office of Special Operations, and the Chairman of the Joint Chiefs of Staff U.S. Army General Lyman Lemnitzer.

Gen. Lyman L. Lemnitzer presented the Operation Northwoods plan to Kennedy early in 1962. Bamford records that the President rejected the plan that March because he wanted no overt U.S. military action against Cuba. Lemnitzer then sought unsuccessfully to destroy all evidence of the plan. The U.S. military planners under Lemnitzer's leadership had aimed to launch a full-scale invasion of Cuba to overthrow Castro. The planning culminated in a series of memoranda and recommendations, addressed in their final form from Lemnitzer to then U.S. Secretary of Defense Robert McNamara on 13th

March 13, 1962. It is, however, not certain that McNamara ever received them, since he now denies any knowledge of the plan.

Lemnitzer's covering memorandum states that the Joint Chiefs of Staff "have considered" an attached memorandum constituting a "description of pretexts which would provide justification for military intervention in Cuba." The attached memorandum, entitled 'Justification for U.S. Military Intervention in Cuba,' asserts that a political decision for a U.S. military intervention "will result from a period of heightened U.S.-Cuban tensions which place the United States in the position of suffering justifiable grievances." World opinion and the United Nations "should be favorably affected by developing the image of the Cuban government as rash and irresponsible, and as an alarming and unpredictable threat to the peace of the Western Hemisphere."

"We could develop a Communist Cuban terror campaign in the Miami area, in other Florida cities and even in Washington," said one document prepared by the Joint Chiefs of Staff. "We could blow up a U.S. ship in Guantanamo Bay and blame Cuba," it continues. "Casualty lists in U.S. newspapers would cause a helpful wave of indignation." Other measures were also recommended: "Exploding a few plastic bombs in carefully chosen spots, the arrests of Cuban agents and the release of prepared documents also would be helpful... We could sink a boatload of Cubans en route to Florida (real or simulated).... We could foster attempts on lives of Cubans in the United States, even to the extent of wounding in instances to be widely publicized." Other proposals included the idea of using fake Soviet MiG aircraft to harass civil aircraft, to attack surface shipping, and to destroy U.S. military drone aircraft. "Hijacking attempts against civil air and surface craft" were recommended, along with the idea of shooting down a CIA plane designed to simulate a passenger flight and announce that Cuban forces shot it down. The Northwoods plan even proposed that if the 1962 launch of astronaut John Glenn into orbit failed, resulting in his death, the U.S. government would publicise fabricated evidence that Cuba had used electronic interference to sabotage the flight (also see Appendix D).[604]

Pearl Harbor and Operation Northwoods together establish quite clearly a historical precedent for current U.S. policy, by demonstrating without doubt that the U.S. government and military are fully capable of undertaking the policy that has been documented here.[605]

Notes

[600] History Channel, 'Betrayal at Pearl Harbor,' 7 December 2001.

[601] Stinnett, Robert B., *Day of Deceit: The Truth About FDR and Pearl Harbor*, Touchstone Books, 2001.

[602] Stinnett, Robert B., 'Pentagon Still Scapegoats Pearl Harbor Fall Guys,' *Providence Journal*, The Independent Institute, Oakland, 7 December 2001.

[603] Borgquist, Daryl S., 'Advance Warning? The Red Cross Connection,' *Navy History*, The Naval Institute, May/June 1999.

[604] Bamford, James, *Body of Secrets: Anatomy of the Ultra-Secret National Security Agency*, Doubleday, 2001. See ABC News, 'Friendly Fire,' 1 May 2001; Shane, Scott and Bowman, Tom, 'New book on NSA sheds light on secrets,' *Baltimore Sun*, 24 April 2001; Spannaus, Edward, 'When U.S. Joint Chiefs Planned Terror Attacks on America,' *Executive Intelligence Review*, 12 October 2001.

[605] Of course, this is not to suggest that the current policy and the past policy/plans are identical.

Appendix D: Excerpts from Declassified Northwoods Documents

Operation Northwoods—The U.S. Military Plan to Manufacture Terror Attacks Against the U.S. to Justify War: Excerpts from Declassified Documents

Operation Northwoods was a plan to stage terror attacks on the U.S., killing Cuban refugees and U.S. citizens, to justify an invasion of Cuba. The plan was developed and proposed by the Joint Chiefs of Staff in 1962, but was never implemented. The Northwoods document is discussed extensively by James Bamford in his book *Body of Secrets*. Bamford's research has been corroborated and confirmed by the authoritative National Security Archive:

"... an independent non-governmental research institute and library located at The George Washington University in Washington, D.C. The Archive collects and publishes declassified documents acquired through the Freedom of Information Act (FOIA). A tax-exempt public charity, the Archive receives no U.S. government funding; its budget is supported by publication royalties and donations from foundations and individuals."

Below are excerpts from the Joint Chiefs' Operation Northwoods document obtained through the Freedom of Information Act:

1. The Joint Chiefs of Staff have considered the attached Memorandum for the Chief of Operations, Cuba Project, which responds to a request* of that office for brief but precise description of pretexts which could provide justification for U.S. military intervention in Cuba.

2. The Joint Chiefs of Staff recommend that the proposed memorandum be forwarded as a preliminary submission suitable for planning purposes. (p. i)

5. The suggested courses of action appended to Enclosure A are based on the premise that U.S. military intervention will result from a period of heightened US-Cuban tensions which place the United States in the position of suffering justifiable grievances. World opinion, and the United Nations forum should be favorably affected by developing the international image of the Cuban government as rash and irresponsible, and as an alarming and unpredictable threat to the peace of the Western Hemisphere. (p. 2)

6. While the foregoing premise can be utilized at the present time it will continue to hold good only as long as there can be reasonable certainty that US military intervention in Cuba would not directly involve the Soviet Union. (p. 2)

3. It is understood that the Department of State also is preparing suggested courses of action to develop justification for US military intervention in Cuba...

8. It is recommended that:

A. Enclosure A together with its attachments should be forwarded to the Secretary of Defense for approval and transmittal to the Chief of Operations, Cuba Project...

b. This paper NOT be forwarded to commanders of unified or specified commands.

c. This paper NOT be forwarded to US officers assigned to NATO activities.

d. This paper NOT be forwarded to the Chairman, US Delegation, United Nations Military Staff Committee. (p. 3)

1. Since it would seem desirable to use legitimate provocation as the basis for US military intervention in Cuba, a cover and deception plan, to include requisite preliminary actions such as has been developed in response to Task 33 o [this may be a 'c'] could be executed as an initial effort to provoke Cuban reactions. Harassment plus deceptive actions to convince the Cubans of imminent invasion would be emphasized. Our

military posture throughout execution of the plan will allow a rapid change from exercise to intervention if Cuban response justifies. (p. 7)

3. A 'Remember the Maine' incident could be arranged in several forms:

We could blow up a US ship in Guantanamo Bay and blame Cuba...

(5) Blow up ammunition inside the [Guantanamo] base; start fires.

(6) Burn aircraft on air base (sabotage).

(7) Lob mortar shells from outside of base onto base. Some damage to installations. (p. 8)

The terror campaign could be pointed at Cuban refugees seeking haven in the United States. We could sink a boatload of Cubans enroute to Florida (real or simulated). We could foster attempts on lives of Cuban refugees in the United States even to the extent of wounding in instances to be widely publicized...

6. Use of MIG type aircraft by US pilots could provide additional provocation. Harassment of civil air, attacks on surface shipping and destruction of US military drone aircraft by MIG type planes would be useful as complementary actions. An F-86 properly painted would convince air passengers that they saw a Cuban MIG, especially if the pilot of the transport were to announce such fact. The primary drawback to this suggestion appears to be the security risk inherent in obtaining or modifying an aircraft. However, reasonable copies of the MIG could be produced from US resources in about three months. (p. 9)

It is possible to create an incident which will demonstrate convincingly that a Cuban aircraft has attacked and shot down a chartered civil airliner enroute from the United States to Jamaica, Guatemala, Panama or Venezuela. The destination would be chosen only to cause the flight plan route to cross Cuba. The passengers could be a group of college students off on a holiday or any grouping of persons with a common interest to support chartering a non-scheduled flight. (p. 10) ...

Backword: Where would we be without our Wars?

A Perspective, by John Leonard

The Most Dreaded Enemy of Liberty, James Madison, August 1793

"Of all the enemies to public liberty war is, perhaps, the most to be dreaded, because it comprises and develops the germ of every other. War is the parent of armies; from these proceed debts and taxes; and armies, and debts, and taxes are the known instruments for bringing the many under the domination of the few. In war, too, the discretionary power of the Executive is extended; its influence in dealing out offices, honors, and emoluments is multiplied; and all the means of seducing the minds, are added to those of subduing the force, of the people... [There is also an] inequality of fortunes, and the opportunities of fraud, growing out of a state of war, and... degeneracy of manners and of morals... No nation could preserve its freedom in the midst of continual warfare...

The powers proposed to be surrendered to the Executive were those which the Constitution has most jealously appropriated to the Legislature...

The Constitution expressly and exclusively vests in the Legislature the power of declaring a state of war... the power of raising armies... the power of creating offices..."[606]

Wars are started by deliberate provocation much more often than people think. Even without the mass of evidence assembled by Ahmed, it is clear that military actions by a strong country against a weak one require a provocation to appear acceptable. Yet weaker nations avoid provoking conflict, in order to survive. Thus, to instigate an unequal battle, an attack scenario has to be arranged by the strong country elite against its own people in a deliberate, clandestine way, in order to mobilize them. It is a formula of: *provocation, invocation, retribution, and redistribution.*

Far from being an unprecedented shocker, suspected government complicity in 9/11 builds on an august and cynical tradition. "It's the oldest trick in the book, dating back to Roman times; creating the enemies you

---

Notes

[606] Thanks to Gore Vidal for contributing this model quotation. Online text from www.sumeria.net/politics/dreaded.html.

need," wrote political gadfly Michael Rivero in 'Fake Terror—The Road to Dictatorship.'[607]

"The state-sponsored schools will never tell you this, but governments routinely rely on hoaxes to sell their agendas to an otherwise reluctant public. The Romans accepted the Emperors and the Germans accepted Hitler not because they wanted to, but because the carefully crafted illusions of threat appeared to leave no other choice."

Rivero recounts how the unscrupulous Crassus became military despot: by the simple ploy of blockading Spartacus' escape from Italy, he cornered the reluctant rebel into marching on Rome. The Romans caught Spartacus, but they never got their Republic back again.

When America was colonized a millennium later, the Native Americans were even more outmatched. Strangely, they are always depicted on the attack, and no peace treaty granting them any useful land ever seemed to hold...

The new America that took their place was a phenomenon — a powerful nation without natural enemies. Impregnable behind ocean barriers, a wealthy ally to be courted, a melting pot linked by family bonds to all peoples, a fearsome military power in its own right, after 1865, and above all, undisputed owner of real estate unencumbered by the conflicting ethnic claims of the Old World — here was a great power no one had any reason to tangle with.

Holding such a strong hand, America's robber baron elite could dare to believe in a manifest destiny of unbridled scope. But how in the world to project America's power, when no one in that world dared to attack it?

Manufacturing villains proved to be a simple matter for our efficient captains of industry. Even incidents like the Boston Tea Party, or the introduction of slavery into the Mexican province of Texas, might be viewed as early provocations that paid off in colossal redistributions of real estate. The modern period of American militarism can be marked from 1898, with the U.S. annexation of Cuba, Puerto Rico, Guam, the Philippines and Hawaii.

---

[607] In www.whatreallyhappened.com/article5/index.html, Rivero gives these examples of democracy hoaxed: the sinking of the Maine, 1898; the Reichstag burning, 1933; Pearl Harbor bombardment, 1941; LBJ's war powers gained by the fake provocation of the Gulf of Tonkin, 1964 — all common knowledge — plus, with depressing regularity in recent years, Bush Sr. luring Saddam Hussein to attack Kuwait, Clinton's bombing of the Sudan, Afghanistan and Kosova, and the OKC bombing.

The Spanish-American War was the test run of America's imperialist strategy. This "conflict" was started the modern (unconstitutional) way, without declaring war. America stationed a ship, the Maine, in Havana harbor, which blew up.[608] The blast was blamed on Spain, inventing an excuse to annex her tottering, but world-straddling empire. Media spin, known in those more forthright days as "yellow journalism,"[609] was perfected to excite patriotic blood lust.

And it was all done under the pious cloak of anti-colonialism, to protect the goodwill America held in the world! and to replace the old empires with a more sophisticated and universal means of global dominance.[610] At home, conditioning of the insular American public with pollyannish patriotic lies has been wildly successful. Americans think of imperialism as a communist epithet, or a thing of the past, which we freed the world from.[611] At the same

---

[608] Concerning the Maine, Rivero writes: "In 1975, an investigation led by Admiral Hyman Rickover examined the data recovered from a 1911 examination of the wreck and concluded that there had been no evidence of an external explosion. The most likely cause of the sinking was a coal dust explosion in a coal bunker imprudently located next to the ship's magazines." (Imprudently or intentionally, we'll never know.) See also Patrick McSherry, 'The Loss of the Battleship Maine and the World Trade Center Towers: An Historical Comparison,' at www.spanamwar. com/MaineWTC.htm. McSherry finds a coal dust explosion makes poor physics, and thinks the Maine was sunk by a small mine placed next to the powder magazines, by Cuban revolutionaries who wished to elicit a U.S. intervention against Spain (how convenient!) Also, Christopher Conway, in 'The Birth of U.S. Imperialism – An Introduction to the Spanish-American War,' offers a short history with links about the dawn of U.S. imperialism in Latin America, at www.geocities.com/athens/ithaca/9852/usimp.htm.

[609] A field led by Pulitzer's "yellow" papers, which went on to give the name to America's most-coveted journalism award.

[610] America has perfected a more purely capitalistic, abstract form of imperialism than the old colonial systems. She does not send people to settle lands, having plenty of land already. It is enough for her to control the major financial and resource flows, through local satraps, and without exposing her own citizens to the temptation of 'going native.'

[611] CIA specialist William Blum's *Rogue State* sardonically characterizes our plight of unawareness: " 'The American Empire:' to the American mind, these words sound like an oxymoron [a contradiction in terms, like 'large small']. Suggesting to Americans that their country has a compelling

time, basking in a total victory for American culture and business interests, we subconsciously assume that the world owes every good thing to America – as well as virtually all its resources.

Americans are a good-hearted people, but ill-informed.[612] There is a curious closed-mindedness, dating back at least to the "Know-Nothings" of Andrew Jackson's day. It is easily exploited. The self-censorship of American media, owned by interlinked interests, allows no inkling that our comfy domesticity is only one side of a cynical imperial system. Our so-called left or liberal political wings are more of the same. Domestic issues and interest groups are paramount, and determine the entire foreign policy agenda. Pluralism and democracy for home consumption, absolute power politics abroad.

Empire, as perfected by ancient Rome, was noted for two axioms: *bread and circuses*, and *divide and conquer*. In modern translation, consumer and media saturation[613] at home, balance of power in foreign policy.

---

lust for political, economic and military hegemony over the rest of the world, divorced from any moral considerations, is akin to telling them of one's UFO abduction — except that they're more likely to believe the abduction story." See also notes 616 and 623.

[612] Development specialist Dr. J. W. Smith, Research Director of the Institute for Economic Democracy in California, quoted in www.mediamonitors.net/mosaddeq32.html: "No society will tolerate it if they knew that they were responsible for violently killing 12 to 15 million people since WW II and causing the death of hundreds of millions more because their economies were destroyed ...While mouthing peace, freedom, justice, rights, and majority rule, all over the world state-sponsored terrorists were overthrowing democratic governments, installing and protecting dictators, and preventing peace, freedom, justice, rights, and majority rule... All intelligence agencies have been, and are still in, the business of destabilizing undeveloped countries to maintain their dependency and the flow of the world's natural wealth to powerful nations." The mainstream media, of course, are in the business of "mouthing" the official line.

[613] The motto of communist propagandists was "repetition is the mother of reason." It is amazing how easily one can be hoodwinked by this simple ruse.

For instance, the demonization drills done on Saddam Hussein. An average dictator became the devil himself - "give a dog a bad name and hang him." Then keep talking about democracy. Never mind that the USA supported the Shah of Iran, whose secret police were at least as brutal, and then gave

Power balancing had been refined into an art by great little Britain, cunningly leveraging her modest potential between shifting alliances to retain the strategic edge. But the fall of the Spanish empire foreshadowed the decline of the British and French colonial systems, too. Joining forces, the pink and green rivals still proved unable to defeat the Central European powers in the Great War.[614]

Britain chose to lend her mantle of supremacy to the United States, a nation she could always influence by her skill in psychological warfare, through the famous Special Relationship.

The stage was set by an unforgettable atrocity, the 1915 sinking of the Lusitania by a German torpedo, since documented as an incident of US-UK provocateurship. The liner was painted and armed as a warship, and intentionally navigated at slow speed without escort into waters where a U-boat torpedo attack was as inevitable as it was fatal – she served double duty as a munitions transport. The 700 passengers were hostages whose death had been carefully planned by Anglo-American psychological warfare experts.

Still, another attack on the USA was needed to get the doughboys "over there." Such a suicidal move was the last thing the Germans would have dared try, as they hoped against hope for American friendship. Yet, with undercover cunning and a big dollop of yellow journalism, a "virtual" attack was arranged. A secret telegram, in which a German official mused about what might be done *if* America declared war on Germany, was hyped by the White House and the media into – "America under attack."[615]

Now, instead of an anti-colonialist crusade, the U.S. cast itself as a white knight, with a garbled slogan about making the world safe from Germany — then a democratic monarchy.

Saddam chemical weapons to wage war on the more democratic but less desirable (less plutocratic) movement that replaced him!

[614] Some Viennese believe Prussia's dirty tricks department triggered the 1914 conflict by arranging the Serbian attack on the Austrian Crown Prince in Sarajevo, in a double play for leadership of Central Europe over rival and ally Austria, as well as a victorious war with Britain and France.

[615] John Cornelius, 'The Balfour Declaration and the Zimmermann Note,' *The Washington Report on Middle East Affairs*, Aug. 1997. See also Lenny Brenner, dissident Jewish historian, in *Zionism in the Age of the Dictators*, www.marxists.de/middleast/brenner/index.htm; and other Jews of conscience at dmoz.org/Society/Politics/Nationalism/Zionism/ Opposing_Views.

The War on Freedom

The American Century was on, and a game called "Enforce the Rule of Might Makes Right, and Still be Liked" began.[616] Is it coincidence that the 20th century was the bloodiest and most depraved since the dawn of time? By destroying the balance of power and destabilizing Europe, Woodrow's war planted seedbeds in Germany and Russia[617] for the most colossal massacres ever known.

In the nineteenth century, Germany was also a rising power with an unbroken string of military victories. Now that the slogan, America Under Attack, has been emblazoned on a billion TV screens, it is worth noting how provoking war can end. From the Third Reich's No. 2 Man, Hermann Goering, at his Nuremberg trial, sentenced to hanging despite his candor:

> " 'It is always a simple matter to drag the people along... All you have to do is to tell them they are being attacked, and denounce the pacifists for lack of patriotism and exposing the country to danger."[618]

---

[616] Stephen Peter Rose, Harvard University, Kaneb Professor of National Security and Military Affairs, Director of the Olin Institute for Strategic Studies, in *Harvard Magazine*, May-June 2002: "A political unit that has overwhelming superiority in military power, and uses that power to influence the internal behavior of other states, is called an empire. The United States [is] an indirect empire, to be sure, but an empire nonetheless.... The maximum amount of force can and should be used as quickly as possible for psychological impact – to demonstrate that the empire cannot be challenged with impunity. Now we are in the business of bringing down hostile governments and creating governments favorable to us. Imperial wars end, but imperial garrisons must be left in place for decades to ensure order and stability. This is, in fact, what we are beginning to see, first in the Balkans and now in Central Asia." Decades? How handy to have an open-ended "war on terror."

[617] Prof. Gerhard Rempel of West New England College, in 'The Russian Revolution of 1917,' shows how Lenin initially supported war to weaken capitalism. In spring 1917, [as an opportunistic demagogue,] he came out for "peace without annexations," to wrest popular support from the moderates. Allied pressure on the moderate 'Menshevik' government to keep up the war on the Eastern front [and spare Western lives] sealed the fate of Russian democracy. At http://mars.wnec.edu/~grempel/courses/stalin/lectures/ Rev1917.html.

[618] Steve Gowans, Goering's testimony at the Nuremberg War Crimes Trials, quoted in 'Charlie Brown and the Brownshirts,' www.mediamonitors.net/gowans41.html; the article stresses that

Sound familiar? Goering pleaded that engineering an enemy attack is the *standard operating procedure* everywhere to whip up and mobilize people for war. Hitler, Goering and Goebbels were probably behind the infamous burning of the Reichstag, or Parliament; in any case, they certainly made the most of it. This "communist attack" consolidated their power, in a double play that is a mark of undercover action: creating the illusion of a ruthless enemy, while also conveniently putting Parliament out of commission.[619] After that, it followed naturally for Stalin's Russians and Hitler's Germans to mutually frighten each other into the great conflict the Nazis expected to win.[620]

Americans keep falling for the same war-provoking trick, like Charlie Brown over Lucy's football. In the full quote Goering emphasized that it works in *any* political system: "Why of course the people don't want war. Why should some poor slob on a farm want to risk his life in a war when the best he can get out of it is to come back to his farm in one piece? Naturally the common people don't want war neither in Russia, nor in England, nor for that matter in Germany. That is understood. But, after all, it is the leaders of the country who determine the policy and it is always a simple matter to drag the people along, whether it is a democracy, or a fascist dictatorship, or a parliament, or a communist dictatorship. Voice or no voice, the people can always be brought to the bidding of the leaders. That is easy. All you have to do is tell them they are being attacked, and denounce the peacemakers for lack of patriotism and exposing the country to danger. It works the same in any country."

America's high-tech weapons industry has improved on Goering's recipe, so that "poor slobs" don't have to be conscripted; a U.S. military career is well-paid, with less risk of violent death than driving a taxi—except, of course, for the poor farmers on the receiving end.

[619] Ian Mulgrew, '9-11: George W. Bush had nothing to do with it... did he?', *Vancouver Sun*, Feb. 23, 2002: "Even dullards can appreciate that anthrax sent to a top Democrat and to the U.S. media helped unify the nation behind the war effort while literally shutting down Congress -- a remarkably useful outcome for Dubya and his gang." A concise and cheerful putdown of the most glaring holes in the official 9/11 story. Now at www.indymedia.org/front.php3?article_id=140623.

[620] Hitler was able to play the anti-communist card to win over skeptical German industrialists. Curiously, the Bush family, no newcomers to melding political and business interests, got their start as key Hitler supporters. Prescott Bush, father of George Bush Sr., was Hitler's banker and propaganda manager in New York, until FDR confiscated his holdings

Let's move along to Pearl Harbor, on Hawaii (annexed, like California, in a subversive putsch,[621] turning the Pacific into an American lake). Declassified files recently revealed that FDR was even more cunning than the "conspiracy theorists" believed. He not only let the Japanese attack Pearl Harbor – he first executed an 8-point plan to provoke and lure them, ensuring that they saw no alternative other than to attack.[622]

These few well-documented, elementary facts about the way we have always gone to war are enough to lead a neutral observer to conclude, even from a great distance, that the complicity of the executive branch in 9/11 is far more likely than its innocence. But distant, neutral observers do not show up on our screens much. We are not Martians with telescopes, but emotionally patriotic human beings, swimming in a media soup of

in 1942 under the Trading With the Enemy Act. See Webster G. Tarpley and Anton Chaitkin, *George Bush: The Unauthorized Biography*, at www.tarpley.net/bush2.htm. Also www.onlinejournal.com/Archive/Bush/bush.html for a review of *Blowback,* and *Old Nazis, the New Right, and the Republican Party*, exposing post-war collaboration of conservative U.S. government circles, the CIA and State Dept. with ex-Nazis, of whom six were on George Bush Sr.'s campaign team. Of course the Bushes were not the only profiteers. IBM founder Thos. Watson is accused of micro-managing the automation of the Nazi death camps from New York, see www.villagevoice.com/issues/0213/black.php. See also *The Progressive Review*, 'Behind the Bushes,' covering Bush team members and backers, including "Enron-Afghan" connections.

[621] See 'Hawaii is not legally a state!' at www.whatreallyhappened.com/HAWAII/hawaii.html. Documents how Hawaii was "stolen" by "private American citizen" settlers, backed up by the U.S. Army, in tactics similar to the founding of the California and Texas "Republics." More info at the Hawaiian Sovereignty website, www.hawaii-nation.org/.

[622] Robert B. Stinnett, *Day of Deceit: The Truth About FDR and Pearl Harbor*. Stinnett, who served in the U.S. Navy with distinction during World War II and who retrieved the official documents, doesn't quite break with the end-justifying-means syndrome to condemn FDR, because he acted to make the world safe from the Germans, and for the Bolsheviks, though he admits they probably would have wiped each other out anyway. See Appendix C, p. on page 321, 'Pearl Harbor and Operation Northwoods.'

disinformation and distractions, with our flag waving at us from every spare surface, from billboards to bottlecaps. [623]

America was immensely powerful in 1945, yet she was well-tutored in the balance of power, too. Truman ordered his commanders to let the Red Army walk into Eastern Europe. Stalin, the nasty piece of work whom FDR had rescued from Hitler, needed no training in the role of bogeyman that he got from Nazi central casting. The Communist threat served as a seemingly permanent pretext for half a century of grotesque military budgets. The American machine must be stimulated, force-fed on conflict, to make it grow.

Were our boys held back then to spare American casualties? That was the excuse for the U.S. re-introduction of the Mafia into Italy, after its eradication by Mussolini. More likely, this was meant to hobble the ingenious people who invented fascism, while Germany was neutralized by splitting it in two. Did top strategists then favor incompetent communism as a convenient method of preventing Russia from ever being real competition?

Finally Japan, tricked into war with the U.S. over the Pacific, was rewarded by being the only country ever hit with nuclear weapons—again ostensibly to save American soldiers' skins—*but those two unnecessary bombs were the single biggest war crimes of all time.* They were primarily a

---

[623] Overuse of flags and slogans is a sure sign of a totalitarian system. Here, again, American ingenuity has vastly improved on Old World populist dictatorships, to create the first truly total form of totalitarian rule. Total, because "voluntary." Our system doesn't "wake the baby" by forcing its children unwillingly into the mold of a "New Man," but flatters them that by munching on its outputs, they already represent the apex of human possibilities. Dissidents are not jailed, but co-opted, ignored and lost in the deluge of a hundred channels, all blathering the same seductive consumerist messages. No one masters foreign languages that might subvert their views, and the Happy Home Gulag is secured by two great moats, the Atlantic and Pacific, which few of the workaholic inmates ever get enough time off to cross over. See also notes 594 and 627.
Logic and rhetoric have been banned from our curricula. Without training in clear thinking or exposure to dissent, as captives of rote education and sold-out media, there is no need to worry about losing our freedom of thought: it is already an illusion. If you take only one idea from this book, take this: look up the Army's Psy-Op Techniques Manual, with its myriad tactics of fallacious reasoning, obfuscation and brainwashing. Learn to see through the tricks that bombard us, and let your brain declare its independence. At www.freerepublic.com/focus/fr/546409/posts .

warning to Russia and the whole world of American supremacy. Not too surprisingly, the Russians obligingly responded, and the "Commie" threat was soon neatly spiked with nuclear warheads.[624] Then, hobbled by NATO, Europe lost her sovereignty, too.

Drunk on their superpower status, America's "elites" forgot, if they ever cared to know, that cooperation, not power, is the recipe for global happiness and prosperity. While maintaining the public mask of benevolence more adamantly than ever, America's real policy was now Realpolitik. A declassified memo features State Department planner George Kennan insisting that we must jettison "ideals" in order to maintain our 50% of world resources with only 6.3% of the population.[625]

---

[624] In *Rogue State*, Wm. Blum writes: "Dropping of the A-bomb was not the last shot of WWII but the first shot of the Cold War." Blum "compiles a record of the United states involvement, since World war II, in genocide, war crimes, use and training of foreign military police offices in torture, harboring terrorists and war criminals, use of biological and chemical weapons against civilians, assassinations, kidnapping and many other exposures of the true nature of U.S. foreign policy. 'From 1945 to the end of the century, the United States attempted to overthrow more than 40 foreign governments and to crush more than 30 populist-nationalist movements struggling against intolerable regimes. In the process, the U.S. caused the end of life for several million people, and condemned many millions more to a life of agony and despair.'"—From a Barnes & Noble online customer review.

A recent such attempt came on April 12, 2002. See Ted Rall, The Ugly American Redux, 'Bush Backs a Botched Coup in Venezuela,' www.uexpress.com/tedrall/. Also, the Spanish judge who prosecuted Pinochet wants Henry Kissinger to tell Interpol a few things about U.S. involvement in torture and murder in Latin America. On Radio Netherlands, 'Kissinger wanted for questioning,' April 19, 2002, www.rnw.nl/hotspots/html/spai020419.html.

[625] George Kennan, in a 1948 planning memo: "We have about 50 per cent of the world's wealth, but only 6.3 per cent of its population... In this situation, we cannot fail to be the object of envy and resentment. Our real task... to maintain this position of disparity without positive detriment to our national security. To do so we will have to dispense with all sentimentality and day-dreaming... We need not deceive ourselves that we can afford the luxury of altruism and world-benefaction... We should cease to talk about vague and... unreal objectives such as human rights, the raising of living standards, and democratization. The day is not far off

With the ignorant misconception that the world economy is a zero-sum game, half-educated think-tankers jettisoned not only "ideals," but the minimum bases of civilization, and even of modern capitalism, in favor of dog-eat-dog barbarism. The Enlightenment endarkened—Adam Smith, the pioneering thinker of capitalism, John Stuart Mill and the Utilitarian philosophers of freedom and responsibility, and all the other moral leaders who taught us about *enlightened* self-interest, Keynes and his teaching of the multiplication of prosperity, of win-win economics – all became mere fig leaves, gracing the superstition that might makes right—the base belief of bandits and bullies.

Madison warned of the connection between war and "degeneracy of manners and of morals." Can America at home really insulate itself from this crass immorality abroad? Is it any wonder that in America, civilization is a quaint synonym for technology? That our icon is the gun, divorce is our norm, and culture is a competition to strike new lows of vulgarity? Or was our Enlightenment flawed from the start, when the Jeffersonians tried to hold slaves and humanitarian ideals at the same time?

We proclaim that all human beings are equal – but to what, when we value money, power, speed, fame, almost anything, before humanity? This makes us at once a very-rich-and-powerful, and a very-poor-and-weak country: with an incidence of homelessness off the chart, and incarceration as one of our fastest growing business sectors.[626] So we look the other way, comforting ourselves with flags and self-praise, while America drops ever farther behind in the quality-of-living rankings.[627] Why worry, when there is still money to be made, franchising our weapons systems and our brand of empty materialism worldwide, until our cultural globe is wrapped in one-size-fits-all plastic.

---

when we will have to deal in straight power concepts. The less we are then hampered by idealistic slogans, the better." This fascist manifesto is quoted in Nafeez M. Ahmed, 'America in Terror – Causes and Context: The Foundational Principles of Western Foreign Policy and the Structure of World Order,' www.mediamonitors.net/mosaddeq12.html.

[626] The Bush Brothers, governors of Florida and Texas, conspired to deprive 57,700 purported "felons" of the vote in Florida – swinging the election. See Rep. Cynthia McKinney, Thoughts On Our War Against Terrorism, April 13, 2002, www.counterpunch.org/mckinney0413.html.

[627] See Carl Haber, 'American Illusions,' the plaint of a horror-struck returned expatriate, at www.mediamonitors.net/carlhaber1.html.

Kennan's zero-sum fallacy[628] is the key. If America would realize that "what goes around comes around," she is capable of world wonders far more miraculous than the war provocations our elite contrive to involve each generation in foreign affairs. If Americans could overcome false pride, and see the world as a two-way street, they could have a much richer life.

The Kennan memo that surfaced did not spell out specific 'non-idealistic' methods, but he did make clear his allegiance to the heinous creed of "the end justifies the means." His emphasis on "maintaining disparity" gives a clue, too: it isn't enough for us to be rich, a lot of other people have to be kept poor. We are familiar with the terms subversion and destabilization from Cold War anti-communist rhetoric, but in fact, Kennan's plan requires the U.S. to undermine much of the rest of the world by a double standard — democracy (of sorts) at home, any dictator who will cooperate abroad.[629]

Stalin was just one in a long line of voodoo icons and handy despots who underpinned the Kennan policy, like the CIA-trained protégés, Sadman Hussein, Noriega, and Osama bin Laden. The arch-villain Hitler, no less, proved useful even after his death,[630] as a justification for colonial expansion into the Old World and a new, rich field, the Middle East—at the end of the colonial era in Asia, and well after the discovery of oil.

The West encountered an inconvenient stumbling block to Kennan's global creed of greed — a few tribes of dusty Bedouins, bowing down to an other God than the almighty dollar, and sitting on seas of oil. Of course,

---

[628] For example, 'Major Issues For Vaccine Development in Developing Countries,' shows that the world-wide *one-time* costs to eradicate a disease can be less than the *annual* savings for the U.S. alone. At www.brown.edu/ Courses/Bio_160/Projects2000/VaccineIssues/Issues.html. Yet the U.S. is the world's stingiest wealthy country with "foreign aid."

[629] An online corpus of materials on subjects like the exporting of havoc can be found at sites like free.freespeech.org/americanstateterrorism/ books/Subject.html, and www.thirdworldtraveler.com/ TWTwebsite_INDEX.html.

[630] Brenner (see note 615 above op. cit.), documents how top planners in the World Zionist Organization scuttled humanitarian efforts to rescue European Jews from the Nazis. While they did not provoke the Holocaust, their key strategists saw it as the key to international support and the emigration of survivors to Palestine. This complicity in the mass murder of millions of their own has never been prosecuted, but it is one answer to those who ask, Would *our* leaders sacrifice thousands of their own people?

some of us might neutron nuke[631] them off the map, to avoid having to live within our own means. But the white knight costume and local satrap charade have served so well so far. Why ruin a good thing, when big arms sales to all sides there keep campaign coffers full, and help save the Middle East for servile sheikhs and "the only democracy" in the region.

Indeed, the consummate colonial Empire, the United Kingdom, knew that the Middle East is "a vital prize for any power interested in world influence or domination," since control of the world's oil reserves also means control of the world economy.[632] And the new superpower, the United States, already had a lively interest in world domination. A declassified secret document from 1953 records that: "United States policy is to keep the sources of oil in the Middle East in American hands."[633] Clearly, the United States aimed to dominate and control Middle East affairs to ensure its regional monopoly on resources, thus ensuring its leverage over the world economy, and consolidating its global hegemony.

U.S.-U.K. policy in the Middle East was clear: to suppress any movement threatening Western domination of the region. In 1958, a secret British document[634] articulated this policy and its ramifications, which included the demolition of "Arab nationalism" (meaning the indigenous population's desire for self-determination, the sacred principle to which Wilson gave lip service at Versailles):

> "The major British and other Western interests in the Persian Gulf [are] (a) to ensure free access for Britain and other Western countries to oil produced in States bordering the Gulf; (b) to ensure the continued availability of that oil on favourable terms and for surplus revenues of Kuwait; (c) to bar the spread of Communism and pseudo-Communism in the area and subsequently to defend the area against the brand of Arab nationalism."

---

[631] Jeffrey St. Clair, 'Trigger Happy – Bush administration hawks want to deploy "mini-nukes" against Osama bin Laden,' at www.inthesetimes.com/issue/25/26/news2.shtml.

[632] Introductory paper on the Middle East by the UK, undated [1947], FRUS, 1947, Vol. V, p. 569.

[633] NSC 5401, quoted in Heikal, Mohammed, 'Cutting the lion's tail: Suez through Egypt eyes,' Andre Deutsch, London, 1986, p. 38.

[634] File FO 371/132 779. 'Future Policy in the Persian Gulf,' 15 January 1958, FO 371/132 778.

The antipathy to "Arab nationalism" may be a relic of colonial policy after the First World War. The British Empire aimed to dismantle Ottoman Turkey, which had been the Muslim caliphate for four centuries and encompassed the areas of Syria, Iraq, Lebanon, Palestine, Jordan and much of Saudi Arabia. Local divisions were perpetuated by relying on pro-West Arab leaders with local tribal or religious followings, none whom, however, had a claim to popular leadership. Plans to sponsor uprisings were improvised by British officers in the Arab Bureau in Cairo. Sir Arthur Hirtzel of the India Office has candidly admitted that British aims were to divide the Arabs, not unify them.

This chaotic and bloody colonial programme succeeded in fracturing the Arab world into numerous impotent client regimes. The arbitrary creation of borders within what was formerly a single empire, carved the region into several divided segments, giving birth to twelve previously non-existent nations.[635] In all of these fictional nation-states, pro-West leaders were forcefully installed to execute Western instructions. This entire process involved the manipulation of the political environment to ensure the establishment of impotent client-regimes, whose social and economic administration was subservient to Western interests. This inevitably resulted in the impoverishment and repression of the Arab people under their newly formed, illegitimate governments. These regimes thus were dependent on the West for their sheer survival, in all significant respects.[636]

Americans need to stop, think and ask ourselves: Do policies that conflict with our ideals, with what we want for ourselves and our own children, really serve our interests? U.S. Deputy Defense Secretary Paul Wolfowitz said on this subject: "If people are really liberated to run their countries the way they want to, we'll have a world that will be very congenial for American interests."[637]

This counter-democratic policy had deep roots in the historical context of colonialism. Between 1820 and 1840, Mohamed Ali Pasha, "the Egyptian Napoleon," had the temerity to challenge Western hegemony by industrializing and uniting Egypt, Arabia and Syria. Britain and Austria sent

---

[635] The parallel to the post-colonial experience of Latin America and Africa could not be more exact, two continents that have been relegated to irrelevancy in world councils.

[636] See Said K. Aburish, *A Brutal Friendship: The West and the Arab Elite*, Indigo, London, 1998.

[637] 'For Wolfowitz, a Busy Life Being a Lightning Rod for Bush,' The New York Times, April 22, 2002.

forces to crush him. The trade route over Suez was kept for the crown, and the Islamic world was kept divided, dependent and under-industrialized to this day.[638]

To prevent any more such incidents, a colony was needed, as a wedge and a listening post between North Africa and the Middle East. The master stroke was to use the Jewish nation as a proxy, who would defend the land as their own—an idea introduced by prime minister Palmerston, and promoted later by Disraeli. The repatriation of the Jews to Palestine—latterly invoked as an alleged grievance by bin Laden—had thus been planned as a geopolitical gambit by Britain as early as 1840. That was the year before she invaded China, to quell resistance to her opium imports that were debilitating Chinese civilization. Today's CIA, with its drug dealing and undercover skulduggery, is merely following this old playbook from "perfidious Albion."

After 9/11, Americans engaged in a perhaps unprecedented soul-searching, including a remarkable effort to understand Islam. Yet, many pundits have obscured the issue by glossing over what are, in my opinion, the key Muslim grievances – the expulsion of the Palestinians by the Zionists in 1948, their continued miserable existence as refugees under Israeli occupation, and the dangers to Muslim and Christian shrines there.[639]

The influential economist and development theorist Samir Amin, Director of the African bureau of the Third World Forum, observes in the

---

[638] See 'An alternative path: the case of Egypt, Muhammed Ali and modernization,' Supplementary Readings in the History of the Ottoman Empire, Consortium for Middle Eastern and African Studies (CMEAS), University of Alberta, 1997, at www.humanities.ualberta.ca/ottoman/module4/tutorial4b.htm. After 1917, the Ottomans were replaced by the anti-Islamic strongman Kemal Ataturk, who made Turkey a Western bridgehead to Central Asia and the Middle East, and a regional industrial power.

[639] Background data: The West Bank of the Jordan and the Gaza Strip are the two remnants of Palestine remaining after the area currently known as Israel was ethnically cleansed in 1947-48. They were occupied in a "pre-emptive strike" made by Israel in 1967, after a series of preparatory provocations against its neighbors (see R. W. Howe, *Weapons: the international game of arms, money, and diplomacy*, 1980), and partly demilitarized during the "Oslo peace process," although the Gaza Strip retained the nickname of "concentration camp for 1.3 million people." See also http://dmoz.org/Society/Issues/Warfare_and_Conflict/Specific_Wars/Middle_East/Israel-Palestine.

United Nations University study *Maldevelopment: Anatomy of a global failure* that:

> "Zionism is a reactive response of Jewish communities to the oppression they suffered through centuries of European history...[Yet,] The appeal to pan-European solidarity against the peoples of Asia and Africa is a reality that still means something. Hence Zionism has succeeded in drawing on Western support from the right (and even sometimes the anti-semitic extreme right!) to the great majority of the left... Britain in the 19th century, the United States nowadays – have always deemed it essential to their predominance to maintain Egypt in such a ruinous condition that it could not become the pivot of a revived Arab nation, that is, a genuine partner in the worldwide capitalist system. The plan of creating an artificial European state in Palestine to undermine such a possibility, was dreamed up by Palmerston in 1839, a score of years before Zionism even took shape."[640]

As a regional watchdog dependent on the West for its security, the state of Israel would become a key instrument of U.S. policy in the region. Israel does not deny its strategic role as protector of U.S. interests in the Middle East. Retired Israeli General Shlomo Gazit, former Director of Military Intelligence and West Bank Administrator, has described in detail how, after the Cold War: "Israel's main task has not changed at all, and it remains of crucial importance. Its location at the center of the Arab Muslim Middle East predestines Israel to be a devoted guardian of the existing regimes: to prevent or halt the processes of radicalization and to block the expansion of fundamentalist religious zealotry." [641]

---

[640] Samir Amin, 'The Middle East conflict in a world perspective,' in *Maldevelopment: Anatomy of a Global Failure*, United Nations University Press, 1990, www.unu.edu/unupress/unupbooks/uu32me/uu32me0f.htm.

[641] *Yediot Aahronot*, 1992; cited in Lance Selfa, 'The U.S. and Israel,' *International Socialist Review*, Spring 1998, at www.isreview.org/issues/04/Israel_watchdog.shtml. See also Chomsky, Noam, 'The Middle East Settlement: Its Sources and Contours,' in *Power and Prospects*, South End Press, Boston, 1996, p. 165 and Shahak, Israel, *Open Secrets*, Pluto Press, London, 1997, p. 40-43.

"Gazit noted that Israel asserts its right to intervene militarily in any Arab state facing 'threats of revolt, whether military or popular, which may end up by bringing fanatical and extremist elements to power in the states concerned... The existence of such threats has no connection with the Arab-Israeli conflict. They exist because the regimes find it difficult to

In fact, though, religious animosity makes Israel useless as an overt proxy; this was obvious in the Gulf War, when Israel had to stay out for the U.S. coalition to hold together. The guarantee is rather of instability: *divide et impera,* assuring Jewish *and* Muslim dependency on American arms. No purely political and economic, "Marxian" explanation of the unique neo-colonialist phenomenon of Israel is adequate without weighing in the religious factor, and the complex relationship between the three monotheistic faiths.

In sociological terms, shared Scriptures and the Western sense of a Judeo-Christian tradition left Muslims beyond the pale, an outgroup, fair game. Puritan readings of the Bible found Jewish resettlement of the Holy Land to be the Will of God as early as the 17th century. This idea picked up support as the second millennium neared and the mass persecution of Jews in Europe sharpened. Worse, Christian fanatics even today praise the Lord over the violence in Palestine as a sign of the Second Coming, which they believe will give them eternal life in this body.[642] Purportedly numbering 70 million,

---

offer solutions to their socio-economic ills. But any development of the described kind is apt to subvert the existing relations between Israel and this or that from among its neighbors.'

"After the collapse of the USSR, 'the Israeli role as a strategic asset guaranteeing a modicum of stability in the entire Middle East did not dwindle or disappear but was elevated to the first order of magnitude. Without Israel, the West would have to perform this role by itself, when none of the existing superpowers really could perform it, because of various domestic and international constraints.' "

[642] See dmoz.org/Society/Politics/Nationalism/Zionism/Christian_ Zionism/, www.iraqwar.org/ArmageddonUpdates.htm, and www.virginiawater.co.uk/christchurch/articles/articles.html.
The dirty little secret of tens of millions of American Christian Zionists, dispensationalists, millenialists or what have you: in a nutshell, stranger than fiction, they believe that if the Jews regain "The Promised Land," and are subsequently wiped out in 'Armageddon,' Jesus will raise the believing Christians bodily to Heaven; so what's a few trillion in military aid to nudge prophecy along? "Based" on a few lines of St. Paul: "The Lord shall descend from heaven with a shout... the dead in Christ shall rise first: Then we... shall be caught up together with them... and so shall we ever be with the Lord." In the poetic metaphor loved by the ancients, this merely says that first those who are "dead to the world" ("detached" in the Buddhist tradition) will hear the call and arise (be enlightened, gain permanent wisdom), followed by the rest of us. Are these "born-again Christians"

The War on Freedom

fundamentalist Christian Zionists outnumber Jews in the U.S. by about 10 to one. A strange alliance:[643] divide-and-conquer cynicism met with irrational religion and ordinary racism—the idea of Negroes back to Africa, Jews back to Judea—in a broad Christian Zionist constituency, whose structure continues little changed today.

Of course, New England was also settled by persecuted religious minorities, followed by economic refugees. Colonialism generally has been propelled by such pressures within the mother country. Jewish Zionism also is composed of several major strands. Its founder, Theodore Herzl, a secular nationalist, was happy enough to accept a new homeland outside of Palestine; but without the Holy Land as a magnet, his project had little appeal for the orthodox masses. There were economic migrants among the poorer Jews, plus the financial and business elites. Again, the constellation has not changed much today, with unreligious economic refugees coming to Israel from Russia, radical right rabbis from Brooklyn, and the financial elite helping Israel with their investments and political support.[644] The pressures

---

dead to the world, or just brain-dead? What tea-leaf reader decided Paul wanted us to dynamite the Dome of the Rock? As for the Muslims of the Holy Land, they revere Jesus, and believe the second (and final) coming was Mohamed's – safely past.

Protestant Evangelicalism would appear to be in the last stages of decay into shamanism, making the United States the scariest example on earth of a foreign policy dictated by crazy cultists.

[643] Jonathan Rosenblum, 'Think Again: US Christians care more than US Jews,' *The Jerusalem Post*: "Many of Israel's staunchest supporters in Congress have traditionally come from states with small Jewish populations: e.g.,... John Ashcroft... they consistently line up on the opposite side from the organized Jewish community. These men support Israel not because of the mainstream Jewish community, but despite it... Devout Christians constitute the bedrock of American support for Israel. Such Christians number in the tens of millions. Unlike American Jews, they are not embarrassed by criticisms of Israel in certain left-wing circles... Christian supporters of Israel open up their Bibles and read that Israel is the Promised Land, promised to the Jews." Online at: www.jpost.com/Editions/2001/11/15/Columns/Columns.38205.html. See also Jim Lobe, 'Evangelical Christians and the Sharon lobby,' *Asia Times*, April 27, 2002, www.atimes.com/front/DD27Aa03.html, and www.jewishhistory.com/Occident/volume3/may1845/menasseh.html.

[644] Selfa, op. cit.: "Between 1949 and 1996, the U.S. gave Israel about $62.5 billion in foreign aid--about the same it gave all the countries of sub-

arising between these quarreling elements continue to favor fresh colonial expansion over peace.

Together, this Judeo-Christian coalition, thanks to the native ambition and entrepreneurial audacity of the Jewish elite, and the influence of their highly-placed Christian allies, was able to execute the dangerous decision to create a new homeland in the Old World – or should we say the ancient world, as a site more laden with sectarian controversy and history could hardly have been chosen.

In the 1980's, a new chapter of divide-and-conquer was opened. Zbigniew Brzezinski's remake of the Great Game,[645] unleashing Islamic fundamentalism on Russia, plowed the next fertile seedbed for cultivation of the rare flower of villainy—after seven decades of forced collectivization had tired out the Soviet soil. Ahmed has documented this in detail. I would only reiterate that such villain figures are trained, let loose on the world and lovingly nurtured for decades by the U.S.

Why didn't we topple Saddam Hussein?[646] What would we do without him, or Osama bin Laden?

Special handling has assured that bin Laden escapes after each exploit attributed to him. In December 2001, bin Laden's hiding place in the Tora Bora cave complex was heavily bombed—from the Afghan side—while exits to the safe haven of the Pakistani tribal areas were left virtually unguarded—accidentally on purpose, of course. As the editor of Jane's World Armies put

---

Saharan Africa, Latin America and the Caribbean during the same period. Israel remains the U.S.'s single greatest recipient of foreign assistance, pocketing more than $3 billion in aid each year. But even this figure underestimates the extent of U.S. assistance to Israel... One estimate placed the aid level at nearly $1,400 per Israeli citizen."

[645] Kipling's expression for the geopolitical struggle for Afghanistan, "Roof of the World" and "Silk Crossroads," as played between Russia, Britain and the indigenous Afghans during the 19th century.

[646] The Bush administration is breaking all the rules to fire José Bustani, the exemplary head of The Organisation for the Prohibition of Chemical Weapons, who has been trying to get the U.S. and Iraq to comply with inspections. George Monbiot, writing in *The Guardian*, April 16, 2002, believes the motive is to foreclose the possibility of Iraqi compliance, which would remove the excuse for war. "Bustani has to go because he has proposed the solution to a problem the U.S. does not want solved." At www.guardian.co.uk/Iraq/Story/0,2763,685155,00.html.

it, "the U.S. military campaign, apart from not capturing Mr. bin Laden was, up to that point, staggeringly effective."[647]

At the very least, there is some sort of gentleman's agreement here, like the one with Saddam Hussein. The dictator and CIA protégé has proven immensely useful for his wars against Iran, Kuwait, the Kurds, and his own people. The U.S. lets him hang on to power for decades on the theory *"better the devil you know."* The U.S. is currently eagerly exploring other potential alternatives to Saddam in the hope of installing a more subservient regime in the oil-rich region, based on the same brand of strategy used in the Afghan "test-case."

The devil the U.S. doesn't want to know is the djinn of democracy, which, if unleashed from the Middle Eastern bottle, might spell Muslim unity in place of the subservient fiefdoms that are putty in the hands of U.S. and Israeli policymakers.[648] The CIA and MI6 torpedoed the best chance democracy had in the Middle East when they staged the overthrow of Iran's President Mossadegh – Time Magazine's 1951 Man of the Year[649] – and

[647] Philip Smucker, 'How bin Laden got away,' *Christian Science Monitor*, Mar. 4, 2002, at www.csmonitor.com/2002/0304/p01s03-wosc.html, as well as chat forum with reporter Smucker at csmonitor.com/monitortalk/events/pastevents/0304chatLog.html. See also 'U.S. Protection of Osama,' p. 197 ff . Is bin Laden just "wearing the black hat"for the USA?

[648] Nina Burleigh, 'Missing the Oil Story,' synopsis in *South Asia Voice*, at http://members.tripod.com/~INDIA_RESOURCE/mideastoil.html. Also see Nafeez M. Ahmed, 'The 1991 Gulf Massacre: The Historical and Strategic Context of Western State Terrorism in the Gulf,' Media Monitors Network, www.mediamonitors.net/mosaddeq14.html. Explains how oil policy dictated the carving up of the region into states with artificial boundaries, such as the Emirates, Iraq, Kurdistan, the Zionist project, all under repressive regimes. Quotes a 1953 internal U.S. document: "United States policy is to keep the sources of oil in the Middle East in American hands." Forecasts U.S. dependency on Central Asian oil. Also, in 'Israel: The U.S. Watchdog' (see note 650), " 'The Israeli establishment knows that an Arab democracy will be much stronger than any Arab autocratic regime,' the radical Israeli human rights campaigner Israel Shahak explained. Israel wants an authoritarian Palestinian bantustan in the occupied territories because it knows that 'democracy will strengthen the Palestinians while Israel wants to keep them weak.' "

[649] The Time magazine Man of the Year article on Mossadegh is at www.time.com/time/special/moy/1951.html. The declassified official CIA history of the 1953 coup is at www.iranian.com/History/2000/April/CIA/

replaced him with the Shah and his infamous secret police, in order to keep the Anglo-American lock on oil supplies.

Queen Victoria's planners had an acute grasp of geopolitics; Israel today is indeed the U.S. watchdog in the Middle East.[650] But how is this thumbnail history related to 9/11? Intimately, if we accept the conventional view about "Islamic terrorism" and "Palestinian terror groups." Furthermore, evidence of a Middle Eastern and specifically Israeli connection to 9/11, not yet discussed by Ahmed, is significant and intriguing enough to inspect in brief here, without making a hasty judgment.

On September 10, 2001, the Washington Times printed an article about a report from the U.S. Army School of Advanced Military Studies (SAMS), giving this assessment of Mossad, Israel's military intelligence agency: "Wildcard. Ruthless and cunning. Has capability to target U.S. forces and make it look like a Palestinian/Arab act."[651] The date of publication was an odd coincidence. Had someone caught a straw in the wind?

Cutting up

News reports about these leads are sketchy, but the inexplicable facts they contain are suspicious enough to be addressed in any public inquiry into 9/11. The Washington Post reported, "On Sept. 11, five young Israeli army veterans who worked for a moving company were observed at a park on the Hudson River in New Jersey, snapping photographs of the burning World

---

(first published in The New York Times, April 16, 2000). The role of MI6 and the Anglo-Iranian Oil Co. – today's British Petroleum – can be seen at www.lobster-magazine.co.uk/articles/l30iran.htm, in an excerpt from Mark Curtis' book, *The Ambiguities of Power: British Foreign Policy since 1945* (Zed Press, 1995). Curtis is a former Research Fellow at the Royal Institute of International Affairs in London.

[650] Lance Selfa, 'The U.S. Watchdog,' op. cit., a Marxian analysis characterizing Israel as an artificial state, subsidized by the West to maintain repressive regimes in the region and globally, through armed intervention and assassinations. See also S. Marshall, P. D. Scott and J. Hunter, 'Contracting Out U.S. Foreign Policy,' in *The Iran-Contra Connection*, mentioning Mossad involvement in the Iran arms deals and setting up of Somoza's death squads. Excerpts at www.thirdworldtraveler. com/Ronald_Reagan/ContractingOut_TICC.html.

[651] Rowan Scarborough, 'U.S. troops would enforce peace under Army study,' *The Washington Times,* Sept. 10, 2001, www.iiie.net/Sept11/ MossadTargetsUS.html.

Trade Center and seemingly clowning around. To complicate matters, when authorities arrested them they had box-cutters in their moving van, the types of weapons used by the terrorist hijackers."[652] The Bergen Record provided further insight into the event, reporting that:

"Eight hours after terrorists struck Manhattan's tallest skyscrapers, police in Bergen County detained five men who they said were found carrying maps linking them to the blasts... sources close to the investigation said they found other evidence linking the men to the bombing plot. 'There are maps of the city in the car with certain places highlighted,' the source said. 'It looked like they're hooked in with this. It looked like they knew what was going to happen when they were at Liberty State Park.' Sources also said that bomb-sniffing dogs reacted as if they had detected explosives.[653] The FBI seized the van for further testing, authorities said... Sources close to the investigation said the men said they were Israeli tourists... 'We got an alert to be on the lookout for a white Chevrolet van with New Jersey registration and writing on the side,' said Bergen County Police Chief John Schmidig. 'Three individuals were seen celebrating in Liberty State Park after the impact. They said three people were jumping up and down.' "[654]

Local police had been prompted to intervene after receiving the following FBI alert: "Vehicle possibly related to New York terrorist attack. White, 2000 Chevrolet van with New Jersey registration with 'Urban Moving Systems' sign on back seen at Liberty State Park, Jersey City, NJ, at the time of first impact of jetliner into World Trade Center. Three individuals with van were seen celebrating after initial impact and subsequent explosion. FBI Newark Field Office requests that, if the van is located, hold for prints and detain individuals."[655]

The *New York Times* and *Jerusalem Post* reported that angry, suspicious neighbors had mistaken the group for Arabs "going to unusual lengths to

---

[652] '60 Israelis on Tourist Visas Detained Since Sept. 11,' www.washingtonpost.com/ac2/wp-dyn/A3879-2001Nov22. More details at www.americanfreepress.net/12_08_01/Ashcroft_Talking/ ashcroft_talking.html.

[653] There are many, widely and wildly conflicting reports on the Internet of bomb explosions in the WTC towers after they were hit, e.g., www.cyberspaceorbit.com. See also note 680.

[654] Paulo Lima, 'Five Men Detained as Suspected Conspirators,' Bergen Record, Sept. 12, 2001.

[655] Ibid.

photograph the World Trade Center ruins," "some with themselves in the foreground smiling" and significantly "making light of the situation," posing and laughing on and in front of their moving van, with the scene of WTC destruction in the background.[656] The *New York Post* clarified that witnesses had seen them "cheering" and "jumping up and down" in apparent joy.[657] According to the *Jewish Week*:

> "In the moving van they were driving for their employer, Urban Moving Systems in Weehawken, N.J., the men — ages 22 to 27 and all single — carried box cutters. One had $4,000 in cash, another had a camera, and a third had two passports because he is also a German citizen. They were stopped by police at about 3 p.m. Sept. 11 after two women saw them standing on the roofs of the moving company and their van, smiling as they took pictures of each other with the burning World Trade Center in the background."

The "movers" were all on tourist visas; they were all employed as a team, without work permits, for an Israeli-owned company, and two more employees of the firm were also arrested for questioning by the FBI. Their spokesman was planning to fly to India "to meet friends" on September 14.[658]

The FBI, especially after developing their film, suspected them of being Mossad agents, kept them in solitary confinement and wanted to keep them in custody for at least another 90 days. But the five Israelis refused to give information about their type of military experience, or anything else. The *New York Times* reported coyly that one of them, Paul Kurzberg, the group's effective spokesman, "had trouble" with a seven-hour polygraph test, but "did better on a second try" – in other words, failed them both. Kurzberg had "refused on principle to divulge much about his role in the Israeli army or subsequently working for people who may have had ties to Israeli

---

[656] *New York Times*, Nov. 21, 2001, also, Melissa Radler, 'Israelis mistaken for terrorists may be home soon,' *Jerusalem Post*, 26 October 2001. Trophy photos can be a part of military culture, and the IDF (Israeli Defence Forces) is no exception. See the dissident IDF soldiers' website, http://oznik.com/kolhair13.html; also Inigo Gilmore, 'Israel Probes Trophy Claims,' *The Telegraph*, Oct. 15, 2001: "I remember one terrible photo of the soldiers smiling like children as they stood on the bodies with their boots, really enjoying the moment." At www.palestinemonitor.org/ archives/ israelis_pose_with_dead_palestinians.htm.

[657] Al Guart, 'Trio Who Cheered Attack Face Boot as Illegal Aliens', *New York Post*, Sept. 13, 2001.

[658] Stewart Ain, 'Caught in a Dragnet', *Jewish Week*, Nov. 2, 2001.

352   The War on Freedom

intelligence." Yet Kurzberg's release was soon arranged on the personal order of Attorney General John Ashcroft. The respected New York-based Jewish newspaper *Forward* disclosed that "top-ranking Israeli diplomats" had intervened with Ashcroft on the group's behalf, securing their release and deportation on minor immigration charges.[659]

It has now been confirmed, in spite of official denials, that the group of five Israelis rescued by Ashcroft were, indeed, working for the Israeli intelligence agency Mossad. America's most prominent Jewish newspaper *Forward* reported that: "According to one former high-ranking American intelligence official, who asked not to be named, the FBI came to the conclusion at the end of its investigation that the five Israelis... were conducting a Mossad surveillance mission and that their employer, Urban Moving Systems of Weehawken, N.J., served as a front."[660]

This is more than enough to wonder whether we didn't have several key culprits in 9/11 behind bars, and release them because of high-level U.S.-Israeli intervention. It is worth speculating on the possibilities here. A moving company, for instance, would have been a perfect cover; they could transport equipment in their van, and bring it into the WTC in their uniforms. They absolutely did not cooperate with the police, and in the circumstances, all they had to do was deny everything and wait for help. It came soon, partly in the form of a weepy PR offensive, making them out as bewildered mama's boys and victims of stern justice. Several parallels will be noted between their escape and the Mexican Congress case discussed on page 361.

The dubious activities of these young Israeli intelligence operatives, apparently rejoicing at the impact of the WTC attacks, appears to have had a broader context. FOX News recently reported the FBI's uncovering of large-scale Israeli espionage in the U.S., with a ring of 60 Israeli spies arrested. The Washington Post elaborated in the subheading of an article on the subject that: "Government Calls Several Cases 'of Special Interest,' Meaning Related to Post-Attacks Investigation."

INS officials testified in immigration court hearings that the 60 Israeli spies were "of special interest to the government" – the same pretext for detaining Arabs in connection with the 9/11 investigation. An INS official who requested anonymity said the agency will not comment on the Israelis, but clarified that the term "special interest" means the case in question is "related to the investigation of Sept. 11." The Post also noted that "many of

---

[659] *New York Times*, Nov. 21, 2001; *Forward*, Nov. 23, 2001; *Jerusalem Post*, Oct. 26, 2001.

[660] *Forward*, March 15, 2002.

them [were] held on U.S. government officials' invocation of national security," and had served in special anti-terrorist and intelligence units.[661]

All wiretapping in the U.S. and virtually all telephone billing has been handled for years by two Israeli companies, Comverse and Amdocs — as approved by a somewhat reluctant Congress! Thus, "FOX News[662] has learned that some American terrorist investigators fear certain suspects in the Sept. 11 attacks may have managed to stay ahead of them, by knowing who and when investigators are calling on the telephone."[663]

In the first of a four-part series on an Israeli connection, FOX News correspondent Carl Cameron reported on the detained Israeli spy ring that:

"A handful of active Israeli military were among those detained, according to investigators, who say some of the detainees also failed polygraph questions when asked about alleged surveillance activities *against and in the United States* [emphasis added]… investigators suspect that they [sic] Israelis may have gathered intelligence about the attacks in advance, and not shared it. A highly placed investigator said there are – quote – 'tie-ins'. But when asked for details, he flatly refused to describe them, saying, – quote – 'evidence linking these Israelis to 9-11 is classified. I cannot tell you about evidence that has been gathered. It's classified information.' Fox News has learned that

---

[661] John Mintz, '60 Israelis on Tourist Visas Detained Since Sept. 11,' *Washington Post*, Nov. 22, 2001, www.washingtonpost.com/ac2/wp-dyn?pagename=article&node=&contentId=A3879-2001Nov22.

[662] Brit Hume and Carl Cameron, Fox News Correspondent. Fox ran a series on the Israeli spy ring, then erased the stories from its site. They are archived around the web, e.g. www.angelfire.com/oh2/elevatorbrewing/houston51.htm.

[663] Justin Raimondo has written most extensively on the Israeli-911 connection, see http://antiwar.com/israelfiles2.html.
See also Charles Smith, 'Spying on America,' www.newsmax.com/archives/articles/ 2002/1/16/110443.shtml, "Israeli ingenuity in infiltrating and exploiting the U.S. high-tech industry may be seriously undermining the security and power of the country that is, in fact, the ultimate guarantor of its existence." And, E. Spannaus and J. Steinberg, 'Israeli Spying in U.S. – Exposé Cracks Coverup of Sept. 11, *Executive Intelligence Review*, www.larouchepub.com/other/2001/ 2849isr_spies_911. html: "Investigators within the DEA, INS and FBI have all told Fox News that to pursue or even suggest Israeli spying through Comverse is considered career suicide."

one group of Israelis, spotted in North Carolina recently, is suspected of keeping an apartment in California to spy on a group of Arabs who the United States is also investigating for links to terrorism."[664]

The detained Israelis, in other words, had been part of a vast intelligence operation that had very possibly been tracking the hijackers, and had both the means and the opportunity to discover the terrorist plot. Indeed, somewhat ominously, the U.S. government has refused to disclose the already existing "evidence linking these Israelis to 9-11," ensuring instead that it remains "classified."

The FOX News series also detailed extensive Israeli penetration of U.S. defense and government facilities. A larger group of as many as 120 "Israeli art students" were arrested after 9/11 for suspiciously "casing" high-security government facilities, while pretending to sell paintings. "The detained Israelis served in Israeli military intelligence, surveillance, and explosive ordinance units." An even larger ring of Israelis without visas left their sales jobs so quickly after September 11 that the company that hired them was temporarily closed down. These people may have been in surveillance, perhaps in preparation of further "simultaneous attacks,"[665] which were foiled or called off as it became apparent that September 11 had been quite enough.

French intelligence expert Guillaume Dasquié, who is Editor of the respected newsletter Intelligence Online and co-author of *Bin Laden: The Forbidden Truth*, reveals the contents of a classified 61-page report by a U.S. interagency task force led by the Drugs Enforcement Administration (DEA), whose Office of Security Programs was first confronted with "unusual behavior of young Israeli nationals who had gained access to DEA circles." The Israeli "art students" are, in fact, members of an Israeli intelligence network operating in the U.S., consisting of "around 20 units composed of between four and eight members each." Dasquié continues:

> "A few of the operatives are well known in the Israeli intelligence community. The report cited the names of Peer Segalovitz (military registration number 5087989) and Aran Ofek, son of a renowned two-star general in the Israeli army. The network targeted some of the most sensitive sites in the U.S., such as Tinker Air Force Base near Oklahoma City. Indeed, the U.S. Air Force's Office of Special Investigation sent a letter to the Justice Department on May 16 of last

---

[664] FOX News, Dec. 11, 2001.

[665] See also notes 662 and 711.

year to ask for assistance in a case against four Israelis suspected of spying: Yaron Ohana, Ronen Kalfon, Zeev Cohen and Naor Topaz."

The Israeli intelligence operatives, under their cover of "art students," "cultivated contacts with Israeli information technology companies based in the U.S. and serving as regular suppliers to various U.S. federal agencies, such as Amdocs."[666] The DEA document, whose authenticity is confirmed by accounts from official U.S. intelligence sources,[667] continues to record that: "The activities of these Israeli art students raised the suspicion of [the DEA's Office of Security Programs] and other field offices when attempts were made to circumvent the access control systems at DEA offices, and when these individuals began to solicit their paintings at the homes of DEA employees. The nature of the individuals' conduct, combined with intelligence information and historical information regarding past incidents [involving Israelis, leads the DEA] to believe the incidents may well be an organized intelligence gathering activity."

There were scores of encounters between federal agents and Israelis describing themselves as art students, who in fact appeared to be attempting to gain access to sensitive U.S. offices and military installations. Paragraph 82 of the document records, for example, how MacDill Air Force Base intelligence officers were warned in March 2001 of the Israeli students' efforts. A month later, another special alert warned of "possible intelligence collection effort" by the Israelis at Tinker Air Force Base in Oklahoma City. U.S. counterintelligence officials issued a bulletin on March 23, 2001, asserting the existence of an "ongoing security threat" in the form of intelligence agents operating as "Israeli National Art Students that are targeting government offices selling 'artwork.'"[668]

---

[666] Credit goes to U.S. columnist Justin Raimondo for his lucid summary and compilation of these facts in '9/11: The Truth Comes Out,' Antiwar.Com, Center for Libertarian Studies, California, March 8, 2002, www.antiwar.com/justin/j030802.html.

[667] Ted Bidris reports in 'U.S. Deports Israeli Spy Suspects,' Associated Press, March 5, 2002, that: "The DEA report was first obtained by a French Web site that specializes in intelligence news, Intelligenceonline.com, and confirmed Tuesday as authentic by DEA spokeswoman Rogene Waite in Washington."

[668] For in-depth discussion of the DEA report and related facts see John F. Suggs, 'The Spies Who Came in from the Art Sale,' *Weekly Planet* (Tampa Bay), March 20, 2002, www.weeklyplanet.com/2002-03-20/news_feature.html. In a separate case, the ADL (Anti-Defamation

The *Weekly Planet* reports that "addresses of many" of the "Arabs under scrutiny by the U.S. government" systematically "correspond to the specific areas where the Israelis set up operations." One extremely pertinent example is "an address for the Sept. 11 hijacking leader, Mohammad Atta," which is "3389 Sheridan St. in Hollywood, Fla., only a few blocks and a few hundred feet from the address of some of the Israelis, at 4220 Sheridan." The strange coordination between Atta and Israeli intelligence operatives is not an isolated case. About a "dozen Israelis, including the alleged surveillance leader, had been based in Hollywood, Fla., between January and June [2001] – quite possibly watching Arabs living nearby who are suspected of providing logistical support to Osama bin Laden's network." Indeed, ten of the 19 Al-Qaeda hijackers lived in Florida, bolstering conclusions reported by a FOX News reporter that "the students-cum-spies might have gained advance knowledge of aspects of the Sept. 11 terrorists" – or even worse, may have been directly involved in some way.[669]

Unfortunately, these facts have been shoved out of the confines of mainstream cogitations, and are now blithely ignored. "The biggest story of our time, of Israel spying on all branches of the government, on all our intelligence agencies – in the CIA, the DEA and the White House itself," observed Carl Cameron on a CSPAN TV show, "is not picked up by the leading newspapers like the New York Times and the Washington Post."[670] The authoritative military and intelligence analysis service Jane's Information Group similarly criticizes the resounding silence on a subject which of course is of critical importance to U.S. national security, not to mention a proper understanding of 9/11: "It is rather strange that the U.S. media, with one notable exception, seem to be ignoring what may well prove to be the most explosive story since the 11 September attack, the alleged breakup of a major Israeli espionage operation in the United States, which aimed to infiltrate both the Justice and Defense departments, and which may

---

League), which fights alleged anti-Semitism, has been found guilty of spying on up to 10,000 Americans, including many Jews (and of defamation itself, by false accusations of anti-Semitism). See Barbara Ferguson, Arab News Correspondent, 'ADL found guilty of spying by California court,' April 25, 2002, at www.arabnews.com/Article.asp?ID=14650; or, *The Progressive Review*, on ADL spying for South Africa's apartheid regime, http://prorev.com/feb26.htm.

[669] Ibid.

[670] Mohamed Hakki, 'What tiger?', *Al-Ahram Weekly*, January 24-30, 2002, Issue No. 570, www.ahram.org.eg/weekly/2002/570/in1.htm.

also have been tracking al-Qaida terrorists before the aircraft hijackings took place."[671]

The case of the Odigo Company is perhaps the icing on the cake. Odigo is an Israeli-based instant messaging software company with New York offices in the vicinity of the World Trade Center. The online Washington Post news service Newsbytes reported that officials from the firm "confirmed today that two employees received text messages warning of an attack on the World Trade Center two hours before terrorists crashed planes into the New York landmarks... the company declined to reveal the exact contents of the message or to identify the sender." Alex Diamandis, vice president of sales and marketing, confirmed that the workers in Odigo's research, development and international sales office in Israel "received a warning from another Odigo user approximately two hours prior to the first attack... the employees recorded the Internet protocol [IP] address of the message's sender to facilitate his or her identification."[672] The Israeli daily *Ha'aretz* has elaborated that: "Micha Macover, CEO of the company, said the two workers received the messages and immediately after the attack informed the company's management, which immediately contacted Israeli security services, which brought in the FBI." The FBI has remained tight-lipped about the results of its investigation ever since, although tracking down the original sender through the IP address is hardly a complicated task.[673] The incident suffices to quite strongly suggest that someone in Israel, at least, had advance warnings of the attacks – and in light of the data discussed previously, may have derived warning from Israeli spies carrying out intelligence operations around Al-Qaeda terrorists in the U.S.

Another provocative collection of evidence on Israeli involvement I have had the luck to find, thanks to Media Monitors Network, is a book being published in Germany by journalist Wolfgang Eggert:[674] :

1. 1999: Israel's new military strategy, to evolve from a regional to a world power which will carry out attacks farther afield in the Islamic

[671] *Jane's Information Group*, March 13, 2002.

[672] Brian McWilliams, 'Instant Messages To Israel Warned Of WTC Attack,' *Newsbytes*, September 27, 2001, www.newsbytes.com/news/01/170583.html.

[673] Yuval Dror, 'Odigo Says Workers Were Warned of Attack,' *Ha'aretz*, April 24, 2002, www.haaretzdaily.com/hasen/pages/ShArt.jhtml?itemNo=77744&contrassID=/has%5C.

[674] Wolfgang Eggert, *Angriff der Falken*, (*Attack of the War Hawks*), ISBN: 3-935845-05-7.

world,[675] precisely foreshadows "The War on Terror" in its scope and methods. Eggert argues that Israel could not risk forging Arab unity by carrying out the strategy alone, but must operate behind the shield of U.S. mobilization.

2. 2000: Israel begins to carry out the plan by cooperating with India over Kashmir. Soon after, Pakistan holds the Indian and Israeli secret services responsible for the explosion of fundamentalist violence there.

3. 2000: Months after Pakistan and Afghanistan are named as spheres of activity in Israel's new global military doctrine, both countries accuse Israel of supporting Islamic fundamentalist terrorists in their own countries.

4. 2000/1: In January 2000, eleven "Muslims"—Afghans or Palestinians with Israeli passports—are detained by authorities at Calcutta airport on their way to Bangladesh, but are soon released on pressure from Israel. Indian secret service people thought their mission was to infiltrate *"an organization like bin Laden's"* from Muslim Bangladesh. They had been on the lookout for eight Afghans whom they believed were planning to hijack the flight.[676]

5. 2001/3: Andrej Kosjakov, former Deputy Chairman of the Soviet Union's Espionage Oversight Committee, testifies that Israel carried out studies on aerial terrorist action in early 2001.

6. 2001/4: Soon after Sharon's election, months before September 11, a firm owned 50% by the Israeli government prematurely cancels its lease on its extensive offices in the WTC and moves out.

7. 2001/9: A veritable host of discrepancies concerning the alleged hijackers.

8. 2002: On March 6, 2002, France's most serious newspaper *Le Monde* reports that one of the tasks of arrested Israeli spies was to "monitor Al-Qaeda terrorists in America, *without informing the American authorities*."

Which ones? we might ask. The money to be made by shorting airline shares is small crumbs to the windfall that could come from foreknowledge of oil prices. The price of gasoline dropped sharply after 9/11 to 90 cents,

---

[675] From a Salzburg daily, Jan. 28, 1999, and *Jane's Foreign Report*.

[676] Subir Bhaumik, BBC's eastern India correspondent, 'Aborted mission Investigation: Did Mossad attempt to infiltrate Islamic radical outfits in south Asia?' *The Week of India*, Feb. 6, 2000, www.the-week.com/ 20feb06/ events2.htm.

then bounced back to $1.60, after a deal with Russia and a squeeze on Iraq. Pocket money for top American officials with links to the oil industry and the State Department?

Are we really so different from Russia, where oilogarchs occupy the Kremlin?[677] Curious how the new bear-hugging friendship comes with an accord to parcel out Muslim oil territories between the great rivals. Chechnya[678] for Putin, the rest for Bush, and no more side-swiping about human rights. Curious, too, how closely Bush has followed the Putin playbook to popular support.

On September 23, 1999, just one week after the second bomb blast in Moscow, residents in an apartment block in Moscow-Ryazan found bags in their basement containing a substance that looked like hexogen, the explosive used in the first two apartment bombings. The local FSB (secret police) department announced that day that an act of terrorism had been prevented. However, the federal FSB later said it was just a training exercise.[679]

Because agents of the FSB, the secret police, were seen and their car identified leaving the scene of the crime, the FSB had to switch their cover story to the training alibi. Officially and in the mass media, the Chechens were blamed, although *no suspects were found*. Sound familiar? The apartment bombings put Putin the politician on the map, galvanizing popular support for a new war in Chechnya, with him as fearless leader. Oddly enough, Putin had previously been head of the FSB. And Bush Sr. was CIA Director. Why try a new recipe, when old ones work?[680]

[677] Judicial Watch, April 1, 2002, "the recent spate of terror attacks on Israel has lent new urgency to the need for former President Bush to resign from the Carlyle Group." At www.judicialwatch.org/1685.shtml.

[678] Nafeez M. Ahmed, The Smashing of Chechnya, http://mediamonitors. net/ mosaddeq5.html, quotes testimony from numerous reliable sources that "FSB officers were caught red-handed while planting the bomb," and that the war against Chechnya had been planned six months earlier...

[679] A Chechen website reports that after falling out with Putin, who closed down his TV stations, the powerful tycoon Berezovsky began campaigning from his London exile for an investigation of the Ryazan incident, but without making much of a dent on mass opinion. At www.ichkeria.org/a/ 2002/1/com2201-en82227.html.

[680] According to aerospace engineer Joe Vialls, the Cessna that hit the White House in 1994 was probably a test run for a remote autopiloted plane bombing, see www.geocities.com/roboplanes/cessna.html.
One theory circulating on the Internet is that the Boeings were steered

Israeli-Russian-Indian "anti-terror" cooperation[681] bore fruit after 9/11, too, as the scenario of multiple "Islamic terror" attacks on a world-wide front was played out. Fundamentalist terrorists bombed the parliament in Kashmir (Reichstag *again?*), Hindu national passions were invoked, and soon pogroms were unleashed against Muslims in India.[682] Pakistan was brought to the brink and shown the abyss.

---

from the ground by remote control. It explains how such inadequate pilots as the hijackers could carry out their approach patterns. This has been partly corroborated officially: "Investigators later determined that [Flight 77] had been flying on autopilot on its path over the Pentagon," (M. Wald and K. Sack, *New York Times*, syndicated in The Atlanta Constitution Journal, Oct. 16, 2001, at www.accessatlanta.com/ajc/terrorism/investigation/1016tapes.html.) The planes that hit the WTC reportedly also displayed the rapid aileron flutter characteristic of an autopilot closing in on its transmitter. Since the minimum electronics would be only a small transmitter for the autopilots to lock onto, this hypothesis doesn't tell us much about who did it, as cheap remote-controlled vehicles can be found in toy shops. Interestingly, Flight 93, which was apparently destined for the White House but crashed in Pennsylvania, struggled and failed to hold course, that is, without the benefit of an autopilot.

A really wild theory is that only one plane really crashed, the one in Pennsylvania. The passengers were supposedly transferred to it from the other flights at a military airfield, and someone stole 3 Boeings. It is averred the Pentagon attack was really a truck bomb, because no airplane wreckage was shown. This theory made a stir in France, where a book on it, "L'imposture effroyable," reportedly sold out in two hours. It purports to explain how 4 flights could be so empty, when full flights were the rule.

[681] Reuven Paz, ICT Academic Director, 'Israeli-Indian Cooperation for Counter-Terrorism,' an Israeli description of a wave of high-level meetings on "anti-terror cooperation" between Israel, India and Russia, mid-2000, is at www.ict.org.il/articles/articledet.cfm?articleid=114.

[682] On Bush's coattails, India's Prime Minister Vajpayee has franchised his own War on Freedom, arousing fears among liberal Hindus for "the world's largest democracy." See Siddharth Varadarajan, 'I salute you, Geetaben, from the bottom of my heart,' in *The Indian Times*. Geetaben was a Hindu woman, blown to pieces on March 25 by the ruling Hindu separatists for falling in love with a Muslim man. "For all his fulminations against jehad, Mr Vajpayee's ideology is equally jehadi. His party does not believe in people living in peace, in ensuring that the citizens of India — whether Hindu, Muslim or other — have the wherewithal to live as human

Provocation, invocation, retribution, and redistribution—the legions are drawing lots to carve up a defenseless Islamic world.

The Smoking Gun

A full-blown investigation into the facts surrounding the Israeli connection to 9/11 is of immense importance. For there can be little doubt that this brief documented overview confirms an Israeli connection to 9/11.

One does not need to jump to conclusions about 9/11 from the track record of suspected Israeli undercover operations over the decades in the U.S. and elsewhere. Buried in the far recesses of Google, away from skimming net surfers, for deep-sea trawlers only, as it were, I found astonishing reports of how Israeli agents were caught red-handed in a bombing attempt, in Mexico City, on October 11, 2001.

Why Mexico? A good answer was posted on Pravda's English-language forum, by an American who commutes across the border to work:

"Shortly after the 9/11 incident, Gallup took a poll in a lot of countries, and it turned out that in all of Latin America, support was very low for the planned US war effort. Mexico had the lowest margin of support, with only 2% of the population in favor of a war. This probably dropped to even less than that shortly after the poll was taken when Mexican papers revealed the connections between the Bush and Bin Laden families, and much hay was made of that by editorialists.

---

beings. The BJP does not respect the rights of citizens or of the nation as a whole. Instead, a bogus, hollow ideology of 'Hindutva' has been erected to cover up their utter contempt for the rights of the people of India." The old party trick of Waving the Flag to hide robbery and murder.

See also *Hindustan Times*, April 26, 2002, 'Gujarat toll is 2,000, and it was genocide: Report': "The brutal violence unleashed in Gujarat following the burning of 58 Hindu train passengers claimed nearly 2,000 lives, a fact-finding report says... the economic loss suffered by Muslims all over the state totals a staggering Rs 35 billion. Also, mobs linked to the Gujarat government and the ruling BJP destroyed or damaged nearly 270 mosques. 'Even during the unspeakable horrors that communities inflicted on each other in 1946 and 1947, all organs of the state had not been directly involved in stoking the fires,' it said. 'Not so in Gujarat, 2002.'" The report was issued by the Hindu editors of an anti-sectarian magazine, *Communalism Combat*. At www.hindustantimes.com/nonfram/270402/dlnat09.asp.

One may well ask if the "War on Terror" is really a War of Terror.

Meanwhile, Mexican president Vicente Fox and foreign minister Jorge Castaneda (whose mother is Jewish, by the way) declared that Mexico was behind Bush and that they would even send troops if Bush wanted them to. [The late Castaneda Sr. also served as foreign minister in his day.] This was met with outrage in Mexico, and since Mexico is actually the most influential country in Latin America... a bad sign for those who had a vested interest in the progress of the war party.

This has been discussed [in the Mexican media] as the only possible reason for the attempted terrorist act on the part of the Israelis... Hispanics are the largest minority in the US, of which Mexicans make up the largest block."

Mexican editors unanimously took this for an attempt to turn the public relations tide for the U.S. war, just as I have been suggesting that one effect of the 9/11 attacks was to turn the PR tide for Israel.

The botched bombing thus points to a convergence of aims, an alliance of Bush's war in Central Asia, and Sharon's war on the Palestinian refugees.

Now to the misdeeds. Two Israeli citizens sneaked past security into the Chamber of Deputies – Mexico's Congress or Parliament – posing as cameramen. When they aroused suspicion, security guards found that they were armed with: 9-mm plastic Glock pistols (undetectable by metal detectors), nine grenades, several sticks of explosives, three detonators and 58 cartridges.

Obviously – and if being caught red-handed is not obvious to you, and you want them caught after they blow the place sky-high, and come running out in the melee, disguised and armed to the teeth; or if you think this kind of thing happens all the time, and that any connection between 9/11 and 10/11 should simply be ignored – then I can't help you, and you might have bought a cookbook instead of wasting your day reading these 400 pages, or maybe you could try getting into the U.S. Congress with all that paraphernalia yourself – obviously, this was supposed to be another Reichstag or Srinagar.

Srinagar is the capital of Kashmir, where India's puppet government sits. On October 1, 2001, its Parliament building was truck-bombed in a bloody attack, threatening the wobbly Pakistani government with a two-front war between India and the U.S. forces in Afghanistan. Passing strange. As the Pakistani journal Dawn put it: "those responsible for that bombing were friends of neither Pakistan nor the Kashmiri people, raising some questions about whose friends the bombers were."[683]

---

[683] Dawn Internet Edition, www.dawn.com/2001/10/23/op.htm.

So are the two south-of-the-border terrorists, Ben Zvi and Smecke, rotting in a Mexican jail? Editorialists commented that any Mexican caught with explosives in the halls of Congress would be *"hundido,"* "a goner." Our daring Lavoners were gone soon enough, alright, from their jail to freedom.

In a flurry of damage control, the Israeli embassy interceded, Sharon sent a special envoy, strings were pulled, the story was spiked, and everyone went home. Yes, just like home – the land of the free, and home of the brave;[684] where seldom is heard a discouraging word, and Israeli spy networks, on Fox News today, are '404 Not Found' tomorrow.

Pravda does mean Truth, after all.

And funny thing, the story of two Israeli agent provocateurs, caught red-handed with explosives in the Chamber of Deputies, is still up there for all to see, on the website of *La Cronica de Hoy.*[685]

No honest observer can turn a blind eye to this inexplicable sequence of events. The Israeli role must be investigated as part of a broad full-blown public inquiry into 9/11, and we should not fear the conseque⁀ ⁀es – a proper inquiry can only help confirm who is truly innocent and truly ⁀ ⁀ty. If Israeli intelligence operatives were guilt-free, then an investigation would exonerate them, and end any more speculations on this subject once and for all.

The Pattern of Provocation

Yet, at face value, it is hard to interpret the available data in a less than damaging light. There is in fact a rich history here, showing that the clandestine activities of Israeli agents in the U.S. prior to 9/11 are nothing new, but merely the extension of longstanding military intelligence policies. Indeed, it would not be the first time that Israel has shown the scorpion's habit of biting the hand that feeds it.[686] Menachim Begin[687] led the 1946

---

[684] Among the elect feeding at the Great Trough of the Potomac, I would apply the term 'brave' to no man but Rep. Cynthia McKinney.

[685] 'La PGR investigará si los israelíes son terroristas,' *La Cronica de Hoy,* www.cronica.com.mx/2001/oct/12/nacional07. See also Procuradora General de la Republica, 'La PGR Informa Sobre la Situación de los Sujetos Detenidos en la Cámara de Diputados,' www.pgr.gob.mx/cmsocial/bol01/oct/b69701.html.

[686] One precedent occurred during the 1967 war, when Israeli warplanes and torpedoes nearly sank an American spyship, probably to prevent interference with the planned invasion of Syria's Golan Heights. See the USS Liberty survivors' website, www.ussliberty.org.

Zionist truck bombing of Jerusalem's King David Hotel, timed to spur British troop withdrawals and give Zionist militias a free hand against the poorly armed Palestinians, taking the lives of just under 100 British guests.[688] Little wonder that the public in the Middle East is convinced that Mossad had a hand in on 9/11. Who else? they may well ask.[689] As locals, they may be less dependent on commercial media reports. As the world gets smaller and more wired together, we may all become locals...

Advanced electronic surveillance plus old-fashioned infiltration by paid informers should have provided Washington seamless information about the Boeing bombing plot—especially if the adversary was the very high-profile bin Laden.

After September 11, a chant of loud moans was heard on Capitol Hill about America's weakness in "human intelligence." Yet, in fighting the Afghan war, America knew very well how to marry its high technology with local collaborators on the ground. The same principle should apply to espionage. Is the Middle East off limits for American intelligence? Or is it easier for America to use proxies there?

Israel's Mossad,[690] for one, is not short of field agents, and is no stranger to the old trick of war provocation. Undercover action by Oriental Jews

---

"Every time anyone says that Israel is our only friend in the Middle East, I can't help but think that before Israel, we had no enemies in the Middle East." - Jesuit Fr. John Sheehan.

[687] Begin was a leader of the Jewish underground, the Irgun, and of the Likud party. He served as Prime Minister, and shared the 1978 Nobel Peace Prize with Anwar Sadat.

[688] 'Mid-East: Palestine Time-Line,' Index of articles on 'Recovered History,' from *The Progressive Review*, http://prorev.com/recovered.htm. James O. Pittman, 'Negotiation Strategy in Hostage Situations,' *U.S. Army Medical Department Journal*, May-June 1996, http://das.cs.amedd.army.mil/journal/J9636.HTM: "Menachim Begin, the former head of the state of Israel, who began his political growth as a member of the Irgun Zvai Leumi (IZL), eventually rising to lead the IZL and participated in the bombing of the King David Hotel in Jerusalem in the name of Zionist liberation from British rule."

[689] For a summary of Arab reasoning about 9/11, see M. Amir Ali, 'Destruction of the WTC and the Pentagon,' www.mediamonitors.net/mamirali2.html. Also, 'Who Benefits Most?,' /mamirali1.html.

[690] "Mossad" means 'By Way of Deception,' the title of an article by Robert I. Friedman, *The Village Voice*, April 6, 1993. Skeptically he

posing as Arabs was a standby of early Zionist tactics.[691] Spies do more than observe and report; they can also infiltrate an enemy organization as provocateurs, to instigate actions that backfire on it. Any observer of the Mideast crisis will note how regularly and severely the Palestinians hurt their own cause with ill-considered attacks. Surely the 9/11 bombing was catastrophic for the Taliban, whether they were behind it or not!

It may seem far-fetched to entertain the possibility that bin Laden himself could consciously be a double agent. It is also virtually irrelevant. The method is more sophisticated than that. Conscious or not, double or dupe, the effect is the same; either way, he has been fostered for a purpose. In a terror organization, the ready-to-die cannon fodder are only the bottom level. They have handlers, or operators; these have managers, who select the targets. Once the organization is infiltrated, it is easy enough to taint their ideas and influence them in the wrong, outrageous direction. One has only to help them carry out their fantasies of wronged revenge – at required targets and times.[692]

---

recounts an interview with Victor Ostrovsky, who believes Mossad was behind the 1993 WTC attack. See www.textfiles.com/conspiracy/wtcbomb3.txt. After talks with further Israeli intelligence sources, Friedman concluded in a later article, see note 698, that Ostrovsky's hunch was right.

[691] The Department for Jewish Zionist Education, 'Early Operations of Israeli Intelligence,' www.jajz-ed.org.il/juice/service/week1.html, recounts operations of the "Arab Platoon of the Palmach... the elite strike force of the Haganah." See also Nafeez M. Ahmed, 'Occupied Palestine and the Politics of Terrorism: Post-Modern Colonialism, Suicidal Rage and the Propaganda System,' www.mediamonitors.net/mosaddeq34.html, quoting official Israeli sources openly welcoming Hamas terror attacks. "This ruthless line of thought seems to explain why Israel has targeted Arafat while leaving Hamas untouched."

[692] Of interest in this respect is a series of interviews by Christopher Bollyn, 'Intel Expert Says 9-11 Looks Like A Hollywood Show,' at www.conspiracyplanet.com, 'WTC: Enemy Within.' Three top German intelligence officials are interviewed, who insist the attacks were impossible without the support of a state spy agency. The most outspoken of the three experts, "Andreas von Buelow, served on the parliamentary commission which oversees the German secret services, while a member of the Bundestag (German parliament), from 1969 to 1994, and wrote a book, *Im Namen des Staates (In the Name of the State)* on the criminal activities of secret services, including the CIA.

The book for devious minds on the subject of infiltration is written in the blood of Israeli-Palestinian terrorist attacks. Israeli undercover work has evolved into a sophisticated pillar of state strategy, from amateur beginnings in the 1950's, when the exploits of some provocateurs became public. In the Lavon affair, Israeli "private citizens" blew up American and British property in Egypt, blaming it on the Muslim Brotherhood, but were caught by the police.[693] The bombing of synagogues in Iraq by Zionists inciting their brethren to flee to Palestine also became public knowledge.[694] Today, the

---

"Von Buelow told AFP that he believes that the Israeli intelligence service, Mossad, is behind the September 11 terror attacks. These attacks, he said, were carried out to turn public opinion against the Arabs, and boost military and security spending. 'You don't get the higher echelons,' von Buelow said, referring to the masterminds. The organization doing the planning, such as Mossad, is primarily interested in affecting public opinion. The planners use corrupt 'guns for hire' such as Abu Nidal, the Palestinian terrorist who von Buelow called 'an instrument of Mossad.... The BND (German secret service) is steered by the CIA and the CIA is steered by Mossad." The terrorists who actually commit the crimes are what von Buelow calls 'the working level,' such as the 19 Arabs who allegedly hijacked the planes on September 11. 'The working level is part of the deception,' he said. 'Ninety-five percent of the work of the intelligence agencies around the world is deception and disinformation,' which is widely propagated in the mainstream media creating an accepted version of events. 'Journalists don't even raise the simplest questions... those who differ are labeled as crazy.'"

[693] British journalist David Hirst, 'The Lavon Affair,' in *The Gun and the Olive Branch*, 1984; excerpts at www.mideastfacts.com/lavon_hirst.html . The scandal brought down the Israeli government, but the plotters got a hero's welcome home.

[694] See first-hand testimony on this policy from an Iraqi Jew, Naeim Giladi, 'The Jews of Iraq,' *The Link*, published by Americans for Middle East Understanding (AMEU), Vol. 31, No. 2, April-May 1998. "About 125,000 Jews left Iraq for Israel in the late 1940s and into 1952, most because they had been lied to and put into a panic by what I came to learn were Zionist bombs," recalls Giladi. "The principal interest Israel had in Jews from Islamic countries was as a supply of cheap labor, especially for the farm work that was beneath the urbanized Eastern European Jews. Ben Gurion needed the 'Oriental' Jews to farm the thousands of acres of land left by Palestinians who were driven out by Israeli forces in 1948... Documents, including some that I illegally copied from the archives at Yad Vashem, confirm what I saw myself, what I was told by other witnesses, and what

primary payoff of terror is for Israeli hawks, to neutralize their peace movement and gain command of domestic public opinion; the mainstream view becomes identified with "justified vengeance," even over-kill against "savages" who "target women and children."

The New Zealand Herald learned how Israeli infiltration worked in the Achille Lauro hijacking, from an ex-Mossad agent who exposed the atrocity as an Israeli "black propaganda operation."[695] A Palestinian double agent working for Israel had instructed his charge, extremist leader Abu'l Abbas, to seize the cruise ship and make a cruel example to "show them." Like the Israelis, Abbas was against the 'compromise' peace agreement then on offer; in addition, disguised Israeli agents paid him hefty bribes to boost his courage. The payoff was the infamous and tragic dumping overboard of the old Jewish-American gentleman in a wheelchair—which turned out to be a stunning propaganda hit for Israel.

Furthermore, a major terrorist group, the Abu Nidal organization, worked regularly for Israeli pay:

"Middle East expert Patrick Seale writes: 'Israeli penetration of Palestinian organizations was common, but it was clearly not the whole story. Most intelligence sources I consulted agreed that it was standard practice to use penetration agents not simply to neutralize or destroy the enemy but to try to manipulate him so that he did one's bidding without always being aware of doing so... Abu Nidal's murdering Palestinian moderates was connected with [former Israeli Prime Minister] Begin's determination never to negotiate with Palestinians for fear of losing the West Bank. For Begin, the moderates, who wanted to negotiate, were the real danger and had to be eliminated... What is curious is that Israel has never punished Abu Nidal's

---

reputable historians and others have written concerning the Zionist bombings in Iraq, Arab peace overtures that were rebuffed, and incidents of violence and death inflicted by Jews on Jews in the cause of creating Israel." See Giladi's book, *Ben Gurion's Scandals: How the Haganah and Mossad Eliminated Jews*, AMEU, 1992. Also *Christian Science Monitor*, May 22, 2002, 'How Israel builds its fifth column - Israel's Palestinian puppets:' "the recruitment of collaborators has become a crucial plank of Israel's security," www.csmonitor.com/2002/0522/p01s04-wome.html.

[695] According to testimony of ex-Mossad agent Ari Ben-Menashe, at www.howlingatthemoon.com/pacific_jihad_OCT2000.htm. More on Mossad is found in books like *Gideon's Spies* by Gordon Thomas, and *By Way of Deception* by ex-Mossad agent Victor Ostrovsky.

organization... His genius has been to understand that states will commit any crime in the name of national interest.' "[696]

The Abu Nidal terror was particularly wanton and suited to exploitation by Israeli propaganda: Italian and Austrian airports, a Greek cruise ship, all targets in countries sympathetic to the Palestinians, and the bombing pinned on the PLO by Israel to justify the 1982 invasion of Lebanon.

Evidence also links Israel's intelligence agency Mossad to the 1988 Pan Am / Lockerbie bombing, [697] in an incident that also shows up the opportunistic aspect of U.S. "retribution for terror acts." Mossad sources were seen to manipulate the trail of evidence, making it clear that the bombing might be a Mossad "false flag operation." Yet blame was cavalierly shifted between Libya and Palestine, until the flavor of the week in the White House fell on Qaddafi.

---

[696] American journalist David Hoffman, *The Oklahoma City Bombing and the Politics of Terror*, Constitution Society, 1998, 'Ch. 14 – A Strategy of Tension,' at www.constitution.org/ocbpt/ocbpt_14.htm. Also gives inside details of the Rabin assassination; saying that Rabin arranged the attack on himself for political gains, intending it to be foiled, but the secret service Shin Bet let it go through. Allegedly the same kind of thing happened in Oklahoma City and the first WTC bombing in 1993. Bush had reason to be nervous on September 11... Hoffman reviews the evidence of government prior knowledge of the Oklahoma City bombing in this highly acclaimed and meticulously researched tome, introduced by U.S. Rep. Charles Key.

See also Congressman McCloskey, writing in *The Washington Report* in 1986, on Israel blaming Abu Nidal attacks on Arafat's PLO, at www.washington-report.org/backissues/022486/860224001.html; and John Cooley of the *Christian Science Monitor,* on Begin's use of this tactic to invade Lebanon, www.washington-report.org/backissues/080684/840806007.html.

[697] Russell Warren Howe, who has followed the Lockerbie case for ten years, reviews compelling evidence that the Pan Am bombing may have been a Mossad black propaganda stunt in 'What if the 'Lockerbie bombers' are innocent?', *The Mail & Guardian* (Johannesburg), April 26, 1999, www.mg.co.za/mg/news/99apr2/26apr-lockerbie.html. Similarly, Bill Clinton used the bin Laden embassy bombings against the Sudan, without a shred of justification: Nafeez Mosaddeq Ahmed, 'United States Terrorism in the Sudan,' www.mediamonitors.net/mosaddeq16.html.

There have been even more persistent and detailed reports, for instance by Village Voice correspondent Robert Friedman, that Mossad was involved in the first World Trade Center bombing in 1993.[698]

Allowing ourselves to indulge in speculation by theoretically extending this historical pattern to the events of September 11, we see that only a select few liaison personnel and top officials would need to know of such a double play. Clearly, this would be a far superior plan to riskily trying to winnow American undercover agents willing to sacrifice thousands of their fellow citizens, for whatever geopolitical gains.

The quid pro quo? Provocation is a perennial cover for Israel's ongoing strategy of "creating facts on the ground," by steadily occupying more land, "an acre and a goat at a time," and building up its military potential.

> "Barak and Sharon both belong to a line of political generals that started with Moshe Dayan" *(Ha'aretz)*. This breed of generals was raised on the myth of... the sanctity of the land. In a 1976 interview, Moshe Dayan, who was the defense minister in 1967,[699] explained what led, then, to the decision to attack Syria. Syria was conceived as a serious threat to the security of Israel, and a constant initiator of aggression towards the residents of northern Israel. But according to Dayan, this is 'b------t'—Syria was not a threat to Israel before 67: 'Just drop it... I know how at least 80% of all the incidents with Syria started. We were sending a tractor to the demilitarized zone and we knew that the Syrians would shoot. According to Dayan (who at the time of the interview confessed some regrets), what led Israel to

---

[698] Robert I. Friedman, 'Mossad link to first WTC bombing' at www.americanfreepress.net/09_16_01/, recapping a 1993 Village Voice article. The author learned from Israeli intelligence sources that the supposed PLO terrorist Ajaj was a paid scapegoat, a petty Palestinian criminal, whom the Israelis recruited out of jail to be their stooge. 'Deported' by Israel to Pakistan, he went on to Afghanistan before coming to New York and infiltrating Sheikh Abdel-Rahman's clique. Victor Ostrovsky is cited as saying that CIA support for the Afghan mujahideen was directly supervised by Mossad.

[699] Israel's stunning victory in the Six-Day War renewed the dream of a Greater Israel. See John Mitchell Henshaw, 'Israel's Grand Design: Leaders Crave Area from Egypt to Iraq,' in *The American Mercury*, Spring 1968, at www.mediamonitors.net/johnhenshaw1.html. War-weary as most of the Israeli public is today, the dream dies hard; it has resurged as the New Global Military Doctrine.

provoke Syria this way was the greediness for the land—the idea that it is possible 'to grab a piece of land and keep it, until the enemy will get tired and give it to us.'" [700]

Crises are created to torpedo peace talks, then packaged as Israel's "restraint" and "retaliation" by our media.[701] The essential strategy has been candidly articulated – in private of course – by Israeli Defence Minister Moshe Dayan:

> "[Israel] must see the sword as the main, if not the only, instrument with which to keep its morale high and to retain its moral tension. Toward this end it may, no it must, invent dangers, and to do this it must adopt the method of provocation – and revenge…and above all, let us hope for a new war with the Arab countries, so that we may finally get rid of our troubles and acquire our space."[702]

Provocation, invocation, retribution, redistribution.

---

[700] Tanya Reinhardt, Israeli journalist, in 'Evil Unleashed' at www. mediamonitors.net/tanya11.html. Water supply is Israel's real goal in the Golan Heights.

[701] Cal. State Univ. Prof. Kevin MacDonald has established that at least 59% of U.S. newsprint and screen media are in the hands of our Jewish minority, just 2.5% of the population. At http://indymedia.org/front.php3? article_id=176000&group=webcast. A psychologist and eminent sociologist, MacDonald has contributed illuminating insights on Judaism as a highly successful competitive group strategy, and on pervasively recurring anti-Semitism as rooted in resentment of Jewish separatism and competitive success. A sympathetic, balanced, and courageous critic, he writes, "The IQ of Ashkenazi Jews is at least one standard deviation above the Caucasian mean," while also mentioning negative aspects, such as clannishness and an attraction to collectivist ideologies. See www.csulb.edu/~kmacd/ vitae.htm for a list of his published works. For ongoing critiques of U.S. media bias, see Palestine Media Watch, www.pmwatch.org.

[702] Quoted from a May 1995 entry in the personal diaries of former Israeli Prime Minister Moshe Sharatt; cited in Livia Rockack, Israel's Sacred Terrorism, Arab-American University Graduate Press, Belmont, Massachusetts, 1986. See Nafeez M. Ahmed, 'The Blood on Israel's Hands,' www.bargione.co.uk/Blood_on_Israel.htm.

Even a brief timeline of the Bush and Sharon presidencies raises an eyebrow. The Al-Aqsa Intifada started with a wilful provocation—the degradation of the second most holy site in Islam, barred to non-Muslims, by the murderous intrusion of the sadist Ariel Sharon, butcher of the refugee camps,[703] with his bodyguard of hundreds of soldiers, on September 28, 2000. His aim was to shatter the Oslo "Peace Process," with its looming risk that Nobel Prize aspirant Clinton just might get the Palestinians to accept the demeaning offer of quasi-statehood in a smattering of bantustans.[704]

The derailment policy had its cost: the uprising became a serious setback in world opinion, and a source of deep anxiety about Israel's future. But Sharon's Intifada got him elected. Soon after he – and Bush – took office, the ECHELON Bojinka warnings started. Then he started to lose battles in his Brussels war crimes trial, but not his taste for more massacres, as became horrifyingly clear a year later.

Sharon came twice to Washington, for personal talks. Arafat was never invited, as if to seal his fate. It was a done deal from day one. Bush washed his hands of Jerusalem, letting the devil take the hindmost.[705] As world

---

[703] For updates on the War Crimes trial of A. Sharon, see www. indictsharon.net. The Sri Lanka Daily Mirror likens Sharon to King Herod, who sent soldiers to kill the young. Ameen Izzadeen, 'Herod and the Holocaust,' www.dailymirror.lk/inside/worldw/020405.html.

[704] Former Israeli minister Abba Eban's sly phrase, "The Palestinians never miss an opportunity to miss an opportunity," can be read more than one way... With America's total supremacy and backing, and Israel's own armed might, diplomacy and compromise lost their attraction. Israel had used the Oslo process, 1993* – 2000†, to gain time, expand its settlements in the occupied territories, cut the costs of occupation by outsourcing discipline to the Palestinian Authority, the PA, and paper over differences between Israeli hawks and doves. PA decision-makers were co-opted with economic incentives, which evaporated, along with private Palestinian investments, after the new uprising (Intifada).

[705] Washington's extreme one-sidedness or "tilt" has become painfully apparent to the whole world, after the demise of Clinton's brand of double-talk. Bush subscribes slavishly to the Israeli line, even at its most incoherent, as in "The strange affair of Karine A: Israel's official account of the Palestinian Authority's connections with a ship found loaded with weapons makes little sense, writes Brian Whitaker," at www.guardian. co.uk/Archive/Article/0,4273,4339656,00. html. In other words, it bore some marks of a false flag operation aimed at Arafat – and Iran, which had started to get chummy with Washington.

opinion turned sharply against Israel and even the U.S., Palestinians could hardly believe their luck. What had happened to the expected Israeli public relations counter-offensive? Might we dare guess that 9/11 was it?

Two weeks before September 11, a high-level Mossad delegation came to Washington, carrying Bojinka warnings; then another top-level Israeli visit for the week of September 11 was cancelled. Since that awful day, Bush and Sharon read from the same page in taking their wars to the "enemy," folks who happen to be hereditary owners of the real estate they want.

Immediately after the 9/11 attacks, Israeli spokesman Bibi Netanyahu crowed publicly, "It is very good," because it would strengthen American support for Israel.[706] As if to confirm his sentiments, using the 9/11 "War on Terror" as justification, Sharon soon began escalating the Israeli-Palestinian conflict, pummeling civilian infrastructure in the West Bank and Gaza on the pretext of fighting terrorism.[707]

See also links at http://dmoz.org/Society/Issues/ Warfare_and_Conflict/ Specific_Wars/ Middle_East/International_Policy.

[706] Gleeful Israeli reactions quoted in Israel Shamir, 'Orient Express,' Sept. 14, 2001, http://shamir.mediamonitors.net/september142001.html.

[707] In an e-mail to Al-Awda@yahoogroups.com, April 6, 2002, reporting on a phone call to his family in Ramallah during the Israeli invasion, Rima Al-Alamy wrote: "houses were run down by tanks on the heads of the families. Houses been set on fire with children still inside them. Children and ladies were taken as human shields by the Israelis. Many dead and wounded left in the streets due to the intense bombardment throughout the night and till now. One of the witnesses said that she counted 30 dead bodies were lying in front of her house in the street."

See the report by Phil Reeves, of *The Independent*, "Amid the ruins of Jenin, the grisly evidence of a war crime,' 16 April 2002, at http://news.independent.co.uk/world/middle_east/story.jsp?story=285413:

"A monstrous war crime that Israel has tried to cover up for a fortnight has finally been exposed.

A residential area roughly 160,000 square yards about a third of a mile wide has been reduced to dust. Rubble has been shovelled by bulldozers into 30ft piles. The sweet and ghastly reek of rotting human bodies is everywhere, evidence that it is a human tomb. The people, who spent days hiding in basements crowded into single rooms as the rockets pounded in, say there are hundreds of corpses, entombed beneath the dust, under a field of debris, criss-crossed with tank and bulldozer treadmarks.... He was

The plans for this massive military escalation had been long in the making. In the first weeks of the Al-Aqsa Intifada, before any Israeli civilian casualties had occurred, Barak's government had already dusted off its strategy of invading and destroying the Palestinian Authority. The respected Israeli commentator Prof. Tanya Reinhart of Tel-Aviv University observed:

"The assault would be launched, at the government's discretion, after a big suicide bomb attack in Israel, causing widespread deaths and injuries, citing the bloodshed as justification... Many in Israel suspect that the assassination of the Hamas terrorist Mahmoud Abu Hanoud, just when the Hamas was respecting for two months its agreement with Arafat not to attack inside Israel, was designed to create the appropriate 'bloodshed justification.' "[708]

As the American Jewish political scientist Prof. Stephen R. Shalom of William Paterson University, New Jersey, records: "In November 2001, there was a week-long lull in the fighting. Sharon then ordered the assassination of Hamas leader Mahmoud Abu Hanoud, which, as everyone predicted, led to a rash of terror bombings, which in turn Sharon used as justification for further assaults on the Palestinian Authority." Hamas, a major detonator of violence, was reportedly financed by Israel to undermine the PLO, during the Israeli occupation of Lebanon in the 1980's.[709] Thus, having provoked the spate of unconscionable suicide bombings in the first place, Sharon exploited the predictable Israeli civilian casualties as justification for a new series of massive military offensives in the Occupied Territories.[710]

Writing in July 2001, Jeffrey Steinberg[711] finds new Prime Minister Sharon confident of a free rein from President Bush for his war drive: "Indeed, on July 6, testifying before Congress, Defense Secretary Donald

---

trembling with fury and shock. 'This is mass murder. I have come here to help but I have found nothing but devastation. Just look for yourself.'

All had the same message: tell the world."

[708] Tanya Reinhardt, in 'Evil Unleashed,' op. cit.

[709] *Ha'aretz*, December 21, 2001.

[710] See Shalom, Stephen R., 'The Crisis in Palestine,' ZNet, April 2, 2002, www.zmag.org/content/Mideast/shalomcrisis.cfm.

[711] Who needs Nostradamus? Jeffrey Steinberg, in 'Sharon War Plan Exposed: Hamas Gang Is His Tool,' *Executive Intelligence Review*, July 20, 2001, predicted that "simultaneous terrorist actions against American targets" will pave the way for Sharon's expulsion of the Arab population. At www.larouchepub.com/other/2001/2827sharon_hamas.html.

The War on Freedom

Rumsfeld acknowledged that a war crisis would give the Administration leeway to crank up defense spending, from the current 3% of GDP, to 8-10%." (I thank you, Carlyle thanks you.) Steinberg continues prophetically,

> "Hamas teams are also reportedly activated—with clandestine Israeli backing—to target American assets in Europe and the Middle East. An 'Islamist' terrorist attack against an American target, Sharon believes, would assure U.S. blessings for whatever 'retaliation' Israel might take against Iraq, Iran, or Syria."

Indeed, the respected journal The Israeli Insider reported in mid-July that according to the authoritative intelligence newsletter Jane's Foreign Report, a "high casualty suicide bombing" against Israeli civilians would provide the pretext needed to implement existing war plans:

> "Chief of Staff Lt.-Gen. Shaul Mofaz presented the government…with an updated plan for an all-out attack on the Palestinian Authority. The London-based Foreign Report reported that the plan calls for an invasion of Palestinian-controlled territory by some 30,000 Israeli soldiers…As reported in the Foreign Report this week and disclosed locally by *Ma'ariv*, Israel's invasion plan – reportedly dubbed Justified Vengeance – would be launched immediately following the next high-casualty suicide bombing, would last about a month and is expected to result in the death of hundreds of Israelis and thousands of Palestinians."[712]

The Hebrew Israeli daily Yediot Aharanot reported in grim detail the escalation of Sharon's war plans in mid-June 2001: "…the Israeli military and political leadership are aiming, eventually, at a total destruction of the Palestinian authority, and, with it, the process of Oslo…What can they be after?…

> "…a simple solution of annexation of the occupied territories would have turned the occupied Palestinians into Israeli citizens, and this would have caused what has been labeled the 'demographic problem' – the fear that the Jewish majority could not be preserved. Therefore, two

---

[712] Ellis Shuman, 'Is Israel preparing to dismantle the Palestinian Authority?', *Israeli Insider*, July 12, 2001, "MK Michael Kleiner [chairman of the Herut Party] called on Israel to either assassinate or topple Arafat… even if it meant the Hamas would take his place. According to Kleiner, the entire world recognizes the Hamas as a terrorist organization, so Israel's continued efforts against a radical Palestinian leadership would not be condemned." At www.israelinsider.com/ channels/security/articles/sec_0057.htm.

basic conceptions were developed. The Alon plan consisted of annexation of 35-40% of the territories to Israel, and self-rule or partnership in a confederation of the rest, the land on which the Palestinians actually live.

...The second conception, whose primary spokesman was Sharon, assumed that it is possible to find more acceptable and sophisticated ways to achieve a 1948 style 'solution' – it is only necessary to find another state for the Palestinians. 'Jordan is Palestine' – was the phrase that Sharon coined. So future arrangements should guarantee that as many as possible of the Palestinians in the occupied territories will move there. For Sharon, this was part of a more global world view, by which Israel can establish 'new orders' in the region.

...The first step on this route is to convince the public that Arafat is still a terrorist and is personally responsible for the acts of all groups from the Islamic Jihad to Hizbollah...It is hard to avoid the conclusion that after 30 years of occupation, the two options competing in the Israeli power system are precisely the same as those set by the generation of 1948: Apartheid (the Alon-Oslo plan), or transfer – mass evacuation of the Palestinian residents, as happened in 1948 (the Sharon plan). Those pushing for the destruction of the Oslo infrastructure may still believe that under the appropriate conditions of regional escalation, the transfer plan would become feasible.

In modern times, wars aren't openly started over land and water. In order to attack, you first need to prove that the enemy isn't willing to live in peace and is threatening our mere existence. Barak managed to do that. Now conditions are ripe for executing Sharon's plan, or as Ya'alon put it in November 2000, for 'the second half of 1948.' Before we reach that dark line, there is one option which was never tried before: Get out of the occupied territories immediately."[713]

That option was never taken. Instead, the 9/11 bombing has given Sharon the cover he needed: the Sharon and Bush policies are the shared beneficiaries of 9/11.

Sharon's life-long goal is to expand the borders of the State of Israel to engulf the entirety of Palestine, and if possible, beyond. As Israeli Foreign Minister, Sharon addressed a meeting of militants from the extreme right-wing Tsomet Party: "Everybody has to move, run and grab as many hilltops as they can to enlarge the settlements because everything we take now will

---

[713] 'The Second Half of 48: The Sharon Ya'Alon Plan,' *Yediot Aharanot*, June 10, 2001.

stay ours... Everything we don't grab will go to them [i.e. Palestinians]."[714] Not a surprise, given that in May 1993 Sharon had proposed at the Likud Convention that: "Israel should adopt the 'Biblical borders' concept as its official policy. There were rather few objections to this proposal, either in the Likud or outside it, and all were based on pragmatic grounds."[715] The most far-reaching interpretation of these borders include the following areas: "in the south, all of Sinai and a part of northern Egypt up to the environs of Cairo; in the east, all of Jordan and a large chunk of Saudi Arabia, all of Kuwait and a part of Iraq south of the Euphrates; in the north, all of Lebanon and all of Syria together with a huge part of Turkey (up to lake Van); and in the west, Cyprus."[716]

As if to corroborate, the Washington Times reported in April 2002, during the Israeli invasion of the Occupied Territories, that Israeli Foreign Minister Shimon Peres confirmed Sharon's "plan calling for Israel to annex 50 percent of land in the West Bank." The existence of the plan was originally "disclosed by Ephraim Sneh, the Israeli transport minister," who observed that the annexation plan is "incompatible with a two-state solution," and thus designed to block the emergence of a viable independent Palestinian state.[717]

As we go to press, Sharon is indulging in open warfare in the West Bank with plans to annex half of it, evidently intending to eventually "transfer" – ethnically cleanse – a large fraction of the population. Yet Israeli media present this as a "humane" action, because their foot soldiers risked their lives in action, rather than dropping daisy-cutters. Thus, America's wanton use of overwhelming firepower is an encouragement and an alibi to the world's war criminals, of every stripe.

Conclusions

The executive branch of the federal government has apparently enabled a lethal surprise attack with mass murder against two of the founding thirteen colonies, New York and Virginia. By such an act, the federal government would grossly violate and void its contract with the states, and abrogate its

---

[714] Agence France Presse, November 15, 1998.

[715] Shahak, Israel, *Jewish History, Jewish Religion: The Weight of Three Thousand Years*, Pluto Press, London, 1997, p. 9.

[716] Ibid. p. 10.

[717] Joyce Howard Price, 'Sharon plan for West Bank confirmed,' *Washington Times*, April 22, 2002, www.washtimes.com/ national/20020422-8855812.htm.

own constitutional rights and privileges. Even if you do not accept the complicity argument, it has failed to protect its largest city from the consequences of its overweening foreign policies.

Like a loose handgun, our Federal government has backfired on its owners, the States. The executive has gone to war in defiance of the Constitution, and Congress has abdicated its war-making authority on at least 200 occasions since 1945, according to The Federation of American Scientists.[718] The federal government has proven utterly incapable and unwilling to remedy its chronic and world-threatening sickness.

The war powers have been usurped and abused by the White House at least since the 1840's. A new book sharply assails the totalitarian basis of our modern Union, as laid by Abraham Lincoln, over the rubble of the U.S. Constitution. "Lincoln lusted after Empire. The juggernaut he put in place exterminated the Plains Indians with the same ferocity with which Southern towns and cities were sacked and pillaged."[719] The Indians are in Palestine now – evicted into camps, demonized, and massacred in illegal wars.

The Constitution grants all powers not delegated elsewhere to the States; and delegation of powers is not their abandonment or abuse. Thus, the war powers rightfully revert back to the individual states, and need to be devolved to them, to make such mutual defense agreements as they deem fit.

This works perfectly in the European Union, for example, where people live much more safely than we do, even in small countries, even without ocean barriers, with collective security arrangements—because they don't threaten their neighbors with trillion-dollar "handguns." Because they practice pluralism, not absolutism, in relations between the nations.[720] The last thing anyone needs is a military superpower, a loose cannon on the deck of the world, that can be hijacked by an irresponsible clique. On the contrary, the world will be a safer and healthier place if Europe will reclaim its strategic and military independence in foreign policy. Europeans remember what living under aerial bombing means, and they do not yet have America's

---

[718] Gore Vidal, in *Perpetual War for Perpetual Peace — How We Got To Be So Hated*, a new book on 9/11, Waco, McVeigh, and interventionism.

[719] Prof. Thomas J. DiLorenzo, *The Real Lincoln: A New Look at Abraham Lincoln, His Agenda, and an Unnecessary War*, reviewed by Paul C. Roberts in 'War on terrorism a threat to liberty?', at www.washtimes.com/commentary/20020321-90276020.htm, 3/21/2002.

[720] If the nations of Asia – the Islamic world, China, India, Russia, Japan, and others – unite as the EU has done, they can not be challenged in their own sphere, and will retain their fair share of world resources.

sheer one-track mind about the profit motive. What the world needs is to see more of Europe's wisdom and sense of balance.

How did Switzerland, a cold and rocky spot with few resources, become the world's richest country? By its habits of neutrality and local autonomy, where the cantons collect a lion's share of revenue. Is it coincidence that the arguably unconstitutional Internal Revenue Act of 1913 passed just in time to give the Feds the wherewithal to wage an insane Great War in Europe? Yet, our states still have the right to secede...

DiLorenzo writes that Lincoln and his generals should "have been hanged as war criminals under the Geneva Convention of 1863." In our time, complicity – whether indirect or direct – in the Pearl Harbor and WTC attacks is also a treasonable crime against humanity, which should be prosecuted.

But we have gone too far along the Roman road to a military society of pawns in bondage to bread and circuses. Appealing to the political system, writing letters to Congress, may not do much.[721] A more promising avenue would be to work from the grass roots. Individual states could pass Belgian-style, universal, no-immunity war crimes laws, or legislation applying the principles of equal access,[722] affirmative action and anti-monopoly to the problem of media influence, as proposed by the Russian Jewish democrat,

---

[721] Those who wish to participate in letter-writing campaigns may see www.radicalpress.com/news/activistskit.htm. The site contains some good evidence on government complicity, and on the Enron affair.

[722] Liberal Jewish journalist Robert Scheer, 'The Palestinian Side Must Be Told,' *Los Angeles Times*, April 23, 2002: "The traditional absence of acknowledgement in U.S. news reporting of the ongoing victimization of the Palestinians, powerless from the beginning of their displacement half a century ago, is callously immoral. Moreover, no group is so safely denigrated in the mass media of this country, particularly in film, as "the Arabs," who became the enemy of choice in post-Cold War movie-making in such films as "True Lies." And no group is as underrepresented in the media work force; there are more than 3 million Arab Americans, yet it is exceedingly rare to find one working as a newspaper reporter or TV news personality. The American Society of Newspaper Editors doesn't even include Arabs or Muslims in its annual monitoring of groups underrepresented in the nation's newsrooms. Surely, if there were even a sprinkling of people in the news biz who were hearing from relatives in Ramallah or Jenin, it would influence the way events are interpreted." At www.robertscheer.com/1_natcolumn.

Israel Shamir. [723] Relatives of WTC victims should sue the federal government for manslaughter damages in their county courts, and get their local newspapers to write about it.

Even if complicity – or systematic negligence – were at a level below the president, he ratified the attacks, like Hitler did the Reichstag burning, by seizing on their political benefits, and suppressing investigations of intelligence failures. Bush's bombast about evildoers sounds almost Hitlerian, too – he "protests too much." Gore Vidal and Noam Chomsky are perfectly right to say we got a taste of our own medicine on 9/11, that it is no wonder the U.S. is detested by citizens of lands we destroy. But that is only the lesser half of it. To my mind, at least, we have abundantly shown that in all likelihood, the suffering Manhattan tasted must have been co-produced in Washington – and very possibly in Tel Aviv. [724]

It is impossible to know at this stage how much "Islamic terrorism" is a volcanic reaction to half a century of festering injustice in Palestine[725] – apartheid, squalid refugee camps fenced off from luxurious new Jewish settlements, the chicanery of military occupation – and injustice under repressive Arab regimes, too; how much is intentionally provoked, and how much is false flag operations – but for certain, the world-wide cost of added security measures must be enormous.

---

[723] In fact, existing FCC rules forbid media monopolies, but are observed chiefly in the breach. Furthermore, in February 2002, Fox TV won a suit in federal court requiring the FCC to justify any such restrictions. See 'FCC Ownership Rules Under Seige,' at www.mediamergers.com/fcc1.html.

[724] Websites on Mossad as a suspect in a "false flag" operation on 9/11: http://groups.yahoo.com/group/anti-crusade, best links on the 9-11 plot. www.nocturne.org/~terry/wtc_4000_Israeli.html#4000, researches press reports to debunk the story of 4000 missing Israelis or Jews in the WTC. http://external.nj.nec.com/homepages/wds/wtcbomb, by W. D. Smith, 9/15/01, adds two and two together. Ditto from ex-ISI director Hameed Gul, interviewed by UPI roving reporter de Borchegrave, www.unitedstates.com/news/ content/733287/mossad.

[725] What is most unbearable to the stateless Palestinians is the frustration at the world's double standard; as human rights makes gradual advances elsewhere, they alone are demonized and excluded from this process. Sociologists have a word for it: immiseration – more than the specific difficulties of one's condition, it is the perception of unfairly being kept worse off than others that hurts the most, psychologically.

America's complicity in the rape of Palestine[726] seems to have opened a Pandora's box that only a shocked and awakened America might close again. Instead, mentally lazy attitudes prevail with us: "why don't the Arabs just pull up stakes and move?" or "they're all crazy there anyway," which amount to justifications of ethnic cleansing. If you manage to explain provocation intrigue, you get: "it's their own tough luck if the Arabs let the Israelis trick them." Such "losers-weepers" rationalizations ignore all our own canons of justice.

1. We recognize differing degrees of murder; passion or desperation at injustice is an extenuating circumstance; cold-blooded calculation an aggravating one. The proverb says, "Whom the gods wish to destroy, they first drive mad."

2. Concealing guilt and shifting the blame on an adversary multiply the severity of a crime.

3. Those who arrange a crime and give the orders do bear a greater burden of guilt than those who carry it out. Without reducing the guilt of those who follow their orders, they bear responsibility both for their own acts and those of their underlings.

4. There are always criminals and desperadoes, and it is the government's job to stop them. If it collaborates with them instead, then that is the most heinous crime.

5. Because a small minority from any oppressed group can be drawn into a black propaganda plot, or become extremists or guerrillas in response to repression, millions of its law-abiding members suffer ten-fold retaliation. Such is the atrocity of collective guilt, as we know from Lidice and Guernica.

And Jenin. Our civilization has made strides in recognizing and applying these principles – but only in certain spheres. 9/11 notwithstanding, it is still a white man's world.

Militarily, of course, Israel is unconquerable. With hundreds of nuclear warheads, 4000 main battle tanks, and its own digitally enhanced fleet of

---

[726] Gore Vidal in his foreword to Israel Shahak's *Jewish History, Jewish Religion*: "John F. Kennedy told me how, in 1948, Harry S. Truman had been pretty much abandoned by everyone when he came to run for president. Then an American Zionist brought him two million dollars in cash, in a suitcase, aboard his whistle-stop campaign train. 'That's why our recognition of Israel was rushed through so fast.' [It] unfortunately resulted in forty-five years of murderous confusion, and the destruction of what Zionist fellow travellers thought would be a pluralistic state." True, Truman was already a Christian Zionist.

American fighter-bombers, it has double the firepower even of the U.S. in the region. "Israel can field 19 divisions of ground troops, by some counts; the United States boasts 13 divisions worldwide." [727]

Yet it is a fractured and war-weary society. Suffering the cycle of violence and cruelty that sprang from the Nazi death camps, that rebounds throughout the region and reaches even our shore; in spite of the determination to be free of persecution, and an enormous competitive spirit, at heart its people just want to be accepted by their neighbors and live a normal life:

"We rejoice in the avowed proposal of the Peace Congress to put into practical application the fundamental principles of democracy. That principle which asserts equal rights for all citizens of a state, irrespective of creed or ethnic descent.... We protest against the political segregation of the Jews, and the re-establishment in Palestine of a distinctly Jewish state as utterly opposed to the principles of democracy..." [728]

That was the American Jewish petition to Woodrow Wilson, at the 1919 Paris Peace Conference (who ignored it, for his own reasons).

Be your bogeyman bin Laden or Sharon, the whole boiling cauldron of the Middle-East crisis would subside of its own accord, if only the U.S. could switch from military aid for apartheid and bantustans[729] in Palestine to moral support for pluralistic democracy in Israel. Could it be that without Israel, we

---

[727] David Wood, 'Israel no longer dependent on U.S. military assistance,' *The Seattle Times*, April 9, 2002. " 'We have created an 800-pound gorilla,' said Kenneth Brower, an independent military consultant in Washington, assessing decades of U.S. military aid to Israel." At http://seattletimes.nwsource.com/html/nationworld/ 134433612_israelmilitary09.html.

[728] Source: www.nmhschool.org/tthornton/.

[729] Nafeez M. Ahmed, 'Apartheid in the Holy Land: Racism in the Zionist State of Israel,' a paper presented at the NGO Forum of the UN World Conference Against Racism, 20 August 2001for Islamic Human Rights Commission, draws on specialist work on this subject; see www. mediamonitors.net/mosaddeq11.html. Also, Lance Selfa, op. cit. note 650, "Norman Finkelstein argues that the language in the accords outlining the PA's powers matches nearly word-for-word the legislation setting up the Transkei bantustan in South Africa." With a mild difference: the Boers didn't expel the black population bodily, nor did America deport the Indians to Canada or Mexico.

could not find the enemies a growing body needs, or field-test lethal new means of destruction from our labs?

Yet how dangerous the game is for Israel. As we know, the history of the Jewish people is a tragic one. Time and again, resentment at their separate sense of identity and their competitive success has erupted into a terrible backlash of violence. Jewish fear of anti-Semitism is real,[730] even when the object of fear is sometimes imaginary. Yet there is no question that real hostility to Jewry is on the rise since Sharon's Intifada. What seems surprising, given this people's gifts of intelligence and psychological astuteness, is the cyclical failure to anticipate which actions incur hatred. The reason may be that anti-Semitism, as the external threat that cements Jewish group cohesion, became a totem exempted from analysis.[731]

On my brief visit to Jaffa, the iconoclastic Israeli dissident Israel Shamir underscored a point, and the *ikon* he broke for me was a taboo of the first water. To hear Shamir, Israel is only the tail of the dog; seekers of a solution to the Mideast crisis should direct their attentions first to the American Zionist lobby, and its media czars.[732] After all, we are able to blame "yellow journalism" for the Spanish American War. Shamir points at American media that display only a fraction of the courage to dissent that you will find in Israel's *Ha'aretz*; and the extremism of our "more Israeli than Israel" revanchists who keep them that way, who keep Israel that way, a safe six thousand miles away from the front lines.

Now these are hypotheses we need to be able to inspect, if we are serious about ending the cycle of violence. Our social scientists have developed powerful analytical tools. What good can it do to use them on quaint tribes, and hide the mirror from our own society or nationality?

---

[730] Quoted from Hertzberg by Prof. MacDonald in 'Indoctrination and group evolutionary strategies,' 1998: "Survey results from 1990 indicated eight out of 10 American Jews had serious concerns about anti-Semitism, and significant percentages believed anti-Semitism was growing although there was no evidence for this, while at the same time 90% of Gentiles viewed anti-Semitism as residual and vanishing."

[731] So strong is the taboo against analyzing anti-Semitism that it escapes notice that the very word is a misnomer. The main Semitic race are the Arabs; Judaism is a religion, so a more exact term would be Judeophobia. Meanwhile, we have no word for enmity to Arabs or Muslims.

[732] Israel Shamir's 'Fiesta of St. Fermin,' at www.israelshamir.net/fiesta.htm, may be the last word on the subject.

Isn't that what "Know Thyself" is all about?

All we know is the enormity of our unprecedented loss on 9/11, and even greater losses in past foreign wars. We don't know who is running foreign policy in our country – our elected representatives, or a clique with its own agenda? How can we know for sure our President would be safe taking his orders from us, when a popular President could be assassinated, without the culprits ever being caught? We don't know why we, the American public, have to pay for the losses from the plundering of Enron, like we took the hit for the BCCI bankruptcy.[733] Will we ever know what really happened to that huge budget surplus we no longer hear about, that was going to finance so many fine things?

We have no way of knowing what will hit us next, nor where our country is being taken. If we do not resolve 9/11, the next calamity will be worse still, because We the People are not masters in our own house. A criminal clique is running it their way. Be they CIA or KGB or Mossad or military industrial complex, it is up to the American people to find them out.[734]

---

[733] Brian D. Quig, B.C.C.I.: 'Bank of Crooks and Criminals International – U.S. Government One of its Biggest Customers,' www.dcia.com/bcci.html, quoting *Time Magazine*, July 29, 1991: "'B.C.C.I. is the largest corporate criminal enterprise ever, the biggest Ponzi scheme, the most pervasive money-laundering operation and financial supermarket ever created for the likes of Manuel Noriega, Ferdinand Marcos, Saddam Hussein and the Columbian drug lords.' A significant part of this story involves B.C.C.I.'s 'stealth-like invasion of the U.S. banking industry by secretly buying First American Bankshares --- whose chairman is Clark Clifford' [end of *Time* quote]... the attorney who drafted the original charter for the CIA at the direction of John Foster and Allen Dulles... B.C.C.I. maintained what its insiders called a 'black network' which was engaged in international bribery, blackmail, and assassination of government officials at the highest levels. The CIA used B.C.C.I. to facilitate funding of the Contras, illegal arms sales to Iran and Iraq as well as the arms supply to the Afghan resistance." Among many other writers, the author also points to CIA involvement in large-scale drug imports, in "The Phony Drug War."

[734] The way they are going, the authorities will never find them, in spite of massive jailing and racial profiling – another fine reason to suspect an inside job. "The world's biggest criminal investigation has yielded meager results... Police across the United States and Europe have arrested nearly 1,400 people in connection with the attacks on New York and Washington.

To deserve the names democracy and freedom, we should have gotten to the bottom of this decades ago, find whoever they are, and clean our government of this infection.

Our motto is still "land of the free, and home of the brave." Can we live up to it – or is it for criminals only?

Dr. Johnson quipped: "Patriotism is the last refuge of a scoundrel." He meant that true patriots uphold our ideals. They do not trample on them while invoking and abusing our national symbols.

"Beware the leader who bangs the drums of war in order to whip the citizenry into a patriotic fervor, for patriotism is indeed a double-edged sword. It emboldens the blood, just as it narrows the mind. And when the drums of war have reached a fever pitch, and the blood boils with hate and the mind has closed, the leader will have no need to seize the rights of the citizenry. Rather, the citizenry, infused with fear and blinded by patriotism, will offer up all their rights unto the leader, and gladly so. How do I know? For this is what I have done. And I am Caesar. "[735]

The end can never justify the means. We will be safe in our homes when we and our representatives remember that, and live by it. Those who tell us it can, are following the "consequentialist" doctrine of desperadoes and dictators. They are no leaders, but liars, who bring us to evil ends.

California,
Easter 2002.

*continued at **www.waronfreedom.org/update.html***

But they have charged only one of them in connection with the worst terrorist outrage in history." Peter Ford, 'Legal War on Terror Lacks Weapons,' *The Christian Science Monitor*, March 27, 2002, www.csmonitor.com/2002/0327/p01s04-woeu.html. See also Charley Reese on "the War on Terrorism," in 'Going Nowhere Fast,' May 13, 2002, http://reese.king-online.com/Reese_20020513/index.php. Yet note who was arrested with bombing materials in the U.S.A., and then released: six Israelis with plans to bomb a nuclear plant (www.whatreallyhappened.com/israelswithnukes.html); two Israelis speeding away after midnight near a naval base, with traces of TNT, RDX, false papers and a fake alibi (www.indybay.org/news/2002/05/128816.php); and two JDL leaders with materials for a pipe bomb (www.cnn.com/2001/LAW/12/12/jdl.arrests/).

[735] Words of Julius Caesar, according to a popular online urban legend.

Index

Tree of Life Books - Bianca's Backlist

Acres Of Diamonds, by Russell H. Conwell. The classic by a self-made man who lived to open opportunities for millions by teaching "all good things are possible!" Let him point you to your "Acres of Diamonds." The complete edition, 160 pages, ISBN 0-930852-26-5, $10.95

Adventures In Kinship With All Life, by J. Allen Boone with Paul Leonard. Heart-warming, true stories of the the world of silent communication, a bond of trust between people and animals of all kinds. Thoughtful tales salute the divinity within all creatures and cultivate a gentle reverence toward all life. 128 pages, ISBN 0-930852-27-3, $12.00

Anne Hutchinson, Unsung Heroine of History, By Winnifred K. Rugg. America's first feminist, female minister, and martyr, Anne came from comfort in England to rugged, four-year-old Boston. An all-male clergy met her zeal with inquisition and banishment, followed by her tragic death with young children. 350 pages, ISBN 0-930852-30-3. $19.95

How to Conquer Cancer, Naturally. Dr. Johanna Brandt, diagnosed with cancer, shared her journey back to wellness in this remarkable book on "The Grape Cure." 96 pages, ISBN 0-930852-35-4, $9.95

The Prophet of the Dead Sea Scrolls, by Rev. Upton Clary Ewing. Pre-Christian origins of the New Testament in the mysteries and devout practices of the ancient Essene sect. New evidence on the Crucifixion exonerates the Jews. 176 pages, ISBN 0-930852-26-5, $11.95

The Unknown Life of Jesus Christ, by Nicolas Notovitch. Where was Jesus and what was he doing from age 12 to 30? The amazing account, from an ancient manuscript the author found in a Tibetan lamasery in the 1890's. Read about his perilous journey as you uncover the mystery. References, maps. 56 pages, 8 ½" x 11", ISBN 0-960285-01-6, $10.00

Shipping and handling in USA: Priority mail: $4 first item, $1 ea. add'l. Media Mail: $2.50 first, $0.50 each additional item. 40% discount to booksellers. Mail check or money order to: Tree of Life Books, P.O. Box 126, Joshua Tree, CA 92252. Info: www.treelifebooks.com, treol@earthlink.net. Credit cards: www.waronfreedom.org. Or order from: Amazon, Baker & Taylor, Barnes & Noble, Bookpeople, Borders.